# Language and Logos

(Photo: Billett Potter)

# Language and Logos

Studies in ancient Greek philosophy
presented to G. E. L. Owen

Edited by Malcolm Schofield and
Martha Craven Nussbaum

CAMBRIDGE UNIVERSITY PRESS

Cambridge
London   New York   New Rochelle
Melbourne   Sydney

Published by the Press Syndicate of the University of Cambridge
The Pitt Building, Trumpington Street, Cambridge CB2 1RP
32 East 57th Street, New York NY 10022, USA
296 Beanconsfield Parade, Middle Park, Melbourne 3206, Australia

© Cambridge University Press 1982

First published 1982

Printed in Great Britain at the Pitman Press, Bath

Library of Congress catalogue card number: 81-12217

*British Library Cataloguing in Publication Data*
Language and logos.
1. Owen, G. E. L.
2. Philosophy, Ancient – Addresses, essays,
lectures
I. Schofield, Malcolm
II. Nussbaum, Martha Craven
III. Owen, G. E. L.
180    B171

ISBN 0 521 23640 1

# Contents

# Preface

These studies are offered to Gwil Owen on the occasion of his 60th birthday with respect, gratitude and affection. Their writers are all either pupils of his or younger scholars who, while not formally his pupils, would wish to acknowledge the stimulus of his talk and thought at a formative stage in their own philosophical histories. The volume contains fifteen chapters, all concerned in one way or another with aspects of the role played by reflection upon language in the thought of Plato, Aristotle, and other ancient Greek philosophers. It would have been as easy and as appropriate to persuade a quite different team of authors to write essays in Gwil Owen's honour on some quite different subject – say, Greek science and philosophy of science – no less close to his heart. So this book is dedicated to him with the good wishes, expressed by many to the editors, of a much greater number of pupils and others, on both sides of the Atlantic, than are assembled between these covers. Our thanks go to all who have helped us by their co-operation or advice, particularly our publisher Jeremy Mynott, who has made the project possible.

M. S.
M. C. N.

# Introduction

Since the end of the Second World War, the academic study of Greek philosophy in Britain and North America has changed almost out of recognition. One fairly crude index of the change is the huge growth in the numbers of scholars active in the subject, the volume of their publications, and the variety of their interests. Harder to characterise is the way in which scholarly study of the ancient texts has, without losing in historical scrupulousness or historical imagination, become much more a first-order philosophical activity than it was in the first half of the century. Such changes require moving causes. This volume salutes the work of a scholar and philosopher whose influence on the development of study of Greek philosophy in the last 30 years is second to none.

There have been three major channels through which G. E. L. Owen has made his influence felt. Pride of place must go to the series of masterly essays which he has given us since the early fifties, transforming the state of the art. In Parmenides and Zeno he has shown us, in place of the dogmatic monist and the sophist of the textbooks, the inventors of philosophy as we now understand it, or more specifically of a tradition of profound and subtle metaphysical argument. He has demonstrated how Plato in the theory of Forms gave classic expression to a seductively simple picture of the relations between language and the world, but then in his later dialogues fought his way self-critically to a more penetrating understanding of their complexities. G. E. L. Owen's first venture in this field was made in a celebrated paper on the *Timaeus*; subsequently he has explored it in essays devoted to the *Parmenides*, the *Sophist* and the *Politicus* and to Aristotle's *On the Ideas*. Aristotle, indeed, has been as central to his thought as Plato.

He has interpreted in many richly detailed and far-ranging studies
first Aristotle's rejection of the theory of Forms and the theory of
the relationship between science and philosophy of which it forms
a part; and then Aristotle's construction of a more sophisticated
and congenial account of the workings of language, and of a rival
philosophy of science and scientific method. These now classic
essays have persuaded many philosophers that Greek philosophy
holds greater rewards than they had ever conceived. What has
attracted the working philosopher in G. E. L. Owen's work is its
satisfying match of style to subject matter. By his own searching
and versatile attention, sympathetic but not reverent, to arguments and the philosophical impulses which generate them, he
has made his readers aware, as few other scholars do nearly so
well, of the depths, subtleties and complexities of the great Greek
philosophers. In the space of an article the whole range and unity
of a thinker's concerns are illuminated.

Many others have found the same illumination by their atten-
dance as graduate students at Professor Owen's weekly seminars
in Oxford, then Harvard, now Cambridge, or in his supervision
of their first researches. Those seminars have generated an electric
sense of intellectual exhilaration and discovery among their participants. They and he have helped one generation of graduates after
another to assimilate the principles of their craft and to discover
their own philosophical gifts.

It is not only graduate students who have benefited from
Professor Owen's conception of research as a collaborative enterprise. In 1957 he initiated with Ingemar Düring the celebrated
series of triennial international Symposia Aristotelica, which
continue as they began to bring together the leading workers in
the field and to foster progress in many areas of Aristotelian
scholarship. After he had left Oxford for Harvard in 1966 he
founded in New York an ancient philosophy group that was
designed to draw together some of the widely scattered workers
in the subject for monthly discussion. This flourishing body was
replicated by a British counterpart in 1975, upon his return to
England: the junior group meets in London to read the *Metaphysics*
of Aristotle, and has recently published its own commentary on
Book Z.

The contributors to this volume have addressed themselves to
topics in Greek philosophy close to the centre of G. E. L. Owen's

preoccupation with the place of language in philosophy. Some take up themes which he has made the subject of published writings; others subjects on which he has lectured or discoursed in seminars, but not published; others again topics more remotely connected with his teaching. Taken as a whole, the book gives a fair indication not only of how and where his impact upon the study of Greek philosophy is felt most today, but of the general character and direction of research in the field at present.

Although G. E. L. Owen has often lectured on Heraclitus, he has never devoted a published essay to his thought. Chapters 1 and 2 of our book provide original and much-needed accounts of his epistemology and of the place of language, and the metaphor of language, within that epistemology. Wiggins' Heraclitus is an exponent of the Principle of Sufficient Reason, Hussey's of a Rule of Intrinsic Meaning: the one leads to a realist, the other to an idealist interpretation of Heraclitus' cosmology. Heraclitus' idea that language is a main source of insight into reality was apparently endorsed in cruder form by the obscure figure of Cratylus. And it is Cratylus' version of the theory (as presented by Plato) which is discussed in chapters 3 and 4 by Schofield and Williams. Readers will notice agreement between them on the general drift of the dialogue – i.e. on its devastating scepticism – reinforced by diversity of approach and by a different selection of points of focus.

In chapter 5 Annas considers at greater length a topic in the *Cratylus* on which Williams touches briefly: its theory that knowledge requires a *logos* consisting in analysis into elements. Her main object is to cast light on the appearance of this theory in 'Socrates' dream' in the *Theaetetus*, which, as she shows, yields up a powerfully attractive notion of a hierarchical structure for knowledge, not (as Ryle thought) the beginnings of a syntactic conception of the proposition. This latter conception, and its connection with the problems of falsehood, are taken up in chapter 6. Here McDowell pushes further forward lines of interpretation of the *Sophist* first opened up by G. E. L. Owen, and offers new solutions to some of the toughest problems in that difficult dialogue.

Chapters 7 and 8 are devoted to the debate in Plato's Academy about the theory of Forms. Moravcsik argues that in the second part of the *Parmenides* Plato himself paves the way for a transcendental argument for the existence of Forms, construed not as paradigms or subjects of predication but as entities *sui generis*. Fine reconsiders the critical arguments of Aristotle's fragmentary treatise *On the Ideas*, which like Part II of the *Parmenides* has been the subject of a powerful essay by G. E. L. Owen. She posits a dilemmatic structure, hitherto unnoticed, for the strategy of the work, and discerns two subtly distinct 'one over many' arguments in Alexander's reports of its contents.

Aristotle's own thought is the concern of chapters 9 to 14. These chapters are organised by theme rather than by treatise. They deal with a variety of issues in metaphysics and philosophy of explanation: Aristotle devotes less consideration than Plato to specific questions of language, but accords to certain general ideas about language a pervasive role, sometimes explicitly enunciated, in all his philosophising; and he does not sharply distinguish talk of definition from talk of essence, talk of explanation from talk of principles of reality, or in general talk about what we say from talk about what there is.

In chapter 9 Bostock scrutinises the relationship between Aristotle's theory of the logical form of change and his criticisms of his predecessor's substantive physical enquiries. He suggests that Aristotle is not altogether clear on the character of the relationship, and that this unclarity has a significant bearing on some of the fundamental difficulties with which Aristotle wrestles in his theory of predication. Natural change, and in particular the reproduction of species, is the topic of chapter 10. Cooper there argues that the idea of teleological explanation which Aristotle introduces to account for such processes is not, as some scholars have held, one which we project on to reality and justify in terms of the illumination it brings us: ends are embodied in the very structure of nature and are not themselves to be explained, reductively or otherwise, by any external principle.

Matthews takes up Aristotle's distinctive notion of accidental unity in chapter 11. He provides a subtle account of Aristotle's grasp of the concept of identity proper, and interprets the doctrine of accidental identity as a resourceful response to still unresolved problems of referential opacity and the like. Much here turns on our understanding of Aristotle's object in distinguishing uses or senses of 'the same' – or indeed of any other expression. And in chapter 12 Irwin attacks the general question of whether Aristotle has a theory or concept of meaning at all. He argues against G. E. L. Owen for a negative answer: but he relates Aristotle's concept of signification to his theory of scientific method, so memorably expounded by Owen in his essay *'Tithenai ta phainomena'*. The interpretations of that essay are pushed further in chapter 13 by Nussbaum, who ascribes to Aristotle a conception of science as operating within the limits of language and thought contained in our shared human experience, and without reliance on unconditionally guaranteed foundations. The limits of language and thought are also the topic of chapter 14, in which Sorabji argues for the superiority of Plotinus' treatment of thinking and its propositional structure to Aristotle's, and touches incidentally on Nussbaum's theme of Aristotle's valuation of scientific enquiry.

Sorabji's paper testifies to the interest which philosophical scholars in the analytic tradition are now taking in later periods of Greek philosophy. So too does the final chapter of the book. In it Burnyeat expounds and assesses the debate between the Stoics and their sceptical opponents about sorites arguments. He contends that while contemporary philosophers see the sorites as problematical mostly for philosophy of language, the ancients thought the lessons it taught were mostly epistemological. His essay sheds light at once on his philosophical topic and its history, and thus fittingly concludes our tribute to G. E. L. Owen.

# 1    Heraclitus' conceptions of flux, fire and material persistence

## DAVID WIGGINS

Even when they are most worthy of amazement, things of daily occurrence pass us by unnoticed.

Seneca, *Quaestiones Naturales* 7.1.1

It can be hardly be supposed that a false theory would explain in so satisfactory a manner as does the theory of natural selection the several large classes of fact above specified. It has recently been argued that this is an unsafe method of arguing; but it is a method used in judging of the common events of life and has often been used by the greatest natural philosophers.

Charles Darwin, *Origin of Species*

## I    *Heraclitus and the Milesians*

1.1 In recent decades there has been a tendency among scholars to question whether Heraclitus was, in the same sense as the Milesians were, a *cosmologist*: '[Heraclitus'] real subject is not the physical world but the human condition, which for the Greeks means the condition of mortality . . . Like [his] substitution of Fire for [Anaximenes'] Air, any changes in detail must have been designed not to improve the physical scheme in a scientific sense but to render its symbolic function more drastic.'[1]

1  Charles Kahn 'A New Look at Heraclitus', *American Philosophical Quarterly*, 1 (1964), 189–203. It would be wrong for me not to qualify the disagreement I shall note in the text by the acknowledgment of how much I have found both to agree with and to admire on the subject of Heraclitus in Kahn's book *Anaximander and the Origin of Greek Cosmology* (New York and London 1960), esp. 187–97.

Kahn's new book, *The Art and Thought of Heraclitus* (Cambridge 1979), came to hand as this essay was reaching its penultimate draft; but it has enabled me to make a number of improvements in detail. I have also taken over from Kahn the felicitous (and felicitously ambiguous) expression 'elemental form'. Since Kahn's new book is not a repudiation of the doctrine I have quoted from his 1964 article, I have ventured to let section 1.1 of this essay remain as it was before I saw the new book.

I seize the first opportunity to thank the editors and Edward Hussey and Richard Sorabji most sincerely for the efforts that each of them has made at various stages to save me from the errors born of amateurish enthusiasm. I wish I could now blame them for every howler that remains.

It would be foolish to deny that problems about mortality, fallibility and the human perspective were an important part of Heraclitus' main subject. But this is not inconsistent with his having seen himself as answerable in the first instance to the same questions as the Milesians, whatever his reservations about their would-be *polymathiē*:

One thing is wisdom: to understand the plan by which all things are steered through all things (B41).

One from all and all from one (B10).

It is wise to hearken not to me but to my *logos* and to confess that all things are one (B50).

Thales, Anaximander and Anaximenes had been concerned not only with particular phenomena that aroused their curiosity but also with the description and explanation of the world as a whole: How did the world come to exist and to be what it is? And now that it does exist, what sort of thing is it, and how does it maintain itself? Heraclitus inherited these questions from the Milesians, and he asked others of his own, about the soul, and about human destiny, cognition and language. I shall contend that the new problems were seen by Heraclitus as requiring an unconditional willingness on his part to attempt some better than merely symbolic response to those of the Milesians. Indeed, if the reading that I shall propose for certain passages is accepted, then it will appear that he saw himself as positively obliged to improve upon his predecessors' cosmological theories.

1.2 There is a second affinity I claim to find between Heraclitus and the Milesians. If we are to trace any pattern in the doctrines that have come down to us as his, we need to see him as exploiting just as recklessly as his Milesian predecessors did what is sometimes called the Argument to the Best Explanation:[2] If *q* is the best explanation why *p* holds, then, if *p* is true, *q* must be true too.[3]

Whatever G. E. L. Owen may make of the ascription of the method to Heraclitus, it is he who must bear some considerable

2 See Gilbert Harman, 'The Inference to the Best Explanation', *Philosophical Review*, 74 (1965), 88–95; Paul R. Thagard, 'The Best Explanation: Criteria for Theory Choice', *The Journal of Philosophy*, 75 (1978), 76–92, to whom I am indebted for the initial quotation from Darwin. Thagard mentions the Peircean and Leibnizian parallels. There is also an interesting affinity waiting to be drawn out with Collingwood's doctrine that '*questions are the cutting edge of the mind*'.

3 The 'must' has 'if *p* then *q*' as its scope here; and of course it does not connote the metaphysical necessity of *q*.

part of any blame or credit that it provokes. For it is one of Owen's contributions to our understanding of Greek philosophy to have drawn attention to the central part (insufficiently remarked in modern times) that is played in Greek thought by the idea of Sufficient Reason.[4] Owen has traced the idea from Leucippus, Parmenides and Melissus[5] back to Anaximander, where Anaximander's mastery of Sufficient Reason is brilliantly demonstrated by his replacement of Thales' supposition that water is what holds the world up by the insight (cf. Aristotle, *de Caelo* 295b11) that the earth is held up by nothing and simply stays where it is because it is in equipoise with other things, there being no reason for its shifting in any particular direction.

What is the connection between Sufficient Reason and the Argument to the Best Explanation? Suppose nothing holds true unless there is reason for its so holding. Then if *p* is true, something must be true which explains why *p* is true. But then it must be possible to argue backwards – albeit against the direction of implication – and infer from *p*'s truth whatever best explains why *p*. The Principle of Sufficient Reason gives us the Argument to the Best Explanation[6] then, and in doing this it suggests a research strategy – the same strategy which Charles Darwin seeks to justify in the passage of *Origin of Species* prefixed to this essay. Any phenomenon that is observed calls for explanation. But, wherever explanation is called for, one should postulate as true that which best explains the phenomenon, regardless of whether the putatively explanatory fact is in any way directly observable. Improving and amplifying the precept a little, it is natural to expand upon it as Plato did: when we have several explanations of distinct phenomena arrived at in this manner, we must test our explanations and the consequences of our explanations for consistency with one another and with everything else we believe.

4  See, for instance, 'Plato & Parmenides on the Timeless Present', *The Monist*, 50 (1966), 317–40. I understand that Owen has developed the theme further in his Sather Classical Lectures and in other recent work with which I am not acquainted.

5  For various statements of the principle or approximations to it, see Xenophanes A28; Parmenides B8, 9; Melissus B1–2; Leucippus A8, B2. See also Plato, *Phaedo* 98–9, 108E–109E; *Timaeus* 62E12ff.

6  There are doubts about the opposite dependency – doubts that one may suppose can only be cleared up by an elucidation of 'reason' diverging from, e.g., Leibniz's interpretation of what counts as sufficiency. A full treatment of all this would divorce teleological conceptions of sufficient reason (Socrates, Plato, Leibniz) from anti-teleological conceptions. For Heraclitus' anti-teleological stance see B52, B124 ('The fairest order in the world is a heap of random sweepings').

Then, in the light of our findings under that head, we must revise and modify or develop our explanations. Which being done, we must go on, find more phenomena to explain, use these explananda to gain favour for more hypotheses, and then collect all our hypotheses together in order to test the new accumulated total commitment for consistency, plausibility etc . . .

No articulate statement of this method is to be found in Greek philosophy before Plato reaches for the Method of Dialectic in *Phaedo* and *Meno*, and tries in the *Republic* to marry it up with the idea of ultimate explanation in terms of the Good, which Leibniz inherited from him and brought into a quite special relation with Sufficient Reason. Nor is there any fully explicit statement of the Principle of Sufficient Reason before Parmenides. So sceptics will say that primitive natural philosophers such as the ones we are concerned with could not possibly have engaged in reasoning that wants so sophisticated a description. But to this I would reply first that Anaximander and Heraclitus and their successors were not primitive thinkers; and, second, that even if they were, we should still need to remember that very simple patterns of reasoning can satisfy very complicated theoretical descriptions. (Think even of the syllogism in Barbara.) The sophistication of the description we have to give in order to see the argument from the best explanation as a rational argument is no reason not to credit the Milesians (however methodologically unconscious they may have been) with the corresponding procedure – or with the conviction that is made for the method, that we live in a universe (as Edward Hussey puts it) of 'order, lawlike regularity and intellectually satisfying construction',[7] susceptible of truly general, all-embracing explanatory hypotheses that stand in no need of qualification or adjustment *ad hoc*. (Cf. B41 etc., quoted in 1.1.)

1.3 From the nature of the hypothesis, the claim that Heraclitus and the Milesians have a common method can only be judged by the coherence and order that it will eventually discover to us if we see these men as building up their world-picture in response to the demands made upon them by the principle of Sufficient Reason and in the light of the precept always to argue back to the best explanation. In the interim, some more immediate conviction of

7 Edward Hussey, *The Presocratics* (London 1972), 17.

Heraclitus' continuity with the Milesians may be created by reconsideration of the familiar text where it seems that Heraclitus makes allusion to Anaximander. This is the correction that Heraclitus seems to offer of Anaximander's doctrine of mutual reparation. Anaximander had said:

Whence things originate, thither according to necessity they must return and perish [that is, back into the same components]; for they must pay penalty and be judged for their injustice in accordance with the assessment of time (B1).

It would appear that Heraclitus found much to agree with in this opinion, offering an excellent gloss on Anaximander's most probable meaning:

Cold things grow warm, warm cools, moist grows parched, dry dampens (B126).

But there was a fault that Heraclitus found with Anaximander:

One must understand that war is universal, strife is justice, and that absolutely everything happens by strife and by necessity (B80);

and he denounced Homer (cf. Aristotle, *Eth. Eud.* 1235a26 [+ scholiast on *Iliad* xviii 107] = A22) for saying 'Would that strife would perish from among gods and men', complaining that Homer did not see that he was praying for the destruction of the universe.

Now it is scarcely denied by anybody that B80 is a clear and (by Heraclitean standards) respectful allusion to Anaximander.[8] What has been insufficiently remarked is that such a disagreement between the two of them only makes sense against some background of agreement. What was this background? Only one answer readily suggests itself. They agree in wanting to explain the maintenance of the world order. Evidently they also agree that the maintenance of the world order (or the maintenance, had we better say in Anaximander's case, of this particular whorl off the *Apeiron*?) must be managed from within a definite store of something or other. Unless this were agreed, why otherwise should there be any need for what Anaximander calls *requital for injustice* and what Heraclitus prefers to see as *mere exchange* – one thing's superseding another, as one piece replaces another on a

8 Cf. Vlastos, 'On Heraclitus', *American Journal of Philology*, 1955.

square in the game of *pessoi*? (Cf. B52) If the two agree that this sort of process must be postulated, the disagreement between them relates only to the proper view to take of the justice or injustice of the process they otherwise agree about.

Here of course I am guessing – as I believe everyone interested in either Heraclitus or Anaximander ought to be obliged to guess. And obviously the guess must be pitted against any rival suggestion about what the background of agreement was. But this particular suggestion, together with the special idea that it imports of the autonomic steering or regulation of the world order, has the signal advantage of engaging well with information that we have from Aristotle about his predecessors. Aristotle says that one of their concerns was that coming to be and passing away should not give out.[9] On my reading, Anaximander and Heraclitus will be prominent examples of philosophers with this preoccupation.

1.4 Such familiar reflections will lead into others. In Anaximander certain questions appear to have been left open about the origin and continuous renewal of the world as we know it. Presumably B1 was his most striking contribution to the problem. But Heraclitus himself *closed* these questions. Not only was

this cosmos made neither of god nor of man, but always has been, is and always will be, an everlasting fire going out in measures and kindling in measures;[10]

the steering too (or the governance of the world as we know it) is said by Heraclitus to be from within, not, as it may have been for Anaximander, by the Boundless from without. (Cf. on Anaximander, Aristotle, *Physics* 203b7ff.) For whatever Heraclitus' thunderbolt is, whatever his Zeus may be, and whatever the relations may be between thunderbolt and Heraclitean fire (per-

---

9 Cf. *Ph.* 203b15–30, 208a8–9; *GC* 336a14–18; Burnet, *Early Greek Philosophy* (London 1908²), 60.

10 B30 (in part). Aristotle is thought to have been the first to assert that the *kosmos* was not created. But B30 suggests that he was anticipated in this not altogether satisfactory move by Heraclitus.

Aristotle asserts (*Cael.* 279b12) that all his predecessors believed that the *kosmos* had a beginning, though many denied (280a11) that matter had a beginning. To reconcile B30 with Aristotle it seems best to locate the difference Aristotle sees between himself and Heraclitus in the *periodicity* of things. Aristotle contemplates little or no variability from *the kind of world order that is familiar to us*, Heraclitus an orderly eternal periodicity. See 4.1, 4.2.

haps these things can be debated), thunderbolt is or stands for something inside the world; and

Thunderbolt steers all things (B64).

But then, if the steering of the *kosmos* was from within and if the maintenance of its order and vital activity was a question that required an answer, the idea of autonomic regulation that appears in the Anaximander fragment was exactly the idea that Heraclitus needed. One can scarcely imagine a more natural continuity between the doctrines of two independent thinkers, where the second knows the work of the first and improves or simplifies or develops it.

## 2    A hypothetical reconstruction of the scaffolding of Heraclitus' theory of flux

2.1 I embark now on the hazardous and experimental work of the reconstruction of the philosophical motivation for Heraclitus' world view – a necessary task, but one that was speculative even in early antiquity. So far I have credited him with a Milesian method – the method of postulating whatever appears the best explanation of a phenomenon. I have quoted his conviction of the unity of things (which, as the reader will have guessed, I want to see as related to one consequence of that method). And I have implicated him in what I argue to have been a Milesian question about the maintenance of the world's motion, order and vital activity. To complete that stage of the reconstruction I have to ask what observations or phenomena can be expected to have given him the *question* of the constant renewal of the world and made it as pressing as the fragments cited in 1.4 above have suggested to me that it was. The most natural answer would appear to be:

(a) the everyday observation of the conspicuous but not man- ifestly ubiquitous disintegration of terrestrial *order*, and the observation of the constant transmutation and decay of terrestrial *substances*;

(b) the equally familiar observation of the habitual tendency of terrestrial *motions* to run down;

(c) the observation of the continuation, in spite of all this, of the world that we know, replenished by creation, growth, and new motion. When one substance ceases to exist, another takes its place. When one motion is spent, others appear and inherit its impetus.

Observations (a) (b) (c) suffice to justify the postulation of a theory of reparation. But what else beside these things did Heraclitus observe and seek to explain and bring into harmony with them? He is credited with all sorts of hypotheses about sun, moon and stars as bowls of fire, and about the periodic and regular inclinations of these bowls. Such hypotheses, if Heraclitus really propounded them, were evidently designed to explain differences of night and day, or the warmth and coolness of the seasons. I am disposed to agree with the sceptical historian of science D. R. Dicks[11] that it is 'doubtful whether any of this [would-be astronomical detail] represents even approximately what Heraclitus thought'; but the detailed accuracy of the reports matter far less than a presumption which they help to sustain, that such celestial happenings were among the phenomena that Heraclitus treated as explananda. Dicks is surely right again when he declares, on the basis of fragments such as B94,

The sun will not transgress his due measure: otherwise the Erinyes, the ministers of justice, will find him out[12]

and B100

. . . the cycles the sun presides over, in order to determine and adjudicate the changes and seasons that produce everything,

that 'two things in particular struck [Heraclitus] when he contemplated [the cosmic] order, first the fact of its continuity, and second its periodicity'. But if this is what is impresses about the heavens, then how is the apparent anomaly, diversity and small-scale disorder of terrestrial phenomena and the limited persistence of ordinary continuants to be subsumed under *one* order of nature with celestial imperishability, continuity and periodicity? Surely what underlies celestial stability must be some regular lawlike process or processes. Nothing less will suffice to explain celestial phenomena. But if so, then, despite appearances, regularity of process must underlie terrestrial phenomena too – unless we are to breach the *a priori* requirement of unity (see B41 etc. quoted in

11 D. R. Dicks, *Early Greek Astronomy to Aristotle* (London 1970).
12 Cf. B120, on which see Kahn, *Anaximander*, 197.

1.1). In the name of unity, which is only another aspect of Sufficient Reason, the orderly process that is manifest in the heavens must be something that the natural philosopher can recklessly hypothesise to hold absolutely everywhere, and so upon earth – in spite of the apparent contrast between the perishability of terrestrial bodies and the apparent imperishability of heavenly ones. The conviction of unity ('one from all and all from one') forces us to see the terrestrial order as continuously renewed in spite of disintegration and change; and the celestial order as subject to continuous processes of change in spite of its regularity, periodicity and everlastingness. But if unseen elemental processes are uniformly regular and directed, then anomaly is an illusion that results from our imperfect understanding of their interaction, and, if all involve change, then permanence or apparent cessation of activity represents equilibrium (temporary equality, not armistice) between unseen forces that are opposing one another actively.

2.2 When he reaches this point Heraclitus has advanced well past the observational-cum-hypothetical stage of scientific theorising that I began by describing. He is offering redescriptions of phenomena themselves in terms more theory-contaminated than any that our senses could offer, and then reconceptualising the classes of terrestrial and celestial phenomena in defiance of observed differences.

The hidden joining/harmony is stronger than the visible one (B52).

One hypothesis leads to the necessity for another. Inasmuch as every one of the elemental processes hypothesised must, unless resisted by others, take over the whole world, the belief in the continuance of the world obliges him to believe in the irresolubility (by treaty, by exhaustion, or by any other means) of the struggle in which they are locked. Strife is ubiquitous and universal. But being the instrument of renewal and restitution, it is also just.

2.3 So much for a first attempt at reconstruction of how we may find it intelligible that Heraclitus makes perpetual process or change the model by which to redescribe everything. We have motivated the idea of a flux that is ubiquitous, incessant, exceptionless and all-embracing, and in virtue of which not only all living things flow but absolutely all perceptible things – stones, rocks, even the sun (cf. B8) – flow (cf. Aristotle, *Metaphysics* 987a33, 1078b14, Melissus DK B8). And, seeing Heraclitus in this light, we find nothing to astonish us in Plato's report that:

Heraclitus said that everything is in a stage of change and nothing stays stable, and likening things to the flow of a river he says that you could not step twice into the same river (*Cratylus* 402A)[13]

or in Aristotle's testimony:

And some say that all existing things without exception are in constant movement, but this escapes our perception. Supporters of this theory do not state clearly what kind of motion they mean or whether they mean all kinds (*Physics* 253b9–12).

It is plain that those physicists who assert that all sensible things are always in motion are wrong . . . They mostly conceive this as alteration (things are always in flux and decay, they say), and they go so far as to speak even of becoming and perishing as a process of alteration (ibid. 265a2–7).

It is true that someone may still ask why we should believe that everything in heaven and earth is in flux and participates in a hidden harmony of opposites. But the ready answer to that question is that Heraclitus' argument or doctrine is simply a bold generalisation from certain special cases or phenomena. It was the height of madness to extend his theory from these phenomena to absolutely everything. But before one derides the theory for that reason one should ask how else Sufficient Reason is to be reconciled with the convictions that our senses make it nearly impossible for us to abandon, about earth and sky and the seemingly continuous motion and renewal of the *kosmos*. (And how else, we can then reflect, is the ordinary behaviour of colliding bodies to be explained, unless *all* bodies contain opposing processes?)

13 In 'Natural Change in Heraclitus', *Mind*, 60 (1951), 38–42, G. S. Kirk has sought to cast doubt on Plato's testimony here. He has done this in the name of doctrines of measure and reciprocity between opposites whose attribution to Heraclitus he has made very persuasive. My exposition of these doctrines is indebted both to this article and to Kirk's *Heraclitus: The Cosmic Fragments* (Cambridge 1954). I also believe Kirk reconstructs the river fragment correctly. (Cf. 2.5 below: if Heraclitus also said that you could not step into the same river twice, that is a hyperbolical restatement of what is said soberly and correctly in B12.) But against Kirk, I should claim that, on a more correct understanding of change than Plato achieved when he departed from the everyday conception to which Heraclitus was party, there is no conflict of any sort between the measure doctrine and the doctrine of universal flux.

2.4 What further ancient evidence can be adduced for Heraclitus' involvement in this way of thinking? Two points at least can be confirmed, one being general and the other an indispensable point of detail.

First, the reconstruction makes goodish sense of a report of Plato's that is certainly intended to collect up Heraclitus' as well as other philosophers' opinions:

Coming to be, and what passes for being, are produced by change, while not being and ceasing to be are produced by inactivity. For instance, the hot, or fire, which we are told actually generates and governs everything else, is itself generated by means of movement and friction; and these are changes. Moreover the class of living things is produced by means of those same processes . . . The condition of the body is destroyed, isn't it, by inactivity and illness but to a great extent preserved by exercise and change . . . *States of inactivity rot things and destroy them whereas states of activity preserve them* . . . So long as the heavenly cycle and the sun are in motion, everything is and is preserved, in the realms of both gods and men; whereas if that motion . . . were brought to a standstill, everything would be destroyed (Plato, *Theaetetus* 153A–D, trans. J. H. McDowell).

In the second place, confirmation is to be found in Diogenes Laertius for the way in which I have claimed that Heraclitus combines an ontology of substances – the belief in what we should call substances – with his belief in universal flux:

The totality of things is composed out of fire and is dissolved into it. Everything comes to be in accordance with fate, and the totality of things is harmoniously joined together through *enantiodromia* (running in opposition) (D.L. ix 7 [=DK A1]).

The word *enantiodromia* – whatever it was that prompted it to Diogenes – is tailor-made for the account that our reconstruction has been forced to give of continuants, of permanency, and of the appearance of cessation of activity.

2.5 And here at last we arrive at the river fragment. For reasons that will become more fully transparent in 5.1 below and following, the version that I accept as likely to be closest to Heraclitus' official statement of his doctrine (no matter what other poetical or rhetorical effects he may have attempted) is Kirk's reconstruction:

Upon those who step into the same rivers different and again different waters flow. The waters scatter and gather, come together and flow away, approach and depart (Fragments 12 and 91; text, contamination and translation after Kirk, *Heraclitus, The Cosmic Fragments* (Cambridge 1954), 367–84).

The river is at once an eminent and observable instance of flow and a metaphorical hostage for myriads of invisible cases of heavenly and celestial flux.[14] It is also an eminent instance and metaphysical hostage for processes of renewal which Heraclitus sees as resulting from the equilibria or superpositions of opposing forces that underlie substance. In this reconstruction the fragment will remind one forcibly that Heraclitus' thinking is untouched by Parmenides. Heraclitus is not concerned with how it is conceptually possible for a substance to survive through change as that very same substance.[15] Why (unless one is sophisticated enough or muddled enough to be confused by identity and persistence) should that be a problem? What he asks is how a thing could survive unless it did change. A substance can persist through time, but only by virtue of constant process, and if *work* is done:

The barley drink disintegrates if it is not constantly stirred (B125).

The barley drink was a drink made of barley-meal, grated cheese and Pramnian wine (to which on one well known occasion when Odysseus was her guest, Circe added honey and magical drugs).[16] Being neither a mixture nor even a suspension it separated and reverted rapidly to its constituents unless it was stirred vigorously. What the barley drink stands for is at once conditional persistence and the tendency towards disintegration which Heraclitus sees as so general that order, renewal and arrest of disintegration are what need explaining. He explains them without explaining them *away*, however; and if we accept that, with the barley drink as with everything else, what work explains is renewal and persistence, and if we also remember the correction to Anaximander, then we shall be led to one more reflection that belongs here: wherever one substance does persist by work and through process being set against process, there

14 For the idea of a phenomenon going proxy for a whole class to which it may itself belong, I am greatly indebted to Edward Hussey (see chapter 2 below). Cf. also here Philip Wheelwright, *Heraclitus* (Oxford 1959), 44, from whom I borrow the Goethean phrase 'eminent instance'.

15 One of the editors has informed me that, in his courses of lectures on the Presocratics, Owen has expressed a similar opinion.

16 Cf. Homer, *Odyssey*, 10, 234 and 326.

will always be other substances which, for just that reason, did not benefit by the application of work, or had it withdrawn from them.

2.6 I shall return in section 5 to the misunderstandings that Heraclitus' doctrine has provoked in the minds of those who have been schooled to put strange constructions upon ordinary descriptions of change and find philosophical difficulty in the idea of a changing substance. But in the interim, let us complete the first statement of the Heraclitean doctrine that persistence and numerical identity require change. It is important that this is not the doctrine that some continuant substance or stuff persists through *every* change – a Milesian idea which the Heraclitean doctrine of process is in flight from. Nor is it the doctrine that an individual substance can persist provided that just any change befalls it. Admittedly, there is a great need for an account of what changes promote or allow the survival of a particular sort of continuant and what changes will entail destruction. This really is a good problem. (My own answer to the problem would depend on the natural distinction between answers to the question *what a thing is* and *what it is like*.[17] I claim that once we focus on the foundations of this distinction, which is almost the same as that between substantive and adjective (cf. Aristotle's *Categories* 1–5), it will appear plainly that particular concepts of continuants of this or that natural kind both *require* of their compliants certain sorts of change and also *delimit* the changes that such compliants can undergo except on pain of extinction: see below, 5.3.) But it is not clear that Heraclitus himself, enjoying the good fortune of writing before the waters had been muddied, saw any of this as an urgent or intractable problem, or even *as* a problem.[18] He takes the concept of change for granted. But he does not therefore misconceive it.

## 3 Fire

3.1 If 2.5 is correct, we must expect that, as one force or another force temporarily prevails in the struggle at any place, there will be a shift in the locus of equilibrium. And wherever this shift occurs

17 See my *Sameness and Substance* (Oxford 1980), especially chs. II–III.
18 Martha Nussbaum has put it to me that B36 and Heraclitus' other remarks about watery souls indicate an interest in this problem, and that the river fragment does too, though less clearly.

we have seen that we must expect a gradual but continuous run-down of substances going past their *acme* in favour of others that are in progress towards their *acme*. We must expect this because Heraclitus supposes that there is a limited store of that in virtue of which there can be any processes at all. If, however, we now speculate with Heraclitus about the long-term general tendency of the struggle of elemental processes and of everything that depends on this struggle, then we have a chance to plait together at last the following ideas: the unity of things, perpetual flux, the just or equitable replacement of one thing by another thing, and *fire*.

The interpretation of Heraclitus' theory of fire that I want to propose rests on the following fragments:

This world or world-order, which is the same for all, no one of the gods or men has made; but it was ever, is now, and ever shall be, an ever-living Fire, kindling in measures and going out in measures (B30).

Fire lives the death of earth and air lives the death of fire, water lives the death of air, and earth of water (B76).

The turnings of fire are first sea; and of sea half is earth, half whirlwind (B31A).

Earth melts back into sea and is measured by the same tale as before it became earth (B31B).

All things are an exchange or requital for Fire, and Fire for all things, like goods for gold and gold for goods (B90).

B30 appears to assure us that the kosmos is a perpetual fire. Yet fire is extinguished. So fire itself is not the only elemental form. B31A and B31B tell us about fire's particular turnings or transformations into other things, e.g. into sea and earth. But B90 encourages us to suppose that, when sea changes into earth and back again, there is something that is not lost at all. And surely Heraclitus thinks the same applies in the cases where fire is condensed into sea or sea congeals into earth as when earth melts back into sea and sea evaporates back into fire (which Diogenes Laertius says Heraclitus says is the process by which fire is nourished). If so, then Heraclitus must think that, whatever happens, no fire is ever lost in the cycle of transformations ('Beginning and end are shared in the circumference of a circle', B103). If everything else is to fire as goods are to gold, then that cannot help but mean that the total fire-value of fire, sea and earth (plus *prēstēr*, plus whatever else) taken together is constant. Suppose then that we were to try to think of Heraclitus' fire not as a particular form or stuff but as the agent of all process – or as the determinable of process itself. If we give in to this temptation, we are not the first to do so. See the discussion of the etymology of 'Zeus' and *'dikaion'* in Plato's *Cratylus* 412D:

> Those who suppose all things to be in motion conceive the greater part of nature to be a mere receptacle, and they say there is a penetrating power which passes through all this and is the instrument of creation in all, and is the subtlest and swiftest element . . . this element which superintends all things and pierces all (*diaion*) is rightly called just (*dikaion*) . . . [When] I begin . . . to interrogate [these philosophers] gently . . they try to satisfy me with one observation after another . . . One says that justice is the sun . . . [one says] it is fire itself . . . another says, No, not fire itself but the hot itself that is in the fire (quoted by Kirk, *Heraclitus*, 363.).

Suppose now that we see some trace here of a Heraclitean conception of Fire, or of something that those who had the whole text of Heraclitus found that they had to say in order to sustain their stance as Heracliteans. Then what I believe we shall conclude is that, without having any notion of how the relevant measure of process would be constructed, Heraclitus committed himself to the idea that the total quantity of process is constant. I do not mean that he had the conceptual resources to make this last claim explicit. He has to prefer such expressions as the metaphor we encounter in B90. But if we try to transpose what he says there into something more literal, and then collate that with B31B, no smaller claim will do justice to the advance he has made from the Milesian standpoint. Fire is no more that out of which all things are made than gold is a constituent of all the things that buy and sell in the market place. Gold is one stuff among others. But it is that by reference to which, or that in terms of which, all other stuffs can be measured there. Fire is for the world order, then, what gold is for the *agora* – the measure. Extending Heraclitus' metaphor, one may go on to say that, notwithstanding the local extinguishing of fire, and notwithstanding temporal variation in the proportions of the elemental forms (see below, section 4), the great cosmic enterprise as a whole trades neither at a loss nor at a profit; but, in virtue of a reciprocity between processes that are getting their way and processes that are falling back, the books always balance exactly. However much the assets are redeployed or transformed, the *capital* is constant as measured in measures of fire.

A comparison between fire, conceived as Heraclitus conceived it, and energy, as that was conceived in eighteenth–nineteenth century physics, would be anachronistic, but perhaps only relatively mildly so. Many plain men have scarcely any better idea of what energy is than Heraclitus had of what fire was. But most of us have *some* conception of energy. The common idea, and the idea that holds our conception of energy in place and holds Heraclitus' conception of fire in place, is the idea of whatever it is that is conserved and makes possible the continuance of the world-order. 'Fire' is Heraclitus' counter for that, 'energy' (or energy plus matter, conceived independently of energy in nineteenth-century fashion) is ours. A physicist would be needed to take the point further. But that does not mean that Heraclitus cannot have taken it this far.

3.2 This sort of reading of B90 and B31A,B is not new. I find that Vlastos and others[19] have anticipated it:

[B90] identifies fire as the thing that remains constant in all transformations and implies that *its* measure is the same or the common measure in all things . . . The invariance of [fire's] measure is what accounts for the observance of the *metron* in all things, and fire is therefore that which 'governs' or 'steers' all things (G. Vlastos, 'On Heraclitus', *American Journal of Philology* 76 (1955), 360–1).

But the very mention of energy in the modern sense will prompt others to remind me that it took European science two hundred years from the death of Galileo and at least one long and vexatious metaphysico-scientific controversy concerning *vis viva* to assemble the ideas of work and of potential energy (as distinct from kinetic energy), to gather the other fruits of the conceptual labours of Leibniz, Bernouilli, Helmholtz and others, formulate the principle of the conservation of energy, and then at last see the principle of the conservation of the *sum* of kinetic and potential energy tested by the efforts of Joule. I also expect to be informed that by the importation of the idea of energy one lays oneself open to the charge of systematic falsification of Heraclitus, a thinker

19 E.g. Kahn, in his *Anaximander*, and J. L. Mackie, in an unpublished paper of 1941.

much more primitive (it may be said) than any who can be recognised in this portrait.

Such a charge would rest on a misapprehension both of what I am saying, and of the conceptual provenance of the conservation principle. To make out my interpretation I do not have to credit Heraclitus with any conception at all of that which is the sum of kinetic and potential energy, where kinetic energy is $\frac{1}{2}mv^2$, or even to credit him with our conception of energy as the power of doing work, where work is conceived as force times distance moved (or whatever). Nor do I have to credit Heraclitus with any cleverness that would have carried him any great distance in physics itself. I have only to credit him with having asked a question and then conceived of there being something or other whose conservation would help to answer that question. So far as I am concerned there is nothing more than this to the *rapport* between the energy that modern science has established to exist in the world and the thoughts of Heraclitus. I cannot forbear however to add that, whatever the complexities of arriving at an idea of energy sufficiently precise for the conservation principle to be tested and proved, one part of what eventually and painfully discovered it to human beings was a stubbornly ineradicable prejudice that is even older than philosophy:

An effect is always in proportion to the action which is necessary to produce it. René Descartes (*Oeuvres* I [A.T.]. See pp. 435–448)

There is always a perfect equivalence between the full cause and the whole effect (Leibniz, Reply to Abbé Catelan in *Nouvelles de la Republique de Lettres*, Feb. 1687, quoted in Hidé Ishiguro, 'Pre-established Harmony *versus* Constant Conjunction', *Proc. Brit. Acad.* 63 (1979), 241).

No working cause can be destroyed totally or in part without producing an action equal to a decrease in the cause (Johannes Bernouilli, *Opera Omnia* Vol. 3, p. 56, Essay no. 135, ch. 10, §1).

The author [Clarke] objects that two soft or non-elastic Bodies meeting together lose some of their *Force*. I answer, No . . . The *Forces* are not destroyed but scattered among the small parts; but the case here is the same as when men change great Money into small (Leibniz: Fifth letter to Samuel Clarke).

Why are Leibniz and Bernouilli so sure? Though they proved to be right, they have no empirical evidence that it was so. Maybe the answer to this question has to do with the ultimate unintelligibility of the idea that anything could come from nothing. But the most striking demonstration of the naturalness and simplicity of this underlying thought can be found in the words that Joule spoke in St Anne's Church Reading Room, Manchester, in the 1847 address in which he first described for the world at large his experimental demonstration of the conservation principle:

You will be surprised to hear that until very recently the universal opinion has been that living force could be absolutely and irrevocably destroyed at any one's option. Thus, when a weight falls to the ground, it has been generally supposed that its living force is absolutely annihilated, and that the labour which may have been expended in raising it to the elevation from which it fell has been entirely thrown away and wasted, without the production of any permanent effect whatever. We might reason, *a priori*, that such absolute destruction of living force cannot possibly take place, because it is manifestly absurd to suppose that the powers with which God has endowed matter can be destroyed any more than that they can be created by man's agency; but we are not left with this argument alone, decisive as it must be to every unprejudiced mind. The common experience of every one teaches him that living force is not *destroyed* by the friction or collision of bodies. We have reason to believe that the manifestations of living force on our globe are, at the present time, as extensive as those which have existed at any time since its creation, or, at any rate, since the deluge – that the winds blow as strongly, and the torrents flow with equal impetuosity now, as at the remote period of 4,000 or even 6,000 years ago; and yet we are certain that, through that vast interval of time, the motions of the air and of the water have been incessantly obstructed and hindered by friction. We may conclude then, with certainty, that these motions of air and water, constituting living force, are not *annihilated* by friction. We lose sight of them, indeed, for a time; but we find them again reproduced. Were it not so, it is perfectly obvious that long ere this all nature would have come to a dead standstill.

How much of this would be unintelligible to a Presocratic philosopher?

## 4    *Periodicity and variation*

4.1 Among the many loose ends I have left hanging here (many of which would still hang loose, I fear, even if we had the whole book instead of fragments), let me attend to just one. What in this picture will explain periodicity, and night and day and the seasons? It seems clear that Heraclitus thought of these as corresponding to variations in the quantity or distribution of elemental forms air, sea, *prēstēr*, earth, etc. Diogenes Laertius reports

Heraclitus as maintaining that the earth gave off bright exhalations which nourished fire and produced day by igniting in the circle of the sun; whereas the sea gave off dark exhalations which nourished moisture and by their periodic increase produced night. But luckily there is nothing to force me to try to adjudicate upon the accuracy of this report. For however it is interpreted, the report (like the *verbatim* fragments themselves) leaves unanswered what is the most pressing and interesting question: what causes or steers or controls these variations themselves?

Perhaps we can supply the deficit in our evidence here (or in Heraclitus' own book) by adducing the words of the zealously Heraclitean author of the Hippocratic treatise *de Victu*, which Bywater had the happy idea of printing with his collection of fragments of Heraclitus:

Fire can move all things always, while water can nourish all things always; but in turn each masters or is mastered to the greatest maximum or the least minimum possible. Neither of them can gain the complete mastery for the following reason. The fire as it advances to the limit of the water lacks nourishment, and so turns to where it is likely to be nourished. The water as it advances to the limit of the fire finds its motion to fail and at this point falls back (*de Victu* 1 3).

The explanation is thoroughly Ionian in spirit and it fills a gap in the Heraclitean theory. If we wished, and if we trusted Diogenes Laertius enough, it could be complicated and diversified by deployment of the two sorts of exhalation he mentions. But what matters is the leading idea. Every elemental process or force wants to take over the whole world, but, the closer it comes to that objective, the harder it finds it to follow up its victories, and the better conditions then become for the forces that are ranged against it to rally themselves. If we see this as a sort of feedback arrangement, then we have only to suppose that the requisite and inevitable adjustment is always slightly delayed, or that there is always overcompensation in the adjustments, in order to explain periodicity. We can see periodicity as resulting from a kind of 'hunting' between opposite and equally unstable or unmaintainable states of an unceasing struggle.[20]

20 We can take this idea over from the author of the *de Victu* as a complementation of Heraclitus' doctrine. But of course we should note that he has resolved in an overdefinite way certain difficulties – most notably Heraclitus' apparent need for a matter-principle quite independent of fire. Anticipating Aristotle's criticism of monistic condensation and rarefaction theories (*GC* 330b10), this author allows water to enjoy an

4.2 The *de Victu* certainly fills out the Heraclitean world-view. But more still needs to be said about periodicity. It has often been supposed that there is a conflict here between the testimonies of Plato and Aristotle. Aristotle says in the *de Caelo* 279b12:

That the world was generated they are all agreed, but generation over, some say that it is eternal, others say that it is destructible like any other natural formation. Others, again, with Empedocles and Heraclitus believe that there is alternation in the destructive process, which takes now this direction now that and continues without end.

There is other evidence of a complementary kind that is hard to dismiss. Simplicius says (*de Caelo* 94, 4):

And Heraclitus says that at one time the kosmos is burned out and at another it rises again from fire according to certain definite cycles of time in which he says it is kindling in measures and going out in measures. Later the Stoics came to be of the same opinion.

And again in *in Physica* 23, 38 Simplicius quotes Heraclitus as saying that:

There is a certain order and determined time in the changing of the kosmos in accordance with some preordained necessity.

There is also DK A13, which consists of passages of Aëtius and Censorinus and amounts to the claim that Heraclitus thought that there was a great year whose winter was a great flood and whose summer was an *ekpurōsis* (conflagration). It appears that Heraclitus and Linus supposed that the cycle consisted of 10,800 years. This is a not inconsiderable body of evidence. But many have felt that there was some conflict between all this and what Plato says in *Sophistes*:

The stricter Muses [e.g. Heraclitus] say 'in drawing apart it is always being drawn together.' The milder [e.g. Empedocles] relax the rule.that this should always be so and speak of alternate states, in which the universe is now one and at peace through the power of love, and now many and at war with itself owing to some sort of Strife (*Sophistes* 242E).

What scholars have concluded from these testimonia is that we have to choose between an oscillatory or Aristotelian interpretation of

autonomy for which we have no Heraclitean authority. Insofar as Heraclitus himself offered any account of the differentiation of kinds of process or kinds of thing, he seems to have explained differentiation of things by reference to the difference of the processes underlying them, and differentiation of processes simply – alas – by a metaphor: 'God is day and night, winter and summer, war and peace, surfeit and hunger, but he takes various shapes, *just as fire, when it is mingled with spices, is named according to the savour of each*' (B63, trans. Burnet).

Heraclitus and a Platonic interpretation in terms of instant reciprocal tension between opposites. Heraclitean scholarship itself has
long oscillated between the two interpretations. Tension theorists
have ignored or sought to discredit A13 and Aristotle *de Caelo*
279b12, while oscillationists have even supposed that they had to
tinker with the interpretation of what seems to me to be one of the
clearest of Heraclitus' fragments. This is B51, a fragment whose
proper paraphrase is surely:

They do not grasp how the discord of things is in fact a perfect accord.
[What we have here], as with a bow or lyre, is the harmonious
reciprocation of opposites, or opposing tendencies.[21]

Now anyone who sees a conflict here should start by noting
that there is in fact no consistent opposition between Plato and
Aristotle in this matter. In another place Aristotle confirms a
steady state reading of B51:

Heraclitus says that 'it is what opposes that helps' and that 'from
opposing tones comes the fairest harmonia' and 'that everything happens
in accordance with strife' (EN 1155b4).

And, so soon as we understand the doctrine of fire properly, I
suggest that there need be no real conflict at all between oscillation
and reciprocal tension. The world is in a steady state of rapid
flux;[22] but this steadiness simply consists in the conservation of
process or fire. Heraclitus' theory of the world requires reciprocal
tension if it is to accommodate substance; and it requires oscillation if it is to accommodate periodicity. But there is simply no
problem in combining both features, or in allowing continuous
variation in the overall proportions of the elemental forms, if we
will only see the conservation of fire in terms that are abstract
enough. What then about *ekpurōsis*, which oscillationists like
Charles Kahn now admit into Heraclitus (in reaction against
Burnet and Kirk)? The idea of periodic annihilation of everything

---

21 Whether we read *palintonos* or *palintropos* – whether we consider the lyre or bow in
repose, strung in tension against itself (*palintonos*), or consider the bow or lyre's
tendency to return into that state after the withdrawal of the interfering force of the
archer or lyre player (*palintropos*) – it makes little difference, I believe. Either way, this is
a steady state theory, presented in a manner consistent with a potentially very abstract
account of what the steadiness consists in (it is a steadiness such as to require a total
balance of universal agitation), and consistent also with periodicity or seasonal
variation.

22 A phrase I steal from Rudolf Schoenheimer (one of the founders of modern biochemis-
try; see *The Dynamic State of Body Constituents* (Cambridge, Mass. 1942)).

by fire is rationally objectionable (how can fire differentiate itself again?), and it spoils the accord with the *de Victu* passage. But nor is it forced upon us by textual evidence. For there is nothing in the conservation of fire, seen now as the conservation of quantity of process, to exclude the possibility that Heraclitus thought that every 10,800 years (or whatever) the sea rises to its maximum possible extent and takes over all it can, provoking an equal and opposite reaction in which fire conceived as an elemental form reaches out to *its* maximum extent, scorching almost everything.

## 5   Identity through time

5.1 Finally I turn to flux and identity through time. In point of general Heraclitean doctrine I have accounted Plato a reasonable witness.[23] But as a critic I think he was less excellent; either that, I would claim, or his influence has been pernicious.

An entirely typical statement of the mental condition into which we have lapsed in certain matters ever since Plato is to be found in Frege's introduction to *Foundations of Arithmetic*:

If everything were in continual flux, and nothing maintained itself fixed for all time, there would no longer be any possibility of getting to know anything about the world and everything would be plunged in confusion (p. vii).

The general context is of course arithmetic but the assertion itself carries no such restriction, and the confusion it evinces between flux and chaos echoes a well known argument in Plato's *Theaetetus* 182. This argument distinguishes between two kinds of change – moving in space and undergoing alteration – and it then claims that nothing can be involved in both simultaneously:

Socrates   Let us ask them 'Are all things, according to your doctrine, in motion and flux?'
Theodorus  Yes.
Socrates   Have they then both kinds of motion which we distinguished? Are they moving in space and also undergoing alteration?
Theodorus  Of course; that is if they are to be in perfect motion.
Socrates   Then if they moved only in space, but did not undergo

---

23 Even though he offers us a misstatement of the river paradigm. But here there is interaction between the virtues of the witness and the vices of the critic.

alteration, we could perhaps say what qualities belong to those moving things which are in flux, could we not?

Theodorus That is right.

Socrates But since not even this remains fixed – that the thing in flux flows white, but changes, so that there is a flux of the very whiteness and a change of colour, so that it may not in that way be convicted of remaining fixed, it is possible to give any name to a colour, and yet to speak accurately?

Theodorus How can it be possible, or possible to give a name to anything else of this sort, if while we are speaking it always evades us, being, as it is, in flux?

(Translated H. N. Fowler)

The standard interpretation of this passage reads the argument as pointing to a precondition of identifying or individuating anything through time. Thus Owen wrote in his article on Plato's *Timaeus*:

Plato points out that if anything . . . were perpetually changing in all respects, so that at no time could it be described as being so-and-so, then nothing could be said of it at all – and, *inter alia*, it could not be said to be changing. If an object moves, we can say what sort of thing is moving only if it has some qualitative stability (182C9–10); conversely, to have complete qualitative flux ascribed to it, a thing must have location . . .[24] So no description of any process is possible if we can say only that its constituents are changing from or to something and never that they are something (cf. *Tim.* 37E5–38A2, where it is allowed to say only what a *gignomenon* was and will be; the White Queen offered Alice jam on the same terms).[25]

On the basis of *Theaetetus* 182 it has seemed that Plato either concludes that knowledge of material particulars is impossible (a familiar nineteenth–twentieth century interpretation) or concludes that, if there is to be intelligible description of perception and the objects of perception themselves (which are never this or that in themselves,[26] but only becoming), then the contention that 'everything flows' or 'everything constantly changes' must be mitigated somehow.[27] And here the enemies of Heraclitus have

24 The omitted passage reads: 'Nor can any quality of the object, such as its whiteness, be claimed as a subject of this unqualified change: any change would be "change to another colour", and to apply "whiteness" to a colour-progression is to deprive it of determinate sense' (182D 2–5). This anticipates a variant interpretation offered by John McDowell at pp. 180–4 of his annotated translation (Oxford 1973).

25 G. E. L. Owen, 'The Place of the *Timaeus* in Plato's Dialogues' *Classical Quarterly*, n.s. 3 (1953), 85–6; cf. I. M. Crombie, *An Examination of Plato's Doctrines* (London 1962–3), II, 27.

26 Cf. Plato, *Timaeus* 49D7–E6.

27 At least for instance to the extent of according sufficient stability to a class of *qualia* in terms of which the perception and description is possible of *gignomena* (cf. McDowell, op. cit.).

rejoiced in Plato's supposed refutation of him, and the friends have either (Kirk, Reinhardt) sought to deny that Heraclitus ever said that 'everything flows' or (in the case of Guthrie) acknowledged their embarrassment but sought other Heraclitean concessions to stability and permanence (e.g. the doctrine of fire).

Both these reactions are equally mystifying. How could Plato's demonstration, however it should be interpreted, possibly prove the incoherence of the claim that 'everything flows' or 'everything constantly changes', which is all that Plato says that Heraclitus said? The accepted answer seems to be that for a world to be rationally intelligible there must be some landmarks, and for there to be landmarks there must be some continuants. But continuants have to be individuated (the argument continues) and under conditions of Heraclitean flux it is impossible that there should be any rational basis in the properties or behaviour of things for a difference between good and bad hypotheses about which changeable continuant $x$, included in an inventory of items existing at one time, should be counted as coinciding with which changeable continuant $y$, included in an inventory of items existing at a later time. Heraclitean flux, it is then said, removes the whole point of the questions that these hypotheses set out to answer. But if that is the argument, it is unconvincing. Only if one confused flux with chaos could one possibly suppose that this basis was lacking in the world that Heraclitus describes. Why should not the principle that 'steers all through all' and the unending and irresoluble struggle of opposites furnish us with a natural order in which there is a sound, non-arbitrary basis on which to distinguish between good and bad hypotheses about which perishable continuant coincides with which? Heraclitus' *kosmos* is lawlike, and lawlike at several levels of description. There is constant change, and most substances eventually perish. But the perishable changeable substances are *continuants*, which can be traced through time so long as they persist – right up to the moment when they are replaced by other things.

5.2 A logical difficulty may perhaps seem to lurk in elucidating how exactly we understand as readily as I think we do understand the phrase 'all the time everything is changing in all respects'. There are puzzles of what Russell called impredicativity to be uncovered here. But these are not the difficulties that Plato and his latter day followers are urging; and 'all the time everything is changing in all respects' is not quite what Plato reports Heraclitus as having said. Plato says that Heraclitus said that everything was on the move, was in a state of change, or flowed. But even if Heraclitus had said that all the time everything was changing in all respects, we could still dispel impredicativity in the natural way (whatever that is) that controls our manifest intuitive understanding of the claim (e.g. reading Heraclitus as saying that all the time everything there is at that time is changing in respect of all its completely determinate *qualia* in every empirically definable property range): and it would then be hard to see why, even in a world satisfying this stringent specification, a persisting thing should not remain for the while within the set limits of transformations that preserve its integrity, and be reidentified there through simultaneous continuous change of position, continuous motion, continuous replacement of its constituent particles *and* continuous change of qualities. What is the difficulty supposed to be?

'If anything . . . were perpetually changing in all respects, so that at no time could it be described as being so and so, then nothing could be said of it', Owen wrote (in a sentence that only the occasion of the present volume can excuse or explain my picking out for such disobliging, officious and pedantic treatment). But I protest that 'man' or 'river' or 'barley drink' or whatever does not stand for a respect of change in which a thing 'perpetually changing in all respects' changes. That is not what we let ourselves in for when we say that a thing is changing in all respects. And that is not what we ought to mean by such a respect – or what Heraclitus would have meant if he had said this (see below 5.3). Indeed, if we say of an individual thing that *it* is changing all the time, then we must already have excluded counting 'man' or 'river' as a respect in which that thing changes. It is true that the objection might give trouble if Heraclitus wanted to assert of rivers and men and such things that they only *come to be* (become) and never *are* anything. But there is no evidence that he did want to confine the being of rivers and men to 'becoming'; and it is evidence against his having had this desire that there is no trace of the Cratylean denial of substance in Heraclitus' writings. Heraclitus writes happily of 'rivers', 'souls', 'the barley drink' – of continuants, that is. To insist that he really thinks of these things as processes, not as continuants, is to try to make a contrast that is quite anachronistic – and, on top of that, a category mistake. Processes are regular or gradual or fitful, take time, have temporal parts. None of this holds of rivers, even if rivers correspond to a certain class of processes, or supervene (as Heraclitus could be paraphrased as saying) upon certain classes of processes. In fact the rubbish that philosophers have sometimes talked about rivers or men not being but only becoming seem to be entirely of Plato's and other post-Parmenidean philosophers' confection. If (as I suppose) there is no clear trace of such linguistic revisionism in Heraclitus, then we should not carry this post-Parmenidean philosophical hang-up to the fair-minded assessment of the claim which is the strongest claim that anyone can prove Heraclitus to have made about flux, viz. that everything is on the move or flows.

5.3 Aristotle derides Heraclitus; but there is an Aristotelian insight from which any even-handed critic might see Heraclitus' doctrine as properly entitled to benefit.[28] 'River' or 'man' answers in the category of substance the question 'What is it?', and this is a question that Aristotle found good reasons of theory to contrast with the question 'What is it like?' The two questions correspond to a categorial distinction among predications of *substance* and predications of *quality*, and our very identification of continuants depends on our distinguishing the first sort of predication from the second. Surely this is the distinction that we have just seen to be presupposed to the proper understanding of the claim that individual substances are changing all the time in all respects. No doubt there are many changes which aren't any substance's changing. But every time some substance does change, what we typically have is a qualitative change. (When a thing ceases to exist, that results from a change in it. But existing and then ceasing to exist, though a change, is surely not itself a respect in which the thing itself changes.) To change is to come to deserve a different description in respect of *what one is like*, not to become different in respect of fundamental predication in the category of substance or in respect of *what one is*. Thinking that substances

---

28 Which makes it all the worse that Aristotle was simply helping himself in his *Meteorologica* (357b28–358a3), without acknowledgement of any sort, to the thoughts and perceptions of the philosopher he belittled so frequently.

supervened upon universal process, Heraclitus is not charitably interpreted by anyone who accepts or understands Aristotle's distinction as maintaining that at every moment every substance changes in respect of its being this or that very supervenient substance.

## Conclusion

6.1 It is sometimes claimed nowadays (by Michael Dummett, for instance, in *Frege: Philosophy of Language*) that the proper foundation of philosophy is not the theory of knowledge but the theory of meaning. The theory of meaning, as we have got it, was born out of the theory of logic, which is a subject that pre-Socratic speculations such as Parmenides' played their indispensable part in bringing into existence. Except perhaps by serving as a butt for Aristotle, who needed to find a philosopher open to the charge of denying the Law of Non-Contradiction, Heraclitus contributed nothing to these speculations. Nor did logical or semantical puzzles impinge upon Heraclitus. They were not the sort of thing to engage with the intellectual passions of such a man. *A fortiori*, Heraclitus did not have the logical equipment to distinguish opposition from contradiction (say), or identity from exact similarity. But so far from concluding from this that he must then have been tempted to confuse them, I have drawn the conclusion that, not having the equipment to distinguish them, he did not have the logical equipment to confuse them either. (Just as he lacked the equipment to formulate the absurd hypothesis that a thing's principle of individuation is a respect in which that thing can change.)

A finished philosophy of logic will be an instrument of special philosophical power. Removing all distortions and obstructions that now impede us from getting a clear view of this aspect of ourselves, it will purify our understanding of our own beliefs; and, working in this way, it may one day reveal to us, as through a medium of utter transparency, a world of wonderful plainness. But, as the long history of the manufacture of lenses and other magnifying instruments might prompt one to suppose, such a philosophical instrument (however easy it is to describe) is neither easily invented nor easily manufactured. After the logical labours of many men of genius and good sense, our philosophy of logic and language is scarcely in sight of partial completion; and even now the colours of the rainbow vexatiously and constantly obtrude themselves in the philosophical magnifications that have been achieved. One need not deny that, if philosophy needs any foundation, then its ultimate foundation is the theory of logic and meaning. But so long as such instruments only approximate to perfection, it is no bad thing if at least some philosophers proceed as if philosophy needed no foundation. And one such philosopher is Heraclitus, a thinker best seen as relying on the language itself (not on a philosophy of logic or language or some theory of names or reference or predication) to fix the meaning of what he says.

6.2 It would be an error to suppose that a reliance like Heraclitus' on natural language as non-philosophically construed will automatically entail naïveté, or will carry with it any insensitivity to the question how, if the *kosmos* is as unlike the vulgar conception as Heraclitus says, a human being can think or give expression to the thought that matters are really thus or so. Nor need this reliance entail some blindness to the problem of how the initiated theorist can express his new thoughts in the very same language that the ignorant employ (and he himself employed when he was ignorant of the unity of things). Heraclitus knew that there were those problems. Since the theory of meaning or philosophical logic (as many now call it) has just got us to the point where we can appreciate his contribution to their solution, I shall conclude with some account of this.

Nature loves to be hidden (B123), Heraclitus says, but there are places where the workings of the cosmos will peep out. What can be seen in these places may be interpreted by anyone who has the sense to heed and reflect upon such clues as the river, the barley drink, or the motion of the heavens. If he will attend then, just as the Delphian Apollo 'neither speaks nor conceals but makes a sign', these phenomena can exemplify for him the whole nature of things. He must lay himself open to such eminent instances.

Now it is only by a transaction between things and minds, or designata and their designations held together by a practice, that language itself, not excluding vulgar prephilosophical language, has come into being and been invested with sense, reference and denotation. It is no accident even that *bios* means 'life' and 'bow', and again no accident that *ergon* can mean 'work' or 'thing' or 'reality' and that these ambiguities all combine in such a way that the same set of words can mean either

The name of the bow is life but its work is death (B48)

or

Life is the name assigned but the reality [to which we give it] is the process of dying (cf. B21).

These are bizarre instances, but what they exemplify is the general process by which language comes into being.

When we ask how the *logos* of the world can be grasped by the soul, we must remember that the soul itself is not for Heraclitus something that is alien to reality; it is all of a piece with what it seeks to interpret,[29] being fire or air (and, like all fire or air at hazard from the peril of too much wetness).[30]

Heraclitus lived before the moment when concepts became ideas and took up residence in the head. But, even if concepts had by then taken up residence in the head, Heraclitus' view of the *psuchē* might have saved him from the absurdities of psychologistic accounts of concepts that seek to identify a concept by reference to some mental state somehow annexed to it, and specify the mental state itself not *de re* but in isolation from any outward feature of reality that impinges on the mind or serves as the intentional object of the state. Unlike most philosophers in our tradition, then, Heraclitus cannot even be tempted by the theory that Austin parodies in 'Pretending' (*Philosophical Papers*, 2nd. ed. by J. O. Urmson and G. J. Warnock (Oxford 1970), 254 n.1):

It is only the hair on a gooseberry that stops it from being a grape: by a 'gooseberry' then, we may mean simply a hirsute grape – *and* by a 'grape' likewise simply a glabrous gooseberry.[31]

If one element in that which identifies the concept of what it is to be a gooseberry (which is what the predicate 'gooseberry' stands for) is what the predicate is true of (viz. gooseberries, as they are out

---

29  Cf. Hussey, chapter 2 below; Martha Nussbaum, '*Psuchē* in Heraclitus, 1', *Phronesis*, 17 (1972), 1–16.

30  Kahn argues that air, not fire, is the stuff of the soul in *The Art and Thought of Heraclitus*, 238–40, 248–54, 259.

31  These theories stem from Locke, but Locke's own opinions are too complex, too highly elaborated and too much of a compromise between empiricist and rationalist elements to be fairly parodied. For a perfect statement of a sub-Lockean model, richly deserving such parody, see e.g. James Mill *Analysis of the Human Mind*, ch. IV, section 1.

there in the world, ready and waiting for us to find out what they are and what they are like);[32] and if the predicate's denominating what it in fact denominates is determined not by the match between a mental content and certain objects but by some causally conditioned, practically reliable lien that ordinary men can depend upon *without* knowing what they are depending upon or knowing the nature of the terms of this relation; then it follows that what the thinker who follows Heraclitus' way to truth must refine is not language *per se* or predicates such as 'gooseberry' but conceptions – conceptions of the very same concepts as are unavailable to ordinary men who use predicates like 'gooseberry' without true understanding.

Reading Heraclitus' several fragments about sleeping and waking and grasping how things are, one is struck by the similarity between the state of ordinary men as Heraclitus conceives them and men sleep-walking. If one sleep-walks one finds one's way without knowing what one is doing. Similarly, ordinary men conduct the business of everyday life without getting lost or suffering the sad fate of Elpenor. But they do not grasp properly what they encounter, nor understand what things are, even after they learn to recognize and reidentify them (B17, 26). Here once more, Heraclitus would appear to be in a fortunate position. He does not have the theory and technical vocabulary that it requires to confuse the concept of gooseberry – what it is in nature to be a gooseberry – with thinkers' *conceptions* of gooseberry. (What I mean by the conception of gooseberry is a rudimentary recognitional capacity of ours that may or may not mature into distinct theoretical knowledge of gooseberries.[33]) But, had he possessed the technical vocabulary required to enter into these matters, and had he wished to pronounce on the issue, it would have been open to him (at least in cases like these) to agree with Frege's declaration that 'what is known as the history of concepts is really a history either of our *knowledge* of concepts or of the meanings of words'.[34] The man who has awoken and learned to expect the unexpected

---

32 Cf. chapter 3, section 1 of *Sameness and Substance*, cited at note 17 above.

33 Cf. Leibniz. *Meditationes de Cognitione, Veritate et Ideis* (Gerhardt IV) on clear but non-distinct ideas.

34 G. Frege, *Foundations of Arithmetic*, preface – adjacent to the sentence criticized in section 5.1 above. For the Fregean theory of predicates' sense and reference here espoused see especially Frege's letter to Husserl, 24 May 1891, and again *Sameness and Substance*, chapter 3 *ad init.* (with note 2).

(B18) and to exploit whatever signs nature does afford to him, gains new understanding of what, without thinking, he did already in the world at large. It is in gaining this that he transcends the valueless subjective opinions he once entertained about the world and its contents:

So one must follow what is public, that is what is common and universal to all. For what is public *is* what is common and universal to all. But, although the logos is something common and universal to all, the many live as if they had their very own private wisdom (B2).

It is the universality and publicity of the *logos* and of the reality that the *logos* ordains that makes the philosopher's or scientist's task possible:

Of the *logos* that is given in my book, men are always uncomprehending. They do not understand it before they hear it from me, or when they first hear it. For, although everything happens in accordance with this *logos*, men have no cognizance of this, even though they have encountered the words and things I put before them, as I dissect each thing according to its real nature and show forth how it really is. Other men are not aware what they do when awake, just as they are forgetful of what they do in their sleep (B1).

As for those men who can see no unity and no connections between different phenomena even when they are afforded clues in perception, Heraclitus likens them to the deaf. Because they understand as little of the working of their own language as a Greekless foreigner understands of Greek among Greeks,[35] the senses of ordinary men deceive them instead of informing them.[36] For so long as they use their language only by habit, bad testimony is all they will ever be able to get. Yet even this does not mean that the human condition is simply hopeless, closed in upon its own hopelessness. What determines the identity of concepts and attaches common nouns to their denominata is what men *always did* – even before some men awake from their deafness to their own language. Practice is the anchor (and practice, I would add, can only be adequately described if we describe the objects[37] themselves which men uncomprehendingly responded to in perception and action, and spoke of without knowing what they were saying).

35 Cf. Nussbaum, op. cit.
36 Cf. Leibniz, *Nouveaux Essais* (Gerhardt v 252): '[Les hommes] sont empiriques et ne se gouvernent que par les sens et exemples, sans examiner si la même raison a encor lieu.'
37 For this reading of the doctrine that meaning is use see *Sameness and Substance*, 1–4.

All this, in his own special way, Heraclitus understood. But we have only just begun in philosophy to understand the significance of the thing that he understood. We have found it so hard to understand that thing ourselves that we have never seen that Heraclitus understood it.

6.3 Parmenidean puzzles of being and non-being were no doubt as indispensable to the infancy and maturation of the philosophy of logic and language as the alchemical speculations of some of Aristotle's scientific successors were to the development of chemistry. But the power of Heraclitus – his claim to be the most adult thinker of his age and a grown man among infants and adolescents – precisely consisted in the capacity to speculate, in the theory of meaning, just as in physics, not where speculation lacked all useful observations, or where it needed more going theory to bite on, but where the facts were as big and familiar as the sky and so obvious that it took actual genius to pay heed to them.

# 2 Epistemology and meaning in Heraclitus

EDWARD HUSSEY

To further the understanding of the Presocratics, as intelligent beings looking for a theoretical ordering of the world, has been, among the cherished aims of Gwil Owen, one to which he has repeatedly recurred and to which we owe some of his most characteristically illuminating work. To this collection in his honour I offer a set of proposals for the understanding of Heraclitus.[1]

## 1 Epistemology: the programme

1.1 The hypothesis to be explored claims that at the heart of Heraclitus' thought there lies a remarkable and characteristic epistemology, and that it is this above all that must first be grasped if his account of the world is to be understood. It will help to begin with a statement of what would be agreed about Heraclitus' epistemology by many scholars.

I shall treat as non-controversial the position summarised in the rest of the present paragraph. Heraclitus is deeply interested in the problem of knowledge. He sharply rejects the claims to be guides

1 An earlier version of this approach to Heraclitus was presented in 'Heraclitus: Meaning and Understanding', a lecture delivered (under the auspices of the Arts Council of Great Britain) in the Serpentine Gallery, Kensington Gardens, London in September 1977, in connection with an exhibition of work by Ian Hamilton Finlay. I am greatly indebted to Ian Hamilton Finlay for the intellectual stimulus of his work in general, and of his response to Heraclitus in particular. This article also owes a great deal to the conversation and encouragement of David Wiggins, as well as to his writings, particularly 'Truth, Invention and the Meaning of Life' (Henriette Hertz Trust lecture, *Proc. British Academy*, 62 (1976), 331–78) and chapter 1 above. Two other recent works from which I am conscious of having profited are: Charles H. Kahn, *The Art and Thought of Heraclitus* (Cambridge 1979) and Thomas Nagel, *Mortal Questions* (Cambridge 1979). For helpful criticism of a first draft I wish to thank Malcolm Schofield and Martha Nussbaum.

to knowledge of (a) ordinary common sense; (b) popular and traditional beliefs; (c) much of traditional Greek religion; (d) the older accepted authorities, Homer and Hesiod; (e) more recent claimants of such diverse kinds as Archilochus, Xenophanes, Hecataeus and Pythagoras. Against all these, and in support of his own account of the world, Heraclitus appeals in the first place to the evidence of the senses. 'All of which the learning is seeing and hearing, to that I give preference' (B55).[2] But sense-perception by itself is not enough; to suppose that it is is according to Heraclitus the mistake of some of those he attacks. 'Much learning does not teach the mind; otherwise it would have taught Hesiod and Pythagoras, as also Xenophanes and Hecataeus' (B40). At least one further step is necessary if we are to know anything: we must interpret sense-experience. 'Bad witnesses to human beings are eyes and ears, when those human beings have alien souls' (B107). The word rendered here by 'alien', *barbarous*, has the literal meaning of 'non-Greek-speaking'. The soul of the perceiver must understand the language in which sense-information is expressed – how far this is a metaphor is not said – and must step from the message as presented by the senses to its meaning. Many fragments of Heraclitus may be fitted comfortably in with this notion of interpretation as the necessary condition for understanding: human failure to know is like the failure to solve a riddle (B56); the Delphic oracle is where the Lord Apollo 'neither speaks nor conceals, but makes a sign' (B93); the nature of things 'loves to hide itself' (B123), and 'latent structure is master of manifest structure' (B54). People in general are vehemently criticised for their failure to understand how things are, and again the forms of the criticism suggest that they fail to interpret what is given them in sense-perception.

In all this, Heraclitus is not obviously at variance with the Milesian cosmologists. It is probably significant that none of them is attacked by name in the surviving fragments.[3]

1.2 There have always been people claiming to have found a hidden meaning in ordinary experience. Some have been great

---

2 References to Heraclitean material will be given in the standard A- and B- numeration of the later editions of Diels–Kranz. (H. Diels, *Die Fragmente der Vorsokratiker*, 6th and later editions ed. W. Kranz, Berlin 1952, etc.).
3 Thales was mentioned by name (B38, see Kahn op. cit., p. 113).

prophets, sages, philosophers or scientists; others, mere eccentrics or charlatans, and others, a mixture. It must not simply be assumed that Heraclitus belongs in the first class, nor can it be proved just by the fascination of his prose style or by the fact that he is reported to have propounded a cosmological theory. Some ancient writers do in fact put Heraclitus down as little more than an eccentric: Aristotle, followed by Theophrastus, seems to have seen him as a deranged denier of the law of non-contradiction, who in more lucid moments sketched an incomplete cosmology in Milesian style. On the other hand, the Stoics, followed by some early Christian writers, saw Heraclitus as a sage and a precursor. Neither set of testimonies can simply be discarded; no more can the more oblique and nuanced testimony of Plato and Plutarch.[4] But ultimately it is the fragments which must be the ground of any decision to take Heraclitus seriously as a thinker or a sage, or not to do so.

If Heraclitus is indeed to be taken seriously, it is reasonable to suppose that there must be more to his epistemology than has so far been stated. For the notion of *interpretation*, which plays the central role, is, unless further determined, so elastic as to give no guidance. I propose, as a hypothesis, that Heraclitus' notion of interpretation was implicitly determinate, in ways that are natural consequences of taking seriously the analogy of language.

In full, the hypothesis is as follows:

(1) Heraclitus follows (though he may never have formulated) rules for the interpretation of sense-experience, including at least the four following:

(a) *Rule of No Cancellation*: Nothing may be rejected that is given by ordinary sense-experience; just as the words of a sentence are not cancelled or superseded by the meaning of the sentence. Interpretation adds to what is given, but may not take away from it or alter it.

(b) *Rule of No Extra Sensibles*: To what is given, nothing may be added (in interpretation) that is itself of a kind to be the object of sense-experience; just as the meaning of a sentence does not consist (even partly) of extra *words*, nor does understanding the sentence involve the introduction of extra words.

4 The treatments of Heraclitus by later ancient philosophers, particularly Plato, Aristotle, Theophrastus and the Stoics, are difficult topics which have not been adequately treated in detail. For the early Stoic view, see the useful summary in A. A. Long, *Hellenistic Philosophy* (London 1974), 145–7. Heraclitus as 'melancholic', i.e. manic-depressive: Theophrastus (Diogenes Laertius IX 6).

(c) *Rule of Holism*: Sense-experience, when being interpreted, must be taken as a whole, or at least in naturally determined chunks; just as we can properly interpret only whole sentences, or at least phrases.

(d) *Rule of Intrinsic Meaning*: The interpretation, once found, must be seen as 'given' by and in the sense-experience, not imposed from outside it; just as the meaning of a sentence lies in the words and is determined by them, not imposed on them from the outside.

(2) These rules determine the characteristic shape of Heraclitus' system, which is to be seen as the product of the systematic application of the rules to Heraclitus' own experience.

In the rest of this chapter I try to work out the consequences of this hypothesis and thereby to exhibit the hypothesis as convincing. In sections 1.3 to 1.6, the 'four rules of interpretation' are further considered. In section 2 Heraclitus' view of the world is accounted for as an outcome of the epistemological programme. Section 3 explores briefly the style of Heraclitus and his use of the word '*logos*', both of which, it is claimed, are essentially related to the epistemology. Section 4 offers some general reflections in conclusion. Particularly in sections 2 and 3 the exposition is, of necessity, rather abbreviated and dogmatic; many details are neglected. The interpretation offered has to be judged by its success or failure in accounting for Heraclitus as a whole.

1.3 Rule (a) above, the Rule of No Cancellation, immediately suggests the question: how much of what we ordinarily take as given really *is* given by ordinary sense-experience? It would be impossible to attribute the rule to Heraclitus unless there were signs, as there are, that he was interested in the distinction between data and interpretation. That interest might have been expected. The Milesians' proto-scientific theorising had produced two or three dramatic reinterpretations of ordinary experience; their strangeness, and their natural incompatibility, would force the distinction upon the notice of any contemporary with philosophical sensitivity.

Here Xenophanes is a useful 'control' for comparison and contrast with Heraclitus. Xenophanes reacts to the same situation in a partly similar way, though with less coherence and determination. He appears to want to preserve the unity and lawlikeness of the Milesians' universe, but at the same time to protest against their theorising in the name of a rudimentary empiricism. His own world-view therefore falls apart into (a) a transcendental monotheism, which he himself admits cannot be verified by sense-experience; (b) a bitty cosmology having no overall coherence and no connection with the theology.[5] As Hermann Fränkel has pointed out, the remnants of the cosmology strongly suggest a deliberate 'not going beyond sense-experience', which may be taken as summed up by the Rule of No Cancellation and its stable-mate the Rule of No Extra Sensibles.

The same 'primitive' and 'impoverished' aspect is shown by the cosmology of Heraclitus, though not to the same degree, because there is evidence of a general theory of transformations. It is worth trying out, therefore, the possibility that Heraclitus too followed the Rule of No Cancellation. The report that he said that the sun had 'the width of a human foot' (B3) is not in itself very impressive. But it can be combined with the fragments exhibiting some sort of 'unity in opposites' in situations of ordinary life; the interpretation is controversial (see 2.2 below), but on any tenable interpretation the moral Heraclitus intends is not that the different sense-experiences are mistaken or merely relatively true, but that every experience contributes an essential part of the truth.

From acceptance of the Rule of No Cancellation it follows that all sense-experience is equally good and true so far as it goes. ('Eyes are more exact witnesses than ears' (B101a) – but this is either a statement of the fact that hearsay is not directly given in sense, or makes the point that seeing gives more detailed information than hearing.) Sceptical doubt is allowed no place. Scepticism has a long and honourable part in the history of Greek philosophy, but at the time of Heraclitus there is no evidence that it had as yet gathered and sharpened its weapons. In supposing that Heraclitus accepted the Rule of No Cancellation, one is not therefore obliged to find him defences against scepticism. Still, it is interesting to note that Heraclitus did have a first line of defence against some obvious sceptical arguments. Dreams, for instance, do not have to

5 On Xenophanes' empiricism see Hermann Fränkel, *Wege und Formen frühgriechischen Denkens* (2nd ed. Munich 1955), 338–49; an English translation of these pages, by Matthew R. Cosgrove and Alexander P. D. Mourelatos, appears in Alexander P. D. Mourelatos (ed.), *The Pre-Socratics* (New York 1974), 118–31. Heraclitus' closeness to Xenophanes is rightly seen (perhaps exaggerated) by Olof Gigon, *Untersuchungen zu Heraklit* (Leipzig 1935), 76–8, 149–59.

be admitted as valid sense-experiences by Heraclitus, because they occur when the senses are 'quenched' (B26). To be sure, dreamers may *think* that they are actually seeing and hearing things; but Heraclitus is not committed to saying that what anyone thinks is true. Indeed, dreamers here provide him with a valuable analogy for the common misinterpretation of experience. As for the sceptical arguments from relativity and illusion, they were, if known to Heraclitus, turned into arguments for the unity in opposites.[6]

1.4 Rule (b), the Rule of No Extra Sensibles, is suggested, as already said, by the furniture of Xenophanes' and Heraclitus' universes, which goes nowhere beyond the observable. Here there is a striking contrast with the Milesians (at least Anaximander and Anaximenes), who in postulating infinite stretches of perceptible stuff outside our cosmos, and infinitely many cosmoses, violated the rule in a prodigal way. The attribution of the rule to Heraclitus, then, has some initial plausibility.

1.5 Rule (c), the Rule of Holism, is, unlike the first two rules, fully in accord with Milesian ways of thinking, and indeed with all scientific theorising. There is at least a strong presumption, then, that it was a principle implicitly governing Heraclitus' thought, since as much as the Milesians he aims to exhibit the world as a unity and a system.

It is even possible to argue that Heraclitus himself came close to formulating the rule explicitly. In one fragment he describes himself as 'according to its nature delimiting each thing in turn and showing how it is' (B1). And, once again, part of the moral of the doctrine of the unity in opposites is certainty that one will go wrong, as Hesiod did about day and night (B57), if one considers one aspect or one opposite in isolation.

1.6 Rule (d), the Rule of Intrinsic Meaning, will be the pivot upon which the whole interpretation turns. It is the most far-reaching

6 It is perhaps more likely that later scepticism derived some of its arguments from Heraclitus. The Rule of No Cancellation is expressed later in the Epicurean principle that 'every perception is true', on which see C. C. W. Taylor, 'All Perceptions are True', in *Doubt and Dogmatism, Studies in Hellenistic Epistemology*, ed. Schofield, Burnyeat and Barnes (Oxford 1980), 105–24.

and, if Heraclitean, the most peculiarly Heraclitean. There is admittedly no evidence for anything like it in any of Heraclitus' predecessors, nor is it easy to argue directly for its presence in Heraclitus himself, except by means of the fragments mentioned in section 1.2 above. B107, in particular, has suggested to many students of Heraclitus that the analogy with language must be followed rather closely. To quote the recent commentary of Charles Kahn, for example: 'The world order speaks to men as a kind of language they must learn to comprehend. Just as the meaning of what is said is actually "given" in the sounds which the foreigner hears, but cannot understand, so the direct experience of the nature of things will be like the babbling of an unknown tongue for the soul that does not know how to listen' (*The Art and Thought of Heraclitus*, p. 107 – see note 1 above).

What follows is an attempt to think out and press the analogy rather more closely than Kahn, or any other scholar, seems to have done. The Rule of Intrinsic Meaning says at the very least that interpretations of sense-experience may not be arbitrary: it cannot be that any arbitrary interpretation is correct. For Heraclitus it would be a criticism of the Milesians that they theorised in an essentially arbitrary way. This criticism must have occurred to many Greeks of the period when they observed the grandiose but unfortunately conflicting interpretations of experience offered by Thales, Anaximander and Anaximenes. What would be immediately suggested was the need for stronger restrictions on what was to count as a good interpretation. Part of the answer ought to be to stick closer to sense-experience, as Xenophanes and Heraclitus tried to do. But that alone could not solve the problem of interpretation.

The Rule of Intrinsic Meaning in its positive aspect presupposes, at least, that there does exist a single correct interpretation, of sense-experience as a whole and derivatively of naturally chosen bits of sense-experience. It presupposes, further, that this interpretation is 'given' in some natural way in experience, and is therefore in principle discoverable by human intelligence. So far these presuppositions are familar as part of the faith of the natural scientist, and presumably of the Milesians too. Modern scientists would agree, too, that finding out the meaning of sense-experience is a process rather like that of learning a language. So far, then, the Rule of Intrinsic Meaning may seem to contain no unfamiliar or implausible implication.

Where Heraclitus differs both from the Milesians and from the modern scientist, I suggest, is that for him the language 'spoken' by sense-experience is not one that has to be learnt laboriously by means of empirical investigation. Heraclitus did not reject empirical investigation as useless, but thought that any amount of it would not necessarily by itself lead to any interpretation. Accordingly its results could be anticipated by reflection on what would count as an interpretation satisfying the Rule of Intrinsic Meaning. The most far-reaching implication of that Rule is that if the message of sense-experience is to be seen as indubitably meaningful, it must be expressed in some language which we can know *independently* of sense-experience.

What sort of language could this be, and where could it be learnt? The only realm to which we have direct access without sense-perception is the inner realm of our selves revealed by introspection. Within that realm, we have privileged access to the meaning of our ordinary actions, which may remain uninterpreted for someone else. And if anyone else wishes to interpret them, he must do so in terms of thoughts, desires, emotions and so on, which he can understand from the inside because he himself has had or might have them. Moreover, to be able to interpret the more long-term and large-scale aspects of the behaviour of some human being, we must refer to some very general principles of behaviour, and we can understand them as possible principles of behaviour only by seeing, from within somehow, that they might give a 'meaning' to life as a whole. There is a continuum between the meaning of a particular action and the meaning that some person gives to, or finds in, life as a whole.

Questioning about the meaning of life as a whole was certainly a feature of Greek culture in the sixth century. It is clear that by that time many Greeks felt partly alienated from the Homeric ideals and the Olympian religion in which they had been brought up. The appeal of exotic and esoteric wisdom and cult is shown by mystery-cults, orgiastic religion, Pythagoreanism, and perhaps Orphism.[7] The search for the meaning of life may present itself naturally, to someone partly alienated from his own traditions, as a search for one's own true self. It was a search that Heraclitus also

---

7 On all this, see particularly the classic treatment by E. R. Dodds, *The Greeks and the Irrational* (Berkeley and Los Angeles 1951), chs. II–V. Heraclitus is notably savage in his attacks on mystery-cults, Dionysiac religion, and Pythagoras.

made: 'I looked for myself' (B101). And more encouragingly 'It belongs to all human beings to be acquainted with themselves and be of sound mind' (B115).[8]

Heraclitus' views on the meaning of human life, which diverge widely from traditional Greek ones in spite of an affinity with those of Homer, will be considered later (section 2.4). What is claimed at present, as the final implication of the Rule of Intrinsic Meaning, is that the experience we have of the cosmos, via the senses, has for Heraclitus to be interpreted in the light of the experience we have of our own selves, via introspection. And in giving a long-term, overall interpretation to the behaviour of the cosmos as a whole, we can invoke only the kind of meaning that any human being can see in his existence as a whole. 'What is the plan of the cosmos?' and 'What is the meaning of life?' must be in essence the same question.

In particular, the 'meaning' given by an interpretation of the cosmos must, on this account of Heraclitus, be one that is wholly and directly intelligible from a human point of view. There is no superhuman perspective on the world, and if there is a divine or cosmic intelligence it must be in essence *human*, and see the meaning of its work in just the same terms as a human being would. If this is right, Heraclitus is here too insisting, as with the Rule of No Cancellation, on the validity of ordinary human perceptions. Just as sense-perceptions are not to be set aside by some higher truth, so too the meanings and values that people 'see' in their experience are not to be set aside or reworked in the name of some higher purpose.

So to interpret the cosmos it is necessary to study one's own self, and apply what one finds there to explain the world. Once again, this has been recognised to some extent as a Heraclitean principle by a number of scholars. According to Diels, Heraclitus 'seeks to discover the world-soul from the human soul, and metaphysics from physics. This is the core of his philosophy.' Reinhardt claims that in Heraclitus 'the comparison of the microcosm with the macrocosm . . . confronts us here for the first time as a method, a principle'. Kahn speaks of the 'identity of structure between the inner, personal world of the psyche and the larger natural order of the universe'.[9] None of these scholars, however,

---

8 See on this fragment Kahn's commentary (reference in n. 1 above), 116–17 and 119–20, where its authenticity is defended.

9 Hermann Diels, *Herakleitos von Ephesos* (2nd ed. Berlin 1909), x; Karl Reinhardt, *Parmenides und die Geschichte der griechischen Philosophie* (Bonn 1916), 193; Kahn, *The Art and Thought of Heraclitus*, 20.

has applied the principle in quite the way in which I shall apply it, as a principle of identity of meaning rather than simply of structure.

## 2    Meaning in the cosmos: the programme realised

2.1 What evidence there is about the furniture and general shape of Heraclitus' cosmos allows it to be seen as derived from direct observation by the application of the rules of interpretation. The cosmos is of limited extent, as we see it to be, and nothing was said about what, if anything, lies beyond it (A1, Diogenes Laertius IX.9.). Nor about what keeps the earth from falling. These two points already signal a radical difference from Milesian thought, caused by the rules of No Extra Sensibles and of Intrinsic Meaning. The former prevents the postulation of any sense-perceptible stuff beyond the limits of our observation, the latter makes pointless the postulation of anything whatever that is not to be discerned at work within the sphere of our observation. Anything there might be beyond the finite cosmos, then, would be totally inaccessible and totally irrelevant to human experience.

The whole cosmos is many miles in length and breadth, but perhaps not many miles high. Its furniture is as observed: a fixed and roughly level earth; large stretches of sea; atmosphere; sun, moon, planets and stars. The earth and sea are inhabited by animals, including human beings.

The earth and sea, and the moon and sun, are involved in short- and long-term periodic oscillations between opposite states. The short-term oscillations, of day and night, the phases of the moon, and the cycle of the seasons are directly observed; the long-term expansion of earth at the expense of sea is inferred from observations as the Milesians and Xenophanes had inferred it.

There is a radical difference observable between sun and moon, on the one hand, and the stars on the other. Sun and moon are theatres of oscillation between opposites, and their movements, though following a fixed pattern, are not absolutely uniform and are determined by the fuel supplied by earth and sea. The stars, on the other hand, are invariant in appearance, movements and arrangement; they are seen by everyone as an army of impassive watchers, and that therefore is what they must be. The sun and moon need not even be materially continuous from day to day, and they are not independent of the cosmic oscillations; the stars must be persisting, intelligent beings and though affected by the cosmic cycles they are not essentially changed by them.[10]

2.2 The first step in the further interpretation of this impoverished and primitive-looking cosmos is supplied by the doctrine of the unity in opposites. This doctrine, cardinal in Heraclitus' thought, is itself one of the first fruits of the epistemological programme.

The examples on which the doctrine rests are drawn from common experience. Take sea-water. 'Sea: purest and most polluted water, for fish drinkable and life-sustaining, for human beings undrinkable and deadly' (B61). The facts are well-known, and the conclusion intended by Heraclitus does not seem to be a merely relativist one. Rather, the wording itself, and the Rule of No Cancellation, both suggest that both human beings and fish experience a different part of the essential truth about sea-water.

It has often been thought that this way of reading this and the related fragments leads Heraclitus into absurdity and self-contradiction. If sea-water is 'life-sustaining', without qualification, then (a) it is life-sustaining for human beings, which is contrary to experience; (b) it is equally 'deadly' without qualification, and hence life-sustaining and deadly at the same time for the same creature, which is a contradiction. If we water down the reading by taking 'life-sustaining' as 'life-sustaining for some creatures at some times', the contradiction is avoided at the price of banality.

Most interpreters, from Aristotle onwards, have rightly sensed that Heraclitus is likely to be everything but banal; many have concluded that he is therefore self-contradictory. But this conclusion is not only inherently implausible, it is not required by any of the fragments. There is no necessity to draw it, if we can only remember that here it is a matter of interpreting, of uncovering the 'latent structure' of sea-water. The Rule of No Cancellation assures us that the experiences of human beings and fish correspond to things actually *there*, independently of them, *in* the

---

10 The evidence for which this section aims to account is presented in the standard works: it cannot here be discussed in detail. I see no good reason to doubt that the report (Diogenes Laertius IX.9–11) of Theophrastus about the heavenly bodies is substantially correct, in spite of some difficulties. Direct evidence for the stars as intelligent watchers is admittedly slight, but there are no contrary indications.

sea-water. These things must be what, with Aristotle, we may call powers or potentialities. These are *not* to be explained as undetected kinds of *stuff* working in the water. The Rule of No Extra Sensibles rules that possibility out. They are, however, just 'powers'; and the general doctrine of unity-in-opposites, neither self-contradictory nor banal, is that it is in the essence of things to have an ambivalence in their powers: they possess no characteristic potentiality without admitting also the opposed potentiality. To put it in a slogan, 'essences are ambivalent'.[11]

The application of the doctrine to the cosmos is clear enough in outline. The number of cosmically important pairs of opposites is very limited, and some may be intended to be reducible to others. *Hot* and *cold*, *dry* and *wet*, appear in B126 and are presumably basic: '*quenched*' and '*kindled*' (of the cosmic fire) in B30, and of the soul fire, in B26. Other obviously important pairs appear in B67: *day–night*, *winter–summer*, *war–peace*, *famine–glut*; and the opposition *death–life* plays a part in several fragments. In general, it is the ambivalence of the contents of the cosmos between the opposed potentialities represented by these pairs that underlies and explains the rather limited catalogue of types of physical process. All the observable cosmic periods are oscillations between members of these pairs, and are thereby partly explained.[12]

Not even the fixed stars are exempt from ambivalence of essence and its consequences. They are quenched every sunrise, and they sometimes set (except for a few privileged ones) during the night. Their immortality is genuine, but it is a half-time immortality, exemplifying the general truth (on which see section

11  A full development of this interpretation of unity-in-opposites would require far more space. One important objection is: if the doctrine of unity-in-opposites is really as Aristotelian as is claimed, why should Aristotle himself have misunderstood it so badly? The objection is blunted by the observation that Aristotle all too frequently fastens on and criticises the terminology rather than the substance of his predecessors' doctrines – a practice admirable for the conduct of a dialectical encounter, but deplorable in the writing of the history of thought. Thanks in large part to Gwil Owen, we are coming to see how thoroughly dialectical Aristotle's treatment of his predecessors always is.

12  The vexed question of flux in Heraclitus, and related controversial matters, need not be discussed here. On these questions see the standard works, e.g. G. S. Kirk, *Heraclitus: The Cosmic Fragments* (Cambridge 1954), and W. K. C. Guthrie, *A History of Greek Philosophy*, vol. 1 (Cambridge 1962), 449–54; also Kahn's commentary (note 1 above). A new approach to these problems is provided by David Wiggins in chapter 1 above. I am indebted to Wiggins for showing me the importance for understanding Heraclitus of the concept of *essence*, a point also suggested by Jonathan Barnes, *The Presocratic Philosophers* (London 1979), vol. 1, 77.

2.8 below) that life needs death to keep it going. 'Immortals are mortals, mortals are immortals, living the others' death, dying the others' life' (B62).

2.3 To see cosmic processes as examples of the working-out of unity-in-opposites is, however, only a first step. The 'latent structure', the ambivalent essence, has, merely as such, no meaning. The Rule of Intrinsic Meaning has not yet been invoked. At this point, therefore, we must consider Heraclitus' conception of the *self*, since that is what is claimed to provide the fulcrum for the application of that rule. '*Psuchē*', traditionally translated 'soul', is in Homer and other early Greek writers the word for the self, the bearer of personal identity. It is always a disputable question how much necessarily goes along with identity; Homer seems to doubt whether the self in Hades retains much intelligence, though it is capable of emotion. In the lyric poets, too, '*psuchē*' denotes the emotional side of the personality. In Heraclitus, for the first time, the 'soul' is clearly thought of as being the locus of intelligence and rational, effective action. It functions well when dry, badly when moist. 'A dry beam of light is soul at its wisest and best' (B118); 'Whenever a man gets drunk, he is led by a young child, stumbling, not realising where he is going, his soul moist' (B117). Here there are the beginnings of a theory of psychology, but there is nothing to make improbable the view that for Heraclitus, as for Homer, the *psuchē* is basically the bearer of personal identity, and that it is that self which is discovered by introspection.[13] It is, of course, important for Heraclitus that it is also the *psuchē* which is properly said to be intelligent or the reverse, and effectively active or the reverse. The relation of the *psuchē* to emotion seems to be equally direct, though the fragments are less clear.

The self that becomes known to a human being through introspection is, like Heraclitus' cosmos, something at once

13 On *psuchē* in early Greek, Dodds, *The Greeks and the Irrational*, 136–90, partly corrected by Kahn, *The Art and Thought of Heraclitus*, 126–27, and n. 112. But Kahn seems to me to go astray (a) in supposing that for Heraclitus 'the psyche is primarily a principle of rational cognition' – a view out of line both with early Greek usage and with the totality of the relevant fragments; (b) in consequently rejecting the correct insight of Bruno Snell, *Die Entdeckung des Geistes*, 3rd edn (Hamburg 1955), 36–9, that Heraclitus' concept of *psuchē* marks an awareness of the distinction between the realm of sense-experience and that of introspection. Snell in turn, I believe, exaggerates the contrast between Homer and Heraclitus in this respect; see section 4 below. On *psuchē* in Heraclitus the best treatment is Martha Nussbaum '*Psuchē* in Heraclitus, I' *Phronesis*, 17 (1972), 1–15.

comfortingly familar and disconcertingly odd. It is both unitary and multiform, liable to give itself in succession or even at one and the same time to a variety of incompatible needs, desires, plans and ideals. It is known with great directness, yet is constantly revealing new and unsuspected aspects. 'The limits of soul you will not find out in going about, though you travel along every road: so deep is the account of it' (B45). The search for oneself is slow, unmapped, unending, and contains surprises for the most successful: 'Those who seek gold dig much ground and find little' (B22); 'If one does not expect the unexpected, one will not find it out, untrackable as it is and pathless' (B18).

The Rule of Intrinsic Meaning directs that the understanding of the cosmos must be found by giving it a meaning. The meaning must be found by seeing it as a human self, and interpreting its behaviour as that of such a self. But this in turn is not enough: the whole business will still be meaningless unless each human being can see, within himself, an overall meaning in his individual existence. So Heraclitus needs, to underpin the whole structure, some conception of what it is for an individual existence to have an overall meaning. In one word, the answer to the question is: 'War'.

2.4 The answer 'war' needs some explanation. Heraclitus takes it that the self has a best state (B118, see section 2.3 above). He sees the meaning of its existence as given by its attempt to be always, or for as long as possible, in the best possible state. Here he is on common ground with the aristocratic warrior-ideal of Homer. But the best state of the self is that in which it is dry, and therefore most capable of intelligent thought and action. So a meaning in existence is found in the developing and exercising, to the utmost possible, of the capacities for intelligent thought and action.

Obviously there are, according to the particular circumstances, different lives which might result. But in general Heraclitus holds that the best life must be a life of active struggle, in two senses. First, there is the internal struggle to keep one's self in the best possible state in the face of all sorts of pressures towards the worse. Second, the exercise of the good capacities demands *external* obstacles to be overcome, and the most testing exercise is a conflict against an able and active opponent. Moreover, in the world of human affairs the same struggle between good and bad opposites reappears: certain types of people, certain political groups, and perhaps certain peoples or races, represent the good and the bad, the 'dry' and the 'wet', the followers of glory and of sensual satisfaction.[14]

So the best life is to be a warrior on the side of human excellence. This need not involve actual fighting: Heraclitus himself can hardly have had much opportunity to appear on the battlefield, unless he fought in Darius' army on some of its campaigns. Heraclitus' own warfare is conducted in words. But he too followed his own prescription: 'The best choose one thing in exchange for all else: glory ever-flowing among mortals; the many are glutted like beasts' (B29). The choice of glory is the external aspect of the pursuit of self-perfection, as in Homer, where the warrior has no other reward for his deeds, and no other consolation for his mortality, since existence after death is a miserable affair. For Heraclitus, though, the after-life may well have more to offer. The fragments indicate that a dry soul, after death, will rise into an honoured position in the skies, and perhaps achieve definitive immortality as a star.[15] Even if one becomes a star, of course, the struggle is not necessarily over: stars too may be liable to fall (literally), and there is some evidence that good souls after death have anyway a role to play in the cosmic struggle, as 'guardians' (B63), fitting the watchful guise in which we see the stars. Being a star is itself, of course, a kind of glory.

For Heraclitus, then, the only meaning of existence is given by the long-term ambitions of being a dry soul and becoming a celestial watcher. Existence has a meaning just because such ambitions are capable of fulfilment without being easy to fulfil. There is constant choice required ('The best *choose* . . .' B29), and a need to shape one's whole life and character: 'It is character (*ēthos*) that is one's guardian spirit' (B119); and, from the nature of the soul, a constant internal struggle.

14 Some fragments reveal political ideas; see the well-balanced remarks of Kahn, *The Art and Thought of Heraclitus*, 177–81. The extension to a 'geopolitical' theory is unsupported by direct evidence. See, further, section 2.7 below. I think it likely that Heraclitus admired the Persian monarchy of his time and the Zoroastrianism which Darius had adopted as its state religion, but there is no space to discuss the question here.

15 For the rewards after death, see esp. G. S. Kirk, 'Heraclitus and Death in Battle, fr.24D', *Amer. Journal of Philology*, 70 (1949), 384–93; Kahn, *The Art and Thought of Heraclitus*, 245–59.

2.5 It is now possible to return to the interpretation of the cosmos. So far it consists of a cosmic substratum which is ambivalent between the potentialities for being hot or cold, wet or dry, etc. The changes that occur express these ambivalences. The next interpretative step is to take the opposites as opposed, not merely in the sense of having opposed and mutually exclusive effects, but in the sense of being live forces, with some kind of independent existence, which are engaged in all-out war against each other. In the war, each side aims at the total destruction of the other (though this is never achieved, at least permanently). Only such a reading will account for the emphasis in the fragments on 'war' and 'strife' – (unless we are to take these as tired clichés merely denoting regular transitions between opposite states). More, only such a reading preserves the required interpretative parallel between the struggles of the self and those of the cosmos.

'War is father of all and king of all: some he sets up as gods, some as men, some he makes slaves, some free' (B53). The second part of this will refer both to ordinary human wars, and to internal human struggles; the first part is quite general. 'But one must know that war is general (*xunon*), and that justice is strife, and that all things come to be according to strife and necessity' (B80). In all kinds of struggle there are constraining laws, determined by the nature of things and not convention, governing the possibilities and restricting but not abolishing rational choice. The situation is analogous to that of a formalised struggle such as a board game played according to rules. Not very much can be learnt about the rules of the cosmic struggle, though certain 'measures' and 'proportions' (B30, 31) were preserved, and a fixed exchange-rate in physical conversions existed (B90); certain temporal lengths, too, were fixed for cosmic periods. The details are not here important: what is important is that the rules are not imposed from outside, but determined by the very nature of the struggle, and therefore an essential part of it, so that (correcting Anaximander) Heraclitus can say with emphasis 'Justice is strife.'[16]

2.6 In the struggle, the cosmic substratum plays the role corresponding to that of the self. The self has not only the passive function of serving as substratum for the opposites, but the active

16 On the laws of the cosmic changes, see the works referred to in n. 12 above.

functions also of reasoning and choosing and constructing a way of existence out of the materials to hand. These two aspects of the self reappear in the cosmic substratum, which is also the cosmic intelligence. The struggles of the opposites are, from a different point of view, the struggles of the self (or cosmic intelligence) to constitute itself and plan its existence.[17]

Heraclitus' preferred name for the cosmic substratum, considered as such, is 'fire'. 'Neither any god nor any man made this cosmos, but it was always and is and will be, an everliving fire, being kindled in measures, and being quenched in measures' (B30). From this it is clear that 'fire' here indicates, not actual manifest fire, but a cosmic 'bonfire' serving as substratum to actual fire or to other states. 'Fire' indicates also that the *best* state of the substratum is the hot, dry, fiery state – it is then that it is 'most itself', just as the self is most truly itself when it is intelligent and active: for its other function positively requires intelligent choice, and action to reinforce that choice. The substratum appears also as 'God' in B67: 'God: day, night; winter, summer; war, peace; glut, famine; but he becomes of another kind . . .'

The name 'God', equally, indicates some kind of intelligent and active being, and points to the substratum as intelligent. That there is intelligence at work in the cosmos is also indicated fairly clearly by other fragments: (B64) 'Thunderbolt steers all things'; (B41) there is a steering of all things through all, and (probably) a *plan* governing this; (B78) 'Human character has no knowledge or plan (*gnōmas*), but divine character does'; (B114) there is one divine being or law which 'nourishes' human laws. The whole relationship of cosmic intelligence to the struggle between the opposites is captured by Heraclitus in a brilliant image: that of a boy playing both sides in a board game. 'Everlasting Time (*Aiōn*) is a child at play, playing draughts: a child has the kingly power.'[18] The contest is real, and law-like; the two sides are genuinely opposed and aiming at total victory; and yet one and the same

17 There are a few fragments relating to the self's internal struggles: B110 'It is not better for human beings to get all they want'; B43, the wanton exercise of strength and power (*hubris*) is a deadly danger to the soul; B85, it is hard to fight against *thumos* (anger and related passions); B117 on drunkenness.

18 'Draughts' is a conventional translation; the game of *pessoi* was more like backgammon. The interpretation given here (the boy plays both sides) was (according to Bruno Snell, 'Die Sprache Heraklits', *Gesammelte Schriften* (Göttingen 1966), 145 n.2, who rejects it) given by Leisegang in 1925 (in *Literarische Wochenschrift*, 1 (1925), 51, which I have not seen).

person is playing both sides, and the keener the contest the more the child exercises and develops his intelligence.

The cosmic intelligence is the central point of the whole construction. Such a being is perfectly at home in Milesian cosmology, but may seem difficult to reconcile with the epistemology attributed to Heraclitus in this chapter. In particular, a wise God must presumably have a superhuman, transcendent and privileged way of knowing the world, which would contradict the Rule of Intrinsic Meaning. We seem to have come back to Xenophanes' transcendent divinity, after all.

The way out of this difficulty has already been suggested. The cosmic intelligence is in all essential respects *human*, just as human 'as you or me'. In particular, it is not something perfect and static, but repeatedly changing, making progress and sometimes regressing, in the process of self-creation. It is therefore a human being of an exceptional kind. The contrasts Heraclitus makes between 'human' and 'divine' in point of wisdom and intelligence (particularly B78: 'Human character has no knowledge or plan, but divine character does'; B79: 'A man is called foolish by a god, as a child by a man') are not concerned with the differences between ordinary human beings and the cosmic intelligence, but with the differences (more important for Heraclitus) between the average run of human beings, and the exceptions, whether 'human' in the ordinary sense or not.[19]

2.7 The cosmic struggle, on this interpretation, is intelligible as the struggle of a human self. Conversely, an individual human self has, in choosing the better side, the hope of a cosmic reward. It is natural to guess that there is a closer connection, in the sense that individual human intelligences are component parts of the cosmic intelligence, and that the cosmic struggle is the summed outcome of many individual struggles of individual intelligences, whether these latter are in human or stellar or some other form. The fragments offer little direct evidence either way as to the truth of this guess, but it is still worth considering.

19 The ambiguity, as between God and human beings, of the wisdom attributed in the difficult B41 is well brought out by Kahn in his book, pp. 170–2. The only fragment that seems to attribute a special perspective to God is B102: 'For God all things are beautiful and good and just, but men suppose some things just, some things unjust.' I am not sure that this is even a paraphrase of a genuine sentence of Heraclitus, but if it is it should be dealt with in the same way as B78 and B79.

Is there any evidence, in the first place, that good men naturally co-operate? (In some societies with warrior ideals it has been thought that good men achieve most glory by fighting and killing other good men.) Since Heraclitus sees value in civic life, and criticises political acts of his fellow-citizens of Ephesus, it would seem likely. 'Law' (*nomos*) – which would cover constitutional arrangements as well as civil and criminal law – is what Heraclitus sees as the indispensable unifying element in a city: 'The people should fight for the law as for the city-wall' (B44). In B114 this kind of law is compared with and related to 'the one divine (law)': 'All human laws are nourished by the one divine one.' Just what relationship is intended here is obscure; and in any case the cosmic 'justice' or 'law' is not obviously on the side of either the better or the worse forces in the cosmos. When good men become, after death, 'Guardians of living and of corpses' (B63) some kind of cosmic collaboration is suggested, as it is also by the orderly army of the stars. The cosmic intelligence might be constituted, along the lines of a city, as a collectivity of individual intelligences, with 'better' and 'worse' parties as in a Greek city.[20]

The same tentative conclusion is supported from another direction by the consideration that the vehicle of intelligence is language, and that Heraclitus, in his war against lack of understanding, uses and appeals to the language and the culture that he shares with his audience.

In second place, it is worth asking whether there are any individual intelligences at work in the cosmos apart from human beings and perhaps stars. But here again good evidence is hard to find. At any rate, the changes due to human activity are much swifter and more dramatic than any others in the cosmos.

It is on the earth's surface and on the sea's that the decisive parts of the cosmic drama are played out. The sun is not an independent or continuing participant, but merely a device for reflecting back onto earth and sea and atmosphere some of their own potentialities for change. Its movements and power are determined by the 'exhalations' from the earth and sea below it. So, too, probably, for atmospheric phenomena. What is fundamental is the struggle

20 In international politics, Heraclitus may well have seen the efficient empire of the fire-worshipping Persians as the representative on earth of the 'good' party. The whole topic of Heraclitus' attitude to the Iranian peoples and their religion deserves careful re-examination.

between earth and sea. But this is a struggle in which men can and do intervene; though as yet only on a puny scale. It is not impossible that Heraclitus envisaged, and hoped to help to create, an international alliance of dry souls, which would fight and defeat the resistance of wetter souls, and help the earth to dry up the sea.

2.8 Seen either from the point of view of the opposites or of the substratum, the cosmic process has two opposed aspects: freedom and regularity. This opposition is the ultimate one in Heraclitus' view of the world. As strife, or as self-determination through struggle of the cosmic intelligence, the process is free; as justice, or as the working out of the continual ambivalence of the substratum in endless oscillations, the process is regular and predictable. The opposition is captured by the remark that 'justice is strife' (B80), by the image of the board game, and by the fact that the Sibyl, a prophetess 'with mad mouth', is able in her apparent ravings to 'reach across a thousand years' (B92), i.e. to make correct predictions about the remote future. Heraclitus was aware of this opposition too.[21]

A related problem is: how is a meaning to be given to the *everlasting* existence of the cosmic intelligence? Its existence must be given meaning by an everlasting struggle towards its best state. But the struggle cannot be endless, for then it would be hopeless and pointless. So it must be crowned with success after a finite time; after which, of course, the struggle must begin all over again, in order to renew the meaning of life. It is clear that Heraclitus saw a general pattern here too: continuing life means repeated self-renewal, and self-renewal requires rest, which is a partial dismantling, a sleep or a death. 'It is the same thing which is present as living and dead, as waking and sleeping, as young and old; these change state to become those, and those again change state to become these' (B88). 'In alteration to a different state, it rests' (B84a). The requirements of meaningfulness and of freedom in existence concur to produce a regular and predictable pattern.[22]

3    *Language, meaning and logos*

3.1 Nothing is more needed at present by students of Heraclitus than a commentary on the fragments applying all the resources of

21 Also perhaps B124 (order out of disorder) belongs here.
22 The 'river' and 'barley-drink' fragments (B12, 125) are obviously related – they give examples of identity preserved by continual change. But they introduce additional complications which are here not relevant.

literary scholarship. Such a commentary would approach Heraclitus in the way he himself intended. Valuable preliminary work has been done, most notably in the studies of Snell and Hölscher and in the commentary of Kahn. My aim in this part is to provide a rapid survey of Heraclitus' use of language, and to show how it is related to the theses of sections 1 and 2. In conclusion, his use of the word *'logos'* is considered in the same context.[23]

3.2 Heraclitus addresses himself to anyone who will listen. But not in a spirit of cool exposition. As has often been recognised, his relationship to his audience is that of a preacher. It is the preacher's style that shows itself in the mixture of plainly-worded descriptions and denunciations of ordinary people's behaviour, pregnantly-phrased aphorisms, images and illustrations from ordinary life, and cryptic formulations of higher truths. These are the means by which he tries to win human beings to the insights and the inner state he has himself attained. As has been suggested already, Heraclitus sees the human race as a battleground disputed by the forces of active intelligence and those of weakness and stupidity. He himself is a warrior on the side of active intelligence, and his words are his weapons, designed to have maximum impact over the widest possible range.

Seers, prophets and oracles existed in archaic Greece as in the ancient Near East, and their style of delivery in some cases is recorded and can be compared with that of Heraclitus. So too can that of two great poets, Heraclitus' near contemporaries, in whom the prophetic tone and style sometimes predominates: Pindar and Aeschylus.[24] Heraclitus differs from the average prophet in the important respect that he does not rely on an essentially private revelation. But the needs of the situation as he sees it force him to adopt the same style.

3.3 As a first approximation we may distinguish four principal components in Heraclitus' style; they cannot, of course, always be clearly separated.

23 On Heraclitus' language: Snell, see n.18; Uvo Hölscher, *Anfängliches Fragen* (Göttingen 1968), 'Heraklit' particularly 136–49; Kahn, *The Art and Thought of Heraclitus*.
24 The comparison with Pindar and Aeschylus was made by Diels, *Herakleitos von Ephesos* (n. 9 above), VII; also Kahn, *The Art and Thought of Heraclitus*, 7. A good characterisation of Heraclitean style is in W. Schmid and O. Stählin, *Geschichte der griechischen Literatur*, I i (Munich 1929), 751–3.

(A) The plain style in which he describes and denounces human lack of understanding. The language is straightforward, ordinary and syntactically simple. The tone may be scornful.

(B) Aphorisms in ordinary language, tersely phrased but immediately intelligible in ordinary terms.

(C) 'Parables' or images drawn from ordinary life, again economically phrased, in ordinary language, but with a significance not necessarily even partly obvious.

(D) The cryptic style: a deliberately chosen formulation of important truths using unusual words and elaborate syntax, with one or more meanings more or less concealed.

All of this can be paralleled from the language of prophets, seers and oracles.[25]

3.4 It is the cryptic style that promises to have the closest connection with the thought of Heraclitus as interpreted in the previous sections. For sense-experience presents itself, as an oracle to be divined, in a way that leaves the important structure hidden and only obscurely hinted at. It would not be surprising if Heraclitus expressed himself in a similar way when he had important truths to convey.

The devices used are various. First, there are those that centre on single words. Each single word normally has one ordinary meaning: but it may have two or more. And by its internal phonetic structure or by its phonetic similarity with other words, further meanings or connections may be suggested. In this way, what we would call facts about language and relationships between words are used to indicate more general truths. In some fragments the intention is manifest: (B48) 'The name of the bow is "life" (*bios*) but its work is death' – the linguistic facts make the word an example of unity-in-opposites and thereby show that the thing signified is also an example. Only slightly less obvious are, e.g., B94 (the Erinyes, from *Eris* = strife, as the assistants of Justice) or B32 (the name *Zēnos*, popularly connected with *zēn* 'to

25 For (A) see the material collected by M. L. West, *Hesiod: Theogony* (Oxford 1966), 158–67. For oracular elements see Hölscher (op. cit. n.23), 136–41. Kahn, op. cit., 91, objects that whereas an oracle has only one correct interpretation, Heraclitus intends many; the contrast seems to me more apparent than real. Useful material in W. B. Stanford, *Ambiguity in Greek Literature* (Oxford 1939), chs. VII–X.

live' is and is not appropriate for the one wise thing). Many other examples of latent etymologies could be given. One has even helped to befog the textual criticism of a fragment: in B118 the phrase *'augē xērē'* (dry beam of light) suggests the etymology *auē* (dry) for *'augē'*, and this resemblance has in fact misled scholars into reading *'auē'* for *'augē'* and deleting *'xērē'* as a gloss.[26]

Continuous with etymologies of single words are 'puns', in the sense of manifest verbal resemblances which Heraclitus uses to suggest a relationship of meaning. So in B15 the words *aidein* 'sing', *aisma* 'song', *aidoia* 'private parts' (from *aidōs* 'shame'), *anaidēs* 'shameless', and *Aidēs* 'Hades' are strung together to suggest an accumulation of esoteric connections. Perhaps more important is the resemblance of *xunos* 'common', key word in B2, 80 and 114, to *axunetos* 'lacking understanding' and *xun nōōi* 'with mind'. The common element is *xun* 'together with'. The verb *xunienai* 'understand', which occurs in another key fragment, B51, has a transparent etymology: it means 'to put together'. To understand is then to reconstruct in one's mind a significant unity, re-assembling it from the pieces given in experience.

In some cases, there are grounds for suspecting that *concealed* etymologies or puns are in play. In these cases, the keyword does not necessarily occur in the fragment at all, but 'clues' to it are given. To read Heraclitus in this way is to risk reducing him to a crossword puzzle; nevertheless I shall present two examples for consideration. B94: 'The sun (*Hēlios*) will not transgress measures.' Another name for the sun is *Huperiōn*, which can be read as a present participle, 'transgressing', of the very verb used in 'will not transgress'. B26 is a remarkable assemblage of artfully arranged contrasts and puns, on any reading: 'A human being in the night kindles a light, being quenched in sights: alive, he touches the dead, awake, he touches the sleeping.' Manifestly, the verb *'haptetai'* is used in different senses ('kindles', 'touches'), yet the original connection between the senses is suggested. Beneath the first clause, there is a latent structure given by the various meanings of the word *phaos* or its other form *phōs*: 'man', 'eye' or 'light'. We have to read it thus:

---

26 See the vigorous and convincing defence of *augē xērē* by Kahn in his commentary, 245–6.

| 'A human being, | in the night, | kindles a light, | being quenched in sights' |
| ($= ph\bar{o}s$ = light) | ($=$ not-light) | (*phaos*) | ($=$ *phaea*, eyes = lights) |

i.e.

| 'A light, | in the not-light, | kindles a light, | being quenched in lights.' |

The physical theory of sleep and dreams embodied here is shown by the concealed verbal equivalences to rest upon the interchange and transfer of the opposites *light* and *darkness*.

The other leading device of the cryptic style is ambiguity of syntax and construction. This has often been remarked on, from Aristotle down, and is properly appreciated and thoroughly and sensitively explored in the recent commentary of Kahn. For this reason it need not be considered further here.

3.5 The conclusion suggested by these features of style is that Heraclitus wishes to use language to 'show how [each thing] is' (B1). For this reason, language properly used is cryptic to the uninitiated, just as sense-experience is. Both contain indications pointing in different directions, and both have to be interpreted. The interpreting consists in the finding of a meaning which casts a unifying light, and enables the different parts to be understood as parts of a structure intended by an intelligent being. To understand is literally to 'assemble' the parts. For this reason it seems likely that Heraclitus' own work was meant to be read *as a whole*, though the individual sayings were clearly almost completely disjoint from one another.[27]

A related problem, which may serve as a final test of the line of interpretation that has been offered, is that of Heraclitus' use of the word *'logos'*. The most controversial cases are in B1 and B50: 'Of this *logos* as it is always men prove to have no understanding, both before hearing it and when they have heard it. For though all things came to be according to this *logos* they are like people of no experience when they experience such words and deeds as I set forth, delimiting each thing according to its nature and showing how it is' (B1). 'Listening not to me but to the *logos*, it is wise to concur that all is one' (B50). It has often been remarked that B1, coming as it does at the beginning of Heraclitus' work, presupposes a standard sense of *logos*: 'statement, account', applied to the

---

27 Kahn, op. cit., 87–95, makes valuable remarks about the unity of the whole work and other questions of interpretation.

prose works of the Ionian thinkers, story-tellers, travellers and historians (in this sense, in B108, 'All whose *logoi* I have heard'). In B1 and B50 the fragments themselves show that 'the *logos*' is some account of the nature of things in general terms. Since Heraclitus' work supplied just such an account, it is tempting to suppose that in those fragments 'the *logos*' is just Heraclitus' account of the universe.

Even if we consider only the wording of B1 and B50, however, this interpretation is hardly satisfactory. 'Listening to the *logos*' is distinguished from 'listening to me'; and the *logos* is said to be (or be true) always. This shows that the *logos* exists and has authority independently of what Heraclitus may happen to say; so that it is not in virtue of being Heraclitus' account that it has the properties mentioned. It would be odd, then, if Heraclitus here used such an accidental characterisation of this important entity as that it was the account given by himself.

The conclusion that the *logos* is meant to be a permanent feature of the universe is reinforced by comparing another part of B1 with B45: 'The limits of soul you would not find out by going about, though you travelled every road: so deep a *logos* does it have.' The true account of 'soul' is undiscoverable; to discover it would be to discover the 'limits' (*peirata*) of soul. So, in B1, Heraclitus describes his own activity as 'delimiting each thing according to its nature, and showing how it is' – giving its *logos*, evidently. The *logos* is again conceived as inherent in the thing delimited: a statement of its essence.[28]

The evidence of these fragments, then, without any further interpretation, suggests that 'the *logos*' is a statement about the essence of the universe, and that this statement is to be considered as a permanent feature of the universe. But how can a statement be a permanent feature of the universe? On the interpretation I have been trying to expound, the answer is straightforward. The manifest parts of the cosmic process are an unending, ever-repeated statement specifying the nature of the process as a whole. What Heraclitus specifies in words, the cosmic intelligence states in 'deeds'.

To interpret *'logos'* in this way is not, of course, to exclude the possibility that the other senses of the word (e.g. 'proportion', 'reasoning' in particular) may also be in play here.

---

28 The meanings of *'peirata'* and of 'defining' (*diaireōn*) need more discussion than they have received here or elsewhere. B115, also referring to the *logos* of the soul, is of dubious authenticity.

## 4   *Conclusion*

Heraclitus assumes the tone and the style of a prophet. But his appeal is not to his private revelation, but to common-sense experience. It insists that men could, but mostly do not, interpret that experience aright. What prevents them from doing so, in his view, is presumably habit and mental inertia, which in turn must be presumed to be due to their insufficiently dry souls. His sayings are clarion calls to wake them from their dogmatic slumbers.

Sense-experience rightly interpreted is sufficient for a complete knowledge of the world, its nature and meaning, to be reached. But in order to interpret, we must pay attention to the realm which we know directly but not by sense-experience: the realm of our own selves. We must 'look for ourselves' and construct a phenomenology of our own inner experience. In doing so, Heraclitus becomes aware of his self as something that continually creates and re-creates itself by its own choices, and yet also is an unbounded reservoir of possibilities opposed to the ones it realises. He becomes aware of the strangeness of the self's contemplation of itself. These and other features of his inner life he uses to interpret the cosmos.

Heraclitus' cosmos corresponds to the structure discovered by introspection (so that, as Bruno Snell has noted, even his generalising statements about the cosmos are conveyed in the vivid language of felt experience).[29] It has its changeless essence, which contains opposed potentialities. It chooses now this, now that, in a process which is a struggle and a continual oscillation between opposite states. The course of the struggle is predictable, at least in outline, because it is determined by the law of oscillation, to which all essentially ambivalent things are subject. But the struggle is not a meaninglessly mechanical one: it is illuminated from inside and given meaning by the effort of the cosmic 'self' to realise its *best* state, that of unmixed activity and intelligence, of pure dryness and heat. This is the struggle for each individual self as well. The paradoxes of individual 'weakness of will' recur in the cosmos: the self intends to choose the better, and yet often freely chooses and identifies itself with the worse.

The cosmic self is fully human in the sense that it is structurally identical with a human self. Moreover, individual human selves seem to be fragments, probably the most important fragments, of

29 Snell, 'Die Sprache Heraklits' (above n.18), 132.

it. Human wars, and even the internal psychological struggles of single human beings, are cosmically significant. The reward of the best human selves is that at death they become stars, and as such enjoy a permanent if interrupted individual existence. The others presumably lose all individuality.

This reading of Heraclitus presents him as attempting to overcome some uncomfortable divisions of which Greek writers in the Archaic age show themselves aware: the division between the self and the world as given in sense-experience, the division between the way things are as a matter of brute fact and the meanings that human beings see in them. Awareness of such divisions is present implicitly in Homer, being indeed a precondition of the grandeur and pathos of his warrior-heroes.[30] In the same era as Heraclitus, they are part of the stuff of the great lyric and tragic poetry of Pindar and Aeschylus.

Heraclitus is, secondarily, in reaction against 'science' as represented by the proto-scientific theorising of the Milesians. But he deals gently with these men, no doubt respecting their intellectual vitality and their opposition to traditional and popular ideas. For Heraclitus, these men had at least *tried* to interpret their experience along what were partly the right lines, but they had disregarded some canons of interpretation and as a result their systems were arbitrary.

Heraclitus presents clear parallels with later thinkers, notably with Hegel and Wittgenstein. Any fuller study would have the duty to elucidate these parallels. But Heraclitus deserves study not only for the sake of later thinkers, or for his historical importance as the first metaphysician, but for his own sake: the first metaphysical system is also one of the most fascinating and most philosophically fertile.

---

30 See now the admirable exploration of this aspect of Homer by Jasper Griffin, *Homer on Life and Death* (Oxford 1980).

# 3   The dénouement of the *Cratylus*

MALCOLM SCHOFIELD

In his published writings Gwil Owen has from time to time given us some characteristically stimulating comments on the *Cratylus*. Although he has not devoted an entire essay to the dialogue, it has often been among his favourite topics of discussion. I recall in particular a seminar which he conducted on it soon after his arrival in Cambridge in 1973. I hope he may enjoy this further contribution to the conversation.[1]

## I

The progress of the main argument of the *Cratylus* is clear enough, although not always well understood. Socrates in conversation with Hermogenes propounds a theory according to which a name (i.e. a noun, a verb, or an adjective – but not a word of primarily syntactic function) counts as a genuine or correct name if and only if its nominatum is a real thing and its constitution is naturally suited to its nominatum. The principal test of a name's suitability is its capacity to teach or disclose to us the nature or essence of its nominatum: simply by considering the constitution of a name we should be able to tell what it is the name of (386D–391A).[2]

---

1  I am grateful to my colleagues Myles Burnyeat, Nick Denyer and David Sedley for their helpful comments, which have led me to revise the text of this article at various points and to add some annotation to it.
2  At one point Socrates couples the function of teaching with that of separating or distinguishing things according to their essences (διαχρίνειν, 388B–C). Norman Kretzmann ('Plato on the Correctness of Names', *Amer. Phil. Quart.*, 8 (1971), 126–38) has interpreted this latter function as *taxonomy*, and as the *fundamental* task ascribed to names in Socrates' theory. He observes that the ultimate authority on names is held to be the dialectician (390B–D); and he associates dialectic here with division (cf. e.g. *Phdr.* 265–6, *Sph.* 253).

Socrates then attempts to explain just how a name could be so constituted as to disclose its nominatum. He does so by means of the hypothesis that his own language, Greek, consists of genuine names in the sense required by the theory.

The account he offers of the way in which Greek names can be construed as genuine names is developed in two stages. In the first stage (391A–421C) he assumes that the sort of constituents in a name which are of prime relevance to its teaching function are its *semantic* constituents. His idea is that names will teach us the essences of their nominata if they *define* or at least *describe* them; and the task of the name-maker was therefore to embody in no-matter-what letters and syllables a description of each thing – what Socrates called earlier 'the form of name appropriate to each' (390A, E) and now speaks of as 'the force of the name' (394B, C). Now if names are really descriptions, they must be logically complex, consisting of at least two constituent names, which will have to form a phrase. So this stage of Socrates' account turns out to be an essay in etymology, an attempt to exhibit a vast number of Greek words as compressing within themselves a latent semantic complexity. Thus – to take just one short sequence – *sōphrosunē* is analysed as *sōtēria* (preservation) of *phronēsis* (wisdom); *phronēsis* as *noēsis* (understanding) of *phora* (motion) and *rhous* (flow); *noēsis* as *neou hesis* (desire for the new). Socrates' etymological essay is extended much longer than it needed to be merely for the purpose of explaining what is involved in the notion that names disclose

Contra: (i) We hear no more of 'separation' in *Cra*. The expression is introduced in connection with names largely to make more convincing the analogy with the function of the shuttle (388B1–2). In the immediate sequel (388D–E), as throughout the dialogue, Socrates lays the stress on teaching or disclosure: hence, e.g., the etymological section, as I go on to argue. Of course, if name '$N_1$' discloses the essence of $X$, and '$N_2$' discloses the essence of $Y$, then between them the two names do something to distinguish $X$ and $Y$ according to their natures. (ii) Although διαχρίνειν is a term Plato seldom employs in his theoretical discussions of division (but see *Sph*. 253E1–2) or his practice of it (but see *Phlb*. 52C1), the notion of διάχρισις is certainly billed for important intellectual roles (which probably include that of division) in *Sph*. 226B–D. Gwil Owen has shown us (in 'Plato on the Undepictable', *Exegesis and Argument*, ed. Lee *et al.*, 358–61) how in this connection, as in others, Plato came to see more and more illumination for philosophy and of philosophy in reflective comparison with the operations of weaving. So if *Cra*. was written close in time to dialogues such as *Phdr*. or *Sph*., it would be surprising if the reference to separation, and equally the reference to the dialectician, did not hint at taxonomy. Perhaps we should conclude that *Cra*. is an earlyish middle period work which unsurprisingly fails to associate dialectic firmly and closely with division, and which exhibits an interest as yet inchoate in the potentialities of the weaving analogy.

their nominata in virtue of their constitution. It is true that it includes, particularly in its first few pages (391A–397C), some interesting matter pertinent to the general theory under discussion; and some of the particular etymologies proposed (like that of *sōphrosunē*) are sensible and approximately correct. But for the most part Socrates is occupied in a curious form of amusement, pursued with a good deal of frivolity and with frequent acknowledgment of the forced, arbitrary, fanciful and tendentious character of many of his derivations. Scholars have often suspected some satirical motivation. We can perhaps extract two serious morals bearing on the main argument of the dialogue. Socrates seems to suggest (cf. especially 396C–E) that there is no hope of articulating and applying a properly scientific method of analysis to the vocabulary of an actual natural language in such a way as to extract from names descriptions of the appropriate sort. And he indicates that in any event analysis of an actual natural language can reveal only what its namemakers believed about the essences of things, not (save accidentally) the truth about their essences (cf. especially 400D–401A, 411B–C). Plato represents him as inclined to the opinion, reiterated at the end of the dialogue (439C), that those who gave the Greeks their vocabulary did so upon the mistaken Heraclitean assumption that all things are in flux (411B–C). Such an opinion could not acquire even plausibility without examination of a considerable body of evidence. Hence, probably, one reason at least for the disproportionate length of the etymological section.

The second stage of Socrates' attempt to explain what is involved in the naturalist theory that genuine names are fitted to disclose their nominata runs from 421C–427D. Maintaining his assumption that Greek consists of names of this sort, he considers what should be said about words which figure in the analysis of other words into complex descriptions, but which cannot themselves be subjected to such analysis: e.g. *ion, rheon, doun*. In practice there will be some words of this class which baffle further enquiry, e.g. because they are loan words of foreign origin (421C–D, 425D–426A). But Socrates recognises the need for a general solution to the problem of how elemental names disclose their nominata. The answer he proposes is that they, like other names, disclose their nominata in virtue of their

constitution – but in virtue of their *phonetic* constitution, something which had been discounted as more or less irrelevant in
the treatment of other names. Socrates' idea here is that each of
the phonemes symbolised in the Greek alphabet functions as a
tool which may be used in name-making to *imitate* (or as we
might prefer to say, *represent*) some basic feature of reality.
What makes this possible is the fact that our vocal equipment is
itself characterised by such features at the moment we produce
significant sounds. Thus the tongue is least at rest and most
agitated in pronouncing rho: hence the use of that phoneme in
*rhein* (flow), *rhoē* (current), *tromos* (trembling), *trechein* (run),
*krouein* (strike), *thrauein* (break), *ereikein* (rend), *thruptein*
(crush), *kermatizein* (crumble), *rhumbein* (whirl); 'again, perceiving the internal character of the sound of nu, he [sc. the
name-maker] introduced the names *endon* (inside) and *entos*
(within), with the intention of assimilating things to letters'
(427C1–3). The name-maker will have combined phonemes
and groups of phonemes to make up his elemental names
according to the particular combination of features of reality
exhibited by the object that he wanted a given name to disclose.
The general principle he must have employed in his work is
therefore resemblance (424D6, 427C9). And from this point on
in the dialogue the naturalist theory is assumed to maintain that
a genuine name discloses its nominatum in virtue of a resemblance between the letters and syllables of which it is composed
and the essence of the nominatum (see especially 433D7–E2,
435C2–D1). This holds true with respect to non-elemental
names as much as to elemental (425A6–B3, 427C8–9). Socrates
accordingly adds a further obliquely critical comment on the
etymologies of the first stage of the defence of his theory
(426A3–B2): 'If anyone, no matter why, is ignorant of the
correctness of the primary names, it is impossible for him to
know that of the secondary names, which must be explained by
means of those about which he knows nothing . . . [Indeed] he
must know very well that he will talk nonsense about them.'
One proof of this last contention he might have offered is that in
the original statement of the naturalist theory and in the
etymological essay it was reckoned immaterial what letters and
syllables were chosen by the name-makers to embody the
description appropriate to a given essence; whereas now it has

transpired that choice of letters and syllables is all-important in securing correctness in a name. Yet if the second stage of Socrates' account reinforces his own and the reader's doubts about the first stage, it is presented itself with disclaimers as strong as any expressed during the first stage. Socrates owns both that the general idea of the disclosure of things through imitation in letters and syllables will seem ridiculous (425D1–3), and that his particular notions about the principles governing the constitution of primary names appear to him outrageous and ridiculous (426B5–6).

Nonetheless it is not until the next and final section of the dialogue (427D–440E) that actual argument is advanced against the naturalist theory. The transition from exposition to criticism is marked by a dramatic interlude (427D–428D) in which Socrates urges a re-examination of what he has been saying, and the compliant Hermogenes is replaced as interlocutor by the more stubborn and assertive Cratylus. Cratylus immediately declares himself to be in close sympathy with Socrates' theory, which was originally presented as an explanation of some ideas ascribed to Cratylus by Hermogenes (383A–B, 390D–E). But when he and Socrates apply themselves to consideration of the core thesis of the theory, disagreement between them breaks out. For Cratylus construes it in an extreme fashion from which Socrates dissociates himself. He holds first that every genuine name must be not only so constructed as to be a naturally appropriate representation of its nominatum, but faultlessly constructed for this purpose; and second that names not only furnish us with instruction about reality in virtue of this property, but supply our best and only instruction about it. Socrates' attack on the first proposition runs from 429B–435C, on the second from 435D to the end of the dialogue.

The plan of this final section sets a puzzle about Plato's authorial strategy. At its outset Socrates plainly promises a critical examination of the theory he himself has been developing. He talks of turning back repeatedly to what has been said, and he exclaims upon the dangers of self-deception (428D). But then he proceeds to examine not himself but Cratylus, and not the theory in its original version but in an extreme guise for which he holds no brief. Is not his promise broken? Not through want of a self-examination. It is a familiar fact, stressed by Plato in this dialogue

(384C, 391A; cf. e.g. 422C) as elsewhere, that in his eyes philosophical inquiry (and in particular the elenchus) is a cooperative enterprise: an enterprise in which, as the *Protagoras* tells us (333C), *both* partners put not just the argument but themselves to the test. Nor, as it turns out, is the original version of the theory neglected. As one would expect, in discussing Cratylus's two propositions the interlocutors do advert to many points made in Socrates' exposition of the theory. Even more importantly, criticism of Cratylus's extreme position leads Socrates to imply diagnoses of further grave weaknesses in his own. Thus after obtaining Cratylus's reluctant agreement that we understand names which are naturally appropriate but imperfectly constructed representations of their nominata, Socrates finds himself arguing that we are able to do so because (or partly because) we accept a mere convention governing (or partly governing) their use (434E1–435C2). But this is tantamount to an admission at least that any reasonable naturalism will have to invoke convention in its explanation of how names make their disclosures to us. And that admission entails discomfiture not only for Cratylus (as Socrates stresses, 435A6–C2), but for Socrates himself (as he ruefully acknowledges, 435C2–6). Perhaps it need not follow that the naturalist must entirely abandon his own view of names in favour of the rival conventionalist theory, according to which *all* that matters in a name is that the linguistic community concerned should agree to use it in a determinate way. It seems that for Socrates, however, the discovery that the naturalist theory requires such reliance on the idea of mere convention presents another and decisive obstacle to its acceptance – as though the price which would have to be paid in order to sustain conviction in it has now become altogether too high.[3] He still avers that he is happy with the idea that names should be like things so far as

---

3 This is perhaps a suitable place to draw attention to the fact (emphasised by R. Robinson, *Essays in Greek Philosophy*, 110–16) that the naturalist makes quite unembarrassed use of the notion of νόμος ('law' or 'convention') at another, less crucial point in his theory. The theory provides that a νόμος must be established to ensure that names constructed according to proper naturalist principles *gain currency* among the linguistic community for which they are designed. Names do not, according to the naturalist, grow on trees. They have to be made; and even the best made names still have to achieve acceptance. Hence Socrates' fiction of the νομοθέτης or law-giver (388D–390E), who as Kretzmann remarks serves as the 'personification of an accepted linguistic authority' (op. cit., 128). What Socrates and Cratylus now have to admit is that not merely his acceptance but his authority derives (in part at least) from convention.

possible (435C2–3; cf. C6–D1). But we should read this as nothing more than an expression of vain regret, particularly in view of the considerations he adduces in opposing Cratylus's second proposition: that names provide us with the only and the best instruction about things. Here he reinforces the doubts he had already expressed in the etymological section as to whether the names of a natural language can be trusted to tell one anything more than the conception of the nature of things held by the name-maker (436B–437D). He adds a proof that there must be other and better ways of learning about things than through their names (437D–439C). The proof removes from the naturalist theory any residual attraction it might retain. As Socrates has hinted, its basic concept of imitation or representation evidently cannot bear the weight it is required to carry; and he has suggested, both by comment and by example, that it is possible to make only partial and arbitrary application of the theory (whether at the first or the second stage of analysis) to an actual natural language. So if the basic purpose of instruction which the naturalist wants names to serve is better achieved by other means, why should he not abandon the unequal struggle to recommend his theory to himself or others?

We are now in a position to explain why Socrates is made to address himself, at what we rightly predict to be the final and critical stage of a developing argument, to two absolute and implausible propositions which the preceding discussion has given us no warning of. The heart of the matter is simply that Plato, with unerring dramatic instinct and philosophical judgement, has seen that much the best way to sharpen the issue between naturalism and conventionalism and set it in a proper light is to present it in extreme terms. Once this is done, it becomes clear that the more qualified theory expounded by Socrates exerted whatever attractions it possessed principally because the qualifications, self-deprecatingly expressed or tacitly assumed, were not allowed to exert their full force in the reader's mind. For now Cratylus's extreme naturalist stance compels him to formulate them much more trenchantly; and when they are so expressed, they leave the position which he himself has taken looking weak and partial. Examination of Cratylus's first proposition forces into a proper reckoning the important (and indeed central) role of mutual understanding and communication in the use of language, neglected in the theory Socrates expounded, and the predominant role of convention in their explanation. By the end of that examination Socrates has contrived to make disclosure of the nature of its nominatum seem an inessential function in a name. In his attack on Cratylus's second proposition he tenaciously and effectively *argues* against the trustworthiness of the instruction names might provide (if they were designed for the job). Earlier he had merely suggested that his hypothetical Greek name-maker must have constructed names on the basis of certain suppositions, not known by us to be true and very likely mistaken, about the nature of things. And his proof that there must be better and more direct ways of learning and enquiring about things than through the disclosures afforded by their names gives expression to a thought which had earlier to be suppressed if the development of the naturalist theory was to be read as bearing any resemblance to a worthwhile intellectual project. Plato is surely reminding us here, at the end of the dialogue, that in order to take the naturalist theory of names even as seriously as the *Cratylus* asks us to do, it has been necessary temporarily to forget the existence of such pursuits as mathematics and dialectic. This is doubtless one reason why he introduces the theory of Forms once more into the discussion on his very last page (439C–440E).

It remains a curious and amusing fact that Socrates succeeds in demolishing the pretensions of the naturalist theory of correctness of names without aiming a single argument in the first instance against the version of the theory he himself has propounded. Plato relies throughout chiefly on our sense of what is serious and central and what is absurd and peripheral in philosophy. This gives him ample scope for teasing the reader, as he loves to do, with argumentation that is ambiguous in direction and equivocal in tone. I shall comment in detail on a particular example, the dénouement at 433–5, which has not, I think, been savoured to the full by writers on the dialogue.

## II

It is at 429B that Cratylus, having agreed that correct names are the products of legislation, denies first (like Thrasymachus) that some legislators produce finer work, others inferior, and then more specifically that one name may be better, another worse 'laid down' (*keisthai*; the legal terminology is sustained). Socrates begins by construing this denial as simply equivalent to the thesis he himself has implied (cf. 387C3–4, D7–8), that a name must be correctly laid down (i.e. in accordance with the general requirements of the naturalist theory), or it will not strictly speaking count as a name. The thesis is illustrated by the example of 'Hermogenes': if the birth of Hermes has nothing to do with Hermogenes, then the name 'Hermogenes' has not been laid down for him at all, despite appearances – 'Hermogenes' is just not his name. The next couple of pages of the dialogue (429C–431C) explore an apparent consequence of this position. The apparent consequence concerns the *use* of a combination of sounds which appears to have been laid down as someone's name, but has not really been. Does it follow that if one refers to Hermogenes as 'Hermogenes', one has *pro tanto* failed to say anything at all, because one has not used *his* name? Cratylus claims that it does, and that utterance of 'Hermogenes' in such a context is mere meaningless sound. But Socrates exploits another point made by Cratylus (that although '*N*' may not be the name for *X*, it may be the appropriate name for *Y*) to argue that the naturalist theory *can* allow the logical possibility of a *mistaken* application of '*N*' to *X* by users of the language.

This fascinating stretch of argument, analysed by Bernard Williams in ch. 4, bears out the account of Plato's strategy in the final section of the dialogue which has been offered above. Socrates here launches no direct attack on the naturalist theory. Instead he allows it to damn itself by the absurdities entailed in its defence, and so shows how inadequate it is to account for the actual use of names in speech.

At 431A–C Socrates rounds off his discussion of misapplication of names, and turns rather abruptly to a new topic (the *Cratylus* is not one of the best finished Platonic dialogues). Cratylus's answer about legislators at 429B had been preceded by questions about good and bad workmanship in the crafts. So when Socrates then went on to ask whether names were laid down with varying degrees of excellence, we naturally expected him to be intent on pursuing the question whether, if a name is genuinely appropriate to its nominatum, it is of necessity perfectly constructed. This *is* the topic taken up from 431C–435C; and in these pages of the dialogue the problem whether every name is admirably laid down becomes an issue about the possibility of degrees of excellence in the construction of names (see especially 433B–C).

Cratylus does not like the idea of saying that something is a name, but not admirably laid down (i.e. constructed) (433C). But the only argument he advances is a desperately feeble point about spelling (431E–432A). Socrates offers three arguments against this extreme position. I pass over the first two, which are briefly discussed by Bernard Williams in the next chapter. They show that where there is representation, there must be the possibility of misrepresentation: a conclusion which might lull the naturalist into a false sense of security. For he might cheerfully infer that he can best sustain his theory by rejecting Cratylus's position. And he might watch with a certain satisfaction the manoeuvres by which in the third argument Socrates eventually forces Cratylus to acknowledge that he cannot maintain his absolutism. But as we noticed earlier, this is not the only direction the third argument takes. It further shows that we need to invoke *convention* in order to explain how a comparatively badly constructed name is understood. An appeal to convention on a point of crucial importance to his position cannot please the naturalist, even if he can accommodate it within his theory. In fact the argument is given yet a third dimension, and with it yet another direction still less congenial to the naturalist. Socrates contrives convincingly to suggest that the difficulties he raises for Cratylus's extreme position necessitate outright abandonment of naturalism in favour of the conventionalist theory of names. He achieves this result by predominantly indirect means. For one thing, he is able to exploit the more specific character which sets this argument apart from the first two. By assisting Cratylus to spell out a naturalist explanation of the word *sklērotēs* (hardness), Socrates effectively draws attention once more to the arbitrary and implausible claims about the mimetic properties of different phonemes on which the theory has ultimately to rest. Then again, the natural progress of the argument from preoccupation with the naturalist interpretation of *sklērotēs* to confrontation with the actual realities of the use of words in communication makes the naturalist theory look as irrelevant to a satisfactory account of language as, of course, it is.

So cunning an argument deserves closer scrutiny. In order to facilitate scrutiny both of it and of my interpretation of it (which depends on a reading of the detail as much as on the general structure of the passage), I shall interleave my commentary with translation. I should add that while Méridier's French version of the *Cratylus* in the Budé series is excellent at this point as elsewhere, the most accessible English translators let down the careful student of the passage, Jowett by a characteristic tendency to paraphrase too economically, Fowler in the Loeb by an equally characteristic sloppiness.

We take up the text at the point where Socrates breaks off his second theoretical argument against Cratylus's proposition that every genuine name is altogether admirably constructed. Cratylus had earlier seemed to succumb to the argument (433B6–7), but now makes a half-hearted attempt to dissociate himself from it:

> C. I suppose, Socrates, that I should not fight what you say. But I am not *happy* with the idea of saying that something is a name, but yet has not been laid down admirably.
>
> 433D S. Aren't you happy with this idea – that a name is a disclosure of a thing?
> C. I am!
> S. But does the statement that some names are composed of prior ones, but others are primary, not seem to you to be admirably made?
> C. It does!
> S. But if the primary names are to become disclosures of something, can you suggest any more admirable way of their becoming disclosures than to make them as similar as possible to
> 433E the things which they must disclose? Or are you happier with the way proposed by Hermogenes and many others, that names are compacts and make disclosures to those who have compacted together and possess prior knowledge of the things [sc. which the names are for], and that this is correctness of names, convention, and that it makes no difference whether one makes a compact just as now obtains or whether one adopts the opposite one of calling large what we now call small, and small what we call large? Which way are you happy with?
> 434A C. There is no comparison, Socrates: disclosure of what one discloses not by any chance expression but by a likeness.[4]

Socrates' first two questions to Cratylus sound a little oddly in translation. Their formulation may seem to suggest that a negative

---

4 'Happy with the idea etc.' in this section of text (433C9, D1, E2, 9), as in the concluding paragraph of the whole passage (435C2), translates ἀρέσκει etc. . . . The word is often used by Plato with the force 'agreeable to accept' (of a philosophical position) – e.g. *Cra.* 427E1, *Tht.* 157D7, 189D4, 202C7. Here it is put more colourfully into Socrates' mouth to mock Cratylus's use of it to make an unreasoned refusal to accept the argument that, if names are representations, it must be possible for them to be misrepresentations.

answer is expected. Yet Socrates plainly cannot really be anticipating such an answer. Of course, the pretence of anticipating it
might well be part of an argumentative strategem. But his long
speech at 433D–E does not confirm that possibility. And in fact
recourse to the Greek solves the puzzle. Socrates' first question is
prefaced by an untranslatable *poteron* ('whether', introducing an
alternative question). This shows that the three questions of 433D
together present Cratylus with a first alternative, to which is
opposed the conventionalist alternative (introduced by *ē, hode*) set
out in 433E. One might be tempted to suppose that Socrates
begins presentation of the first alternative only with the long
speech, and that he there offers Cratylus a choice between two
ways in which names disclose things. But strictly speaking, as we
shall see, it is only on the first alternative that names *do* disclose
things. On the second alternative, what they disclose are their
utterers' thoughts or meanings.

It may be felt that the whole passage is an oddity. Why ever
should Socrates, at this or indeed any other stage in the *Cratylus*,
ask Cratylus whether it is the naturalist or the conventionalist
view of names which appeals to him? Cratylus's commitment to
naturalism was made explicit in the very first lines of the dialogue
(383A–B). (Admittedly he was not there represented as upholding
the notion that names disclose their nominata in virtue of resemblance to them; but he accepts it *expressis verbis* at 430A10–B2, and
the whole of the intervening discussion has been built upon that
acceptance.) There is an obvious and natural explanation of
Socrates' procedure. He is signalling to Cratylus (and Plato to the
reader) that they are approaching the decisive point in the whole
argument of the dialogue. This is why he ceremoniously sets out
the two positions between which a choice has to be made, and
gives Cratylus a last chance to reconsider his own attitude to
them – before delivering the *coup de grâce* to naturalism.

> S. Admirably said. Then if the name is to be like the thing, it is
> necessary that the elements from which one is going to compose
> the primary names should bear a natural resemblance to things?
> Let me put the point this way. Could anyone ever have composed
> a picture (to revert to what we were just speaking of) resembling
> 434B some actual thing, if nature did not supply pigments, from which
> the representations in the picture are composed, that are like the
> things which the painter's art imitates? Would that not be imposs-
> ible?

*C.* Impossible.
*S.* Then in the same way names too would never come to resemble anything, if the items from which the names are composed do not originally bear a certain resemblance to the things of which the names are imitations? And the items from which the composing is to be done are elements?
*C.* Yes.

This section requires little comment. It continues the process, begun in the second and third questions of 433D, of eliciting Cratylus's specific agreement to the naturalist theory of primary names originally expounded at 421C–427D. 'Elements' (sc. of speech) translates *stoicheia*, usually rendered by translators as 'letters' in this passage. But I reserve 'letter' for *gramma*; cf. W. Burkert, 'Στοιχεῖον: eine semiasologische Studie', *Philologus* 103 (1959), 167–97.

  *S.* It is time, then, for *you* to take a share in the argument in which Hermogenes was engaged with me a while ago.
434C Now do you think admirable our proposition that rho resembles motion and change and hardness, or not admirable?
  *C.* I think it admirable.
  *S.* And that lambda resembles smoothness and softness and the other things we were just now mentioning?
  *C.* Yes.
  *S.* Now you know that we say *sklērotēs*, the Eretrians *sklērotēr*, referring to the same thing.
  *C.* Certainly.
  *S.* So do rho and sigma both resemble the same thing, and does the form with final rho disclose to them the same thing as the form with final sigma discloses to us? Or does one of the forms not disclose it to one or other of us?
434D *C.* They disclose it to both of us.
  *S.* In virtue of the fact that rho and sigma happen to be alike, or in virtue of their being not alike?
  *C.* In virtue of their being alike.
  *S.* Is it, then, that they are altogether alike?
  *C.* Yes, at any rate so far as disclosing motion equally is concerned.
  *S.* And what of the lambda set in the name? Does it not disclose the opposite of hardness?
  *C.* Well, perhaps it is incorrectly inserted, Socrates – just like the cases of which you were right now speaking in conversation with Hermogenes, when you took out and put in letters where it was necessary – and I think you were quite right. In the present case we ought perhaps to say rho instead of lambda.

Having agreed with Cratylus the basis on which the argument is to proceed, Socrates in this section launches his attack. The interlocutors assume throughout that *sklērotēs* is a genuine name. Cratylus is presumably committed in consequence to the further assumptions that it reveals its nominatum, hardness, in virtue of a resemblance to it, and that it is altogether admirably fitted for this task. Certainly Socrates' attempts to disconcert him have to be understood as directed against these further assumptions. In a way, therefore, it would have been better if he had formally extracted Cratylus's agreement to them at the outset. But there would have been a compensating disadvantage in this more explicit procedure. For Socrates is also addressing himself to the common man (and the common man in Cratylus). And the common man will take it for granted that *sklērotēs* is, in a sense innocent of theoretical commitments, a perfectly good word. He does not need to be refuted, but only to be convinced of the right philosophical explanation of what he quite properly takes for granted.

The shape of Socrates' argument is plainly adapted to the end of showing that names certified as genuine by the naturalist theory need not (*contra* Cratylus) be perfectly constructed resemblances (henceforth I call this line of thought Direction A). His plan is simple. He considers in turn the relevant mimetic properties of the liquids, rho and lambda (hardness, incidentally, had not earlier been associated with rho (426C–E), and Cratylus omits to mention it where he should do, in connexion with the comparison of rho and sigma (434D6), at the end of our section; but there seems no reason to doubt that the Greeks would have recognised rho to be a particularly hard sound). He then introduces discussion of the word *sklērotēs*, and raises two difficulties for the account he presumes Cratylus would give of it, the first turning on the interpretation of rho, the second on that of lambda. Cratylus accepts the second difficulty as a fatal objection to his view that every genuine name is perfectly constructed, and explicitly subscribes to the more moderate position expounded by Socrates. He brazens out the first difficulty (which consists of a delicate hint by Socrates that the Eretrian form of the word lives up to naturalist standards of correctness better than the Attic), but only by the desperate expedient of claiming that the pronunciation of sigma (not implausibly associated by Socrates with breathiness, 427A) is suggestive of motion.

Although the course the argument takes is governed by Direction A, it cannot but suggest an upshot far more radical than the moderate naturalist conclusion that names may disclose their nominata by less than perfect resemblances. The concessions and subterfuges to which it forces Cratylus may readily and naturally lead the reader to see it as supplying pointers to outright rejection of naturalism (hereafter Direction C). Consider the point about the impropriety of including lambda in *sklērotēs*. The presence of lambda is not very plausibly taken as an isolated flaw in an otherwise satisfactory representation of hardness. After all, the only phoneme in the word which has been alleged to resemble hardness is rho, which in the Attic form appears no more nor less frequently than lambda. One might think it more reasonable to hold that the two liquids just cancel each other out, leaving a set of phonemes with no particular tendency to indicate hardness or its opposite. How, in any case, do we know that rho discloses hardness in this context, and not motion (so much stressed at 426C–E)? The fact is that careful scrutiny of the application of the naturalist theory to *any* particular example is bound to impress upon the reader's mind the gaps, implausibilities and arbitrarinesses which lie close to the heart of the theory. Such deficiencies do not preclude the possibility that the names in a natural language might have been constructed in a necessarily unsatisfactory *attempt* to disclose by resemblance the nominata which they signify. As we have remarked, Socrates will continue to the end of the dialogue (439C) to endorse the idea that the vocabulary of Greek is largely the product of a doubly misconceived (because Heraclitean) attempt to do just that. The lesson which examination of examples like *sklērotēs* does bring home is that disclosure by resemblance cannot *be* the criterion of what makes a name a genuine name.

434E S. Well said. But now: do we not understand each other at all when someone says *sklēron*, using the current form, and do you not know what I am saying?

C. I do indeed, but by habit, my friend.

S. When you say 'habit', do you mean to say anything different from 'convention'? Do you not call it 'habit' when *I*, when I utter *this*, have *that* in mind, and *you* recognise that I have that in mind? Is not this what you would say?

435A C. Yes.

The discussion now develops into an enquiry into the explanation that should be given of how we understand a word like *sklēron* which is not a perfectly satisfactory imitation of its *nominatum*. This section of the argument, like its predecessor, can be read in two different ways.

Socrates might want simply to point out that a reasonable naturalist will agree that habit or convention plays a part in our understanding *which* elements in a genuine name should have their mimetic properties discounted, if they do not *all* disclose features of one and the same essence. That would not preclude the name's *counting* as a genuine name just because most or the most prominent of its phonemes *do* disclose by resemblance one and the same essence. The introduction of the notion of convention will then have been designed to indicate that the reasonable naturalist must pay some respect to conventionalism, without having to accept conventionalism as the *basis* of correctness in names. Such a line of reasoning would be a natural extension of Direction A. But because it takes the naturalist further than Direction A towards conventionalism I shall give it a distinct denomination: Direction B.

To discern in these lines a train of thought so qualified as Direction B certainly requires the eye of naturalist faith. I formulate it for two reasons. First, it expresses all that a stubborn and alert naturalist might feel he is forced to concede by the argument of the preceding section (434B–D) – if he were deaf or resistant to the hints of Direction C in that argument, and attended only to Direction A. Second, we shall find Socrates talking in a *later* section as though it is just the limited concession to conventionalism represented by Direction B which his arguments actually require. Taken in itself, however (and indeed, as we shall see, with its immediate sequel), the present section is most naturally read on the assumption that Socrates is pressing towards a full-blooded conventionalism: in short, in Direction C. No explicit indication is given that habit or convention plays just the limited role of enabling us to understand how to discount phonemes irrelevant to a name's mimetic function. What Cratylus appears to agree to in his first reply is rather that our understanding of *sklēron* is due without qualification to habit. And when he goes on to allow that mutual understanding of *any* word is a matter of habit or convention, he again inserts no qualification. He does not explain (as a stubborn naturalist might) that in the case of some words (the genuine names) the convention governing our mutual understanding is itself explained largely by the fact that they disclose their nominata by means of a natural resemblance.

Here, then, is the great dramatic moment of the *Cratylus*. In abandoning his extreme naturalist position, Cratylus does not retreat to a more moderate naturalism. He flops into conventionalism immediately, as Socrates now points out explicitly.

> S. So if you achieve recognition when I utter, a disclosure comes to you from me.
> C. Yes.
> S. But it may proceed from something unlike what I have in mind when I utter, since lambda is unlike hardness (to revert to your example). And if that is so, then surely you have come to terms with yourself, and the correctness of a name turns out to be convention for you – since both resembling and non-resembling letters make disclosures if once they chance to acquire the sanction of habit and convention. Even if habit is very far from being
> 435B convention, it would still not be well to say that it is resemblance which is disclosure, but habit; for that, as it seems, discloses, and it does so by both what resembles and what does not resemble.

Socrates here opts decisively for the stronger line of attack, Direction C (one would add 'finally' were it not for the next section). He makes one further important move before declaring that Cratylus's concessions commit him to a thoroughgoing conventionalism – since he has 'made a convention with himself' (i.e. arrived at a position consistent with his recognition that he understands a word such as *sklēron*, but that he does not do so in virtue of grasping a resemblance). The move consists in introducing the idea that when $X$ understands what $Y$ means when he says something, then $Y$ has *disclosed* something to $X$ – namely his thought or meaning. Socrates takes Cratylus to have conceded that this sort of disclosure does not depend on resemblances at all. He thus ties the train of thought represented in Direction C to the characterisation of conventionalism at 433E specifically in terms of the type of disclosure it allows: disclosure not of what a thing is like (cf. e.g. 422D1–3, 428E1–2), but of a speaker's thought.

A comment is called for on Socrates' debate with himself about whether habit is or is not the same as convention. Discussion of the question gives him, of course, an opportunity to bang home the anti-naturalist conclusion to which he claims to have led Cratylus. But it is a pity Plato did not make clearer his views on the nature of the issue and of its proper outcome. I take it that the final sentence of the present section and the first of the next show that he rightly allows that habit and convention are distinct concepts. I take it also that he means to point out that if we invoke habit to explain linguistic communication, as Cratylus has just done (434E4), we are really relying not just on habit but on something stronger. Our explanation effectively appeals to a tacit convention by which any two participants in a mutual conversation behave according to certain assumptions about each other's beliefs and intentions. Such a convention does, of course, require habit to sustain it. And in the passage in which Socrates comes closest to identifying the two concepts (434E6–8), he gives a characterisation which serves to specify not a convention, but only a habit: the habit of speakers of using '$N$' to mean $X$ and of hearers of taking them to use '$N$' to mean $X$. No doubt it is implied that such a mutual habit must presuppose a convention.[5] Finally, I take it that Plato acknowledges that a naturalist might object (for whatever reason) to an interpretation of his appeal to habit in terms of convention. So, without ceding any ground to the objection, he points out that the appeal to habit alone is sufficient to rule naturalism out of court as an explanation of our understanding of words in speech.

> S. (continues) Since we agree on these points, Cratylus – for I will put down your silence to agreement – it is necessary, surely, that both convention and habit contribute something to the disclosing of what we have in mind when we speak. For, my excellent Cratylus, if you are prepared to turn your attention to number, where do you think you will be able to bring in names resembling each one of the numbers from, if you do not allow this agreement
> 435C and convention of yours to have a certain authority in regard to correctness of names?

After the unambiguous conventionalist conclusion which is pressed home so emphatically in the previous section, it comes as a surprise to find Socrates' summary of what he and Cratylus have agreed couched in such restricted terms as these. On the face of it Socrates now interprets the argument along the lines of Direction B, as committing Cratylus to at least a *limited* conventionalism,

---

5 Although Plato at the end of the day declares for conventionalism on the issue of correctness of names, it is the naturalist position which excites his philosophical imagination and calls forth his analytical powers. He has little to say on the philosophical analysis of the notion of convention: for which see D. K. Lewis, *Convention*, and J. Bennett, *Linguistic Behaviour*.

but not necessarily to the thorough-going conventionalism of Hermogenes. For the sentence about numbers plainly assumes that Cratylus will stick by his insistence on resemblance in names. And notice the carefully qualified phraseology employed: 'convention and habit *contribute something . . .*'; 'agreement and convention *. . . have a certain authority in regard to* correctness of names'. These are expressions suited to suggest merely a degree of conventionalism, such as a moderate naturalist might be ready to accept.

What prompts this unexpected revision in Socrates' assessment of the results of his argument against Cratylus's extreme position? Perhaps he is now recognizing that although one might take the collapse of that position as requiring total abandonment of the naturalist theory, it is logically possible to interpret it as having only more restricted consequences. The numbers example may indicate that Plato has given some thought to what is involved in this possibility. A naturalist might observe that it is a purely contingent matter if the word for hardness in a language contains non-resembling elements which have to be explained away as due to convention; and he might infer that an *ideal* language could therefore dispense with any appeal to convention. Plato has a counter-argument available. If the names of *numbers* are to disclose by resemblance their essences, then such disclosure can *only* be effected by a positive use of convention. For example, we can disclose the differences between 1, 2 and 3 through their names only by some purely conventional device such as giving the name of 1 one syllable, that of 2 two syllables, that of 3 three; and it will have to be agreed by convention that they are designed to signify *numbers* in the first place. This is the one place in the dialogue where we glimpse the idea that representation is not a natural relationship, but is itself subject to convention.

Yet if that is the message Plato hints at in the numbers example, then the supposedly restricted form of conventionalism apparently advocated here turns out in fact to be barely distinguishable from the radical conventionalism of the previous section. And in any case, the unequivocal assertion of radical conventionalism there makes it hard not to read the tone of our present section as ironical. It prepares us to construe 'contribute something' as an understatement for 'govern entirely', and 'a certain authority' as saying in effect 'all authority'. The mockery of 'this [sc. so recently confessed idea of] agreement and convention of *yours*' only confirms this interpretation. Moreover, any reader of the *Republic* will find an inescapable irony in the mere suggestion that numbers could be accommodated within the naturalist theory on any terms whatever. He will simply not believe that Plato could here be taking seriously the notion that sights or sounds could painlessly disclose the essence of number.

So Direction C lies beneath the skin, after all. The same is true of the next and final section of the passage, where Socrates indicates in characteristically ambiguous terms his own considered opinion on the issue debated in the dialogue: 'I am happy with the idea that names should resemble things so far as is possible. But . . .'[6] Many scholars have followed Grote in reading this confession with straight faces, as conceived in the spirit of Direction B. They suppose that Plato seriously intimates that an *ideal* language would conform to the canons of the naturalist theory – if only it were practically possible. I hope I have done enough to convince the reader that he must mean us to prefer a lighter and more teasing gloss in the spirit of Direction C. Plato allows that the idea that names should bear a natural resemblance to their nominata is a congenial and acceptable idea so far as it goes. But he indicates that it cannot be taken very far. The impossibilities which preclude its actualisation are more than merely practical. The case of numbers has shown this decisively enough, despite the brevity of Socrates' presentation. So too has the example of *sklēron/sklērotēs*. It has raised a deep problem for any theory of natural languages which makes their symbols function as natural signs. If they are natural signs of anything, phonemes and morphemes and lexemes each signify many things, partly because they exhibit a multiplicity of aspects. Consequently the naturalist theory of names worked out in the *Cratylus* affords no prospect of a *determinate* account of what any word means or signifies.

6 Notice the emphatic reiteration of κατὰ τὸ δύνατον ('so far as is possible . . .', '*if* it were possible . . .') at 435C1–2, 7, readily explicable on the interpretation offered below. So interpreted, the expression may be compared (as Myles Burnyeat suggests to me) with the 'if . . .' at the end of *Hippias Minor*: 'He who willingly errs, then, Hippias, and does what is base and unjust, will be none other – if he exists – than the good man' (376B4–6). Notice, too, that Socrates' avowal of happiness with the idea that names should resemble their nominata so far as is possible (ἐμοὶ μὲν οὖν καὶ αὐτῷ ἀρέσκει κτλ) is given a touch of irony by its echo of Cratylus' unreasoned refusal to be happy with the idea of their imperfect resemblance at 433C9 (cf. n.4 above). The effect is to weaken our sense that Plato *is* genuinely agreeable to accept the ideal of the naturalist theory.

Fortunately its failure as a theory does not matter. As Plato has given us to understand, it suffices for the correctness of a name that there should be a convention which enables us to use it successfully to communicate with each other.

> S. (concludes) For my own part, then, I am happy with the idea that names should resemble things so far as is possible. But I fear that in truth this dragging in of resemblance is a niggardly business, as Hermogenes commented, and we must make use also of this worthless thing, convention, for correctness of names. For perhaps a name would be most admirably expressed, *if* it were possible, when it was expressed with elements which were all (or 435D as many as may be) resembling (that is, appropriate); but most deficiently in the opposite case.

# 4 Cratylus' theory of names and its refutation

## BERNARD WILLIAMS

At the very beginning of Plato's *Cratylus* Hermogenes explains Cratylus' view by saying that it supposes there to be a certain natural correctness (*orthotēs*) of names; that this correctness is the same for all linguistic groups; and (very strongly) that it has nothing to do with what name anyone actually applies to anything – so that, he is quoted as saying to Hermogenes, 'your name would not be Hermogenes, even if everyone called you that' (383B). This last point implies something which explicitly emerges later, that, for Cratylus, the question whether some word 'N' is the *correct* name of a given item is the same as the question whether 'N' is that item's name at all.

The assumption that the answers to those questions must be the same is not shared by everyone in the dialogue. It is shared by Hermogenes, for reasons which are (roughly) the opposite of Cratylus'. It is not shared by Socrates, whose final position requires us to distinguish the questions; or rather, to put it more precisely, it requires us to make a distinction which can be handily put by us in terms of a possible divergence between *the name of X* and *the correct name of X*, and is often so put in the dialogue, but which can also be expressed, as we shall see later, in terms of two kinds of correctness.

In trying to give some account of Cratylus' theory of names, I shall particularly emphasise that distinction and Cratylus' denial of it. Some of what I include in that theory is not advanced by Cratylus in the dialogue, but by Socrates in the course of his attempt, with Hermogenes, to elaborate a notion of 'the correctness of names' (see 391B for the start of their enquiry); but Cratylus fully adopts their theory (428C), and, whatever other status these conceptions may have, they are (at least in outline) consequences of the general views which are refuted in the argument against Cratylus at the end of the dialogue. Whether Plato displays any independent attachment to them is a question I shall touch on at the end.

According to Cratylus, then, if 'N' is not the name of a given item, it makes no difference if people call it 'N' – or, perhaps, try to call it so: the embarrassment at this point will grow into an objection. Equally, if it is the name of that item, it makes no difference if people do not so call it. The name-relation is purely binary, relating a word and an item. Names can, of course, be of different kinds, and while the first examples are proper names of people, this is not the basic case, and the theory applies to general terms; indeed, it applies to proper names because it applies to general terms. Exactly what kind of item is named by a general term is a question on which the dialogue gives us no help, and it need not concern the present discussion.

What could such a binary relation be? The first level of discussion which contributes to answering the question gives us the principle that if 'N' is the name of a given item, and 'N' can be resolved etymologically into other names, then the combination of those names must be appropriate to the item. But this, clearly, only raises another question; we eventually have to invoke a theory of elements, and these achieve their relation to what is named through imitation (*mimēsis*) (422 seq.), the basic idea, sketchily enough conveyed, being that the action of producing a certain vocal sound resembles some process in the domain of what is to be named. This theory, elaborated in detail through the labours of the etymological section, and presented with an immense degree of irony by Socrates to Cratylus, is agreed by him to represent his view (428C).

We originally saw that Cratylus holds
  (1) If 'N' is the name at all of an item, it is the correct name of that item.
We have now learned
  (2) If 'N' is the name of an item, 'N' bears a certain complex relation to that item.
Let us call that relation *the Ø-relation*. The relation is to be explained in terms of the procedures for resolving names into other names, and, ultimately

(3) the Ø-relation is grounded in the idea of an element of a name being a *mimēma* (430A9) of a process or natural feature.

There is a difficulty lurking in this which Plato seems to mark without pursuing. (3) requires that there should be elements of names which are related to reality through *mimēsis*, but it does not require that they should themselves be names: indeed they are not, and an elementary name – the simplest thing which is itself a name – is, relative to these elements, itself a complex.[1] While the theory permits this, there seems no reason why it should actually require it. Socrates is obviously right in saying at 422B that the correctness of those names that are elementary will have to be tested 'by some other method' – i.e. not by etymological resolution; but it does not follow that they must be resolved into something other than names. They might be names whose correctness is to be tested by a method which does not involve resolving them at all.

It is unclear why the theory should not yield this outcome. There is indeed the point that the ultimate simples are sounds, which, except for the vowels, cannot be uttered by themselves: the nearest we can come to isolating them in speech is to add a further and arbitrary elements to make them pronounceable. This point is of course made at 393E, merely in order to illustrate, early in the argument with Hermogenes, the general idea that the addition or subtraction of some elements need not destroy the effect of a name. But the status of the elements surely raises a question about the theory of the Ø-relation. Why is it that the ultimate elements, when made with a little assistance into isolable names, turn out to be the names of those sounds (or letters), and not names of the natural features to which they are linked by *mimēsis*? The problem for Cratylus should not just be that the word for hardness can be either *sklērotēs* or *sklērotēr* (434C), but that it is not *rh(ō)* itself.

When Cratylus enters the dialogue at 428, he asserts claim (1) of his position in the strongest possible terms, resisting at the same time Socrates' suggestion that 'legislators' (*nomothetai*), regarded as originally imposing names, might be expected to have done their work better or worse. 'So are all names correctly applied (*orthōs keitai*)?', Socrates asks, and Cratylus answers, 'Inasmuch

---

1 The point is discussed by Norman Kretzmann: 'Plato on the Correctness of Names', *American Philosophical Quarterly*, 8 (1971), 126–38.

as they are names' (429B10–11). In reply, Socrates makes explicit the distinction denied by (1), in the form of distinguishing between the view that the name 'Hermogenes' does not apply (*keisthai*) to the third person present, and the view that it does apply, but 'not rightly'; and Cratylus says that it does not apply to him at all, but is rather the name of someone who has the appropriate nature, i.e. to whom that name bears the Ø-relation.

Socrates' essential step in refuting these claims is to show that they leave Cratylus with nothing coherent to say when one introduces the dimension of what speakers actually do with names, a dimension necessarily left out by any view which finds the whole account of naming in the Ø-relation, since that relation is simply a relation between words and things. Socrates' first example (429E) ingeniously introduces the act of addressing someone (*proseipein*) with the wrong name. The example is of one who, in foreign parts, greets Cratylus and says 'Welcome, Athenian visitor, Hermogenes, son of Smikrion!'[2] The question is, does he not even *address* Cratylus, but rather Hermogenes? Or no-one? When Cratylus replies that such a person would seem to him *phthenxasthai allōs*, 'to speak' – one could take it to mean – 'to no purpose', his answer leaves Socrates still with the room to ask (rather oddly) whether what he spoke was true or false; but this elicits the explanation that he would be making a noise, like someone banging a pot, and this retrospectively offers the possibility of a different reading for *allōs*: he would *merely* be producing speech.[3]

This conclusion can be related quite simply to Cratylus' position. It is important that Cratylus does not have to say (what would be simply false) that the speaker addresses Hermogenes rather than Cratylus. He can reasonably say that there is a speech-act, which may be called 'addressing someone by name',

2 Hermogenes' father's name was Hipponikos: 384A8, 406B8. It has been conjectured that Cratylus really was son of Smikrion: cf. Diels–Kranz, *Die Fragmente der Vorsokratiker* (6th edition), II 65.1 and note.

3 This sense of ἄλλως, for instance in Sophocles *Ph.* 947, 'a mere image', is admittedly well attested only where ἄλλως occurs with a substantive (see Jebb, *ad loc.*). But the reading suggested, besides tying up with Cratylus' later remark, has the advantage that it gives him a reply which relates to, and undercuts, *all* the alternatives that Socrates presents in his question. φθέγξασθαι is of course a standard term not only for human sounds, but for animal cries (cf. Arist. *HA* 535a30) and for noises from inanimate things – for instance, a pot when struck, *Tht.* 179D. (I am grateful to the editors for comments on this matter.)

such that there are two separate necessary conditions of its being true that $X$ addresses $Y$ by name:

(i) $X$ addresses (speaks to, directs words to, etc.) $Y$;

(ii) In the course of (i), $X$ uses a name which is a name of $Y$.

It will follow that in the situation which Socrates puts to Cratylus, the speaker does not address anyone by name: not Cratylus, because of condition (ii), and not Hermogenes, because of condition (i). If the purpose of his speaking was to address someone by name, then indeed he spoke *allōs* – even if Cratylus' final gloss on that failure is a little exaggerated.

However, that does not get Cratylus very far, and once the speech-act aspect of the question is raised at all, Socrates is in a position to show that even to understand Cratylus' theory requires one to understand possibilities which Cratylus denies. He shows this, first, with regard to mistakes, and, ultimately, with regard to convention.

Cratylus denied that, in the imagined situation, the speaker addressed anyone by name, since he did not satisfy both the conditions of doing that with respect to any one person. But he cannot deny that the speaker satisfied condition (i) with respect to the man in front of him: he certainly, for instance, spoke to him. Moreover, he used a particular name in relation to him; and Cratylus must know all that, or he could not diagnose the situation as he does. So Cratylus must accept that the speaker performed *some* speech-act in relation to the man in front of him, and indeed he must know what it is for $X$ *to call $Y$ 'N'*. But if so, then he must know what it is for $X$ to call $Y$ 'N' although 'N' is not $Y$'s name, and he is in a position to recognise mistake. Moreover, he must know what it is for almost everyone usually to call $Y$ 'N', and he is in a position to recognise convention.

The argument about mistake is developed in terms of the allocation (*dianomē*) of names. One can identify $Y$ and a particular name independently of one another, and one can bring that name to $Y$'s attention (431A1–2, cf. 430E6–7, very forceful expressions of perceptual confrontation), just as one can bring to his attention a certain picture; and one can claim that what is displayed is his name or picture. Whatever relation constitutes a particular name's being his name – if, for instance, as Cratylus believes, it is much the same relation as constitutes a picture's being his picture – that claim may be false. Even when it is, there has certainly been an allocation; hence there are mistaken allocations of names.

It is important to see what a *dianomē* is. It is an activity which can be performed on either names or pictures in relation to their objects, and, according to Socrates' introduction of it (430D), it has the properties that, in the case of a picture, if the picture is allocated to a person of which it is the picture, then the *dianomē* is correct (*orthē*), while in the case of a name, if it is allocated to the person of which it is the name, then the *dianomē* is both correct and true. This suggests that the *dianomē* does not simply involve the claim 'this is your picture (name)', for in any sense in which that is true or false, as well as right or wrong, with names, it is equally so with pictures. We should rather expect that *dianomē* is an activity which, when done with a name, yields a *logos*, something that can be true, and when done with a picture, does not. We can imagine a wordless *dianomē* of a picture – handing it to the subject, for instance; and we can imagine a partly worded one, in the form of someone's saying, for instance, 'You are . . .' and presenting a picture. The analogy to this in the case of names would be saying 'You are . . .' and presenting a name. But 'presenting a name' is itself a linguistic activity (cf. 387C6 'naming is part of speaking'); and saying 'You are . . .', followed by presenting '*N*', comes to saying 'You are *N*', which, unlike its picture analogue, can be true as well as correct.[4] Of course, there is also a kind of statement that is available in both cases; that statement which Socrates gives, and which in the name case takes the form 'this is your name'.

Nothing here, any more than elsewhere, restricts the discussion to proper names. Indeed, in the picture case it seems that the pictures can be taken as ascribing the general properties of male and female (431A3–4). The model therefore has some potential to destroy those general arguments against the possibility of false-hood, naturally associated with Cratylus' position, which put in an appearance at 429D; and that is recognised, in a rather sketchy way, at 431B. Those arguments rest, in one way or another, on the idea that an expression '*E*' cannot misfit reality, since it must be allocated either to nothing, or to whatever it is that it fits. But this critic must have some conception of what counts as 'fitting', as I have called it, and of what it is that a given '*E*' would fit. But

---

4 Cf. the formulation at 429C6 of the question to which the discussion of *dianomē* helps to give an answer: 'Is someone not mistaken who says *that he is Hermogenes?*'

then he has an understanding of some (at least) statements of the form ' "*E*" fits *that*', an understanding which allows also for the possibility of such a statement's being false; and that possibility is the same as that of '*E*' misfitting reality.

This has the same structure as the *dianomē* argument in the *Cratylus*. Of course, the potential for destroying the argument against falsehood cannot be fully realised until a *general* way is found of locating independently the item which '*E*' fits or misfits, and this is not achieved until the *Sophist*, if then. The point that the *Cratylus* does not achieve this has been made by John McDowell,[5] who points out that 'the function of indicating what is being talked about is not credited to a constituent in the account' but has to be discharged by an act of confrontation. (A similar limitation, it may be said, can be found in the account given by the *Theaetetus*, insofar as that is even partly successful, of false identity statements). The *Cratylus*, however, disclaims any attempt to give a general answer (429D7–8), and what it does say perhaps has a greater potential for being generalised than the criticism allows. McDowell also objects that the *Cratylus'* contribution is not merely limited but misguided, on the ground that it tries to assimilate falsehood to partial accuracy, as though an expression could be discovered to misfit reality only if its general shape were right but other features wrong. But this is to connect the discussion of *dianomē* too closely to what follows. That discussion lasts to 431C3, and indeed relates, though not in very general terms, to the puzzles of falsehood; from 431C4, Socrates takes off on a further discussion (*au*, C4), designed to deal with the Ø-relation itself.

This discussion reverts to issues of name-*giving*, and the activities of a *nomothetēs*. Plato might be thought to invite confusion by moving so easily between name-giving and the use of established words, since the possibilities of mistake are evidently so different in the two. But – as Plato clearly sees – they are different only if certain assumptions are made, assumptions which are denied by Cratylus. According to Cratylus, there is no act which a *nomothetēs* or anyone else can perform to *make* '*N*' the name of *Y* – '*N*' either bears the required Ø-relation to *Y* or it does not. Hence what is called 'name-giving' will be merely a trivial variant on describing. The distinction between name-giving and using an established name will collapse also at the other end of the spectrum, with that radical Humpty-Dumpty view which Hermogenes offers early on (384D1–2, 385A) as one version of what he opposes to Cratylus. As Cratylus assimilates name-giving to describing, so this assimilates describing to name-giving. The view, opposed to both of these, that what is $Y$'s name depends on 'agreement and custom',[6] precisely leaves room for the distinction, since there is an important difference between following a practice and trying to initiate one.

In his attack on the Ø-relation itself, Socrates first shows that there is a conflict between Cratylus' faith in *mimēsis* (his thesis (3)) and the all-or-nothing view that he takes of the name-relation, since *mimēsis* depends on resemblance, and resemblance is a matter of degree. The very notion of one thing's being an *eikōn*, a representation, of another, involves this point; for the only *absolute* notion of resemblance that could be used is that of indistinguishability, but an item indistinguishable from Cratylus would not be a representation of Cratylus, but 'another Cratylus'. The very idea of a representation of $X$, such as Cratylus takes a name to be, already implies at least a selection among the properties of $X$. The following argument, including the examples at 434–5, works from this point to show that we can recognise that '$N$' is the name of $Y$ independently of the exactness of its representation, and this, like the argument about *dianomē*, undermines thesis (1). But it goes further, for the same considerations show that one can recognise '$N$' as the name of $Y$ independently of resemblance altogether. (3) is wrong, and, as Hermogenes said (414C2), getting resemblance to do this job is a sticky business,[7] and we have to fall back on agreement. It is merely custom and agreement that makes a given name the name of a given item, and this excludes not merely this particular candidate for the Ø-relation but any kind of Ø-relation as constituting the name-relation itself.

The conclusion may be put in terms of the conditions for something's being a name; and that could leave it open whether there was some further question about the correctness of the names

6 συνθήκη καὶ ἔθος, the standard phrase in the dialogue: cf. ἔθει τῶν ἐθισάντων, 384D8. As Robinson pointed out, it is only in that passage and in conjunction with that phrase that νόμῳ in this dialogue expresses the contrast to φύσις: see 'The Theory of Names in Plato's *Cratylus*', in *Essays in Greek Philosophy* (Oxford 1969), 112.
7 435C4–5: see the end-note for this translation.

which, as things are, we use. Alternatively, the conclusion may itself be expressed in terms of correctness, as it is at 435C. In those terms, the conclusion will be that agreement and custom govern everyday correctness – they will be the determinants of whether someone has correctly used a name which we have in our language. In that case, the further question that might possibly arise would be about the correctness of our language. We may then distinguish two ways in which questions about correctness may be raised. There are certainly questions of internal correctness, to be settled by reference to our linguistic practices. There may or may not be a question of external correctness, a question about the correctness of our linguistic practices.

Socrates agrees with Hermogenes that custom and agreement are the sole determinants of internal correctness. Hermogenes, however, thinks that there is no further question of external correctness, while Socrates thinks that there is: there are requirements on what a language has to be, which follow from what it has to do. This is the point of the tool analogies at 387 seq. But this, as Kretzmann[8] has made very clear, has nothing to do with any idea of the material properties of words resembling the world, as was claimed in the theory of the $\emptyset$-relation. The resources of the language can be better or worse adapted to the requirements of dialectic, and that will make it better or worse in an external sense, but it will be so only in virtue of its structural properties and the semantic relations of its terms to each other, and not in virtue of their shape or sound or any such feature.

Socrates, then, differs from both Hermogenes and Cratylus in thinking that there are two questions, of internal and external correctness; or, in the alternative formulation, that there is one question about what the name for a given item is, and another about whether the practices that undoubtedly assign it that name are correct. Hermogenes thinks that there is only one question, settled by the appeal to our practices. Cratylus thinks that there is one question, to be settled by the basically external device of the $\emptyset$-relation; but Socrates' own answer to the external question will be on totally different lines from that.

Socrates' conclusions are not formally inconsistent with claim-

---

8 Op. cit., especially 135. [Schofield, however (above pp. 61–2 n. 2), disputes Kretzmann's grounds for seeing in the dialogue a non-Cratylan answer to the question of external correctness. Edd.]

ing that names do as a matter of fact possess some mimetic features; nor do they strictly exclude the aim of remodelling the language so that names acquire such features. Many have thought that Plato does show some real attachment to the mimetic principle. But, so far as the actual language is concerned, the treatment of the etymological enterprise as a whole, and particularly the mimetic aspect, is loaded with irony and warnings (cf. 426B1, the reference to the expert; 428D, Socrates' doubts; and many other passages); while it is a notable fact that Socrates is prepared to rerun the entire diagnosis of the language on lines opposite to the Heraclitean principles which he and Hermogenes have used. He indeed says at 435C2–3 'it pleases me that names should be as far as possible like things', a formulation neutral between explanation of the actual language and aspiration for a better one; but it is permissible to take this as referring to what Socrates indeed claimed long before, that the structure of language should represent the structure of things.

Certainly that is all we should expect Plato to find important. Here one must bear in mind not just the conclusions already discussed, but the powerfully demystifying arguments towards the end of the dialogue about what might be learned from language. Cratylan *mimēsis* is not what makes our names function as names, and, if they display such features at all, the question arises of how they came to do so. They will, at best, be a flickering record of observations made by the *nomothetēs* (as one might say, by human experience). As a recipe for linguistic improvement, again, the mimetic principle has nothing to offer. The functions of language, and the purposes for which it might be improved, are to teach, learn, inform, divide up reality. The knowledge required for that can appear in language only if someone possesses it already; and while there might be point in making that knowledge appear structurally, and thus improving language dialectically, there can be no such point to altering it in the direction of Cratylan *mimēsis*.

Even if it is not formally inconsistent with them, an attachment to Cratylan *mimēsis* is in fact banished by the conclusions of the *Cratylus*. This brilliant, tough-minded and still underestimated dialogue does not only show that the idea of language's having mimetic powers could not explain what language is; it leaves the belief in such powers looking like what it is, a belief in magic.

*End-note*

The phrase at 435C4–5, γλίσχρα ἡ ὁλκὴ αὕτη τῆς ὁμοιότητος, has received various translations. LSJ incautiously offers 'clinging' for γλίσχρα and 'attractive force' for ὁλκή. Jowett[4] treats both this, and Hermogenes' use of γλίσχρως at 414C2, which is explicitly mentioned here, in terms of 'hunger', and *Rep.* 488A2, ὡς γλίσχρως εἰκάζω is usually taken on the same lines: 'how greedy I am of similes'. Others have taken γλίσχρα to mean 'shabby', but this sense (e.g. D.23.208) clearly comes from the notion of tight-fistedness or being sticky with one's money, which does not fit; in any case, it hardly goes well with the comment that the appeal to agreement is something φορτικόν. Neither line pays enough attention to 414C, where the adverb has to be attached to verbs which express the addition or subtraction of letters by the etymological interpreter, while Socrates' reply cites, in the usual ironical tone, conditions that supposedly make these elaborate manoeuvres necessary. This would fit an interpretation of 435 which gives the γλίσχρα ὁλκή as, straightforwardly, 'a sticky haul', like getting a ship to move over a gummy slip-way: one has to work hard to try to keep the resemblance theory moving.*

---

* Anyone who knows Gwil Owen and is interested in ancient philosophy will have learned from him. I myself, though only a part-time student of these subjects, have had the good fortune of being able to learn from him for more than thirty years.

However, I hope, as other contributors must hope, that this book will be read by many people who will never have known Gwil at all. That reflection often tempts contemporaries to reminisce, in the hope of preserving the essence of their friend and teacher for the future. With regard to Gwil as teacher, that temptation need not be indulged. His writings, in their compression, intense power of argument, and brilliantly resourceful learning, convey better than any selection of anecdote what his influence has been.

# 5  Knowledge and language: the *Theaetetus* and the *Cratylus*

JULIA ANNAS

In this chapter I suggest that some passages in the *Cratylus* may give us insight into certain of the difficulties in the notorious 'dream' passage in the *Theaetetus*. This is a modest point, but it has, I hope, less modest implications for our understanding of what Plato is after when he looks for a definition of knowledge. Whatever the merits of this paper, it has a certain appropriateness as my contribution to a volume honouring Gwil Owen; my introduction to working with him, when I was a graduate student at Harvard, was a class on the *Theaetetus* and a paper I wrote on the *Cratylus*. Nothing here survives, I am glad to say, of the content of my early efforts; what I do hope survive are some effects of those lessons in rigour, in patience with the text and in Platonic readiness to lay aside one's own concerns in the attempt to see Plato's as they are. This paper is offered to Gwil as a token, however inadequate, of truly Socratic teaching and friendship.[1]

What is the dream theory *doing* in the *Theaetetus*? At 201C8, Theaetetus, having been convinced that knowledge cannot just be true belief, suggests that it may be true belief plus *logos* or account. This is not an unexpected suggestion to those familiar with Plato's earlier attempts to show that knowledge is the kind of improvement over true belief that results from being able to offer certain kinds of reason and grounds for what is believed.[2] And it is this suggestion, that knowledge is true belief with *logos*, which

---

1 This is a reworking of a paper given in 1977 to an Oxford B. Phil. class on the *Cratylus* and *Theaetetus*. I would like to thank Lesley Brown, with whom I gave the class, for helpful comments both at the time and while I was working on the revised version. The latter has also been greatly improved by generous help from Gail Fine and Malcolm Schofield.
2 At *Meno* 97E6–97A8 knowledge differs from true belief in the 'bond' of αἰτίας λογισμός. *Phaedo* 73A7–10 and 76B5–7 state firmly that knowledge must involve *logos*. Cf. *Symposium* 202A5–9.

Socrates takes to be the 'question before us',[3] the main claim that must be refuted by examining possible interpretations of *logos* (206A1–210A9). Yet Theaetetus does not offer his new definition straightforwardly; his suggestion is introduced as someone else's idea that he has hitherto forgotten (201C8–9) and Socrates, picking up this point, develops it into an elaborate account of a theory that he has 'dreamed of' (201D8–202C6) before subjecting it to equally elaborate refutation at 202D8–206C2. The suggestion that knowledge is true belief with *logos* survives, and is then scrutinised; but why was it complicated in the first place with the dream theory, from which it had at once to be disentangled?

A very general answer to this is provided by the dream theory's most outstanding and ingenious (202D10) feature: the asymmetry it claims in the knowability of composites and of the non-composite elements that make them up. 'The elements have no account [*logos*] and are unknowable, but they're perceivable, and the complexes are knowable and expressible in an account and judgeable in a true judgement' (202B5–7, McDowell translation). Socrates does not attack the claim that knowledge requires *logos*; so far he endorses it (cf. 202C7–D7). Nor does he directly attack the dream theorist's conception of what *logos* is. We might well expect some comment on the bizarre claim that *logos* is the weaving-together of names of perceivable elements (202B2–7); but we find none. What Socrates does seize on is the claim of asymmetry, the claim that composites are knowable but elements not; this is what lengthy argument shows to be an intentional or unintentional joke (206B9–11). So what is bothering Plato is the idea that the *logos* that converts true belief into knowledge might be a process of reasoning whose final points of appeal were entities that were unknowable. Belief, he claims, cannot be made into knowledge by anything that itself rests on inevitable ignorance.[4] The ingenious theory turns out to be a joke because in making composites knowable and elements unknowable it has violated a condition on knowledge: a claim to know cannot be made out by appeal to what one cannot know. Plato thinks it necessary first to clear away the suggestion that *logos* might produce knowledge by

---

3 τὸ προκείμενον, 206C2. The translation is from J. McDowell, *Plato, Theaetetus*, translated with notes, Oxford, Clarendon Plato Series, 1973.

4 Inevitable because the elements *cannot* be known; they are not just hard to know. They are perceivable and so, in a way, obvious to us; but they are, lacking *logos*, not possible objects of knowledge.

appeal to unknowables, before looking more closely at the actual role it might have in turning true belief into knowledge. Hence the dream theory and its refutation, placed before the examination of different senses of *logos*.

So much seems clearly right. But Plato could have made this point in a more general way. Would it not have been clearer, if this were his worry, to have had Socrates simply elicit Theaetetus' agreement to the principle that the *logos* that converts true belief into knowledge cannot itself make appeal to what is unknowable? Why is this point made in the context of the dream theory? The theory has three puzzling features apparently unrelated to that principle: the claim that elements are perceivable, the claim that they can only be named, and the narrow conception of *logos* as a kind of analysis or decomposition of compounds into simple elements. Those who have thought that Plato is here taking time off to attack someone else's theory (Antisthenes being the favourite for owner[5]) have at least tried to do justice to the way that Plato's concern with the dream theory is much more specific and detailed than the overall argument requires.

It has been suggested that Plato wants us to think back to earlier passages in the dialogue where he was also concerned with the simplest elements of perceptual experience.[6] But even if we are reminded of the earlier theories about perception, this alone hardly helps with the present problem; the nature of *logos* has not been treated in the earlier passages, and, even if there were agreement over which, if any, parts of the discussion of perception at 156A ff. Plato wanted to retain, it would still not shed much light on the later passage. In fact nothing so far in the dialogue prepares us for the dream theory. We have to go outside the dialogue to find, if not an individual target, at least general grounds for seeing why Plato might find it attractive, or compelling, to put the suggestion that knowledge-producing *logos* appeals to unknowables in the very specific form that he does.[7] And even if

5 For a demonstration of the irrelevance of Antisthenes, see M. F. Burnyeat, 'The Material and Sources of Plato's Dream', *Phronesis*, 15 (1970), 101–22; cf. W. Hicken, 'The Character and Provenance of Socrates' "Dream" in the *Theaetetus*', *Phronesis*, 3 (1958), 126–45.

6 Cf. H. Meyerhoff, 'Socrates' "Dream" in the *Theaetetus*', *Classical Quarterly*, n.s. 8 (1958), 131–8.

7 To that extent, then, there is a literary failure on Plato's part; the dialogue is not self-contained, since outside knowledge is needed to complete our understanding. (Cf. 197A8 and the whole 'secret doctrine' passage, likewise unintelligible to the reader without footnotes.) In this respect the *Theaetetus* is like other puzzling dialogues of the Academy period, such as the *Parmenides* and *Philebus*. The implications of this for Plato's use of the dialogue form while teaching in the Academy would repay study.

the dream theory were originally thought up by someone else, we have to look to Plato's own interests to see what it is doing here.

The theory of Forms has naturally suggested itself.[8] Forms in the middle dialogues are presented as the end results of thorough and testing processes of reasoning (cf. *Rep.* 531E4–532B4, 533B1–3, 534B3–D1). But some of the ways in which they are characterised at least suggest that they are not themselves to be dissected by any kind of reasoning;[9] rather they allow some other kind of cognition, which is compared to kinds of perceiving.[10] How natural then for Plato to wonder whether, in making the Forms the termini of a kind of reasoning to which they are not themselves subject, he had, ironically, made them unknowable.

But Forms are not directly in Plato's view here. The terminology of the dream theory would not suggest Forms to anyone not determined to find them.[11] None of the senses of *logos* that the *Theaetetus* discusses has much discernibly in common with the middle-dialogues discussions of *logos* which relate that to Forms. And the dream theory discusses *perceptible* elements, and so can be at best a model for Platonic worries about Forms. A concern with Forms explains none of the bafflingly specific features of the dream theory, and to find it here amounts to a version of Cornford's conspiracy theory: we can know that the Forms are crucial to the *Theaetetus* just *because* they are never mentioned.

The elements in the dream theory are not only perceptible. We are also told that they can only be named (202B1–2), whereas the compounds are 'sayable' (*rhētas*, 202B7). The most influential modern intepretation, which I shall label 'the semantic interpreta-

---

8 Cf. W. Hicken, 'Knowledge and Forms in Plato's *Theaetetus*', *Journal of Hellenic Studies*, 77 (1957), 48–53, reprinted in R. Allen (ed.), *Studies in Plato's Metaphysics* (London 1963), 185–98.

9 E.g. the claims in the *Phaedo* that Forms are incomposite and utterly uniform and unchanging (*Phaedo* 80B1–3).

10 The use of the language of sight and touch for Forms in the middle dialogues is too widespread and familiar to need documentation. I would not now accept the view that such language is meant to exclude the possibility of reasoning articulately about Forms. But it does mean at least that the analytical reasoning or *logos* that leads one to Forms needs then to be supplemented by something different; and this will still lead to a problem if one's model of knowledge is of something characterised by precisely this kind of analytical reasoning.

11 McDowell, p. 246, lists points of contact between the dream theory's terminology and mentions elsewhere of Forms. The affinities come, however, all in the criticisms of the theory, not in the ways it is characterised, which is an obstacle to the idea that Forms can help us to elucidate the theory. Of course the theory's failure may have implications for Forms.

tion', argues that it is this apparently gratuitous feature of the dream theory that gives us the key to Plato's interest in bringing it in.[12] On this view, the *Theaetetus* is a stage in Plato's continuing battle against an oversimplified view of the way that language functions, a battle won in the *Sophist* when he distinguishes naming from stating and so escapes from the idea that all words have meaning in the same way, functioning as names do and subject to failure in a likewise uniform fashion. Until the breakthrough that consists in distinguishing referring, the function of single terms, from stating, something that can only be done by a linguistic item that has propositional complexity, Plato does not see how to avoid paradox in any account of falsity and contradiction.[13] The *Theaetetus* does not achieve that breakthrough, but it is on the way. The dream theory distinguishes names from the more complex entities which are a 'weaving-together' of names, and which first allow of stating or judging, as opposed to merely naming (202A8–B7). The dream theory's insistence that the elements can only be named does suggest that an important distinction is being drawn between what names do and the way that more complexly structured bits of language function.

Even for the most optimistic version of the semantic interpretation, there are difficulties in seeing why the elements are perceptible and why the examples we are given of complexes are people (201E2) and syllables (the 'hostages' for the theory, at 202E3–7, are letters and syllables, which are surely instances of what the theory is talking about). For, as McDowell laconically admits (p.240), 'the complexity of a person and the complexity of a syllable are perhaps equally unpromising as instances of the sort of complexity that is involved in what can be said'. But there are also two strong objections to the semantic interpretation, of a more

12 This interpretation, which is expressed most lucidly by McDowell, owes much to Ryle's influential but never-published paper on the dream theory. Cf. also Ryle, 'Letters and Syllables in Plato', *Philosophical Review*, 69 (1960), 431–51, and for criticisms of Ryle's more incautious claims, D. Gallop, 'Plato and the Alphabet', *Philosophical Review*, 72 (1963), 364–76.

13 This account of Plato's 'development', which I have so crudely sketched here, has come under fire, notably in the claim that Plato originally had such a crude notion of naming. Cf. G. Fine, 'Plato on Naming', *Philosophical Quarterly*, 27 (1977), 289–301. Here I am concerned not with its overall plausibility as an account of Plato's views of language, but with the narrower question, whether the dream theory's peculiar features are best explained by seeing it as part of such a development. I argue, in effect, that so seeing it destroys its relevance to its context.

general kind; they are perhaps familiar, but they bear repeating in the present context. One is that the dream theory is supposed to be distinguishing the functioning of a name from the functioning of a propositional complex; but Socrates *refutes* the theory. Why is Plato greeting his own philosophical breakthrough with such hostility?[14] If the distinction between naming and stating is to explain Plato's interest in the dream theory, then either he fails to see the theory's interest, since he refutes it, or he does not commit himself to the arguments he uses against it, in which case the theory stands and the *Theaetetus'* argument has a gap in it. Either way it looks as though Plato doesn't know what he is doing, which is a disturbing conclusion, especially since the *Theaetetus* is such a carefully constructed dialogue. Secondly, this interpretation cuts the dream theory out of its context. For the 'question before us' here (206C2) is whether true belief can be rendered knowledge by *logos*. If *logos* in the dream theory is characterised by the kind of complexity that distinguishes it from naming, then it is needed for true belief as much as for knowledge. In fact, on the semantic interpretation *logos* has really shifted in sense; from being the mark of knowledge (so that it is mere true belief that is *alogos* (201D1)) it has come to mean something like 'sentence' or 'statement' (so that it is the elements that can only be named that are *aloga* (202B6)). So, either the dream theory concerns *logos* as what is distinctive of knowledge, but characterises it much too weakly, or it is concerned with a different sense of *logos*; again, either way Plato seems to be unsure of his own intentions. The semantic interpretation, then, gives us an answer which is wrong in principle to the problem of why Plato develops· the dream theory.

All the same, what this interpretation overstresses is an important fact about the theory that does need its proper stress. Socrates does not just say that compounds are knowable and elements not.

14 McDowell is cautious here; he holds that while the dream theory does represent an important stage of development in distinguishing naming from stating as being different ways of 'putting a thing into words' which go wrong in different ways, nonetheless Plato is not completely clear about this. The issue is complicated by the fact that the dream theory's refutation rests on an unsatisfactory conception of the part/whole relation, one which Theaetetus resists (204A5–6, B2–3, E11–13) and one moreover which is implicitly rejected at *Parmenides* 157C4–E2. (See McDowell, pp. 243–4.) McDowell thinks that Plato shows 'hints of discomfort' with his refutation. But if the dream theory stands, Plato is, in an unparalleled way, allowing a philosophical truth to be rejected at a crucial stage on the basis of an invalid argument. And if the dream theory is rejected, however uncomfortably, then Plato cannot think that it contains insights relevant to the *Theaetetus'* problems.

The unknowable elements are said to be nameable, and only nameable; *logos* enters in only at the level of the compound. So *logos* in the dream theory is not only what may turn true belief into knowledge. It is also thought of as something statable that is made up of names, which name simple elements. This does not, of course, imply that every *logos* decomposes directly into names of simples; only that at some point a *logos* will turn out to be composed, no longer of other *logoi*, but of names; since the names name elements, this will be at the most basic level of analysis. The elements that are named, moreover, are what we, and everything else, are made up of (201E1–2). Such a characterisation of *logos* as the weaving-together of names of ultimate elements is by no means what we expect as part of a claim that *logos* is what makes for knowledge, or even as part of a claim that *logos* cannot appeal to unknowables.[15] This unexpected way in which the dream theory (literally) 'spells out' *logos* should not lead us to treat it as a detachable part of an independent controversy; but some explanation is needed of why Plato thought it relevant to his discussion of knowledge. I shall argue that some explanation is indeed provided by Plato's interest in language and the kind of account that we can give of its functioning; but not in the manner of the semantic interpretation.

So neither Forms nor an interest in propositional complexity will serve wholly to explain why Plato brings in the development of the dream theory. We are back with the initial point that the whole dream theory passage rules out there being a *logos* of compounds whose analysis ended with names of unknowable simples. Has Plato special reason for being worried by this possibility, special motivation for ruling it out before he even discusses the nature of *logos*?

In the *Theaetetus* Plato is reflecting on the concept of knowledge which he has employed very widely in the early and middle dialogues; and one constant feature of knowledge as it there figured is that it involves being able to give an account of what it is that you know, explain to others your claims and their backing. That is why Socrates is, in the early dialogues, so impressed by

---

15  201E1–202B7 develop the notion that *logos* decomposes into names; 202–B7–C8 revert to *logos* as the differentia of knowledge. The sharp break might raise suspicions that Plato is running together two very disparate issues. But we have no reason to think that this is not deliberate; and anyway knowledge comes into the earlier part also (202B6,7).

craftsmen and so unimpressed by people like poets.[16] You do not have knowledge of the content of a poem, however much it is your creation, if you cannot explain and articulate it. Craftsmen, however, uncontroversially know what they are doing; they can explain and formulate the principles of their craft and so give a satisfactory account of it. The only trouble is that there are areas where we would like to have knowledge which are more complicated than that.

It is, then, a constant assumption in Plato that knowledge requires *logos*, account.[17] But this on its own scarcely motivates consideration of the dream theory. What other assumption or assumptions might he be making that together make it especially urgent to show, even before examining what *logos* might be, that *logos* cannot appeal to unknowables?

The most perceptive suggestion here seems to me to be the recent one by Gail Fine.[18] She claims that Plato believes that 'knowledge must be based on knowledge', a principle that she labels KBK. It is no good providing an explanation of what you claim to know, if you then in turn fail to understand the explanation or account that is offered. Now this assumption together with the assumption that knowledge requires *logos* instantly produce a regress. To know any *p*, I must produce a *logos* of it, *q*; but then I must know *q*, and so produce a *logos* of *it*; and so on. The dream theory accepts the *logos*-requirement for knowledge, but only selectively; it rejects it for simples. Plato sees this as an interesting option; but he rejects it because it violates the assumption that knowledge must be based on knowledge.

This is an attractive suggestion; for Plato surely does accept KBK, the principle that knowledge must be based on knowledge, and clearly this has some connexion with the rejection of the dream theory. But there is a problem for the claim that the principle is actually the basis of Plato's rejection of the dream theory. For that theory claims precisely that there is one kind of

16 Cf. *Apology* 22A8–E1, and the contrast between τέχνη and mere ἐμπειρία at *Gorgias* 462–465.
17 Cf. the references in n.2.
18 G. Fine, 'Knowledge and *Logos* in the *Theaetetus*', *Philosophical Review*, 88 (1979), 366–97. Although I disagree with Fine on the overall interpretation of the passage, I have learned much from this excellent article. Fine refers in her n. 1 to M. F. Burnyeat's unpublished paper, 'The Simple and the Complex in the *Theaetetus*', as the stimulus for her paper and the source of some of the terminology she uses. Some parts of that paper are published in the article cited in n.5.

knowledge (knowledge of compounds) which is *not* based upon knowledge, since the elements into which the compounds are analysed are not knowable. If the denial of this claim is assumed in the argument against the theory then Plato will be flagrantly begging the question.[19]

Perhaps we can find an assumption which might be used, together with the assumption that knowledge requires *logos*, to draw further conclusions about knowledge, if we examine the dream theory's peculiar claim about the *asymmetry* of knowability between compounds and elements. With due hesitation I suggest that what motivates Plato here is concern about an assumption which can be expressed very generally as the assumption that knowledge has a hierarchical structure. Since knowledge for Plato is associated with justification and explanation by reference to a body of information, rather than with a search for absolutely certain grounds for holding a particular individual belief, knowledge is for him always systematic. Again, we can appeal to his respect for the crafts: a craftsman can control and use a body of information and skills in a systematic way. But in the middle dialogues we find a further new idea emerging: knowledge is not just a structure, but a structure which is ordered into the basic and the less basic. This idea appears in the use made of *hypotheses* in the *Meno* and *Phaedo* and emerges fully in the central books of the *Republic*, where the seeker after knowledge is driven upwards to ever higher hypotheses, until the final insight into the nature of the unhypothetical first principle allows descent again; what was formerly held without understanding is now understood and so has become truly knowledge. (Cf. *Rep.* 510B2–511E5, 532A1–B4, 533C7–534D1.) Knowledge, then, does have foundations. They are not, though, Cartesian foundations; they support the rest not by providing certain freedom from doubt but rather by being themselves clearly intelligible without reference to the rest, in a way that provides the knower with insight into the rest.

19 Fine claims (p. 368) that 'it is by insisting on KBK that Plato ultimately rejects the dream theory'. On p. 381 she claims that he is relying on KBK in pressing on the dream theorist the first half of his dilemma (203C1–D10): one cannot, as the dream theorist claims, know the syllable SO if knowing it involves analysing it into the unknowable elements S and O. Fine admits that this part of the argument is then weakened, since the dream theorist is precisely not put out by violating KBK; and I would rather follow McDowell (p. 242) in seeing Socrates' argument here as fallacious rather than question-begging. On anybody's view this passage contains some very dubious arguments.

It is hardly new to suggest that this development owes much to Plato's interest in geometry, and to his discovery in geometry of a body of knowledge that was not just systematic but organized into a hierarchy of basic truths and derived truths. Geometers clearly impressed Plato because they could do more than merely enunciate truths in isolation; they could also show the significance of those truths within the body of geometrical knowledge in terms of their dependencies: such and such a result is necessary to prove this, and is in turn proved from that. In the *Republic*, Plato's account of philosophical knowledge clearly owes much to the geometrical model. To say this is not to say that he thinks of philosophical knowledge as a kind of super-geometry proving philosophical theorems, only that he thinks that in any account of knowledge there is an important analogue to the distinction between the basic and the derived: there are ultimate or basic truths (which in the *Republic* concern the nature of goodness) and other truths are comprehended in their due significance only when seen in their dependency from these.[20] As Aristotle reports Plato's own words, it makes a good deal of difference whether one is going to or coming from the first principles (*EN* 1095a32–b1).

This assumption, that knowledge has foundations or a culmination[21] or, whatever the metaphor, an asymmetrical structure, is one which we find heavily entrenched in the middle dialogues. But one can see how Plato might come to see difficulties that are not raised in the *Phaedo* and *Republic*, as to how to combine it with his constant assumption that knowledge requires *logos*. For giving an account of the less basic truths involves reference to the basic truths (something emphatically brought out in the way in which in the *Republic* all knowledge depends on understanding the nature of goodness). To give a *logos* is to give an account that is explanatory, and the truths that provide explanation are taken to be more basic than those for which explanation is provided. But then what will be involved in giving an account of the basic truths? If we have to explain them in their

20 Plato's debt to the geometrical model is brought out in G. Morrow, 'Plato and the Mathematicians', *Philosophical Review*, 79 (1970), 309–33.

21 In the *Republic* the metaphors are predominantly of the soul's *ascent* to complete understanding. Cf., in a comparatively short stretch: 515E6–516A5, 517B4–6, C8–9, 521C2, 525D5–6, 529A9–C3, 532B6–D1. For Plato it is from the heights of knowledge, not the foundations, that we get insight. It is, however, instructively difficult to transfer this into modern philosophical terminology, and I have continued to talk of 'foundations', 'base', etc.

turn in terms of the less basic truths, then why do we consider them to be *basic*? (If goodness must be understood by reference to justice, piety, etc., then why consider the grasp of goodness that is necessary to explain them as being in any way more ultimate than the grasp of them?) However, if we say that the asymmetry lies just in this, that the basic truths need no account given of them, then, given the fact that knowledge requires *logos*, we have made them unknowable.

We can now see why Plato felt a special need to rule out the option that the dream theory represents. If knowledge requires *logos*, and knowledge has a hierarchical structure, then *logos* will lead us to ultimate items of knowledge – its elements or first principles. But we cannot give a *logos* of them, or they will not be basic in a way contrasting with the other items. So perhaps they have no *logos* and thus are unknowable. This is the option that the dream theory offers, and by refuting it Plato shows that he is committed to denying that the *logos* that improves true belief to the point of being knowledge can appeal to or rest on unknowables. The refutation of the dream theory shows us that we are committed to the principle that knowledge must be based on knowledge. Plato's examination of the dream theory now has a clear point: it brings out how two assumptions about knowledge (it requires *logos*, it has a hierarchical structure) force us to recognise a third important point about it: it cannot be based on unknowables.

The analysis of Plato's problems that I have just sketched already explains some of the odd features of the dream theory passage. It shows why Plato assumes there without argument that *logos* is a kind of analysis, a decomposition that ends with elements; for he is thinking of *logos* as something that produces an asymmetrical structure that ends with basic elements. We can also see why the theory's 'hostages' are letters and syllables – *stoicheia* as letters provide a good illustration of *stoicheia* as physical elements or elements of a Euclidean kind, the basic truths of a science or body of knowledge, especially one of a mathematical kind.[22]

What about the other specific features of the dream theory – the frogs at the bottom of every beer mug so far? Does my suggested reconstruction help to show why Plato was concerned to rule out a

22 On the meanings of στοιχεῖον see Morrow (op. cit.), 326–8. Morrow takes it that it is the mathematical meaning that is to the fore. But it is worth noticing that letters of the alphabet could serve as a homely illustration of knowledge: cf. Xenophon, *Oeconomicus*, VIII, 14 (where knowing the order of the letters is distinguished from knowing the letters themselves).

*logos* whose analysis leads us to *names*? or a *logos* whose elements name items that are *perceivable*? Not directly; and perhaps there is no account of the dream theory that can explain everything about it (a nice irony). But at least my suggestion is supported by two passages in the *Cratylus*, where we can see Plato coping with a particular form of the problem about *logos* which he poses in general form in the *Theaetetus*. And the context in which the *Cratylus* problem arises sheds some light on the problematic features of the *Theaetetus* passage.

In the *Cratylus*, Socrates, having initially rejected the idea that there is no such thing as correctness of names (or words[23]) proceeds on the assumption that names do reveal the nature of the thing named.[24] The long middle section of the dialogue consists of more or less fanciful attempts to show this by giving etymologies that bring to light the supposed original reality-revealing forms of names. At 421C3 Hermogenes interposes: Socrates, he says, has been explaining the true forms of names by appeal to bits of names, component parts that are not words in their own right (421C4–5). What is the principle of correctness for these? Socrates mentions, but importantly lays aside, one let-out: they could say that these forms are foreign, i.e. not part of the language.[25] The serious answer recognizes that the kind of explanation of correctness of names that they have been employing involves analysing words into smaller bits, and these into still smaller bits; and that this process must come to an end when we reach the smallest units of speech (the *Cratylus*, drawing no important syntactic distinctions, calls these all names[26]) which are the elements of the other statements and words – ἐπ' ἐκείνοις γένηται τοῖς ὀνόμασιν, ἃ ὡσπερεὶ στοιχεῖα τῶν ἄλλων ἐστὶ καὶ λόγων καὶ ὀνομάτων (422A2–3). When we reach the elements, we can no longer explain their correctness by doing what we have done hitherto, namely analyse compounds into

23 In the *Cratylus* Plato does not explicitly draw the distinction between ὀνόματα and ῥήματα that is drawn in the *Sophist* at 261–2.
24 Cf. 393D1–4, E4–8, 396A4–5, 422D1–3, 423E7–9, 428E1–2. Cf. N. Kretzmann, 'Plato on the Correctness of Names', *American Philosophical Quarterly*, 8 (1971), 126–38.
25 421C9–D7; he is referring back to 409D1–410B1, 416A3–6. The significance of Socrates' rejection of this option will become clearer below.
26 This means only that he is using a very broad and unanalysed notion of 'name', not that he is assimilating the functions of all words to that of names. On this see Fine, 'Plato on Naming', n. 14.

other compounds and eventually elements, but must do it some other way (422B6–8).

At this point we expect Plato to say something on the following lines: the account we give of compounds displays their correctness (or lack of it) by analysing them into their elements; but the correctness of the elements lies in some different principle. But he firmly rejects any such idea. Rather, he insists that there is a *single* correctness of all names, elements or not (422C7–D6); and he concludes, from the fact that the correctness of the compound names lay in revealing the natures of the things named, that the correctness of the element names must be the same (422D8–E1). So he is led to the theory that the element names, the single sounds, are correct when they imitate what they are applied to – not, he insists, in the ordinary sense of 'imitate', but in an artificial sense whereby imitating *does* reveal the nature of what is imitated (422E1–424A6). Hence a knowledge of language involves the ability to separate out properly the real and not apparent elements of language, and to understand the ways that these are mixed and combined like paints (424D4–E5) to produce ever more complex linguistic compounds – names, verbs, complete sentences. (Such knowledge is hard to come by since actual languages are in many ways imperfect – 425A5–C7.)

Now Socrates fully admits that such a theory about the way single sounds correctly reveal reality by imitation seems ludicrous (425D1–2, cf. 426B5–6); nevertheless, he says, we are *committed* to it; it is *necessary* (425D3). For what is the alternative? It is to appeal to a *deus ex machina*, like saying that the original sounds have no account because they are foreign, or ancient, or god-given (425D3–426A3). These are just ways of saying that there is no explanation of the elements although there is an explanation of the compound. And they will not do. They are just 'clever evasions' by someone refusing to give an account (*logon didonai*, 426A2–3) of the correctness of the elements. For 'if anyone is, no matter why, ignorant of the correctness of the earliest names, he cannot know about that of the later, since they can be explained only by means of the earliest, about which he is ignorant. No, it is clear that anyone who claims to have scientific knowledge of names must be able first of all to explain the earliest names perfectly, or he can be sure that what he says about the later will be nonsense' (426A3–B2; Fowler's translation).

Here we see Plato clearly working with a hierarchically structured notion of knowledge, for the account of how language functions works by analysing linguistic compounds into linguistic simples, which are constantly called the 'elements' or 'first' names. (The translation 'earliest' may wrongly suggest temporal priority, but Plato is clearly not interested in temporal priority as such; the analysis, being etymological in form, treats language as having developed, but a mere appeal to antiquity is regarded as a failure to explain.) The *logos* of language, then, is decompositional, and our knowledge of language as a whole is based on our knowledge of the elements of language. Knowledge of the simple sounds is thus the foundation of our knowledge of the rest; if it goes wrong then the whole lot goes wrong, however well-structured, just as a geometrical proof goes wrong if there is an initial error, however consistent the rest (436C8–D4; cf. *Rep.* 533B6–C5).

Plato is also, clearly, pressing the *logos*-requirement for knowledge. We don't have knowledge of language if there is something in our account of it of which we can give no account. It is no good appealing to something essentially arbitrary, like divine production or foreign origin, for this is giving up on explanation, and *this* vitiates a claim to have knowledge. Plato finds himself committed to the claim that knowledge cannot be based on lack of knowledge; it cannot be produced by an account that appeals at the most basic level to what is arbitrary and unknowable.

The same point is made in reverse, as it were, near the end of the dialogue, where Plato reverses the course of the reasoning of 422–426. At 434A3–435B3 Socrates demonstrates by means of an example that simple sounds cannot reveal the natures of things by imitating. The Athenian word for hardness is *sklērotēs*; however, the Eretrean word *sklērotēr* functions equally well or badly to express hardness, and anyway both contain contain lambda, whose function is supposed to be expressing the opposite of hardness. On the basis of this single example (which is far from convincing[27]) Socrates concludes right off that language as a

---

27 Cratylus has a point when he suggests (434D9–12) that the lambda ought not to be there; in earlier passages Socrates had freely admitted that actual languages fall short of the ideal (425A5–B3), and it is not clear why a point about the way we do, in fact, get around using a particular expression is allowed to overturn the possibility of knowledge when possession of knowledge would avowedly revise some of our beliefs about language as it is. (Cf. 394A1–C8.)

whole does not function by imitating or revealing the nature of its object; this attractive theory (435A6–C6) is jettisoned and it is agreed that the way language functions depends partly on mere convention and custom. Plato is arguing so rapidly because he is assuming that a failure to give an account of the elements is thereby a failure to give an account of any of the compounds. And he moves equally rapidly to the conclusion that we lack real knowledge of language; from now until the end of the dialogue he explores the implications of the conclusion that language is, because it is not something we can give a rational explanation of, not something that we can know; knowledge can only be of what is suitably non-arbitrary.

The *Cratylus* passages, then, show us what happens when, in the search for knowledge of language, the conviction that knowledge requires *logos* is joined by the conviction that the *logos* in question will proceed by analysing compounds into basic elements. Pressing these two requirements brings home the fact that *logos* is needed all the way down; we haven't given an account of language and its functioning if our account of the elements of language is essentially arbitrary. Nothing is explained, and so known, if anything is left unexplained, and so unknowable.

This result is strikingly similar to the result of Socrates' refutation of the *Theaetetus'* dream theory: there cannot be a *logos* that gives knowledge of compounds by decomposing them into unknowable elements.

Can we go further – is the *Cratylus* theory actually an example of the pattern shown in the dream theory – an example in a way that would explain why the dream theory has the curious special features that it has? There are striking similarities; but none of them can be carried through to provide a wholly convincing explanation. The *Cratylus* certainly gives us a decompositional model of *logos*: what matters for giving an account, and thus for knowledge, is what is basic – knowledge of the letters is necessary for knowledge of the resulting compounds (syllables, words[28]). But this does not form a unique connexion between the *Cratylus*

28 *Cratylus* 424C5–425A5, *Theaetetus* 206A1–B11. (The same point is foreshadowed at *Republic* 402A7–B3.)

and the *Theaetetus*; a decompositional or analytical model of *logos* is readily suggested by the idea that knowledge comes with explaining the derived by reference to the basic, an idea which is widespread in different contexts in the middle dialogues. And between the *Cratylus* and *Theaetetus* the metaphor at least for the combination of compounds from simples changes from the painter's palette to weaving.[29] The *Cratylus* does show us a decomposition of *logos* into elements which are names, and only names; but these seem to be simple sounds as opposed to whole words, whereas in the dream theory the simplest names do seem to be whole words as opposed to statements (cf. 201E2–202A5.)[30] And while the *Cratylus* names do seem mostly to name perceivable elements of reality, this is not uniformly the case,[31] whereas the dream theory does not seem to envisage any alternative for the elements but perceivability.[32]

But even if the *Cratylus* theory is not an example of what the dream theory is talking about in its special features, the similarities are still striking. The *Cratylus* theory about the nature of language contains features similar to those found baffling in the dream theory: a decompositional *logos* ending with names of perceivable elements. And Plato's response is also instructively similar. In the *Cratylus*, in trying to gain knowledge of a particular phenomenon – language – by offering a *logos* of it that analysed it into simple elements, he faced and accepted the conclusion that unless

29 *Cratylus* 424D4–425A5, 431C4–8, 434A3–B7; *Theaetetus* 202B. Weaving appears as a metaphor for combination alongside mixing in the *Sophist*, and predominates in the *Statesman*.

30 Thus the *Theaetetus* opposes λόγος to ὄνομα in a way that the *Cratylus* does not. But this is not conclusive evidence of a major shift of ideas given the *Cratylus*' very broad notion of naming.

31 Most of the examples of actual 'etymological' analysis in the *Cratylus* concern perceivable items; but there are stretches where highly abstract nouns are considered (cf. 411A–421C). The idea that all words reveal reality by means of the way their component sounds imitate aspects of reality, although it would obviously suggest an ultimately 'empiricist' analysis, does not have to be taken that way. The issue is rendered confusing by the confusing status in the dialogue of Heraclitean ideas; most of the etymologies are said to support a Heraclitean world view and hence unsurprisingly make reference to perceptible features, and, although some anti-Heraclitean etymologies are offered (437A–C) and Heracliteanism is rejected at the end of the dialogue, no alternative account of language is presented.

32 It may be, though, that the dream theory by making elements perceivable merely allows that we have some access to them which is not mediated by a *logos*. (Cf. Fine, 'Logos' p. 376, and Burnyeat, p. 121.) On such a broad construal of perception (as, roughly, what we intuit rather than reason our way to) the dream theory might not exclude as a perceivable element anything that the *Cratylus* would include as an imitable feature of reality.

the claim to knowledge was to be withdrawn, the *logos*-requirement must apply to the elements as much as to the compounds. And, persuaded that he could not provide such a *logos* for the elements, he did withdraw the claim to knowledge.

The *Cratylus* shows Plato already making use of the principle that knowledge must be based on knowledge. But, if this is the case, why do we find him in the *Theaetetus* feeling the need to establish the truth of that principle by the refutation of the dream theory? (For I have claimed that this is what he does, rather than assuming it for the purposes of refuting the theory.) The answer is surely that it is one thing to find a principle obvious and another to make it the subject of one's reflections and to try to provide it with some 'argumentative support. The main concern of the *Cratylus* is not the nature of knowledge but the nature of language, and the only actual casualty of the argument is the particular *logos* of language put forward, namely that words function by revealing reality. Plato shows no awareness that the problem he has hit upon is a quite general problem about knowledge, given what he accepts as true of knowledge.[33] The *Theaetetus*, reflecting upon the concept of knowledge rather than uncritically using it, generalises the result that the *Cratylus* has unwittingly attained: it would be no good offering another *logos* in place of the unsuccessful one, for any *logos* (of the required decompositional kind, it is assumed) must analyse knowables into knowables. This is a condition on *logos* whatever else *logos* turns out to be.

The *Cratylus*, then, helps to show us why the *Theaetetus'* dream theory is not intrusive in the examination of whether true belief with *logos* amounts to knowledge. Because knowledge requires *logos*, and because Plato is thinking of *logos* as analysis or decomposition, since he is thinking of the resulting knowledge as being asymmetrically structured with basic and derived elements, he sees it as important to insist that *logos* make no appeal to

33  In the *Cratylus* the *logos* of the elements of speech is rejected, not because it imports a regress, but because it does not answer to experience; in this context at least Plato has failed to appreciate the full extent of the problem. But there is anyway something odd about the argument here. At 422E1–424A6 Socrates insisted that letters do not imitate in the ordinary sense of sounding like, but in the sense of showing what the thing is like. But at 434A3–435B3 Socrates finds fault with the results of considering what the words sound like. If Plato had stuck more closely to imitation as characterised at 423E7–9, he might have concluded that his account of how letters imitate was at fault not because it failed to answer to the role of sound in actual language, but because it made the letters do what the words were supposed to do by virtue of their composition from the letters.

unknowables even before any further questions about it are faced. And he does so in a context very like the context in which, in the *Cratylus*, the same point emerged about a particular *logos* that was put forward, a *logos* about the functioning of language.

But the *Theaetetus* ends without a satisfactory definition of *logos*, and, hence, without a satisfactory definition of knowledge. Plato has no defensible characterisation of what knowledge is. Is this wholly or partly due to his rejection of the dream theory? If knowledge requires *logos* and *logos* is analysis, then the end-points of analysis, as well as the starting-points, will require *logos*. But then we have a regress: the end-points of analysis are, after all, subject to analysis. We are forbidden to stop the regress by saying that the end-points have no analysis; that would make them unknowable. But we can hardly just live with the regress. It looks as though all Plato's requirements for knowledge, taken together, make knowledge impossible. To know anything I must offer a *logos* of it; but this either imports unknowables or starts a regress of *logoi*.

The end of the *Theaetetus* shows us only that Plato felt enough discomfort arising from holding together all his convictions about knowledge to prevent his offering any positive characterisation of it. There are several ways in which he might have dealt with the situation.[34] Again I think that the *Cratylus* is useful here, because it indicates rather clearly, though by default, the kind of answer that Plato should have made.

What Plato needs is a distinction between different ways in which things can be known; the compounds are known in one way, the elements in another. This is *not* a demand for analysis to give up and be replaced at the elements stage by a kind of intuition that takes its place. When Socrates is troubled by the claim that the

---

34  Fine ('*Logos*' n. 19) claims that Plato comes to commit himself to an 'interrelation model' of knowledge in which justifications circle back on themselves; 'if the circle of our beliefs is sufficiently large, and the interconnections suitably comprehensive, the links in the circle are transformed from true beliefs into pieces of knowledge' (p. 397). If so, then Plato has abandoned or transformed the hierarchical conception of knowledge found in the *Phaedo*, and in the *Republic* and *Cratylus*; for there he denies that consistency in a set of beliefs can amount to knowledge unless they are suitably grounded in a way that does not reduce to that consistency (*Cratylus* 436C8–D4, *Republic* 533B6–C5). The issue is too large to go into here, and much depends on how one is to interpret remarks about the structure of knowledge in the later dialogues (e.g. the 'methods' of collection and division, and *Philebus* 55C–59D).

elements of language are of foreign origin, he was dissatisfied by appeal to what is *arbitrary*: no intuition, whether replacing or supplementing reasoning, is going to fill the gap. What is needed is not an alternative to *logos* and explanation that comes in when they run out, but a more Aristotelian distinction between two kinds of rational cognition: the reasoning that gets us to the basic elements of a science and the insight we have into the basic elements in the light of the reasoning that got us there. (Cf. *APo.* I 3; *EN* VI 3, 6.) For such insight or *nous* is not an alternative way of knowing which replaces reasoning and explanation; it is just the insight that comes from having the understanding that covers and controls a whole field of study.[35] (Indeed, in the *Republic* Plato implicitly distinguishes the reasoning that leads us to see or grasp the basic principles of goodness, and that grasp of the ultimates itself;[36] unfortunately he does not see the relevance of this to the kind of problem that he faces in the *Theaetetus*.)

Certainly in the *Cratylus* Plato shows no signs of recognising that elements might be known in a way different from the compounds that they make up. And the reason for this is plain: he thinks that the *logos* offered of the elements cannot be different from the *logos* offered of the compound. There is, he says, a *single* correctness of all names, whether primary or most complex (422C7–8). He offers a reason for this (C8–9): they do not differ at all in being names. That is, all distinguishable parts of language, from complex sentences down to single sounds, while they differ in other respects, are the same in being names, i.e. parts of language that reveal the nature of what they name. But this reason does not offer us much in the way of independent support for

35 On this see J. Barnes, notes on *Posterior Analytics*, II, 19, pp. 248–60 of Barnes, *Aristotle, Posterior Analytics* (Oxford, Clarendon Aristotle Series, 1975); L. A. Kosman, 'Explanation, Understanding and Insight in the *Posterior Analytics*', in *Exegesis and Argument: Studies presented to Gregory Vlastos*, ed. E. N. Lee *et al.* (Assen 1973: *Phronesis*, Supplement 1); J. Lesher, 'The Meaning of *Nous* in the *Posterior Analytics*', *Phronesis*, 18 (1973), 44–68. The contrary view, that *nous* is a 'pseudo-performance to confer on first principles the status demanded by Aristotle's view of scientific knowledge' is defended by T. Irwin, 'Aristotle's Discovery of Metaphysics', *Review of Metaphysics*, 31 (1977), 211–29; cf. Irwin, 'First Principles in Aristotle's *Ethics*', *Midwest Studies in Philosophy*, vol. III, 252–72. I am more convinced by M. F. Burnyeat, 'Aristotle on Understanding Knowledge', in *Aristotle on Science: 'The Posterior Analytics'*, ed. E. Berti (Padua 1981).

36 This is not a two-stage model of knowledge; the insight does not add anything to what is already known, but is the state of understanding achieved by one who has successfully completed the dialectical reasoning that Plato thinks necessary for comprehension of goodness. See ch. 11 of my *Introduction to Plato's Republic* (Oxford 1981).

Socrates' claim – for why would we consider these syntactically heterogeneous items all to be *names* unless we thought that a single account could be offered of them all?

We have seen that Socrates regards himself as compelled (425D3) to offer the account of linguistic elements that he does, not because of its independent merits but because he thinks that the *logos* offered of compounds and elements must be a uniform one. Of all Plato's convictions about knowledge and *logos* that we have seen, this one seems the weakest. What Plato most needs is Aristotle's great insight that the kinds of explanation and justification that we offer for what we believe cannot be reduced to a single kind: they are ineliminably plural. The sort of explanation that satisfies a geometer is inappropriate in practical matters, and *vice versa*.[37] Plato never envisages this. At different points in his writings he comes to mean rather different things by '*logos*', but one possibility that never occurs to him is that his different ideas might not be mutually exclusive, that *logoi* might be of more than one kind. It is Plato's insistence on giving a single account of giving an account, a single *logos* of *logos*, that prevents him from drawing distinctions that would have been helpful in his deep and chronic troubles over the concept of knowledge.

37 *EN* 1094b23–1095a2. Cf. *Metaph.* 1006a4–11, 994b32–995a16; *PA* 639a1–15.

# 6 Falsehood and not-being in Plato's *Sophist*

JOHN MCDOWELL

1. For me, G. E. L. Owen's 'Plato on Not-Being'[1] radically improved the prospects for a confident overall view of its topic. Hitherto, passage after passage had generated reasonable disagreement over Plato's intentions, and the disputes were not subject to control by a satisfying picture of his large-scale strategy; so that the general impression, as one read the *Sophist*, was one of diffuseness and unclarity of purpose. By focusing discussion on the distinction between otherness and contrariety (257B1–C4), Owen showed how, at a stroke, a mass of confusing exegetical alternatives could be swept away, and the dialogue's treatment of not-being revealed as a sustained and tightly organised assault on a single error. In what follows, I take Owen's focusing of the issue for granted, and I accept many of his detailed conclusions. Where I diverge from Owen – in particular over the nature of the difficulty about falsehood that Plato tackles in the *Sophist* (§§5 and 6 below) – it is mainly to press further in the direction he indicated, in the interest of a conviction that the focus can and should be made even sharper.

2. By 256E5–6 the Eleatic Stranger (ES) can say 'In the case of each of the forms, then, what is is multiple and what is not is indefinite in number.' Yet it is only at 258B6–7 that Theaetetus is allowed to announce the availability, at last, of the application for 'what is not' that was needed in order to flush the sophist from his refuge. Why was it not available already at 256E5–6? What is the relation between the application for 'what is not' vindicated in the earlier passage and the application vindicated in the later passage?

1 In *Plato, I: Metaphysics and Epistemology*, ed. Gregory Vlastos (Garden City 1971), 223–67.

We can make the question more pressing. What was needed in order to capture the sophist was a non-paradoxical characterisation of the sort of unreality a semblance has, and of falsehood (236D9–237A9, 239C9–240C6, 240C7–241B3). Ultimately the first task is merged into the second (264C10–D5).[2] Now when the ES tackles the second task, the backward reference (263B11–12) with which he seeks to justify his use of the expression 'what is not' is to 256E5–6: the *earlier* of our two passages, not the one in which Theaetetus notes the participants' acquisition of the equipment necessary for their project of pinning down the sophist. But if the project required the ES to go beyond 256E5–6, how can the reference back to the earlier passage be appropriate in its execution?[3]

I shall deal with this composite difficulty by dividing it. First (§3 below) I shall consider the relation between the passages in which 256E5–6 and 258B6–7 are embedded, in abstraction from the question how either is related to the final characterisation of falsehood. Then (§4 below) I shall return to the latter question.

3.  256E5–6 expresses a generalisation of the results of 255E8–256D10. So its employment of 'what is not' must be warranted by the fact that each form or kind *is not* indefinitely many others, as change is not rest (255E14), the same (256A5), other (256C8), being (256D8); that is, in that it is other than – non-identical with – each of them. If, then, we were to consider the expression '(is) not beautiful' within the framework constructed in this passage, we should find ourselves understanding it so as to be true of anything other than the form or kind *beautiful*; no less true, then, of Helen or Aphrodite than of the snub-nosed Socrates, and hardly a plausible reading for day-to-day uses of the expression (cf. 257D10). So it would be unsurprising to find the ES moving beyond 255E8–257A7 – where we are supposed to have been made comfortable with the use of 'is not' in statements of non-identity – in the direction of making room for the use of 'is not' in statements of negative predication.

2 Owen, 250, 259.
3 See Edward N. Lee, 'Plato on Negation and Not-Being in the *Sophist*', *Philosophical Review*, 81 (1972), 267–304, at p. 299 n. 53. (The difficulty is more serious than Lee allows: the treatment of falsehood is not just 'one of [Plato's] major "analytic" problems', but the very problem alluded to at 258B6–7.) James P. Kostman, 'False Logos and Not-Being in Plato's *Sophist*', in *Patterns in Plato's Thought*, ed. J. M. E. Moravcsik (Dordrecht 1973), 192–212, acknowledges inability to explain the reference to 256E5–6 (197, 210 n. 11).

And I believe that is indeed what we are meant to find in the passage that starts at 257B1.[4]

Not that the enterprise of 257B1 ff. is to be conceived as disconnected from that of 255E8–257A7. Together the two passages constitute a careful step-wise response to Eleatic doubts about 'is not'. The first does not merely assume that 'is not' is acceptable in statements of non-identity, but painstakingly works for that conclusion. And the second, in arguing that 'is not' is acceptable in statements of negative predication, employs a strategy essentially involving the materials that have proved useful in the first.

(1) It has been accepted that the nature of *the other* is all-pervasive (254D4–E7). The ES begins the first passage with particular exemplifications of that conclusion: not (brazenly) statements like 'Change is-not rest', but (cautiously) statements like 'Change is not-rest' (the negative particle is ostentatiously annexed, by word order, whose effect I have tried to capture by hyphenating, to the name of the kind than which change is being said to be other, not to the verb). We may be hard pressed to see a real distinction here. But it was the negating of the verb 'to be' in particular, not negation in general, that Parmenides found unintelligible. The ES is starting with something that should be uncontentious: something against which, as it stands, no Parmenidean strictures apply. The upshot, indeed, will be that the puzzling distinction marks no real difference; but in the dialectical circumstances this needs to be argued, not assumed.

The ES proceeds innocently through a series of examples of the form presumed uncontentious: 'Change is not-rest' (255E14), 'Change is not-the-same' (256A5), 'Change is not-other' (256C8). Then he unsheathes his knife. Being was one of the five kinds of which it was agreed, at 254D4–255E2, that each is other than all the others; so anyone who has allowed the first three examples to pass, as true in virtue of the fact that change is other than rest, the same, and other, has no ground for protest when, in virtue of the structurally indistinguishable fact that change is other than being, we insist on what is in fact another example of the same form: 'Change is not-being' (256D8). Moreover, the same can be said of

---

4 A *caveat*: when I write, as I shall, of the 'is not' of non-identity and the 'is not' of negative predication, I do not mean to imply that Plato aims to distinguish senses of 'is not' (and correspondingly of 'is'). See Owen, 257–8.

any other kind (other than being itself) (256D11–E2). It is clear now that we must abandon any hope of accepting the negative statements that constitute the natural expression for the pervasiveness of otherness, while divesting them of counter-Eleatic significance by insisting that being is not what is negated; and the ES now takes himself to be entitled to relocate the 'not' in statements of non-identity like the first three examples – statements other than those in which one term is being itself. The puzzling distinction vanishes, shown up as empty; and, on the strength of 255E3–7, the ES can conclude that each kind or form is-not all of the indefinitely many others.[5]

(2) The second passage also attacks (on a less restricted front) a Parmenidean refusal to make sense of 'is not'. The ES diagnoses the refusal as based on a mistake about negation: that of supposing that the addition of 'not' yields an expression for the contrary of what was meant by the original expression (257B1–C4).[6] In the case of, say, 'not beautiful', the mistake does not have the effect of depriving the negative expression of meaning altogether. The meaning of 'ugly' is a perfectly good meaning, even though it is wrong to assign it to 'not beautiful'. But in the case of 'is not', the mistake is destructive. An expression that meant the contrary of what 'is' means would mean, if it meant anything, the same as what would be meant, if anything could be, by 'in no way is'; and this is an expression for which no use (as distinct from mention) can be found, even in attempts to formulate in the material mode the thought that it has no application (237B7–239C8, on 'in no way being'; recalled, in terms of 'contrary of being', at 258E1–259A5).[7]

The ES works up to the destructive form of the mistake from a consideration of the non-destructive form. What makes it possible to say significantly of something that it is not-beautiful – what

5 Cf. Owen, 233–4, n. 21. The 'both . . . and . . .' construction is strained, on Owen's construal of 256C11–12; and the strain is unnecessary, given the evident intelligibility of the line of thought I have set out.

6 See Owen, passim: e.g. 231–2. (It seems perverse to take 257B1–C4 as anything but an introduction, no doubt partly promissory. to what follows. Cf. Lee, 268–9; and, differently, Frank A. Lewis, 'Plato on "Not"', California Studies in Classical Antiquity, 9 (1976), 89–115, at pp. 111–12, n. 19.)

7 The mistake would undermine statements of non-identity too: (1) has dealt piecemeal with that application. Note that it would not help to protest that we should be considering not 'is not', but 'is not . . .' If to negate being is to deny all being to one's subject, thereby defeating one's attempt to speak of it, then it cannot make any difference if one writes (say) 'beautiful' after the incoherent 'is not'.

ensures that the expression 'not beautiful' is not condemned, whenever uttered, to fly out vainly into a void, so much empty chatter – is not (as the erroneous view might have it) that, should the statement be true, the negative expression would strike home against the subject's being *ugly* (for such statements can be true even though their subjects are not ugly); but rather that the negative expression, if uttered in a true statement, would strike home against some attribute *other* than *beautiful*, possessed by the subject (257D10–11). (It is not that the erroneous view, applied to 'not beautiful', generates a worry about idle chatter; that it does not is precisely what is meant by describing this application of the view as non-destructive. But an adherent of the view would be saddled thereby with an account of why admittedly 'safe' examples of negative expressions are safe, as 'not beautiful' is, which could not but make 'is not' problematic.)

I intend the phrase 'strike home against' as a counterpart, coloured in the interest of conveying a feeling for what I take to be the ES's point, for drabber terms that Plato uses: 'indicate' (relating expressions and things, 257B10) and 'utter . . . of' (relating utterers, expressions, and things, 257D10). We should not, I believe, commit Plato to the view that the relation in question, between negative expressions and things (specifically, something like attributes) other than those meant by the words negated, is in any strict sense a semantic or meaning-determining relation.[8] Compare the tolerance of phrases like 'true in virtue of'. Sometimes we should decline to fill the gap, in '"Socrates is not beautiful" is true in virtue of . . .', with anything that would not count as displaying the sense of the quoted sentence. But this does not mean that we necessarily reject, for all purposes, such claims as this: '"Socrates is not beautiful" is true in virtue of Socrates' being snub-nosed'; and it is at least not wrong to say that the form or kind, *snub-nosed*, is other than the form or kind, *beautiful*. Of course such remarks do not begin to look like a determination of the sense of 'not beautiful'.

It can be tempting to elaborate them into such a determination – either reconstruing 'other than' as 'incompatible with', and analysing 'Socrates is not beautiful' as 'Socrates has some attribute incompatible with being beautiful', or leaving 'other than'

8 For this crucial point, see Lewis, 112 n. 27.

meaning what it does in 255E8–257A12, and using a universal quantifier: 'All Socrates' attributes are non-identical with being beautiful.' Commentators have not been reluctant to succumb to these temptations on Plato's behalf. But an interest in either sort of elaboration is, to say the least, not obviously present in the text.[9] (Incompatibility figures in accounts of the *Sophist* only because its proponents cannot see how Plato can achieve his purpose without it; and I think the same goes for the universal quantifier imported by those who rightly jib at an unannounced shift in the sense of 'other than', but take the same view of the purpose.) This unconcern with analysis need not seem a defect, if we see the ES's project as what it is: not to give an account of the sense of phrases like 'not beautiful', but rather to scotch a mistake about what entitles us to our confidence that they are not idle chatter, that they do indeed have the precise sense that we take them to have. (No need, in executing this project, to produce any substantive theory about what that sense is.)[10] The mistake is worth scotching here, not for its own sake, but because if it is allowed to pass in this case it can be carried over to undermine our confidence in the intelligibility of 'is not'.

We might put the ES's point about 'not beautiful' thus: 'not beautiful' is to be understood, not in terms of the contrary of *beautiful*, but in terms of that part of the nature of otherness that is set over against it. My suggestion is that 'understood in terms of' (at least in the affirmative component of this thesis) is best not taken as promising an analysis. 'Not beautiful' means exactly what it does, *viz. not beautiful*; the role of the notion of otherness is in an explanation, at a sub-semantical level, of why we do not need to fear that such a semantical remark is condemned to vacuity.[11]

9 See Lewis, 105–6; 113 n. 40.
10 An attribute can be other than *beautiful* without being (ever) appropriately mentionable as that in virtue of which something is not beautiful. In order to *guarantee* that what is true in virtue of some fact expressible in terms of otherness is that something is *not* beautiful, Plato would need the commentators' extra apparatus. But he does not need extra apparatus for his different purpose. His point is this: what the attributes that *can* be cited in the role in question have in common is that they are *other* than *beautiful*. (See Lewis, 104.) This suffices without further ado to correct the error about contrariety, which is what threatens the intelligibility of 'is not'. (It is not to the point to object that someone who is, e.g., long-haired has an attribute other than *beautiful*, but is not necessarily not-beautiful on that account. This contradicts no thesis of Plato's. Cf. David Wiggins, 'Sentence Meaning, Negation, and Plato's Problem of Non-Being', in Vlastos, op. cit., 268–303, at pp. 291, 294.)
11 Here I diverge from Lee's thesis that otherness plays a novel, 'constitutive' role at 257C5 ff. What seems correct is this: 255E8–257A12 yields nothing that could be called 'the nature of the not beautiful' (in the sense which that passage could countenance, the not

The ES proceeds to the case of negating being by generalising his point about 'not beautiful' (258A1–2, 4–5, 7–9), and then representing the case of 'is not' as a further instance of the generalisation (258A11–B3). But the inference by instantiation can be understood also as a matter of reformulating the generalisation:[12] 258A11–B3 introduces the idea, not of a part of the nature of otherness contrasted with being as such (whatever that might mean), but of a part of the nature of otherness contrasted with being . . . (e.g. with being beautiful). We can capture the movement of thought as follows. The thesis from which the ES generalises – that *not beautiful* is to be 'understood in terms of' (see above) otherness than *beautiful* – could be written thus: (*being*) not beautiful is to be 'understood in terms of' otherness than (*being*) *beautiful*. When the ES instantiates the generalisation with respect to being, what happens is, in effect, that 'not' shifts back to the hitherto implicit verb, and the complement recedes out of focus. The point becomes this: *not being* (*e.g. beautiful*) is to be 'understood in terms of' otherness than *being* (*beautiful* – to stay with the same example).[13] Only the mistake about contrariety – which has been adequately refuted by the discussion of the case, presumed uncontentious, in which 'not' does not go with the verb 'to be' – could make it seem that the change in the placing of 'not' makes a difference.

4. If I am right, the not-being welcomed at 258B6–7, as what was needed in order to pin down the sophist, is the not-being that

beautiful – e.g. the attribute *snub-nosed* – is rightly so called, not by virtue of its own nature, but by virtue of partaking in the form of otherness: cf. 255E4–6); whereas 257C5 ff. is concerned with something of which it can be said that its nature is being not beautiful (258B8–C4). But Lee's 'constitutive' role for otherness seems problematic. He explains it in remarks like this: 'The determinate sense of "*x* is not tall" . . . lies precisely, but lies entirely, in saying that tall is what *x* is not' (295); but this would scarcely cut any ice with Parmenides. It seems preferable to relocate Lee's distinction: 255E8–257A12 equips us to understand a supervenient role, and 255C5 ff. a constitutive role, for the notion of *being not beautiful*; the notion of otherness plays a semantic role in the former passage and a sub-semantical role in the latter. (The only semantical thesis suggested by the second passage is to the effect that 'not beautiful' means *not beautiful*; I believe this captures in semantical terms the point of the implicit thesis that the nature of the not beautiful is being not beautiful.)

12 See Lee, 282 n. 21.
13 Owen (239 n. 33) objects to supplying 'part of' with 'the nature of being' at 258B1, on the ground that it implies the reductive thesis (i.e. insistence on detaching 'not' from the verb 'to be': Owen, 236–41). But if the notion of a part of the nature of being were established, as applying to such items as *being beautiful*, the reading Owen objects to could make the point in my text, precisely without implying the reductive thesis. A better reason against 'part of' is that the notion of parts of the nature of being has not been established (see Lee, 283–4).

figures in *negative* predications like 'Socrates is not beautiful.' (That statement attributes not-being to Socrates in that it says that he is not – beautiful.) When the sophist's escape is blocked (cf. 264B9–D9) by the production of a non-paradoxical characterisation of falsehood, the point, in the example chosen, is evidently that a false *affirmative* predication attributes what is not to its subject (263B9). Part of our composite problem (§2 above) was to explain why pinning down the sophist requires the materials of 258B6–7, not just those of 256E5–6. So we need to explain how the ES's description of a false affirmative predication, in 263B, can be seen as an application of the conceptual equipment established in the discussion of negative predication.

This component of the problem is easily solved if we understand the 'is not' of 263B as arrived at by a 'converse' reformulation of the 'is not' of 258B6–7. The earlier passage signals vindication of the legitimacy of 'is not' in statements like 'Socrates is not beautiful'; that statement can be reformulated as claiming that *beautiful* is not in relation to Socrates, and now we have the terminology of 263B (capturing the falsity of 'Socrates is beautiful').[14] This answers the question why we have to wait until 258B6–7 before being told we have what is needed for pinning down the sophist: what 263B requires is (a 'converse' version of) the 'is not' of negative predication, which is not yet available at 256E5–6.[15]

The other component of our composite problem was to explain why it is appropriate for the treatment of falsehood to refer back to 256E5–6, even though the conceptual equipment it needs was not yet established in that passage. We can now see at least the outline of a solution to this problem too. The ES's vindication of the 'is not' of negative predication builds essentially on the fact that, whatever attribute one takes, there are plenty of attributes other than it – the negative part of what was said at 256E5–6. If the use of 'is not' at 263B is nothing but a transformational derivative of the 'is not' of negative predication, the ES's entitlement to the

---

14 On the 'converse' idiom, see Michael Frede, *Prädikation und Existenzaussage* (Göttingen 1967), 52–5, 80, 94–5; Owen, e.g. 237–8. As will emerge, I think there is less of this idiom in the *Sophist* than is commonly thought.

15 No doubt the equipment of 256E5–6 would serve for an account of falsity in identity statements. But it would not be generalisable to cover false predications, whereas the account of false predications could be applied to identity statements ('*The same as Socrates* is not about Theaetetus').

former must be justified by precisely what justifies his entitlement to the latter. So it is exactly to the point for 263B11–12 to hark back, past the treatment of negative predication, to the foundation on which that treatment builds.[16]

There is a complication, resulting from the usual way of understanding 263B11–12 and 256E5–6. What we find at 263B11–12 is this: 'For we said that in the case of each (thing) there are many (things) which are and many which are not.' On the usual view, this relates to its context as follows. Universal instantiation of its negative part, with respect to Theaetetus, is supposed to yield, as something the ES could address to Theaetetus, 'There are many (things) which are not in relation to (in the case of) you.' Then '*In flight* is not in relation to you' (263B9, with 'in relation to you' supplied from 263B4–5, 11: the ES's account of the falsity of 'Theaetetus is in flight') is an exemplification: it cites one of the many such things which the instantiation assures us there are. On this view, then, 263B11–12 is taken to contain 'converse' uses of 'is' and 'is not', with the universal quantifier 'each (thing)' binding what would be in the subject place in a more straightforward formulation. The force is: in the case of everything (including Theaetetus), there are many things that it is (e.g. seated) and many that it is not (e.g. in flight). Since 263B11–12 purports simply to repeat 256E5–6 ('we said', 263B12), the standard view imposes a structural parallel in the interpretation of 256E5–6: again, 'converse' uses of 'is' and 'is not', with the universal quantifier binding what would be in the subject place in a more straightforward formulation. Here, then, the force is: in the case of each form, there are many things that it is and an indefinite number that it is not (that is – this is all that 255E8 ff. has licensed – an indefinite number with which it is non-identical).[17]

These interpretations evidently raise a difficulty about 'we said', at 263B12. On this reading, 263B11–12 does not simply restate what was said at 256E5–6; it makes two tacit modifications – modifications which, in view of its bland claim to be a repetition, we should be constrained to regard as surreptitious. First, the range of the universal quantifier is extended, from forms to

16 In fact, as we shall see, 256E5–6 is more straightforwardly relevant to the 'converse' use of 'is not' than this outline explanation suggests: not just obliquely relevant through its bearing on the non-'converse' basis of the transformation.

17 See, e.g., Owen, 235.

everything (including Theaetetus). Second, the negative part of
the generalisation is extended from denials of identity to cover
negative predications as well.

Can these modifications be incorporated into an overall interpretation that solves our problem: that is, one that gives 257B1 ff.
the sort of importance in the final characterisation of falsehood
that 258B6–7 would lead us to expect, and accounts for the fact
that 263B11–12 refers back to 256E5–6? It could be claimed,
plausibly enough, that the modifications are licensed by 257B1 ff.,
given that that passage extends the scope for acceptable uses of 'is
not' precisely from statements of non-identity between kinds or
forms to statements like 'Socrates is not beautiful' (§3 above). But
the surreptitiousness is still a mystery. It constitutes, in effect, a
pretence that nothing of importance for the project of 263B has
happened since 256E5–6. Thus, even if *we* can see 257B1 ff.
playing the role we have been led to expect, we find *Plato*
unaccountably refusing to acknowledge it.[18]

18 Owen (260) conspicuously fails to appeal to 257B1 ff. in explaining the tacit modifications. What Owen explains is not the extension in the later passage, but the restriction
to non-identity in the earlier. The idea seems to be as follows: Plato wants to be able to
say, of *any* attribute, that it is not (in relation to some subjects) (259); this desideratum
can be met for pervasive forms like being, identity, and difference only if the 'is not' is
understood as that of non-identity; hence that is what figures in 256E5–6. But: (1) Why
the putative desideratum? Not for 263B: Plato would hardly be at pains to secure that
'*In flight* is not about Theaetetus' should seem an example of a general kind of truth
(examples of which hold about all forms, including the pervasive ones), when the move
needed to construct the general kind of truth (understanding the 'is not' as that of
non-identity) actually renders problematic the status of the 'exemplification' (in which
the 'is not' is precisely not to be so understood). (2) The putative desideratum is not
enunciated by 256E5–6 as Owen interprets it; he takes 256E5–6 to say, not that any
attribute is not in relation to something, but that an indefinite number of attributes are
not in relation to every form. Of course the indefinite number, in any case, will be all
the attributes other than the topic form itself, including the pervasive ones. But we have
no reason to suppose Plato wants to be able to say 'an indefinite number' because he
*anyway* wants to be able to say 'all' (to include the pervasive forms), and *consequently* has
to understand 'is not' in terms of non-identity; rather than that he finds himself able to
say 'an indefinite number' (or 'all', if he had felt like it) because he is *anyway*
understanding 'is not', at this stage, in terms of non-identity. (3) It is not the restriction
to non-identity in 256E5–6 that needs explaining. If we do not believe that Plato
unpardonably helps himself in mid-argument to a new construal of 'other' (as we
should not: Owen, 232 n. 19), we must regard non-identity as fundamental in his
anti-Eleatic strategy. What more natural, then, than that he should begin on 'is not' by
making room for its use in statements of non-identity? As for what does need
explaining: against Parmenides, it takes more than the mere observation that *beautiful, in
flight*, etc., are non-pervasive kinds to justify going beyond 256E5–6 so as to allow
oneself the use of 'is not' in negative predications (or 'converse' counterparts thereof).
Owen's suggestion that the observation is enough to explain the 'tacit extension' leaves
no room for 257B1 ff., understood as a careful defence of the use of 'is not' in negative
predications.

Is it possible, then, to eliminate the tacit modifications: to understand 263B11–12 as nothing but a repetition of 256E5–6?

This requires us to suppose that 'in the case of each (thing)' at 263B12 can be glossed, from 256E5, as 'in the case of each of the forms', and that the negative part of 263B11–12 involves nothing but statements of non-identity. It would follow that the relation between 'There are many (things) that are not about (in the case of) each (thing)' – the negative part of 263B11–12 – and '*In flight* is not about (in relation to) Theaetetus' – the ES's account of the falsity of 'Theaetetus is in flight' – cannot be one of exemplification. However, so long as 'about each (thing)', in the generalisation, is understood as supplementing 'converse' uses of 'is' and 'is not', it seems impossible to see what else the relation could be, and the tacit modifications seem unavoidable. The key to an alternative reading is the possibility that the 'about' phrases function differently. As before, 'about Theaetetus' supplements a 'converse' use of 'is not', in '*In flight* is not about Theaetetus'; but we can take 'about each (thing)', at 263B12, to constitute a simple quantifier phrase (like 'concerning everything' in, at least, logician's English), binding what the subjects of *non*-'converse' uses of 'is' and 'is not' are said to be and not to be; and similarly with 'about each of the forms' at 256E5.[19]

The force of 256E5–6, on this alternative reading, will be as follows: in the case of each of the forms, what is (it) is multiple and what is not (it) is indefinite in number. There is no problem about understanding this as a conclusion from what precedes it, so long as we see that the generalisation ('each. . . (it). . . (it)') picks up, not the role of *change* in the preceding demonstrations, but the role of, for instance, *the same*. In the case of the form, *the same*, change both is it (256A7–8) and is not it (256A5 'is not-it', convertible to 'is-not it' after 256D8–9: §3 above).[20] Just so, in the case of every form, there are many things (or at any rate many forms; forms are all that the ES's variables have so far ranged over) that are it and an indefinite number that are not it.[21]

The meat of the remark, in the context of Plato's anti-Eleatic project, lies in its negative component; and of course I do not

19 The preposition *'peri'* governs different cases in 263B11 and 263B12, and the same case in 263B12 and 256E5.
20 We are likely to suppose that 'is' functions differently in its two occurrences; but Plato seems to suggest, rather, that the difference of function is in what replaces 'it' (256A10–12). See Owen, 258 n. 63. (Cf. n. 4 above.)
21 R. S. Bluck, *Plato's Sophist* (Manchester 1975), considers taking 256E5–6 this way round, but rejects it on the ground that on this interpretation the passage does not have the right inferential relation to 256D11–E3 (158). But as regards the negative part,

pretend that it makes any doctrinal difference whether we suppose
the ES to say that in the case of each form it is not an indefinite
number of others, or that in the case of each form an indefinite
number of others are not it. The point of the second reading is not
that the substance is different, but that it permits us to extract an
appropriate sense from the text without understanding 'in the case
of each of the forms' as supplementing 'converse' uses of 'is' and
'is not'. This way we can take 263B11–12 to say, as it purports to,
the very same thing, without threatening the intelligibility of its
relation to the claim that *in flight* is not in relation to Theaetetus.

The claim that the form, *in flight*, is not in relation to Theaetetus is a claim on whose availability, to capture the falsity of
'Theaetetus is in flight', the ES insists. He needs to defend the
claim against an Eleatic objection to the effect that its use of 'is
not' makes it undermine itself, offering, so to speak, to deprive
itself of a topic. Not at all, says the ES. That which is not, in the
relevant sense, is not that which utterly is not (long since
dismissed), but that which *is* other[22] (than that which is in

whatever we can say to explain the inferential relation which, taken one way round, it bears
to 256D11–E3 (or, better, 255E8–256E4) – and Bluck says something (158–9) – will serve
equally well for the inverted reading; and the positive part, on either view, needs
generalising beyond anything said in 256D11–E3 (my view makes it a perfectly intelligible
extension of the results of 255E8–D10). Two further possible objections: (1) If 256E5–6
said (as Owen implies: 235, 254) that about each form what is not is more numerous than
what is, it would be an objection that, taking the passage my way, this would be false of
pervasive forms: all the forms that are not *the same* are *the same* – in the relevant senses – and
there is one more form that is *the same*, viz. the same itself. But 'many' does not exclude
'indefinite in number', and the text leaves it open that in some cases the many may be *more*
than the indefinite number. The distinction is adequately explained by the fact that with
non-pervasive forms there are fewer exemplifications of the 'is . . .' component. (In the
case of each form, what is it is – at least – multiple, and what is not it is indefinite in number.)
(2) On my view, 257A4–6, where *being* is the *subject* to 'is . . .' and 'is not . . .', cannot be (as
is often said: see, e.g., Lee, 282, n. 21) an instantiation of the generalisation of 256E5–6,
where the quantifier binds what *follows* 'is . . .' and 'is not . . .' But the affirmative part of
257A4–6 ('being is its single self') never looked, on any view, like an instantiation of
256E5–6. (And, given the reversibility of statements of non-identity, the negative part
follows by instantiation from 256E5–6 taken either way round.)

22  *'Onta hetera'* ('things that are other'), 263B11. Cf. Wiggins, 295: he renders the relevant
sentence thus: '[i.e. it says] things which are², but different things which are² from the
things which are¹ respecting Theaetetus'; and he takes 'are²' as synonymous with 'are¹' – 'In
*Theaetetus is flying* the kind Flies is¹ because it applies to *something* even if it does not apply to
Theaetetus.' It must be on this foundation that Wiggins bases the idea that Plato 'persists in
seeing Socrates' being able to purport that "Flying is respecting Theaetetus" as explained
by there being such a *genos* as Flying (rather than vice versa)' (298); there being such a *genos*
being for Plato, Wiggins thinks, a matter of its having an extension (cf. also 287). But where
Wiggins has Plato (deplorably) insisting that the meaningfulness of 'Theaetetus is in flight'
requires that *in flight* be *instantiated*, what Plato in fact insists is that *in flight* is *other* (than what
is in relation to Theaetetus); this is not Wiggins's dubious condition for the statement to be
*meaningful*, but a perfectly correct condition for it to be *false*.

relation to the subject[23]). And the 'is' I have stressed, which emphasises that the claim does not deprive itself of a topic, cannot now be queried; for it has been accepted, at 256E5–6, that for every form there *are* plenty of forms that are not (because they *are* other than) it. This fills out our outline answer to the second component of our composite question; it shows how it can be that, although 263B uses 'is not' in a way that is established only in the course of 257B1 ff., it is nevertheless entirely appropriate for it to justify its doing so by a restatement (just that, not a surreptitious improvement) of 256E5–6.[24]

5. It may seem back to front to broach only now the question of what puzzle about falsehood the sophist is supposed to hide behind. But this way we can let our interpretation of the problem be influenced by the desirability of finding Plato saying something to the point in response to it.

Many commentators suppose that the puzzle about falsehood is on these lines: the falsity of a false belief or statement would have to consist in the fact that the *situation* or *state of affairs* it represents is an utter nonentity, something totally devoid of being; but there is no coherent way to express such a 'fact' (237B7–239C8), so no coherent way to formulate a characterisation of falsehood made inescapable by a correct understanding of what falsehood would be (if there were any such thing).[25] However, when the ES comes to use the dangerous phrase 'what is not' in the characterisation of falsehood, his point, as we have seen, seems to be that the falsity of 'Theaetetus is in flight' consists in its attributing what is not to its subject, in that *in flight* is not in relation to Theaetetus. And if the puzzle was the one about situations or states of affairs outlined above, this response (on its own at least) seems irrelevant. The sophist might reasonably object:

23 This would translate *'ontōn . . . peri sou'* at 263 B11. But *'ontōn'* is very dubious: in favour of the manuscripts' *'ontōs'*, see Frede, 57–8. Even so, it is natural to supply *'tōn ontōn'* ('than the things that are') between *'hetera'* and *'peri sou'*.

24 Owen (260) gives a clear statement of the relevance of non-identity between attributes to the justification of the 'is not' of 'converse' negative predication, but does not see that this removes the need to interpret 263B11–12 as modifying 256E5–6.

25 See especially Wiggins. For a variant, Owen, 245: he uses the word 'situation', but what he has in mind, as missing from reality when the statement 'Theaetetus is in flight' is false, is the flight of which the statement accuses Theaetetus. (This is in an account of *Tht.* 188C9–189B9. But the difference on which Owen insists (243) between that passage and the *Sophist*'s puzzle lies not in the content of the puzzle but rather in Plato's attitude to its materials.)

Attributes, like *in flight*, are not the sort of thing that I thought a description of falsehood in beliefs and statements would have to represent as not being. And it was not in the sense you exploit – not being in relation to something – but in precisely the sense you agree is problematic – not being anything at all – that I thought a description of falsehood would have to represent my different items, situations or states of affairs, as not being. You have not shown that the description of falsehood I found problematic is not compulsory, dictated by the nature of the concept of falsehood; and you have certainly not shown that it is not problematic.

Some commentators are sensitive to the vulnerability of 263B, considered as a response to the puzzle about situations; and they shift attention to the passage (261C6–262E2) that leads up to the explicit discussion of truth and falsity in statements. There the ES distinguishes (in effect) between a kind of sentence-constituent whose function is to make clear what is being talked about and a kind of sentence-constituent whose function is to make clear what is being said about it. The commentators draw the obvious moral: a sentence (one of the simple kind Plato considers, at any rate) gets its purchase on reality through its possession of a sentence-constituent of the first kind. And they suggest that any inclination to protest against 263B, on the lines envisaged above, would stem from a failure to grasp this point. Worrying about the apparently total absence from reality of states of affairs answering to false statements, or of what would be components of such states of affairs, answering to the predicates of false statements, would manifest a lack of enlightenment about the localisation, within sentences, of the relation that gives them their bearing on the world.[26]

But the puzzle about situations is a deeper puzzle, and the objection to 263B, considered as a response to it, is a better objection, than Plato's strategy, on this view of it, gives them credit for being. The puzzle turns on the thought that the falsity of 'Theaetetus is in flight' should consist in the fact that the state of affairs that the sentence offers to represent, or perhaps the flight in which an utterer of the sentence would accuse Theaetetus of being engaged, is nothing at all. And that thought, properly understood, is absolutely *correct*; it needs no support from a half-baked conception of how speech has its bearing on reality, such as would

26 See Owen, 263–5.

be undermined by the distinction drawn at 261C6–262E2. In conjunction with 237B7–239C8, the thought threatens to undermine the possibility of falsehood; what we should need in order to neutralise this destructive effect is, not the considerations of 261C6–262E2 (which are powerless for this purpose), but something to show us why a description such as 'dealing, in thought or speech, with what is in fact nothing at all' (which might figure in a characterisation of falsehood on the lines of what this puzzle represents as problematic) does not incoherently represent the thought or speech it applies to as (genuine thought or speech, but) possessing no subject matter. And the *Sophist* contains no trace of the necessary distinction.[27] Of course it is possible that Plato simply fails to deal adequately with the difficulty he tackles – fails to see its full depth; but charity recommends that we credit him, if possible, with better success at a different project.

261C6–262E2 does indeed, obliquely and inexplicitly, undermine a paradoxical argument for the impossibility of falsehood. But it is an argument distinct both from the commentators' puzzle about situations and from the difficulty about falsehood that is the *Sophist*'s main concern.

What the passage's differentiation of functions would correct is a position indifferent to, or ignorant of, the distinction between mentioning something and saying something; and such a position does make appearances elsewhere. The idea might be expressed on these lines: the unit move in the language-game of informative discourse (occupying a position analogous to that which we might ascribe to statements; but that term carries a burden of logical theory that includes at least the missing distinction) is the putting into words of some thing. A dim perception that the minimal informative performance must have some complexity (the point of which 261C6–262E2 evinces a clear, if partial, perception) can, in the absence of the distinction, yield only the requirement that

---

27 For the distinction, see Wiggins, 274–5. Owen suggests (246) that in the *Sophist* Plato does not want to deny that 'we can speak of mythical centaurs or chimerical flights' (such items are not wholly devoid of being, since we can say that they are). But on Owen's own account (229) the dialogue contains no direct evidence of hospitality to the chimerical. And there is nothing in the *Sophist* (or in *Prm.* 160B6–161A5, also cited by Owen) to show how the acceptability of reference to the chimerical, on the ground that its target is not devoid of being, might be reconciled with the thought – surely acceptable on some construal – that such 'items' as the flight of which Theaetetus is falsely accused are in fact nothing at all. So long as this thought is not disarmed, it must remain unclear how 237B7–239C8 can fail to have its full destructive effect.

the thing put into words must be constituted of parts, so that the putting of it into words can be a complex performance by virtue of consisting in the successive mentioning of the parts.[28] This position would undermine the possibility of contradicting another person's remark: the best one could hope to achieve would be a change of subject.[29] Equally, it would undermine the possibility of speaking falsely. Failure to put a certain thing into words cannot constitute false speech: for either one will have put a different thing into words, and so spoken truly (though with a different topic); or else one will have failed to put anything into words, which is the nearest we can come, in the terminology I have adopted to express the position that lacks the crucial distinction, to the conclusion that one will not have said anything at all.[30]

This crude position makes no explicit appearance in the *Sophist*.[31] But 261C6–262E2 says exactly what is needed to correct it. And it seems plausible that some terminological apparatus, introduced at 262E5 and used at 263A5, A9–10, C5, C7, is meant to signal Plato's awareness of the bearing of 261C6–262E2 on the crude position. The crude position lends itself to a slogan on these lines: 'A thing can be put into words only by its own form of words.'[32] This slogan encapsulates the destructive effect of inability, or refusal, to distinguish mentioning and saying: any attempt to formulate the notion of error in a form of words succeeds in describing only idle chatter, or else a flawless capturing in words of some other thing. Having drawn the necessary distinction, Plato continues to use the possessive to express the 'about' relation, now safely localised, between (what we can now without risk of misleading describe as) statements and things (263A5, A9–10; 'about me' and 'mine' are interchangeable). The terminology irresistibly suggests an echo of the old slogan,

28  See *Tht.* 201D8–202C5; cf. Aristotle, *Metaph.* 1024b26–1025a1.
29  Cf. *Euthd.* 285D7–286B6.      30  Cf. *Euthd.* 283E7–284C6.
31  *Pace*, apparently, Owen, 241, claiming that '237B7–E7 is a version of the familiar paradox'. In fact (as Owen immediately concedes) that passage does not purport to undermine the notion of falsehood. There is no reason to take it as addressing anything except the *Sophist*'s question: how is it possible to mention or speak of (not 'say') what is not?
32  See *Tht.* 202A6–8; cf. *Metaph.* 1024b32–3. ('Form of words' here represents '*logos*', the noun cognate with '*legein*'. Ordinarily these might be translated 'statement' and 'say'; but as '*legein*' here expresses the notion, straddling those of mentioning and saying, that I am rendering by 'put into words', I use a term similarly free of unwanted theoretical connotations for '*logos*'.)

verbally almost unaltered, but now rendered quite innocuous: 'A thing can be talked about only by a statement of its own.'

The puzzle about falsehood thus obliquely disarmed by 261C6–262E2 is perceptibly less sophisticated than the difficulty about situations or states of affairs outlined above. The notion of a state of affairs is the notion of something with a complexity of a different kind from that of a mere composite thing; it is the notion of a chunk of reality with a structure such as to mirror that of the proposition or statement it would render true. Anyone who could genuinely be credited with possession of this notion would already have advanced beyond a stage at which he could be instructed by 261C6–262E2. And, as I urged above, this would not immunise him against a worry, should he conceive it, about the utter absence from reality of the states of affairs represented by false statements or beliefs. Something similar holds for the notion of a component of a state of affairs answering to the predicate of a statement (the crude position precisely lacks the equipment to effect any such singling out); and for a worry about the total absence of such an item from reality when a statement or belief is false.

Although the difficulty about falsehood generated by the crude position (unlike the puzzle involving situations or states of affairs) is cogently answered in the course of the *Sophist*, the crude position cannot easily be read into the passage in which the dialogue's official problem about falsehood is set out in detail (240C7–241B3). Not-being figures in the crude position's difficulty in that one of the candidate descriptions of falsehood it suggests and portrays as problematic (the other being, irrelevantly for present purposes, in terms of change of subject) is: a form of words such that what it puts into words is not (is nothing at all). The problem about this is that in the attempt to characterise the form of words as false we undermine its bearing on reality. Now the *Sophist*'s paradox is directed against both of two distinguished kinds of falsehood: both falsehoods that represent what is not as being (240E1–4, understanding *'doxazein'* at E3), and falsehoods that represent what is as not being (240E5–9). The threat to the former of these, if this were all that we had to consider, might perhaps be assimilated to the problem posed by the crude position. But this will hardly do for the latter, where the fact that what is represented (as not being) is *what is* ensures that whatever difficulty there is about the falsehood's purchase on reality does not arise in a comparable way. No doubt the fact that what is is represented *as not being* generates a difficulty that could be expressed as one about the falsehood's hold on reality. It remains the case, however, that the *Sophist*'s problem evidently arises in rather different ways for affirmative and negative falsehoods; there is a complexity here for which the crude position has no counterpart.[33]

6. What, then, is the *Sophist*'s difficulty?

Bearing in mind the desirability of finding something to the point in 263B, we should understand the disjunctive characterisation of falsehood at 240C7–241B3 in terms of attributes. Thus an example of the kind of falsehood that represents what is as not being might be 'Theaetetus is not seated', uttered when Theaetetus is seated. This represents *seated*, which is, as not being; that description correctly captures the statement's falsity if we take 'is' and 'not being' as 'converse' uses and supply 'in relation to Theaetetus'. The other kind of falsehood is illustrated by the example actually discussed in 263B, 'Theaetetus is in flight'. This represents *in flight*, which is not, as being; again, that description correctly captures the statement's falsity if we take 'is not' and 'being' as 'converse' uses and supply 'in relation to Theaetetus'.

Why should the sophist find these characterisations of falsehood problematic, so that their putative incoherence affords him a hiding place? Because he makes the mistake we have seen that the ES devotes himself to correcting: he cannot see how 'is not' could be anything but a synonym for 'has the contrary of being' or 'utterly is not' (note how these latter expressions figure in the problem-setting passage: 240D6, E2, E5), and he can find no coherent    significance    for    it    under    that    interpretation

---

33 Owen's remark (265) 'Falsehood had appeared an abortive attempt to mention something' appears to miss this complexity. I am taking it that 236D9–237A9 announces, without precise detail, the difficulties about images and falsehood spelled out in 239C9–240C6 and 240C7–241B3. (237A3–4 might be taken to imply a simpler paradox, turning on the idea that a falsehood itself – sc. the content of a false belief – is not. But all that the lines say is that we are committed to the being of what is not when we claim that falsehood occurs: a commitment we can understand 240C7–241B3 as explaining.) Cf., e.g., Wiggins, who extracts a puzzle to which Owen's remark would be appropriate from the earlier passage together with 237B7–E7 (cf. n. 31 above), ignoring the complexity of the later passage (268–71); and I. M. Crombie, *An Examination of Plato's Doctrines*, II (London 1963), who suggests (505–7) that the later passage introduces a new (and spurious) difficulty.

(237B7–239C8). So it seems to him that when we try to capture the falsity of 'Theaetetus is in flight' by saying that it represents *in flight*, which *is not* (in relation to Theaetetus: given the mistake, the addition does not help),[34] as being, we must be talking nonsense; and when we try to capture the falsity of 'Theaetetus is not seated' by saying that it represents *seated*, which is (in relation to Theaetetus), as *not being*, we describe the statement as talking nonsense, and hence contradict ourselves if we also describe it as significant.

This paradox is utterly disarmed by the ES's painstaking demolition of the Eleatic mistake about negation. Once the mistake has been corrected, it suffices simply to restate the characterisation of falsehood that had seemed problematic; this time carefully avoiding the erroneous equation between 'not being', on the one hand, and 'opposite of being' or 'in no way being', on the other.[35]

If we understand the *Sophist*'s problem about falsehood on these lines, we can see Plato's response to it as an unqualified success. (Contrast the interpretation in terms of situations or states of affairs: §5 above.) What makes this possible is that – to stick to the less complicated case of affirmative falsehoods – we regard the sheer unavailability of anything answering to the words 'in flight', in the false statement 'Theaetetus is in flight', not as a *premise* in an argument purporting to show that a description that captures the statement's falsity is incoherent (an independently obvious reformulation, that is, of the claim that the statement is false); but rather as an *inference* from the claim (which does, in fact innocuously, capture the statement's falsity) that what answers to the words is not (in relation to Theaetetus). The former problematic unavailability (the unavailability of the flight of which the statement accuses Theaetetus) is indeed a concomitant of the statement's falsity; and it is not something with which Plato shows us how to cope. (See §5 above.) The latter unavailability (the unavailability of the attribute or kind, *in flight*) is simply a mistake, and one which Plato definitively corrects.

It may seem a cost of this reading that it separates Plato's concern in the *Sophist* from the deep philosophical difficulty raised by Wittgenstein when he writes: 'How can one think what is not the

34  See n. 7 above.
35  This is actually done only for the affirmative kind of falsehood; once the diagnostic point is clear, the other kind can be left as an exercise for the reader.

case? If I think that King's College is on fire when it is not, the fact of its being on fire does not exist. Then how can I think it?'[36] But it is surely not a cost but a gain that we find in the *Sophist*, not an unconvincing attempt on that interesting difficulty, but a wholly successful solution to a different one.

It is true that we cannot easily find the different difficulty pressing. Indeed, there may be an inclination to protest: how could anyone suppose that the claim '*In flight* is not in relation to Theaetetus', by trying to describe its subject as not being, incoherently represents itself as lacking a subject altogether? Is it not obvious that not being . . . (for instance not being in relation to Theaetetus) is not the same as utterly not being? But the fact is that it was not obvious to Parmenides, if Plato's diagnosis is correct. According to Plato's suggestion, it was precisely by equating 'not being' with 'being in no way' that Parmenides excluded plurality, qualitative diversity, and change from what can sensibly be affirmed to be the case. The *Sophist*'s puzzle, on the present interpretation, applies the same method in order to cast doubt on the concept of falsehood: an intriguing employment of Parmenides' destructive elenchus at a meta-linguistic level, which would impose limitations (for instance) on the strictures available to Parmenides himself against failures to take his point. But what the puzzle elicits from Plato is a move which, by destroying the foundation, has the effect of dismantling the entire Eleatic position.

36 *The Blue and Brown Books* (Oxford 1958), 31.

# 7 Forms and dialectic in the second half of the *Parmenides*

## JULIUS M. MORAVCSIK

The second half of the *Parmenides* has been a source of puzzlement to generations of scholars, inspiring a wide variety of interpretations.[1] Thanks to the groundbreaking work of Ryle and Owen, one can see this material today as offering serious reflections of conceptual and metaphysical nature. In this chapter I wish to locate the key conceptual problems that Plato addresses in this passage, and argue that Plato is here also defending and revising his theory of Forms.[*]

## I *General remarks*

All attempts at interpretation have to come to grips with the strange structure of the passage. On the surface at least, it seems that the material is arranged into eight arguments; the arguments taken pair-wise contradict each other. This organisation is, however, not very tight. Thus it suggests that it might serve for Plato more as a frame of exposition rather than as the logical back-bone

---

[*] I am delighted to be able to dedicate this essay to Gwil Owen. A lot of time has gone by since those wintry days of late 1958 when we met weekly at Corpus, and he would come rushing in, having had to crank up the old Hillman by hand in order to get to college. My feelings for him deepen as the decades go by. In my heart I know that we still stand for the same ideals of knowledge and humanity that he did and I tried to, in those early days.

[1] For example W. F. R. Hardie, *A Study in Plato* (Oxford 1936), William F. Lynch, *An Approach to Plato's Metaphysics through the Parmenides* (Washington D.C. 1959). The ones I shall mostly refer to are: F. M. Cornford, *Plato and Parmenides* (London 1939); G. E. L. Owen, 'Notes on Ryle's Plato', in *Ryle: a Collection of Critical Essays,* ed. O. P. Wood and G. Pitcher (New York 1970); Gilbert Ryle, 'Plato's Parmenides', *Mind,* 48 (1939), 129–51, and ·302–25 (reprinted in *Studies in Plato's Metaphysics,* ed. R. E. Allen (New York 1965), 97–147; all further references will be to this printing); Malcolm Schofield, 'The Antinomies of Plato's Parmenides', *Classical Quarterly,* 27 (1977), 139–58.

of content. For one thing, after the second argument we find a longer passage on time which begins by stating that we are starting for 'the third time' (155E4); commentators, taking the surface structure too seriously, have been treating this as an 'appendix' to the second argument. Further evidence for the hypothesis that the over-all structure is not meant very deeply is provided by the fact that the arguments are not of equal length. The second one is the longest, and the last four take up much less space than the first four. (The first two arguments occupy 137C through 155D while the last two only 164B through 166B.) Finally, not all of the conclusions reached are equally problematic. The conclusions in 161A–B about likeness and unlikeness are not paradoxical and neither is the conclusion about equality at 161E1–2. Finally, the tension between the last two arguments is not exactly similar to the one between the other pairs.

There is evidence from other dialogues that Plato will use an 'outer shell' to frame an 'inner core' which truly represents the real significance of the dialogue. For example, the structure of the *Phaedo* suggests that the most important issue is the way in which Socrates should die, while in fact that issue turns out to be posterior to the issues of the theory of the Forms and the claim for immortality. The structure of the *Sophist* suggests that the main task is to arrive at an adequate definition of sophistry, while the most important issues turn out to be the relationships between Forms and the analysis of falsehood. Thus one might look beyond the mere structural suggestion of a series of contradictory arguments, and seek to uncover what the real issues are that Plato wants to focus on.

Indeed, the parallels between pairs of arguments divert our attention from an equally significant structural fact. The arguments are not presenting merely conclusions that are unacceptable when considered pair-wise. Each main argument leads to conclusions that are by themselves logically unacceptable. For they either claim that given a set of opposites in which every intelligible element should participate – in various ways – *none* of these will in fact characterise the subject of inquiry, or that all of them do. To claim that a certain entity is neither the same as itself nor different from others, and then to claim that the entity in question is both the same and different from itself are equally unacceptable conclusions. This, by itself, is a strong objection to an interpretation like that of Cornford, which claims that Plato's main purpose is to exhibit a certain ambiguity whose understanding is necessary for the correct apprehension of the Forms.[2] One does not uncover an ambiguity by showing that using a term leads to two equally incoherent interpretations.

Clearly, one of the things Plato wants to show is that over and over again pairs of ways of talking about the subject are inconsistent. But it is equally clear that he regards each of the ways in which the subject is described as unsatisfactory.[3] The task of an adequate interpretation is to uncover the reasons for this. At the same time, the looseness of the surface structure leaves open the possibility that there are certain problems independent of the paradoxicality of the pairs and of the arguments considered individually that Plato wants to air.

What is, then, the subject of the arguments? My claim is that all of the arguments deal with the Form of unity, or 'the One'. Evidence for this claim is provided by the following. In the first half we are told that a real puzzle about Forms would unfold if someone were to show that the Forms partake of the main opposites (129C2–4). This is, of course, exactly what the second half illustrates. Again, in 135D–E we are told that what will follow will shed light on how we should talk about Forms. If none of the Forms serve as the subject matter of the arguments, it will be difficult to see how this promise is cashed in. But the main evidence is that in several passages the subject is characterised as the kind of entity of which things partake (e.g. 157C2, 158B2) and which, in turn, partakes of certain characters (e.g. 160E4). It is difficult to see what other hypothesis about the subject will account for these facts as well as the one favoured by this interpretation. A possible objection to this claim might be that the subject is characterised in places by physical properties. It will be shown later how this fact can be accounted for and not taken as evidence against the thesis that the arguments are about the Form of One.

The following is the outline of the interpretation proposed in this chapter. Plato wants to show that we cannot talk of Forms as entities by themselves, having nothing but 'their own nature'; i.e. that nature in virtue of which partaking of them helps to account

2 F. M. Cornford, op. cit.   3 For example at 142A6–8.

for attributions. But Plato wants to show also that we cannot talk of the Forms as one would of other, ordinary, objects of discourse; i.e. as entities characterised in various ways by one or the other of the pairs of the standard main opposites. And he *also* wants to show that it is incoherent to think of a Form both as an entity that is totally separated from all other abstract objects and as an object that is subject to the ways in which we usually describe an object of discourse. Furthermore, on either of those two ways of conceiving of Forms, participation ('relationships to the others') becomes problematic. Finally, Plato shows that these problems, far from being solved, become even worse if one sets out to give an intelligible account of the denial of the existence of the Forms. In the course of this demonstration Plato says also a number of interesting things about Not-being, relational concepts, and spatial as well as temporal units. Once we see what the upshot of the dialogue is with respect to the Forms, we can see also how the treatment of these other topics becomes relevant.

In view of the above, what conclusions did Plato come to with respect to the Forms? The only alternatives left for him are either to abandon the theory postulating these entities, or – on the basis of arguments that Plato might have found convincing – to insist on the necessity of these postulations, and construe the Forms as *sui generis* entities with participation as a *sui generis* relationship, linking particulars to Forms and Forms to each other. There is evidence that Plato took the latter road; thus laying the ground for the first time for what became known later as 'transcendental arguments'. *Parmenides* 135C and *Philebus* 15D show that Plato regards the existence of the Forms a necessary condition for significant '*logos*', i.e. propositions that yield knowledge and understanding.

Is this a defence of the theory of Forms? If so, it is achieved at a high price indeed. The precise nature of the theory of Forms in the middle period dialogues is not beyond controversy; but it is clear that as initially phrased the theory was supposed to have *explanatory power*.[4] Plato did not think that the intelligibility and truth of certain types of attributions should be explained by the postulation of an undefinable *sui generis* entity that is related in an undefinable *sui generis* way to the spatio-temporal particulars

---

4 For more argumentation see J. Moravcsik, 'Recollecting the Theory of Forms' in *Facets of Plato's Philosophy*, ed. W. H. Werkmeister (Assen 1976) (*Phronesis*, suppl. vol. II), 1–20.

whose nature we attempt to explain. Nor did he think that to account for *a priori* understanding we should posit a domain of *sui generis* entities related in a unique inexplicable way to the world of senses. But this is the position into which he is backed in the *Parmenides*. Thus the postulation of Forms remains, but explaining knowledge must be done by additional means. The additional structure shows the Forms interrelated, both positively and negatively. Hence the interest in Being and Not-being. It also shows the Forms as interlocking units, underlying adequate definitions. Hence the interest in the relational nature of the Forms, and the whole–part relation. Finally, on the basis of the postulation of Forms Plato erects – in the *Sophist* and the *Philebus* – a theory of how measurement and classification can yield knowledge; hence the interest in making the basic units of space and time more intelligible. The Forms are no longer solitary metaphysical atoms, and the world of space and time is no longer as chaotic as it is represented in the middle period dialogues. Tenseless being and tensed or temporal being are no longer as far apart as according to the earlier model.

The problems of attribution, of the unity of definitions, and of the analysis of spatial and temporal minimal units are still with us today. There are no final solutions to these problems, only partial illuminations. Plato provides some, and twentieth-century analytic philosophy provides some more. It is helpful to see the common problems, but in the attempt to relate Plato's thinking to contemporary thought we face two dangers. One of these is the fallacious move from the sound observation that Plato is illuminating some of the concepts that we worry about today to the false conclusion that his constructive work must proceed with the use of some of the tools of modern logical analysis. Or, in other words, the view that if his distinctions or tools do not coincide with ours, then he must have been 'confused'. Space, time, predication, definitions, and mathematical relations admit of a variety of analyses. It is neither a virtue nor a vice in Plato if his tools coincide partly with ours; the merits of his analyses do not depend on the extent of these coincidences.

Finally, why should such a dialogue be called '*Parmenides*'? The work of that philosopher showed that the one entity he posited was such that not much could be said about it by itself. It is reasonable to conjecture that Plato wanted to say the same thing about a plurality of entities, namely his Forms. Parmenides and his followers went on to construct on the basis of their conclusion a negative philosophy. Plato went on to construct a positive philosophy by exhibiting relationships between those entities that, taken by themselves, individually, reduce one to silence.

This general interpretation will be supported by a detailed examination of the arguments. This account – because of limitations of space – will leave out the fascinating treatment of temporal being and tenses in the *Parmenides*. Owen has done much to call attention to this topic; a full treatment deserves a separate work.


## II    *Being dispersed: the positive arguments*

The first argument (137C4–142A8) leads to the negative and unsatisfactory conclusion that the One cannot have any of the characters that are included in the basic set of opposites that – in different combinations – characterise anything taken normally to be intelligible. What key premises lead to this paradox?

At the start we are told that if the One is one, it cannot be many. Thus it cannot have parts or be a whole, since these characters require a subject that is, in some sense, a manifold. We must raise two questions: Why does Plato think that the Form of One must be unitary? Is the source of the problem a logical confusion? Since Plato does not defend explicitly his assumption, interpretations have to rely on indirect evidence. Owen, for example, suggested that the source of the problem is very likely a confusion between identity and predication.[5] There is, however, another way of looking at the matter. For in a further passage it is shown that the One cannot be 'other' or 'same' since it is not in the 'nature' of the One to be other or same; to be one is not identical with being same or other (139C4–D3). This suggests that the difficulty lies not in logic but in the metaphysical conception of the Forms. The Form of One must be unitary in some such way as to explain why participation in *this* Form – rather than in some other – will make the participant unitary. If there is nothing of unity in the nature of this Form, then how will participation or sharing in it explain the unitary nature of the alleged participants? In short, the puzzle affects the *explanatory* value of positing Forms, and it is only

5 G. E. L. Owen, op. cit., p. 349.

tangentially related to matters of logic. If the explanatory force of the hypothesis that there is a Form of One in which the unitary things partake requires that the One be in some sense 'unitary', then there is a problem of how to represent statements of the form: 'the One is one'. But merely recognising an ambiguity between identity and attribution − a recognition that Plato seems to reach in the *Sophist* − will not solve Plato's deep worry which I take to be about the explanatory force of postulating Forms and the participation relation.

It is advisable, then, to say that in the first argument the One is considered as a metaphysical atom; it is a Form that simply 'has its own nature', whatever the implications of this may be for logical representation. This conception is shown to be untenable by the various parts of this argument. For to be a subject of true attributions of items from the realm of opposites the entity must be, in some way, a manifold. If it has no 'parts' in any sense, then it lacks the conditions for intelligibility.

Is this a problem unique to the Form of the One, as Schofield seems to suggest?[6] Passages like *Symposium* 211B1 show that Plato in the middle period thought of each of the Forms as simple in nature. This unitary nature of the Forms was supposed to contrast with the 'many-ness' of the particulars. Once we show each of the Forms to be a manifold, this takes away one of the marks that separated reality from appearance in the middle period. Of course, it also opens up the possibility for the constructive work on definitions and measurement that Plato does in the later dialogues.

In the subsequent sections Plato argues that the One, being without parts, cannot be anywhere. For it is without limits, has no shape, and cannot be in something, i.e. contained; nor can it be contained simply by itself. The details of this argumentation carry several implications for how we should talk about points and their relationship to minimal spatial units. But one might ask whether the general conclusion, i.e. that the One has no spatial location, should bother the Platonist? Should one not think of the Forms as being outside of space and time? These questions suggest the Platonism of the twentieth century; for example the Platonism of G. E. Moore. But as the first half of the *Parmenides* shows, Plato was much less firmly convinced that freeing the Forms from any

6 Malcolm Schofield, op. cit., p. 146.

spatial characterisation would preserve the explanatory nature of the Forms as entities to be participated in.

It is also shown that the One cannot be in 'motion' for to be in motion or change implies not being strictly unitary. This same austere unitary nature also makes it impossible for the One to be at rest. (These conclusions foreshadow the *Sophist* in which the partaking of Rest is analysed as an aspect of the manifold nature of each of the Forms.) It is worth emphasising that this conclusion, reached at 139B3, is surely unsatisfactory for any Greek philosopher. There is nothing that any Greek philosopher would allow as a real entity – except maybe some of the Eleatics – if it is neither at rest nor at motion. The next point, that the One is neither same nor different is equally unsatisfactory for Plato or any other philosopher. This too is derived from the strictly unitary nature of the subject, and the observation that to be one is not identical with being same. (Even though, as the *Sophist* would show, everything must be both one and be the same as itself. Hence the second half of the *Parmenides* lays the ground for the conception of the Forms in the *Sophist* as what we would call today 'intensional' entities.)

The further conclusion, that the One is neither like nor unlike, is not derived simply from the original premise about the unitary nature of the One. Rather, it is derived by the argument that if something has likeness or unlikeness, then it must have sameness and difference. Since the One was just shown to lack these characteristics, it cannot have likeness or unlikeness either. This argument too bears on the *Sophist*. For if one accepts it, then it shows likeness and unlikeness to be 'derivative' basic opposites; i.e. a pair that depends on the other pair of sameness and difference. This would then explain why likeness and unlikeness are not included among the '*megista genē*' of the *Sophist*.

Similar considerations apply to the argument showing that the One cannot be equal or unequal. This too is derived from its lacking sameness and difference, and hence this pair too can be seen as a 'derivative' pair in Plato's scheme.

The argument ends with showing that an object denuded of all of these characteristics cannot be the object of knowledge or perception. The general lesson is clear: objects of '*logos*' and understanding, and instances of being, need to be manifolds in some way.

The second argument (142B1–155E3) is the longest one. Its main conclusion is as unsatisfactory as the conclusion of the first argument, but in a different way. While the first argument shows the One as lacking all of the pair-wise arranged opposites, the second shows the One as having all of these characteristics, thus having as its properties an incoherent set.

The argument starts out by pointing out that the One cannot *be* unless it partakes of Being, and its partaking of Being is not the same as its being one. Since statements of the form: 'The *F* is' are among the simplest assertions as long as the subject is an abstract entity, the first part of the second 'hypothesis' shows that the subject of even the simplest *a priori* assertions must be, in some sense, a manifold.

At 143C3 'the One is' is distinguished from 'the One is one'. Thus Being is seen as distinct from identity. But it does not follow that in 'the One is' we have a purely existential 'is'. The modern reader has to keep in mind the fact that Plato is not dealing with problems of being in the formal mode. On the formal plane the claim that '*x* is *F*' does not carry existential import, and hence that existence and the copula are two entirely distinct notions makes sense. On the material plane it does not. If something is attributively related to something else, then both relata must exist. Furthermore, on the material level, one cannot have one type of being without the other. If something is, then it is also related to some property. Even if this was not clear to Plato in the middle period, this seems to be one of the lessons of the *Parmenides*. Getting clear about the need to see '*logos*' as having its own unity, and to see each of the Forms as a certain type of manifold, does not require cutting up being into identity, predication, and existence. (All of this, of course, assumes that Plato is dealing with a Form in this argument.) In 143A4–5 we are told that the One partakes of Being, and in the rest of the argument it is assumed that other things partake of the One.

Following this we are shown that the One must have its being and its oneness as its parts and is a whole made out of these. Since each of the parts has its being and unity, the One is seen as having an unlimited number of parts, and, in view of the distinctness of the parts, it has also difference.

At this stage of the argument Plato shows that this conception of the One brings with it the Form of Number. This argument can read in different ways. Commentators have usually assumed that Plato wants to generate, somehow, the series of positive integers. But there is also another way of looking at the matter.

Plato asks us to consider the elements whose existence was proved to be necessary if the One is to be. These are: The One, Being, and Difference. We can take these individually and in pairs. Pairs are instances of 2, and a pair as such an instance of 1; these together come to 3. Thus we have examples of odd and even number, and with the introduction of multiplication we have two times, and three times. Thus we have 1,2,3, and the properties of odd and even as well as the operations of addition and multiplication.

Cornford's discussion[7] shows the dilemma one encounters when trying to interpret the passage as designed to generate the series of positive integers. If we allow only 2,3, and multiplication, then we cannot get the prime numbers. If we admit also addition, as Cornford does, then the whole section on multiplication becomes superfluous.

As *Phaedo* 101B–C shows, Plato does not think that numbers are to be generated. The series of positive integers is given as a pre-existing abstract realm. There is nothing in Plato's ontology that corresponds to mathematical operations; the ontology reflects only mathematical truths. (This is perhaps the key difference between Plato's and Aristotle's views on mathematics.) Plato's orientation is truly 'foundational' as one might say today. Thus it is more fruitful to look at this passage from that point of view. Plato's task is presumably not to generate any series, but to ask what the basic concepts are whose interrelations underlie truths involving positive integers. This approach does yield an adequate interpretation. We can analyse any mathematical truths into a combination of odd and even numbers, multiplication, addition and their negatives, and the notions of unit, couple, and trio. (Plato might add the number 3 as basic if 1 is not acknowledged as a number.) The conception of the One as we have it at this stage of the argument yields the instantiations of those concepts (Forms) that are basic to the foundation of mathematics; i.e. these are the elements into which mathematical concepts and truths can be analysed.

7 F. M. Cornford, op. cit., p. 141.

This conception of the One as a manifold brings out some of the problems of participation. We are told at 144D2–5 that the One must be distributed over its participants and be a whole at the same time. *Philebus* 15B–C will raise the same issue, providing no more of an answer than our dialogue. Apparently Plato ended up thinking that this is just one aspect of a *sui generis* relationship that admits no analysis.

Plato operates in this section with the ordinary common sense conception of whole and part. Given this conception, if the One is a whole, it must have also spatial characteristics. It has a beginning, middle, end (145A–B), and it must be – if it is this kind of a whole – both self-contained and contained in something else. The suspicious premise in this piece of reasoning comes at 145E1, 'if it is nowhere, it would be nothing'. But if we reject this premise, then we should be able to give a theory of the modes of being of abstract as well as concrete entities. There is no evidence that Plato had such a theory, or that he even had the tools necessary for the construction of such a theory. The passages under consideration show that he might have come to see the need for such a theory.

The following argument, in which it is shown that the One must be both in motion and in rest, cries out for the clarification of 'motion' and 'rest'. Similar considerations apply to 'same' and 'different'. How can an entity partake of both opposites and still be a Form, not a concrete entity? The problem of the relationality of many of the Forms is not the same as the modern problem of distinguishing properties from relations. For Plato such properties as strength, health, or goodness are relational; i.e. they need to be applied in different contexts, with different criteria of application, and yet with the same core meaning. Working out the logic of this is one of the challenges of the later dialogues.

The conclusions that are yielded by these questionable arguments must have been unacceptable to Plato; for they state that the One must be the same as itself and not the same as itself, different from others and not different from others (146A9–B2).[8] The fact that the argumentation is backed by claims such as the one that every two things must be identical or distinct, or stand in

---

8 F. M. Cornford, op. cit., p. 157 (in a note), relates 146A–B to *Philebus* 24 and to the notion '*apeiron*' that occurs there. But that is a notion applied to determinables that lend themselves to measurement. There is no connection between the 'others' here and that aspect of the ontology of the *Philebus*.

the part–whole relation, supports the interpretation that Plato is exploring the possibility of treating the One in terms that one would treat, in general, any subject of ordinary true assertions. Non-self-identity is deduced from the One being contained in something else. Does this show that the problem disappears if the Forms are construed both as objects of participation and at the same time as without spatial characteristics?

The difficulties of treating notions like Same and Different as traditional opposites (146D5 ff.) spawns further problems. Can one maintain – as Plato does in 147D–E – that a term like 'different' will not change its meaning with each application, even though it will be part of very diverse complexes that contribute to the truth conditions of different assertions? This worry occupies Plato both in the *Parmenides* and in the *Sophist*; he never states explicitly what conclusions he came to. The puzzles about these applications of 'different' underlie also the puzzle about the 'derivative' opposites of like and unlike.

The discussion of the concepts of contact, element, exterior, etc., is of independent interest to Plato. Getting clear about these helps to see the world of sensibles as less of a complete chaos. It also shows in a clearer way how geometry can be applied to the empirically given world.

One can sum up the discussions of Same–Different, Like–Unlike, and Greater–Lesser, as centring on a certain view of the basic opposites. This view can be summed up as the following two claims. (i) One can view these basic opposites as one would view heat and cold; i.e. without any regard of the different completions that form predicates out of these. (ii) Each of these pairs must apply to everything; there can be no neutral ground, and no category-theory according to which some might apply to certain entities. It is beyond the scope of this chapter to see to what extent this view of the opposites is revised in the *Sophist* and the *Philebus*.

We see, then, that the final unsatisfactory conclusion is the result of the attempt to treat the One like a subject of assertions about ordinary objects. An ordinary object would have, at a certain time, one or the other of each pair of opposites; or both but with different relata. Plato is showing both that the One cannot be treated this way, and that treating it this way is in any case inconsistent with an insistence on its being 'just what it is', i.e.

having simply its nature that explains participation. What things participate in, must, in turn participate itself in Forms. We see this from these two arguments. But we also see that the nature of the Forms must remain – if necessary – *sui generis*. What about the nature of participation? This is the question addressed by the next two arguments.[9]

The third argument (157B6–159B1) traces the consequences, for 'the others', of the hypothesis that the One is. Both 157C2 and 158A3–5 describe 'the others' as partaking of the One. Thus it is reasonable to interpret 'the others' as designating all else in reality except the One. The fact that we can give adequate characterisations of both the One and the others is itself support for construing the One as the Form of unity.

It is shown that the others make up a whole, have parts, and make up an unlimited collection. The argument in 158C–D, showing how unity is imposed on what is otherwise something indefinite, seems to point towards the discussions of articulateness in the *Philebus*; with '*apeiron*' having the same role of designating the indefinite.[10]

In deriving the conclusion that the others will have all of the opposites, use is made again of the treatment of opposites such as like and unlike as satisfying the two (false) conditions mentioned above. The claim at 159A6–9 that we need not go through the rest, since we can see from what has been shown that all other attributions will follow, can be justified by the second argument. We saw there, that once one shows that the basic opposites and the pair of likeness and unlikeness applies to an entity, the rest will follow as well. Thus Plato's lack of interest in spelling all of this out in the third argument is not a matter of his becoming bored or tired, or treating this as an exercise, but a matter of his expecting the reader to have followed the logic of the second argument. This argument shows, then, that the conception of the others *sharing* in the One along the analogy of the normal part–whole relation will not do. Of course, having a Form in which things can participate entails that the Form in question must be a manifold – a conclusion not found in any of the middle period dialogues. The fourth

9 G. E. L. Owen, op. cit., pp. 354–5, says that the 'fallacies' involve relationals. Here I try to spell this out in more detail.
10 For more detail see J. Moravcsik, 'Forms, nature, and the good in the *Philebus*', *Phronesis*, 24 (1979), 81–104.

argument shows that if we construe the One as 'just what it is', i.e. having the nature of being what to be one is, then participation of any sort will be impossible.

The argument (159B2–160B4) starts out by stating that if the One is simply 'one', then there can be no partaking of it. But without such participation the others cannot be many, have parts, etc., in short they cannot have any characters at all. Thus this argument shows that partaking of unity in some way is a precondition for an entity to have any characters at all, and hence for the entity to be intelligible. This is, then, a part of the reasoning that leaves the Forms for Plato in the later dialogues as 'transcendental postulates'. It also shows that the status of the others on the hypothesis that the One is 'just one' becomes impossible. Furthermore, since the third and fourth arguments lead to contradiction, Plato shows that the notion of the One as purely unitary and as having the others share in it as parts is an inconsistent conception.

But if the Form is not simply unitary in its nature, and if the participants are not parts in some sense, how can we explain participation? Provided that one is convinced of the need to posit such a relation, it will have to be construed as unique and undefinable. Thus the problem is once more not the general issue of predication, but the explanatory power of the theory of Forms and participation.[11]


III    *Not-Being and the Problems of Negative Dialectic*

In the last four arguments we are to consider the hypothesis that 'the One is not'. Again, in view of what was said above, it would be a mistake to construe this as a purely negative existential, or as a strictly negative predicative statement-schema. Given that Plato saw existence and attribution as two aspects of the same thing, the best way to construe the thesis is to say that on this view the One has no being. The fact that these arguments are shorter than the first quartet does not indicate that they are less important, or that

---

11 Malcolm Schofield, op. cit., p. 154, writes that the problem involves predication and the perhaps unavoidable spatial connotations. But it seems to me that the key problem is not the modern notion of predication but Plato's metaphysical notion of participation and the difficulties that one encounters when one attempts to explain or define this notion.

they do not contain some of Plato's own views. As we saw, the arguments follow a certain pattern; if one proves that the One has, or lacks, opposites *A, B,* and *C,* then one can prove that the One has, or lacks, the rest.

The fifth argument (160B5–163B6) starts with the consideration of the proposition that the One is not. Rather than asking first what this means, it adds the remark that the proposition is intelligible, and then explores what this must entail. One might take the problem at hand to be the general problem of negative existentials. But there is little evidence that Plato had such purely logical, or semantic, interests. His examples do not include such statements as 'Pegasus does not exist.' It is not clear what he would have said about that; he could have said that a statement of this sort is about mental images. His concern is with *a priori* statements which he takes to be statements about the Forms. Analysing negative existentials with an abstract entity as the subject takes on special problems of its own. For, in the case of concepts, intelligibility implies existence. How can we ascribe to a concept, or property, that we understand, non-existence? One might say that Pegasus was not a horse but a figment of someone's imagination; but how can one say that a property that we can make intelligible does not exist? We might say that it has no instances; this would not prove for Plato that it does not exist. So what Plato deals with in this argument are not general conditions of assertability or intelligibility, but conditions applying especially to propositions in which the subject is an abstract entity. If the subject in such statements is intelligible, it must be distinct from all else, and have separateness, or 'this'-ness. In 160E7–161A2 we find a curious argument to the effect that even if the One is not, nothing prevents it from having certain characteristics. This concession is taken back subsequently; it seems that it is introduced here solely in order to carry on the argumentation. This passage cannot be taken as a sign of Plato's separating existence from predication. He seems to be saying, rather, that our argument forces us to ascribe to the One its 'being something' even if we started out denying of it being simpliciter.

The intelligibility conditions on abstract entities are used to argue further that the One, even under these conditions, is unlike others and like itself. Plato deems it so important to spell out these conditions that he departs from the general surface format, and does not ascribe both pairs of the opposites in the same respect, hence leaving these conclusions less paradoxical than their counterparts in the previous arguments. The argument then proceeds by ascribing the usual pairs of opposites to the non-existent but intelligible One, relying on the same unsatisfactory conception of opposites that we sketched above. In 161E3–4 Plato finally takes back his previous concession, and insists that the One, if it has these characters, must somehow *be* as well.

The upshot of this argument seems to be that any intelligible denial of the existence of a property like unity leads to difficulties. It 'will not stand up', so to say. As soon as the denial becomes intelligible, the objects slip back into being. As was said above, this is not a problem analogous to the one about Meinong's golden mountain; it is, rather, restricted to the problem of making the non-existence of abstract objects such as properties intelligible. The fact that some of these positive conclusions remain paradoxical shows that Plato is still emphasising the problems of spelling out the mode of being for the Forms.

In the sixth argument (163B7–164B4) the hypothesis in question is reconsidered by fixing an interpretation for the meaning of the phrase 'is not'. The phrase is taken to signify total lack of being. Given this interpretation, the proposition that the One is not fails to provide the subject with grounds for its being the manifold that the subject of a '*logos*' must be.

Thus here again, as before in some of the arguments, a key problem is the unity of '*logos*'. The subject must be a manifold, the predicate too must be a manifold. Neither manifold can be construed on the part–whole model, and the '*logos*' itself, though a unity, cannot be a sum of parts. As the passages quoted from the *Philebus* and the *Parmenides* suggest, Plato is driven to the view that the unity of '*logos*' is *sui generis*. The worry is not that of Frege; i.e. it is not about the unity of sentences in general. Plato would not be bothered if someone were to show that sentences about spatio-temporal particulars are mere juxtapositions of elements. He never said about those that they are, in some way, '*monoeides*'. The problem is that of propositions involving only Forms; where both subject and predicate are supposed to have a special metaphysical monolithicity, and are yet related in a higher unit, a proposition which by itself must be more than the mere sum of parts.

This line of interpretation provides a natural link between Plato and Aristotle. It shows Plato worried in the later dialogues about the unity of '*logos*' where this involves the Forms; Aristotle, one might say, brings the problem down to earth. He worries about the problem of the unity of definitional '*logoi*', but construes these as not being about Forms, but about species. Neither Plato nor Aristotle wants a definition to be a mere conjunction of characters. Plato seems to retreat to transcendental postulations; Aristotle tries to solve the problem by introducing the dichotomies of form vs. matter, actuality vs. potentiality.

Since the One is not in any way, it can have no characters. Thus the usual negative and unsatisfactory conclusions are reached rather quickly. Thus the One which is not, on this conception cannot be the object of perception or knowledge or 'logos'. This conclusion is clearly unacceptable.

Thus the fifth and sixth arguments together lead us to the conclusion that it makes no sense to describe the One as not being, in the only clear sense of 'is not'. The positive arguments showed that there are difficulties in characterising the nature of Forms. But the negative arguments show that the difficulties are even greater if one attempted to abandon the theory. Given the peculiar nature of the Forms, their denial cannot be given any clear sense. Aristotle must have drawn this conclusion as well. For he does not claim that there are no such things as Forms; rather, he claims that Plato misinterpreted their nature, and that they should be reconstructed as Aristotelian forms. The conclusion that one cannot talk of the simple non-existence of Formlike entities is also accepted in the dialectic of Not-being of the *Sophist*.[12]

The last two arguments deal with the consequences of our negative hypothesis for 'the others'. The seventh argument (164B5–165E1) has as its peculiarity that its conclusions are couched in terms of the language of appearances. This is hardly accidental. Plato does not think that if the One is not, then anything else could exist and partake of various characteristics. He thus introduces – in a way reminiscent of the poem of Parmenides – the 'way of seeming'. The ordinary mortal has opinions according to which the others, even without participation in the One, will appear as indeterminate multitudes. These apparent

12 For more argument see J. Moravcsik, 'Being and Meaning in the *Sophist*', *Acta Philosophica Fennica*, 14 (1962), 23–78 (reprinted separately by Bobbs Merrill).

multitudes are not logical collections of sums that we collect under 'mass-terms'. For those have equality and unequality, as well as unity (in the sense that persistence criteria apply to them). Rather, these are as much as Plato thinks one can reconstruct of the mere opinions of mortals who do not comprehend the need for the articulation of everything as having unity and being a manifold.

The last argument (165E2–166B7) shows that even this talk of semblances lacks any rational foundations. If the One is not, then the others – meaning everything – cannot have or appear to have any of those characteristics that, arranged in pairs of opposites, inform whatever has any credential for being part of reality. Thus the being of the One is shown to be a necessary condition for the being of all else. Plato could have carried out this exercise with any of those Forms in which everything, necessarily, participates. The conclusion at 166C1, 'if the One is not, nothing is', can be read as merely the conclusion of the eighth argument. But it is joined by the next line with the general conclusion; thus one can read the final conclusion of the dialogue to be the conjunction made up of this negative statement and the general summary given at 166C3–5.

What should we say, then, about the second half of the *Parmenides*? Ryle suggested[13] that perhaps Plato thought of the Form of unity that one cannot say of it either that it is or that it is not. It seems to me, however, that there is an asymmetry between the positive and negative arguments. The positive ones point out that certain, initially plausible, ways of describing the Forms will not do. The negative ones show that without the Forms nothing exists, and that the very claim that the Forms do not exist seems to be inarticulable.

The puzzles of the first four arguments leave open the possibility of construing the Forms and participation as *sui generis* entities and relations respectively; philosophical constructs whose nature does not admit of definition or explanation but without which the orderliness of nature and the possibility of understanding cannot be accounted for. In the meantime, reflections on the manifold nature of the Forms and further reflections on unity help us to see how to ascribe more orderliness to the world of space and time;

13  Gilbert Ryle, op. cit., p. 131.

spatial units and magnitudes, as well as temporal descriptions, are shown to be less mysterious, and insofar as they are still fraught with difficulties, these difficulties are not unrelated to the ones we encounter when explicating the nature of the Forms.

No doubt, some of the difficulties are meliorated by Plato's further work on relationality and the nature of the vowel Forms in the *Sophist*. But not all of the problems can be removed that way. Above all, Plato needs to say more about how the Forms, now unique, undefinable entities, relate to each other and thus provide the foundations for definitions of various kinds as well as measurement.

The arguments of the second half of the *Parmenides* raise a number of serious conceptual puzzles. The nature of abstract entities, different types of attributions, and negative *a priori* existentials are problems that haunt philosophy up to this day. While paying attention to these fascinating details I wanted to emphasise also the larger concern with the Theory of Forms that motivated Plato in writing this dialogue. To use Isaiah Berlin's felicitous metaphor, in this dialogue the hedgehog and the fox lie side by side. I hope to have shown that the results are far from being grotesque.

# 8 Aristotle and the more accurate arguments

GAIL FINE

In *Metaphysics* I 9 Aristotle mentions several Platonic arguments for forms. These were set out in detail, along with Aristotle's criticisms, in his essay *Peri Ideōn*, portions of which are preserved in Alexander's commentary on I 9.[1] In this chapter I explore the logic of some of these arguments and the interconnections between them.

Aristotle divides the arguments he discusses into two classes, the less and the more accurate arguments; but he says very little about the basis of this division. I shall suggest that the more, but not the less, accurate arguments are valid arguments for Platonic forms; and I shall claim that although Aristotle is no friend of the forms, he concedes to the Platonists that they are valid arguments for forms. But the concession is coy. For, Aristotle argues, these arguments lead to intolerable results and so cannot be sound. One leads to a vicious infinite regress, the third man, and the other produces forms of relatives, 'of which we say there is no independent class' (*Metaph.* 990b16–17).[2] From this point of view, the less accurate arguments are to be preferred. For although they are invalid arguments for forms, they are valid and, so Aristotle seems to believe, sound arguments for his own universals, the *koina*.[3]

If this interpretation is correct, it suggests an interesting result: that the overall structure of the *Peri Ideōn* is neatly dilemmatic. The

---

1 I use M. Hayduck's text of Alexander's *in Aristotelis Metaphysica Commentaria*, in volume I of *Commentaria in Aristotelem Graeca* (Berlin 1891). The relevant portions of Alexander may also be found in W. D. Ross, *Aristotelis Fragmenta Selecta* (Oxford 1955). A new edition of the *Peri Ideōn*, by D. Harlfinger, appears in W. Leszl, *Il 'De Ideis' Di Aristotele e la Teoria Platonica Delle Idee* (Florence 1975), 22–39.

2 Aristotle says, not that there are two more accurate arguments, but that there are two sorts of more accurate arguments, leaving open the possibility that there is more than one argument of each sort. Alexander records only one argument of each sort, however, and I shall for convenience speak as though there are only two more accurate arguments.

3 This is stated explicitly for the arguments from the sciences and for the one over many. The best manuscripts of Alexander claim that the object of thought fails to prove that there are ideas, but do not also make the further point that they prove that there are *koina*. This further

Platonists can rely on two sorts of arguments for forms, their more and their less accurate arguments. If they rely on their less accurate arguments, they produce invalid arguments for forms. But, Aristotle suggests, there is a compensating advantage; for such arguments can easily be converted into sound arguments for Aristotelian *koina*. If, on the other hand, they rely on their more accurate arguments, they produce valid arguments for forms. But there is an attendant disadvantage; for these more accurate arguments lead to intolerable results and so cannot be sound. The moral seems clear: any tolerable theory of universals must be an Aristotelian, not a Platonic, one.

I do not have the space to consider how Plato might respond to this dilemma, or to ask whether the arguments Aristotle records are to be found in the dialogues. Interesting and important though these issues are, we shall have enough to occupy our attention within the confines of the *Peri Ideōn*. A necessary preliminary to assessing its worth as an anti-Platonic polemic is to understand the arguments it contains; and I shall be content if I achieve that.

## I

In the *Metaphysics* Aristotle says that:

Of the ways in which we prove that there are forms, none is convincing; for from some it is not necessary for a syllogism to result, and from some there are also forms of things of which we do not think there are forms. For according to the arguments from the sciences, there will be forms of all the things of which there are sciences, and according to the one over many argument there will be forms even of negations, and according to the argument that we think of something when it has perished there will be forms of things that have perished; for there is an image of these. Further, of the more accurate arguments, some produce ideas of relatives, of which we say there is no independent class, and others introduce the third man (990b9–17).

Aristotle faults all of the Platonists' arguments for forms – but he thinks different arguments fail for different reasons. And although they all fail, some are at least 'more accurate' than others. What are the different reasons for failure? And how are the more and the less accurate arguments distinguished?

Aristotle says that all the less accurate arguments are invalid

point is made in LF. Whether or not the claim is warranted is a difficult and interesting issue that I cannot pursue here. Even if it is not warranted, however, the crucial point is that the less accurate arguments are invalid arguments for forms, whereas the more accurate arguments are valid arguments for forms.

arguments for forms ('it is not necessary for a syllogism to result'), and that some of them also produce forms in undesirable cases.[4] We learn here why the less accurate arguments fail; and perhaps we can infer what is distinctive of the more accurate arguments. To be sure, the more accurate arguments also produce forms in undesirable cases. But Aristotle never says, as he does of the less accurate arguments, that they are invalid arguments for forms. Perhaps the more accurate arguments, then, are valid arguments for forms.

So Alexander probably believes. In commenting on one of the more accurate arguments, the argument from relatives (AR), he remarks that it

seems more carefully and more accurately and more directly to aim at the proof of ideas. For this argument does not, like the ones before it, seem to prove simply that the common thing is something besides the particulars, but rather that the paradigm is something which is related to things here and is completely. For this most of all is thought to be characteristic of ideas (83.18–22).

Here Alexander seems to suggest that the more accurate arguments are valid arguments for forms. AR is said to be more accurate because it aims to prove that there are paradigms that are completely – and these features are distinctive of Platonic forms: 'The idea's being an idea depends on its being a paradigm' (85.15). To be sure, Alexander is cautious, saying only that AR *seems* to prove that there are perfect paradigms. But we shall see that there is no need for caution; for AR is a valid, if unsound, argument for this conclusion. Further, although neither Aristotle nor Alexander explicitly records the fact, the other more accurate argument in the *Peri Ideōn*, the argument introducing the third man, is also a valid argument for forms.[5] Should we not conclude that Alexander is

4 I take the force of the *kai* at b11 to be: some arguments are not only invalid, but also produce forms in undesirable cases. (Of course, if they are invalid, they do not really produce any forms. Aristotle speaks elliptically; the point he means to make, as the *Peri Ideōn* makes clear, is that if we waive the objection to invalidity, and allow (what is not the case) that these arguments are valid, all is not plain sailing; for the arguments would in any case produce forms in undesirable cases.) A second reading – incorporated in Ross's translation – takes the *kai* to indicate that some arguments produce forms even in undesirable cases (sc. as well as in desirable cases) – with no implication that these arguments are invalid. This second reading does not undermine my general view. For the *Peri Ideōn* shows that Aristotle takes these arguments to be invalid, even if he does not repeat the point explicitly here.

5 H. Jackson, 'Plato's Later Theory of Ideas', *Journal of Philology*, 10 (1882), 255 n. 1, argues that the second more accurate argument is not an argument that leads to the TMA, but the TMA itself. He is followed by Ross; see his commentary on Aristotle's *Metaphysics* (Oxford 1924), I 194, note *ad loc*. Ross in part bases his agreement on the belief that *legousi* must mean 'mention' rather than, as Alexander takes it (83.34; 85.7–8), 'involve'. This view is well criticised by H. F. Cherniss, *Aristotle's Criticism of Plato and the Academy*, I (Baltimore 1944),

correct, and that the more, but not the less, accurate arguments are valid arguments for forms?

Such is the natural inference, and the one I shall defend here. But it has been resisted. Cherniss, for example, notes correctly that in the *Metaphysics* Aristotle calls two arguments 'more accurate'.[6] But, he argues, the second more accurate argument, the one implying the third man, 'is simply the *hen epi pollōn*' – yet Aristotle explicitly says that the one over many shows only that there are *koina*, Aristotelian universals, and not that there are Platonic forms. Hence the suggested explanation of 'more accurate' is inapplicable to the second of the more accurate arguments. Cherniss suggests that it may be inapplicable to AR as well. For here, as we have seen, it is suggested that forms are paradigms. Yet the arguments from the sciences also called forms paradigms (79.7) – but the arguments from the sciences are not accurate; they prove only that there are *koina*. The suggested interpretation of '*akribesteroi*' cannot then be Aristotle's own; Alexander must have 'invented it in the absence of an explanation of the term in his source'. Cherniss suggests instead, taking up a suggestion of Ross, that the '*akribesteroi tōn logōn* seem to be the "more precise" in the sense of the more "abstractly logical"'.

While it cannot be proved that the explanation Alexander provides is Aristotle's own, it can, I think, be shown that Cherniss's reasons for denying that it is Aristotle's are untenable. First, while it is true that the arguments from the sciences, like AR, call ideas paradigms, they are not *valid* arguments for paradigmatism, as AR is. Moreover, AR proves something about the nature of these paradigms, that they are completely in contrast to deficient sensibles. This further claim is neither mentioned in nor implied by the arguments from the sciences; in AR it is to the fore. These facts distinguish AR from the arguments from the sciences, and make it, but not the latter, 'more accurate'.

276 n. 184. Alexander records four arguments that introduce a third man; but only the fourth of these (which I discuss below) is ascribed to Aristotle in the *Peri Ideōn*. The second and third are irrelevant here. The first, however, bears obvious affinities to the Aristotelian and Platonic versions; Alexander ascribes it to Eudemus. I mention this version briefly below (see n. 18), but cannot discuss it in detail here.

6 For Cherniss's account, see pp. 275 f. All quotations in the rest of this paragraph are from these two pages. For Ross's view, see his commentary, volume II, p. 424, note on 1080a10; cf. also volume I, p. 194, note on 990b15. Leszl, pp. 183 f., also accepts this account. L. Robin, *La Théorie Platonicienne* (Paris 1908), 19 n. 16, on the other hand, accepts Alexander's interpretation. But he does not explain or justify his acceptance, and it leads him into difficulties he does not notice; see n. 7, below.

Moreover, while Cherniss is right to say that the one over many argument (OMA) is not accurate in the suggested sense, he is wrong to say that the second more accurate argument is the OMA.[7] Rather, it is a distinct, if related, argument, that I shall call accurate-OMA. Accurate-OMA is distinct from the OMA because, among other things, it, but not OMA, is vulnerable to the third man argument (TMA). Moreover, accurate-OMA, but not OMA, is accurate in the suggested sense. That is to say, it is a valid argument for a distinctively Platonic position.

I consider OMA in section II. In section III I examine accurate-OMA. I show how it fits our interpretation of 'more accurate', as OMA does not. In IV I show that accurate-OMA, but not OMA, is vulnerable to the third man regress. In V I briefly consider AR, and show how it is an accurate argument. In VI I argue that AR, unlike accurate-OMA, is not vulnerable to the third man regress.

## II

I have examined the OMA in detail elsewhere;[8] here I only briefly mention those points relevant to our present concerns.

The OMA consists of three initial premises:

(1) Whenever a group of particulars (*kath' hekasta*) are *F*, some one thing, the *F*, is predicated of them.

(2) The *F* is not the same as any of the *F* particulars of which it is predicated.

(3) The *F* is always predicated in the same way of the *F* particulars.

(1)–(3) are taken to license two intermediate conclusions:

(4) The *F* is separate from the *F* particulars of which it is predicated.

(5) The *F* is eternal.

But:

---

7 Here is where Robin runs into difficulties. He accepts Alexander's interpretation of '*akribesteroi*'; but he also agrees with Cherniss that the second more accurate argument is OMA (p. 21). But as Cherniss correctly notes, OMA is not accurate in Alexander's sense. If one agrees with Alexander's interpretation, one cannot with consistency agree with Cherniss that the second more accurate argument is OMA – as Cherniss sees. His solution, however, is to reject Alexander's interpretation; I take another course, and do not identify the second more accurate argument with OMA.

8 'The One Over Many', *Philosophical Review*, 89 (1980), 197–240. I there provide a translation of the argument.

(6) Whatever is a one over many, separate, and eternal is a form.

Therefore – the general conclusion of the argument – :

(7) The *F* is a form.

For our purposes here, the key steps of the argument are (1), (2), (4), and (7). (1) asserts that whenever a group of particulars are *F,* some one thing, the *F,* is predicated of them. As the context reveals, '*kath' hekasta*' is to be understood here as 'sensible particulars'.[9] Hence (1) licenses predications only for groups consisting of sensible particulars – for groups consisting of sensible large things, or of particular men, such as Callias and Socrates, and so on. The importance of this will become clear later, when we turn to accurate-OMA and the TMA.

(2) asserts that what is predicated of particulars is different from any of the particulars of which it is predicated.[10] (3) asserts that the *F* is always predicated in just the same way, despite the plurality and variability of what it is predicated of; particular men come and go, but this does not affect the continued univocal predication of man. This supports (2); and it also helps to show that what is predicated is eternal or everlasting (*aidion*).

(1)–(3) are taken to prove, via the intermediate steps (4)–(6), that whatever is predicated of a group of like sensible particulars is a form – that is, is a one over many, separate, and eternal. Aristotle objects that it proves no such thing: 'But neither does this argument prove that there are ideas, although it too tends to show that what is predicated in common is other than the particulars of which it is predicated' (81.7–10).

Aristotle's remark is directed against (4), the claim that what is predicated of sensibles is separate from (i.e. exists independently

---

9 Aristotle frequently uses '*kath' hekasta*' to refer to determinate kinds or species, which are 'particular' in contrast to their genera; but the phrase also frequently refers to individuals. In the *Peri Ideōn*, Aristotle seems to use '*kath' hekasta*' only for groups of particulars; and the groups he has in mind consist solely of sensible particulars – particulars such as forms or the prime mover do not, here, count as *kath' hekasta*. This is clear in the arguments from the sciences, where *kath' hekasta* are said to be *apeira te kai ahorista* (79.10) and *aisthēta* (79.17); cf. also the contrast between this health and health *haplōs* (79.24–80.1), with which cf. *Metaph.* 981a5–12 and *Rhet.* 1356b28–35. Similarly, in the OMA, *kath' hekasta* are contrasted with things that are *aidion* (80.13); cf. 80.21, *aei menei*. The object of thought is about *kath' hekasta* that are perishable (82.1–2). When Aristotle is concerned with groups including things other than sensible particulars, he uses '*pleiō*' instead; see below, section III and n. 13. Cf. n. 23.

10 It is crucial to note that (2) – the claim that what is predicated of sensible particulars is different from, non-identical to, any of the particulars of which it is predicated – is not the non-identity assumption (NI) of the TMA: for a definition of (NI), see section IV. (NI) entails (2), but not conversely; see further below, section IV.

of) them. Like paradigmatism, separation is a key feature of forms, and one Aristotle repeatedly attacks; his own *koina*, though different from particulars, are not separated from them.[11]

Aristotle allows that (1)–(3) entail (4a):

(4a) The *F* is different from any of the *F* particulars of which it is predicated.

But (4a) falls short of the claim of separation, the claim needed if we are to prove that there are forms, not merely *koina*. And it is clear that (1)–(3) do not entail (4). (2) says that what is predicated is different from the particulars of which it is predicated; but this does not entail that it exists independently of them. (3) justifies the claim that what is predicated is independent of any *single* particular of which it is predicated; it does not follow, what (4) requires, that what is predicated is independent of sensibles as such, that it could exist whether or not any sensibles did.

(1)–(3) do, however, as Aristotle suggests, entail (4a). They entail this for the simple reason that (4a) simply restates (2). If (4a) (=(2)) is a premise of the argument, it is obviously entailed by the argument.

OMA, then, fails to prove separation, and hence fails to establish (7). But, Aristotle suggests, it is not worthless. Although invalid if (7) is its conclusion, the argument is sound if its conclusion is instead (7a):

(7a) The *F* is a *koinon*.

In *Metaphysics* I 9, Aristotle classified OMA as a less accurate argument. Our interpretation predicts that it is then an invalid argument for forms but, to Aristotle at least, a sound argument for *koina*. And so the *Peri Ideōn* says.

## III

The argument introducing the third man, accurate-OMA, is set out along with the third man itself as follows:

84.22     If (1a) what is predicated truly of many things (*pleionōn*) is also (2a) some other thing besides the things of which it is predicated, being separated from them (*kechōrismenon autōn*) (for this is what those positing ideas think they prove; for this is why,

25     according to them, man-himself is something, because the man

---

11 Aristotle clearly implies that his *koina* are not separated; see 79.15–19; 81.8–10; cf. also *Categories* 2b3–6, 14a7–10. For Aristotle's criticisms of separation, see, among many other places, *Metaph.* 991b1, 1086b6. Not all agree with this interpretation of separation; but the controversy need not concern us here.

is predicated truly of particular men (*tōn kath' hekasta anthrōpōn*),
(1a) these being many (*pleionōn ontōn*), and is other than the
particular men) – but if this is so, there will be a third man.

28    For if what is predicated is other than the things of which it is
predicated and exists independently, and if the man is predicated both of the particulars and of the idea, then there will be a
85.1    third man besides the particulars and the idea. And in the same
way a fourth, which is predicated of this and of the idea and of
the particulars, and similarly a fifth, and so on *ad infinitum*
(84.22–85.3).

In the first paragraph, Aristotle introduces two claims, which I
have labelled (1a) and (2a); these are the premises of accurate-
OMA. He then suggests that the Platonists accept or are committed to these claims; unfortunately, however, the third man regress
flows from them. In the second paragraph, Aristotle explains how
these claims generate the regress.

What exactly are the claims that generate the regress? Cherniss and
others take them to be the premises of OMA, already discussed
earlier in the *Peri Ideōn*. For several reasons, this view is unsatisfactory. First, as I shall show below, OMA does not introduce the third
man. If Cherniss were correct, Aristotle would have failed to
understand the strategy of the TMA. Second, it would surely be odd,
if Aristotle did (falsely) believe that OMA entailed the regress, that
he did not say so in his previous criticism of OMA. Why should he
now repeat OMA, and level a new objection to it? Third, we have
seen that in *Metaph*. 1 9 Aristotle classifies OMA as a *less* accurate
argument; but he classifies the argument introducing the TMA as a
*more* accurate argument. On Cherniss's view, Aristotle is in danger
of contradicting himself, classifying OMA both as a more, and as a
less, accurate argument. Further, we saw that Aristotle seems to
classify OMA as less accurate in part because of its invalidity; and he
seems to suggest that the more accurate arguments are valid
arguments for forms. AR, as we shall see, is a valid argument for
forms; OMA is clearly not. Since the argument introducing the
regress is more accurate, we would like to find an interpretation of it
that makes it, like AR and unlike OMA, a valid argument for forms.

These are reasons for wanting Cherniss to be wrong. And I
shall argue that he is. The argument introducing the TMA is not
the OMA, but a distinct, though related, argument, one that is
accurate in our sense and that does generate the regress.

The structure and language of the first paragraph certainly suggest

that a new argument is involved. To be sure, the long parenthesis at
84.24–7 recalls the previously discussed OMA. Indeed, the verbal
parallels are quite exact: once again, Aristotle speaks of predications
of groups of sensible particulars (*tōn kath' hekasta*, 84.25, 26–7), and
he says that what is predicated of them is other than (*allos*, 84.26)
what it is predicated of. This recalls OMA's (1) and (2), respectively.

But the *gar*-clause introducing the parenthesis suggests that
what stands outside the parenthesis (84.22–3) is not just OMA,
but the underlying motivation behind OMA. The Platonists
accept OMA, Aristotle is suggesting, because (*gar*, 84.24; *dia touto
gar*, 84.24; *hoti*, 84.25) they are tacitly relying on assumptions not
explicit in OMA itself.[12] These tacit assumptions are set out
before the parenthesis, and adverted to at appropriate places
within the parenthesis. They may be formulated as follows:

(1a) Whenever many things (*pleiō*) are F, some one thing, the F,
is predicated of them.

(2a) The F is separate (*kechōrismenon*) from any of the F things of
which it is predicated.

If (1a) and (2a) simply restated the premises of OMA, the first
paragraph would be redundant. But (1a) and (2a) are importantly
different from OMA's (1) and (2).

(1a) differs from OMA's (1) in that it speaks of predications of
groups of many things (*pleiō*) rather than of groups of sensible
particulars (*ta kath' hekasta*). This verbal difference cannot, I think,
be accidental.[13] For, as we shall see, if predications are restricted to

---

12 The structure of the parenthesis is difficult, and admits of more than one interpretation.
I assume that the first *touto gar*, at 84.24, means that it is relevant to introduce 84.22–23,
because this is what the Platonists think they prove. The next *dia touto gar* explains and
justifies this claim. But I do not take this to mean that the Platonists take themselves to
have proved (1a) and (2a) – the *dia touto gar* suggests rather that they take themselves to
have proved an instance of (2a) – viz. (4). I also take *dia touto gar* to refer back, so that it
refers to (roughly!) the same thing as *touto gar*. If it refers forward to the *hoti* – as
Malcolm Schofield has suggested to me – the force of the *gar* isn't clear: it should explain
the *touto gar hēgountai* clause, but doesn't then seem to. If we take the *touto* to refer
backwards, we'll say: 'It's because of this ((1a) and (2a)) that they think there is a
man-himself, i.e. because . . .' That is to say, they think OMA's (1)–(3) are reasonable
because they tacitly assume (1a) and (2a). The fact that (1a) and (2a) are assumed is made
clear in the way '*pleionōn ontōn*' is added to '*tōn kath' hekasta anthrōpōn*'.

13 See n. 9 above. The premises of the accurate arguments, unlike the premises of the less
accurate arguments, use '*pleiō*'; this is appropriate, since both of the accurate arguments
require us to form groups containing forms as as well as sensibles. Notice that '*pleiō*' is used,
as it should be; at 84.22 and at 84.26; '*kath' hekasta*' is used at 84.25, 26–7; 85.1, where its use
is inappropriate. At 84.25, it seems quite clear that it is the fact that a group of sensibles are a
group of *things* that licenses a form: (1a) explains (1); see further below. 85.1 makes it quite
clear that *ideai* are not themselves *kath' hekasta*, although they fall within the scope of *pleiō*.
For '*pleiō*' in the argument from relatives, see 82.12, and below, section v and n. 23.

groups of sensible particulars, the TMA is blocked. Aristotle is quite careful in his use of 'ta kath' hekasta' and 'pleiō' in the Peri Ideōn; and the differences between them are crucial for the TMA. (1a) is then best viewed as a generalised version of (1): it entails (1), but not conversely. If there is a group of like sensible particulars, both (1a) and (1) stipulate that some one thing is predicated of them. If we form a new set, consisting of like F sensible particulars as well as the F which is predicated of them, (1a) but not (1) stipulates that something is predicated of that set. For this new set consists of many F things, not just of many F particulars. Hence (1a) licenses predications in a wider range of cases than does (1).

(2a) differs from the OMA's (2) in two important respects. First, (2a), like (1a) but unlike (1) and (2), licenses predications of groups of many things, not just of groups of sensible particulars. Second, (2a) states that what is predicated is separate from what it is predicated of; (2) states only that what is predicated is different from the particulars it is predicated of. (2a), in this respect, corresponds to the OMA's (4). But in the OMA, (4) was inferred from (2) (with the aid of (1) and (3)); here a separation claim figures as an initial premise, not as an intermediate conclusion. Moreover, (2a) is stronger than (4); it is a generalisation of (4), just as (1a) is of (1). (4) asserts that what is predicated is separate from any sensible particulars of which it is predicated; (2a) asserts that what is predicated is separate from whatever it is predicated of, where predications are not restricted to sensible particulars. If we form a set consisting of sensible particulars and something that is predicated of them, (2a) guarantees that what is predicated of that set is separate from anything contained in the set. (4) guarantees only that what is predicated is separate from any sensible particulars contained in the set – and this leaves open the possibility that it is not separate from the F in the set which is itself predicated of the particulars in the set. This difference, too, is crucial in generating the third man, and we shall be returning to it.

(1a) and (2a), then, are not the premises of OMA; they are quite different claims – just as the structure of the first paragraph requires. And, as we shall shortly see, (1a) and (2a) – but not the premises of OMA – generate a regress. First, however, another point needs making. Aristotle says that it is an accurate argument that is vulnerable to the regress. Are (1a) and (2a) plausibly construed as the premises of an accurate argument, as we have understood accuracy? I think so. In criticising OMA, Aristotle argued that it did not prove that there are forms, because it failed to prove that what is predicated of sensible particulars is separate from them (4). (1a) and (2a), however, obviously do entail (4). For (4) is an instance of (2a). If whatever is predicated of a group of things is separate from anything in the group (2a), then what is predicated of a group of sensible particulars is separate from them; and this is just (4). (1a) and (2a), then, obviously do constitute premises from which separation (4) can be deduced. Hence, they are plausibly construed as the premises of an accurate argument in our sense, what I call accurate-OMA. Accurate-OMA, unlike OMA, is a valid argument for separation, and separation (in the sense of (4)) is a key feature of forms. Cherniss is thus wrong to say that the argument introducing the third man is just the OMA; and he is wrong too to say that it is not more accurate in the sense Alexander describes.

Now I suggested above that accurate-OMA reveals the underlying reasoning behind the OMA. But one might ask why Aristotle should suppose this. The reason, I think, is this. Plato surely sometimes uses a one over many assumption. He also clearly believes that there·are separated forms. Aristotle asks how the assumption and the belief fit together. The OMA suggests one possibility: it uses the assumption to generate the belief. But this results in an invalid argument. Aristotle now suggests the following strategy: 'Let us forget the chief defect of the OMA, its manifest failure to prove separation. I'll give Plato his conclusion. I'll even rewrite the argument so that it is formally valid; hence I substitute (2a) for (2).[14] But as long as we are rewriting Plato's argument, let us ask as well what the real basis of (1) is. Why does Plato believe that there is something predicated of particulars? Not because they are particulars as such, but because they are like. It is the likeness of the many, not their particularity, that the OMA seeks to explain. Hence (1a), the generalised version of (1), simply reveals Plato's implicit reasoning. Now we have a new argument to investigate: a valid argument for separated forms, and one which reveals more clearly than does the OMA why a one over many assumption is invoked.'

---

14 Of course, as we have seen, (2a) is much stronger than (4), the claim that forms are separated from sensibles. But Aristotle is entitled to use (2a) rather than (4) here, for the same reason that he is entitled to use (1a) instead of (1): it is not particularity as such that is important in OMA.

(1a) and (2a) thus accomplish two things: they reveal the implicit reasoning behind the OMA; and they provide Plato with a valid argument for separated forms. Should we now conclude that there are separated forms? Aristotle replies: 'No. For (1a) and (2a) lead to an intolerable regress.'

Aristotle thus in effect offers the Platonists a dilemma: if they rest with the OMA, they have a sound argument for *koina*, an invalid argument for forms; if they accept accurate-OMA, they have a valid argument for forms, but they are then exposed to the third man. Hence reliance on a one over many cannot prove that there are forms.

I do not mean to suggest that Plato is committed to accurate-OMA, any more than he is commited to OMA. But the line of reasoning just rehearsed is a plausible defence for taking accurate-OMA seriously. At least, accurate-OMA is as entitled to serious consideration as OMA itself is. Indeed, it is only when we consider the two arguments together that we can see the full force of a one over many assumption. If conjoined with a separation claim, it leads to an intolerable regress. If conjoined instead with a difference claim, it leads only to Aristotelian *koina*.

## IV

Aristotle argues that accurate-OMA implies that 'there is a third man' (84.27). The third man argument (TMA), as is well known, purports to show that a theory of forms is vulnerable to a vicious infinite regress. Corresponding to a given predicate 'F', the Platonists want just one form, the F; the TMA purports to show that there are an infinite number of forms corresponding to 'F'. Interestingly enough, Aristotle does not say that either AR or OMA implies the TMA; he only says that accurate-OMA does. As we shall see, this is not an oversight; for of the three arguments, only accurate-OMA leads to the regress.

What assumptions generate the regress? The Platonic formulation of the TMA in the *Parmenides* is generally agreed to involve the following three assumptions: self-predication (SP), one over many (OM), and non-identity (NI). These three assumptions have been formulated in different, non-equivalent ways in the literature. The following formulations will suffice here:[15]

(SP) The form F is itself F.

15  For lucid discussion of various formulations of the premises of the TMA, see S. Marc Cohen, 'The Logic of the Third Man', *Philosophical Review*, 80 (1971), 448–75.

(OM) For any set of *F* things, there is exactly one form, the *F*, predicated of the members of that set.

(NI) The form *F* is different from any of the *F* things of which it is predicated.

That these three assumptions are at least sufficient for generating the regress can be seen as follows. Suppose we form a set of large things. By (OM), there is exactly one form, the Large, predicated of the members of this set. By (SP), this form is itself large. Let us now form a new set, one consisting of the members of the initial set as well as of the form, the Large. By a further application of (OM), there must be exactly one form, call it Large$_1$, predicated of the members of this set. By (SP), Large$_1$ is itself large. By (NI), Large$_1$ is different from the form contained in the set (the Large). Hence, there are two forms corresponding to 'large'. If we now form a third set, consisting of the members of the second set and Large$_1$, we will be able to generate a third form corresponding to 'large' – and so on, Aristotle argues, *ad infinitum*. If we must, as the Platonists suppose, recognise the first form, then we must recognise the later ones as well. Hence the TMA shows that there is not, as the Platonists desire, just one form corresponding to 'large', but an infinite number of them.

Does Aristotle identify (SP), (OM), and (NI)? I believe so. At 84.29–30 he identifies (SP): 'man is predicated both of the particulars and of the idea'. Here he assumes that the form Man is itself a man; and this is an instance of (SP). Aristotle also adverts to (SP) in criticising AR, where he says clearly that the form of equal is itself equal (83.26–8). (SP) is a target for many of Aristotle's criticisms of Plato, and he himself consistently rejects it.[16]

---

16 G. Vlastos denies that Aristotle identifies (SP). In 'The Third Man Argument in the *Parmenides*', *Philosophical Review*, 63 (1954), 319–49, reprinted in *Studies in Plato's Metaphysics*, ed. R. E. Allen (London 1965), 231–63 (latter pagination), he suggests (p. 250 n. 3) that Aristotle had (SP) 'not only at his finger tips but almost in the hollow of his hand'; but 'that he did not see what was thus within his grasp is clear from the fact that elsewhere' Aristotle levels an objection to Plato's theory of forms that is not pressed here. But this objection is not relevant in the present context, and Aristotle's failure to mention it shows nothing. In 'Plato's "Third Man" Argument (*Parm*. 132a1–b2): Text and Logic', *Philosophical Quarterly*, 19 (1969), 289–301, reprinted in his *Platonic Studies* (Princeton 1973), 342–62 (latter pagination), he argues that since Aristotle uses 'predication' 'so much more broadly than we use it in our debates over self-predication', we cannot assume that he has the relevant sense of 'predication' in mind here (p. 350 n. 35). But of course the fact that Aristotle uses 'predication' broadly does not show that he cannot isolate a particular use of it on a given occasion. And if Aristotle doesn't think (SP) is involved here, it's not clear why he should say that there is a regress. If, for example, class-inclusion rather than class-membership were involved, there would be no regress. Some of Aristotle's objections to the argument from relatives (83.26–8) also seem intelligible only on the assumption that he understands (SP).

Aristotle also identifies (OM); this is just (1a).

(NI) is clearly identified at 84.27–29: 'the man which is predicated is different from the men of which it is predicated and exists independently'. (NI) is not identical to (2a); but it plainly follows from it.[17]

Aristotle's version of the TMA thus identifies the three crucial premises (SP), (OM), and (NI). Now (OM) and (NI) issue in a straightforward manner from accurate-OMA. (OM) is just (1a); and (NI) follows from (2a). But what about (SP)? (SP) is not an explicit premise of accurate-OMA; but it seems to be tacit.[18] It is the fact that the form $F$ is itself $F$ that explains how $F$ things are $F$; the $F$ is predicated of particular $F$s precisely because, in being $F$ (indeed, in being perfectly or superlatively $F$), it explains the $F$-ness of $F$ things. In that case, accurate-OMA involves the assumptions that lead to the regress. Hence Aristotle is perfectly correct to say that accurate-OMA introduces a third man.

It is important to see that if we substitute (1) for (1a), or (2) or (4) for (2a), the regress fails; hence accurate-OMA, but not OMA, involves the regress. This can be seen as follows. The strategy of the TMA depends upon supposing that one may form a set consisting of like sensible particulars as well as a form, such that this set requires a form over it, one distinct from anything contained in the set, including the form contained in the set. (1a) allows us to form such a set, for it allows predications of any group of like 'things', where these need not be restricted to like sensible particulars. But if we substitute (1) for (1a), we have no license to form a set that includes a form, and not just sensibles. Without that license, the TMA cannot get started.

If we substitute (2) or (4) for (2a), the regress again fails. Suppose we substitute (2) for (2a). All we then know is that the form predicated of the members of a set is different from any of

---

17  (NI) requires only that what is predicated be different from whatever it is predicated of; (2a) states that what is predicated is separated from whatever it is predicated of. (2a) entails (NI), but not conversely. Perhaps Aristotle reasons that although (NI) is weaker than (2a), Plato is committed to (2a); at least, he takes Plato to be committed to separation in the weaker sense of (4), and perhaps he believes that Plato cannot distinguish (4) from (2a). Others believe that Plato cannot distinguish (4) and (NI); see n. 32 below.

18  So Alexander assumes; cf. 85.3–5. Notice that in the argument that leads to the TMA in the Eudemian version, (SP) is explicit; cf. 83.35. (NI), by contrast, which is entailed by accurate-OMA's (2a), is not explicit. It is also interesting that in Eudemus' version, but not in Aristotle's, forms are said to be *kuriōs onta* – the feature Alexander, in commenting on AR, singles out as distinctive of forms. But it is wisely not said that sensibles, by contrast, are deficient; for this is the move that blocks the TMA; see below, section VI.

the sensible particulars in that set. This leaves open the possibility that the form predicated of the members of a set consisting of sensibles and a form is identical to the form in the set.

If we rely on (4) rather than on (2a), we know that forms are separate from sensibles. But (4) does not show that a form predicated of the members of a set containing a form is different from the form in that set. Hence neither (2) nor (4) guarantees what (2a) guarantees and what the TMA requires, that the form predicated of the members of such a set is nonidentical to anything in the set. If the set whose members a form is predicated of contains a form, (2) and (4) – but not (2a) – leave open the possibility that the form predicated of the members of the set is identical to the form in the set. Hence OMA is not vulnerable to the TMA, although accurate-OMA is.

The logical point just pressed is not new. Vlastos noted long ago that if predications are restricted to groups of particulars, the TMA fails.[19] If am right, Aristotle too is aware of the point, and his distinction between OMA and accurate-OMA neatly reflects it.

We have seen so far that accurate-OMA is indeed accurate, and that it, but not OMA, involves a regress. I turn now to the other more accurate argument, AR. I shall argue that it, too, is an accurate argument in our sense. But it is an accurate argument that escapes the TMA.

## V

AR is set out in the *Peri Ideōn* as follows:[20]

19 See Vlastos in Allen, pp. 238 f.; he does not discuss this point with reference to OMA or accurate-OMA. Cohen also suggests that Aristotle restricts predications to groups of particulars in the OMA, thereby blocking the TMA (p. 473 n. 42); he does not ask whether Aristotle nonetheless believes, as Cherniss suggested, that OMA is the argument leading to the TMA. If it is correct to suggest that OMA is invulnerable to the regress, and if Cherniss is correct to say that Aristotle takes OMA to engender the regress, then Aristotle fails to understand the full force of the arguments he presents. On my view, there is no such misunderstanding. This issue is not vivid to Cherniss, who mistakenly believes that the OMA is vulnerable to the TMA; see, e.g., pp. 275, 288 ff.

20 The now classic discussion of AR is that by G. E. L. Owen, 'A Proof in the *Peri Ideōn*', *Journal of Hellenic Studies*, 77 (1957), 301–11; reprinted in *Studies in Plato's Metaphysics*, 293–312 (latter pagination). I use the numbering (i–v) contained in his translation in the article. My translation and account differ from his at some junctures; I touch on some of these differences below, but cannot deal with them all in detail here. For other recent discussions of AR, see Leszl, pp. 185–224; R. Barford, 'A Proof from the *Peri Ideōn* Revisited', *Phronesis*, 21 (1976), 198–219; and C. J. Rowe, 'The Proof from Relatives in the *Peri Ideōn*: Further Reconsideration', *Phronesis*, 24 (1979), 270–81.

I. The argument establishing ideas from (*ek*) relatives is of this sort. When some one identical thing is predicated of several things (*pleionōn*) not homonymously, but so as to reveal some one nature, it is true of them either (a) because they are completely (*kuriōs*) what is signified by the things predicated, as when we call both Socrates and Plato man; or (b) because they are copies of the true ones, as when we predicate man of painted men (for we reveal in their case the copies of men, signifying some same nature in the case of each of them); or (c) because one of them is the paradigm (*paradeigma*) and the rest are copies, as if we were to call both Socrates and copies of him men.

83.5

II. But if we predicate the equal-itself of the things here, it is predicated of them homonymously. For (a) the same definition does not fit them all; (b) nor do we signify the real equals; for quantity in sensibles changes and constantly fluctuates and is not determinate. (c) Nor does anything here exactly receive the definition of equal.

83.10

III. But neither [can they be called equal] by one's being a paradigm and another a copy; for none of them is either paradigm or copy any more than another.

IV. And if someone were to allow that the copy is not homonymous with the paradigm, the same things always follow: that these equals are equal as copies of the completely and really equal.

83.15

V. If this is so, then there is something which is the equal itself and completely equal, by relation to which things in this world, as being copies of it, become and are called equals. And this is an idea, being a paradigm ★and likeness★ of those things which come to be in relation to it (82.11–83.17).

The argument is complex and controversial, and I cannot stop here to defend all that I shall say about it. I shall simply outline those points especially relevant to our chief concerns.

First a terminological point. In the *Categories* Aristotle defines homonymy and synonymy as follows:

Those things are called homonymous of which the name alone is common, but the account of being corresponding to the name is different . . . Those things are called synonymous of which the name is common and the account of being corresponding to the name is the same (1a1–4, 6–7).

On this account, two things are homonymously *F* just in case both are *F*, and the definitions corresponding to '*F*' differ; two things are synonymously *F* just in case both are *F*, and the definitions corresponding to '*F*' are the same. Homonymy and synonymy, so defined, are exhaustive options; and cases of focal meaning – cases where definitions are different though related – are cases of homonymy.[21] Now AR concerns non-homonymous predications, explained as 'revealing some one nature'. I take it that the argument is concerned, therefore, with synonymous predication, and that focal meaning is not relevant here.[22]

Part 1 states three, presumably exhaustive, ways in which a predicate can be applied to a group of things (*pleiō*)[23] not homonymously, but so as to indicate a single nature, synonymously. If *x*, *y*, and *z* are non-homonymously *F* – if they indicate a single nature, are synonymously *F* – then either (a) *x*, *y*, and *z* are fully or completely (*kuriōs*) *F*, as particular men are men; or (b) *x*, *y*, and *z* are copies of something that is fully *F*, as pictures of men are men; or (c) of *x*, *y*, and *z*, one is a model or paradigm, and hence fully *F*, and the others are copies of it, as each member of a group consisting of pictures of men and a particular man are men. In each of 1(a)–(c), a predicate applies fully to something – although, as the case of 1(b) reveals, it need not be to something in the group under consideration. But apparently in every case of non-homonymy, something bears the predicate fully, and so is a model or paradigm of that predicate. Particular men, for example, are fully men, and so serve as models or paradigms of man.

Part 1 tells us that 'man' is non-homonymous, and that particular men are fully men. Hence, if we have a group consisting solely of particular men, we have a case of non-homonymy of type 1(a). Subsequent sections consider another predicate, 'equal'. It seems to be assumed that 'equal', like 'man', is non-homonymous – an

21  This account of the *Cat.*'s definition of homonymy is controversial; so too are my claims that homonymy and synonymy are exhaustive, and that focal meaning is a case of homonymy. For a defence of these claims, see T. H. Irwin, 'Homonymy in Aristotle', *Review of Metaphysics*, 34 (1981), 523–44. Owen, in 'Proof' and in 'Logic and Metaphysics in Some Earlier Works of Aristotle', in *Aristotle and Plato in the Mid-Fourth Century*, ed. I. Düring and G. E. L. Owen (Göteborg 1960), 163–90, believes that focal meaning is not a case of homonymy, but a *tertium quid* between homonymy and synonymy; 'Logic and Metaphysics', p. 179 (or, sometimes, that it is an extension of synonymy; see 'Logic', p. 188). In the later 'Aristotle on the Snares of Ontology', in *New Essays on Plato and Aristotle*, ed. R. Bambrough (London 1965), 69–95, he argues by contrast that focal meaning is 'a sophisticated variant on the idea of homonymy' (pp. 72 ff.). This later view represents a significant departure from 'Proof', and would require significant alterations in his overall account of the argument.

22  Here I differ from Owen, 'Proof', p. 297; 'Logic and Metaphysics', pp. 185 f.; but cf. Leszl, p. 188; Rowe, pp. 277–9. Some of the implications of this view are discussed below, in VI.

23  Note that Aristotle again uses '*pleiō*', not '*kath' hekasta*'. This is appropriate, since AR, like TMA, requires us to form groups consisting of forms as well as sensibles. When Aristotle has sensible particulars in mind, he shifts to, e.g., *ta entautha*, 83.6, to make this clear.

assumption most explicitly acknowledged in the antecedent of
IV.[24] The task, then, is to consider a group of sensible equals, and
to discover in what way it is non-homonymous. Are sensible
equals fully equal, as sensible men are fully men, so that 1(a)
applies? Or do we need, in this case, to turn to (b) or (c)?

In part II Aristotle argues that no group of sensible equals is
non-homonymous in way 1(a); hence the argument highlights an
important difference between sensible men and sensible equals.
Although both are non-homonymous, sensible equals, unlike
sensible men, do not bear the predicate fully. III argues that neither
does 1(c) apply. IV then validly concludes that 1(b) then must:
sensible equals are copies of something that is fully equal, of a
non-sensible model or paradigm of equal. V explains that this
paradigm is the form of equal; and hence there is a form of equal.

It would take us too far afield here to explore in detail why 1(a) and
1(c) do not apply to sensible equals.[25] The reasons are familiar from
Plato's middle dialogues: sensible equals are in various ways
imperfect – they are, for example, subject to the 'compresence of
opposites' – and so none is suited to be a model or paradigm of
equality. 1(a) requires that each sensible equal be a paradigm of
equality; 1(c) requires that at least one sensible equal be a paradigm.
But, so Plato argues in the middle dialogues, and the reasons are
echoed here, no sensible equal can so function; hence, neither 1(a) nor
1(c) applies. And if no sensible equal is a paradigm of equality, yet
equal is non-homonymous, there must be a non-sensible paradigm
of equality, a form of equal – so IV and V validly conclude.

In criticising the arguments from the sciences and OMA,
Aristotle faulted their logic: they did not prove the existence of
forms, but only of *koina*; hence they were invalid if the existence
of forms was asserted as their conclusion. No parallel claim occurs
here or in the discussion of accurate-OMA. Instead, Alexander
says that AR is more accurate since it seems 'more directly to aim
at the proof of ideas' (83.18–19).

And he is evidently justified; for AR is a valid argument for
forms. Its conclusion, first of all, asserts the existence of a

24  Owen, 'Proof', p. 300, and others take the antecedent of IV to be concessive; but this seems
    to me unnecessary. I take Aristotle simply to be making explicit the crucial assumption that
    'equal' is non-homonymous. The point is that, given this assumption, and given that
    neither 1(a) nor (c) applies, 1(b) then must.
25  I discuss these issues, in connection with Plato, in 'The One Over Many'; see also Owen,
    'Proof'.

paradigm that is completely, in contrast to imperfect sensibles. But being a paradigm is distinctive of forms – Aristotelian *koina* are certainly not paradigms. Hence the conclusion of the argument is distinctively Platonic. And, second, the argument is evidently valid. It stipulates three ways of being non-homonymous, and assumes that equal is non-hononymous. It then shows that two sorts of non-homonymy do not apply to sensible equals; and it then validly concludes that the third sort must. Hence AR fits our interpretation of 'more accurate': it is a valid argument for a distinctively Platonic conclusion.

To be sure, the arguments from the sciences also called ideas 'paradigms'. But they did not show or argue that paradigms 'are completely' or that sensibles are deficient copies of them. These further claims – central features of Plato's notorious 'degrees of reality' thesis – are prominent here, and explain how AR, but not the arguments from the sciences, is accurate. It is a valid argument for perfect paradigms, and perfect paradigms are forms, not *koina*. Hence Cherniss's reason for rejecting Alexander's interpretation of '*akribesteroi*' for the argument from relatives collapses.

Although Aristotle does not fault the logic of this argument, we can guess where he would balk. Elsewhere he insists, *contra* part 1, that pictures of men are only homonymously men and not, as Plato believed, non-homonymously so. More importantly, he insists that 'equal' just is homonymous.[26] The fact that the sensible world provides no paradigms of equality does not show that there is another world that does; if we cannot explain how 'equal' is non-homonymous by reference to sensibles, that is just to say that 'equal' is in fact homonymous. We have no license to assume, what AR evidently assumes, that all words are univocal. Plato's simple semantic theory fails. Instead of pressing his alternative account of homonomy here, however, Aristotle contents himself with showing that the form of equal is an incoherent entity. This shows, indirectly, that something in AR is amiss. Despite its validity, then, it must be unsound.

26 For the claim that men and pictures of men are only homonymously men, see, e.g., *de An.* 412b17–22; *Mete.* 389b20–390a16; *Pol.* 1253a20–5; *PA* 640b30–641a6. For the claim that predicates like 'equal' are homonymous, see *Phys.* 248b15–21; *Top.* 182b13–27. Owen touches on these matters in 'Proof', pp. 210–12; cf. also 'Logic and Metaphysics', pp. 188 f.

*VI*

The Platonists, then, have two valid arguments for forms, accurate-OMA and AR. Aristotle insists, correctly, that accurate-OMA is vulnerable to the TMA; no parallel claim is pressed against AR. And in fact AR is not vulnerable to the TMA, even if it is vulnerable elsewhere.

This claim by itself is not new. Owen too argues that the forms generated by AR are immune to the TMA. But he grounds his claim on the belief that AR takes forms and sensibles to be focally related – the form *F* and sensible *F*s are *F*, not in the same sense, but in different though related senses. And he appears to believe that if they are synonymously related – if they are *F* in the same sense – then the TMA arises.[27] I suggested earlier, however, that focal meaning is not relevant here; only synonymy is. And one recent author who agrees with me on this score concludes that therefore the Platonists 'are left wide open to the Third Man argument'.[28] I reject this inference.

The third man is generated, as we have seen, from the conjunction of (SP), (OM), and (NI). AR, I suggested, involves (SP): the form of equal is itself equal (83.26–28); it is a paradigm which sensibles deficiently copy. But (SP) is not sufficient for the TMA; (OM) and (NI) are needed as well. But AR involves neither of these assumptions – not even on the synonymy account.

AR rejects (OM) in two distinct but related ways. First, one over many assumptions – whether like (1) or (1a) – are general in scope; they apply democratically to every predicate. (1) and (1a) apply to 'man' as well as to 'equal'. But AR is more selective. It explicitly distinguishes 'man' from 'equal', and postulates a form only in the latter case. Sensible men themselves provide the requisite paradigm for man; there is therefore no need to search beyond sensibles for a satisfactory paradigm of man; sensible men will do. This shows that, so far as AR is concerned, the TMA does not arise for 'man'; for AR postulates no corresponding form. If we cannot postulate even an initial form, no regress arises.

The second way in which AR rejects a one over many assumption shows that the TMA does arise for predicates like 'equal' either – even though AR licenses an initial form here. The crucial feature of (OM), for the purposes of the TMA, is not what sorts

---

27 'Logic and Metaphysics', pp. 181–90, esp. pp. 185 f.    28 Rowe, pp. 277–9.

of predicates it applies to – just those like 'man' or also those like 'equal' – but rather whether it sanctions forms corresponding to groups consisting of forms as well as of sensibles (to groups of *things* or only to group of *sensible particulars*).[29]

To be sure, the premises of AR, unlike those of OMA, do not explicitly allow predications only over groups of sensible particulars; like accurate-OMA, its premises are stated in ontologically neutral terms, speaking of groups of things (*pleiō*), not of sensible particulars. But AR licenses forms only over groups of suitably imperfect things; and as we have seen, only certain sorts of sensibles are suitably imperfect. If we have a group consisting of imperfect *F*s and a perfect *F*, we have a case of 1(c) non-homonymy; and AR does not license a further form over this set. Since the form of *F* is not itself imperfect, no further form over it is necessary. In sum: AR separates the perfect from the imperfect – and this avoids unrestricted (OM). If it avoids (OM), it avoids the TMA.

One might object that the argument just proffered is inconsistent with the synonymy account. For my argument depends on supposing that imperfect *F*s and a perfect *F* can be *F* in the same sense. Yet just this assumption is sometimes questioned. Vlastos, for example, once wrote that 'if the Form, Largeness, is superlatively large, while large mountains, oaks, etc., are only deficiently large, it must follow that the single word, *large*, stands for two distinct predicates'.[30] But as Owen remarks, Plato at least frequently assumes that a 'predicate applies without difference of meaning to model and likeness alike'.[31] Nor is Plato incorrect in so assuming. Perfect and imperfect *F*s are *F* to different degrees or

29 This point is missed by Cohen, p. 473 n. 41, who suggests that in the *Politicus* Plato rejected his alleged earlier view that there is a form corresponding to every predicate, and thereby rejected the (OM) of the TMA. But restricting the range of predicates to which forms correspond at most blocks the TMA for those predicates that have no corresponding forms; the regress might still threaten for those predicates that do have corresponding forms. The crucial question is not how many predicates (OM) applies to, but rather whether (OM) is construed as (1) or as (1a). The TMA requires (1a).

30 Vlastos, in Allen, p. 253. His account of self-predication on pp. 248–51, however, seems to assume that *F* particulars and the form *F* are *F* in the same sense: if they are *F* in different senses, what does it mean to say that *F* particulars 'resemble *F*-ness in respect of being *F*' (p. 248)? Vlastos seems to believe that the different senses view is also required by separation; but neither does this seem to be correct. The issue is complicated, however, and cannot be pursued here.

31 'Proof', pp. 297 f. I am unsure how to square this (correct) claim with the claim that AR takes models and copies to be focally related since, as Owen agrees, focal meaning involves difference of meaning.

in different ways, but not in different senses. If this is correct – if a distinction between perfect and imperfect Fs is compatible with the synonymy account – then the synonymy account is not vulnerable to the TMA. For even if that account involves (SP), it avoids (OM), as I have just shown.

Reflection on the same distinction – between perfect and imperfect Fs – shows that AR also avoids the remaining assumption of the TMA, (NI). To be sure, AR may involve the claim that forms are separate from sensibles, in that they exist independently of them (=(4)). But this separation claim is quite different from (NI), the claim that forms are different from whatever they are predicated of.[32]

Unlike accurate-OMA, then, AR is invulnerable to the TMA – even if it is vulnerable elsewhere, and even if it involves synonymy.

## VII

Only one of the two more accurate arguments is vulnerable to the TMA. This difference between them is related to another – which in turn raises a puzzle if we turn briefly to Plato.

AR contrasts predicates like 'man' with others like 'equal'. 'Man' applies fully to sensible men; 'equal' does not apply fully to sensible equals. This is the feature which AR exploits in generating forms for predicates like 'equal', but not for those like 'man'. Accurate-OMA, by contrast, generates separated forms of man as well as of equal; and Aristotle uses 'man' as his sample predicate in formulating the regress it leads to. Plato, in formulating the TMA, uses 'large', not 'man'. Why does Aristotle describe a third man regress, Plato a third large regress?

Just as AR avoids postulating a form of man, so Plato in the *Parmenides* (130C) doubts the existence of a separated form of man; and his chief arguments for forms, in the middle dialogues, generate forms only for those relative or incomplete predicates on which AR focuses its attention. If there is no separated form of man, the TMA does not arise in its case. But there are separated forms of equal and of large, and so Plato needs at least to confront

---

32 One might argue that although separation and (NI) are logically distinct, Plato could not distinguish them. This is argued by Vlastos, in Allen, pp. 253 f., and by C. Strang, 'Plato and the Third Man', *Proceedings of the Aristotelian Society*, suppl. vol. 37 (1963), 147–63; reprinted in *Plato: A Collection of Critical Essays*, volume I, ed. G. Vlastos (Garden City 1970), 184–200: see p. 194. I do not believe that their arguments are successful; but the matter cannot be pursued here.

the threat of the regress here. Correspondingly, he formulates the regress using 'large', a predicate for which there is a separated form. In fact, 'large' escapes the regress, for reasons already noticed in considering AR.

Aristotle, however, formulates the regress using 'man', not 'large'. Perhaps he sees that AR contains the materials for avoiding the TMA for predicates like 'large'. But what (Aristotle may have asked) if Plato were to overcome the scruples of the *Parmenides*, and to allow a separated form of man – as he seems to have done by the time of the *Timaeus*? Since 'man' functions differently from 'large', Plato needs another argument to generate a form here. He cannot invoke AR, which trades on contrasting them. Aristotle suggests that Plato will need, at this stage, to fall back on accurate-OMA.[33] But once he does so, the TMA arises. Aristotle suggests, then, that even if forms for predicates like 'large' are invulnerable to the TMA, forms for predicates like 'man' may not be. But even if the form of large is not vulnerable to the TMA, Aristotle's criticisms of AR show that it is vulnerable elsewhere. Aristotle's moral is that Plato's more accurate arguments are not to be received with open arms. Although they are valid, they cannot be sound. The search for sound arguments for universals leads us back to Plato's less accurate arguments, and to Aristotelian *koina*.[34]

---

33 Aristotle may in fact be incorrect. For in the *Timaeus*, where Plato does recognise separated forms for predicates like 'man', he does not use any version of a one over many, but something more like AR. Hence Plato might with reason argue that he need not fall back on accurate-OMA for 'man'. If this is right, then Aristotle is wrong to formulate AR in terms of a contrast between 'man' and 'equal'. Although this might capture a strand of Plato's thought in the middle dialogues, it is a strand that has been rewoven by the time of the *Timaeus*. (For more on the *Timaeus*, see my 'The One Over Many'. Owen, too, suggests that Aristotle's strategy here may be to argue that the form of man must be generated by accurate-OMA (although he does not put the matter in just this way, since he does not explicitly discuss what I have called accurate-OMA), and so is vulnerable to the TMA; see 'Logic and Metaphysics', p. 186.)

34 I am indebted to J. Annas, T. H. Irwin, M. Nussbaum, and M. Schofield for helpful comments. I also owe a special debt to G. E. L. Owen. A seminar of his at Harvard in 1973 first stimulated my interest in the *Peri Ideōn*; his work remains a model of what work in this field should be; and my debt to his views will be obvious to anyone familiar with them.

# 9 Aristotle on the principles of change in *Physics* I

DAVID BOSTOCK

Aristotle opens *Physics* I by stating that an inquiry into nature (*peri phuseōs*), like other inquiries, should begin with an account of the relevant principles (*archai*). He does not tell us what he means by 'nature' – for that we have to wait until book II – and he does not tell us what he means by a 'principle' in this context, but as we read on we may come to think this omission unimportant. For straightway at the beginning of chapter 2 he appears to place himself in the tradition of a series of writers on nature (*peri phuseōs*) whose views on the 'principles' (*archai*) were perfectly well known. Thus Thales held that there was one 'principle', namely water, while Anaximenes selected air and Heraclitus fire; Empedocles again held that there were four principles (earth, water, air, fire), Anaxagoras that there were infinitely many, Leucippus and Democritus that there were just atoms and void, and so on. So Aristotle, it would seem, is preparing to offer us his answer to the question to which these answers had already been propounded by his predecessors: he is preparing to list the ultimate ingredients of the world, and to given an account of how the world is made up from those ingredients. Perhaps this characterisation of what the older physicists were up to is rather oversimplified, but I think it is not worth elaborating their problem now. For it soon turns out that Aristotle's problem is after all an entirely different one. The main theme of this paper is to draw attention to the difference, to ask how far Aristotle himself was aware of it, and to trace some of the consequences of his lack of awareness.

We may begin by noticing that as Aristotle's discussion proceeds it soon becomes clear that the principles he is interested in are not so much the principles of natural *objects* (*ta phusei onta*) but rather of

natural *processes* or *changes*, and in particular *generations*. This theme
enters at the beginning of chapter 4, where the older physicists are
said to *generate* things (*gennōsi*, 187a15) from their single body by
applying opposites or by separating opposites out of it; and it is
firmly established in chapter 5, where the paragraph designed to
show that the older physicists were right to rely on opposites
(188a30–b26) is precisely an argument that things in general *come to be*
from their opposites and *pass away* into them, so the point will hold in
particular for the things that *come to be* by nature (*ta phusei gignomena*,
b25). It is the requirements of change and generation, again, which in
chapter 6 introduce the idea that some third 'underlying' principle
may also be required (189a22–6). And finally, when Aristotle
undertakes to develop his own views on the subject in chapter 7, it is a
general account of change or generation (*genesis*) that he promises us
(189b30–1).

Of course, it is hardly surprising that Aristotle should connect the
idea of nature (*phusis*) very closely with that of change, for it has often
been pointed out that the older physicists understood nature as a
source of change no less than as a principle of static existence,[1] and we
know anyway from book II chapter 1 that Aristotle himself
understood nature in this way: for him, nature is explicitly a principle
of change (*archē kinēseōs*). Besides, he does not entirely lose sight of
the original question of the *ingredients* of natural objects. As we shall
see more fully later, his account of the 'principles' of change is at the
same time intended to reveal the 'principles' of the things that
undergo change, fairly much in the sense of the ingredients they are
composed of. But it is important to notice that when in chapter 7
Aristotle puts forward his own positive account of change he does
not by any means confine himself to *natural* changes or generations.
What he promises us is a completely general account of coming to be,
and in fact the bulk of his examples are taken from non-natural
changes – e.g. a man becoming 'musical' (or better: educated), the
generation of a house or a statue, and so on. Clearly the results are
intended to apply to natural changes, but his own investigations in
chapter 7 are actually of a much wider scope. The inquiry into *nature*,
which promised to be a continuation of the speculations in
fundamental physics begun by Thales and his successors, has
somehow got sidetracked into something altogether more general.

1 See e.g. A. Mansion, *Introduction à la Physique Aristotélicienne* (2nd ed.; Louvain 1945),
   56–65.

Right from the beginning there has been some hint that the problems of the older physicists will be not so much solved as bypassed, for it is a curious feature of Aristotle's discussion that he often seems much more interested in the question of *how many* principles there are than in the question of *what* they are. The emphasis on the number of the principles is apparent in his opening statement of the problem in chapter 2 (184b15–25), and it can be seen as dictating the strategy of the arguments that follow. For the only thinkers who receive any extended criticism are the Eleatics who adopted just *one* principle (chapters 2 and 3), and Anaxagoras who adopted *infinitely many* (chapter 4). Other thinkers are not criticised. Instead Aristotle seeks to extract what is common to them all, and by the time he has finished with his predecessors (chapter 5) the only point of this whole discussion that survives is that they all made use of opposites (*enantia*). These opposites were of very different sorts, and sometimes a physicist would make do with just one pair of opposites, and sometimes would invoke several, so the question would certainly seem to arise: *which* pair or pairs of opposites ought really to be adopted as fundamental in our explanation of the physical world? Should we take hot and cold, dense and rare, up and down, love and strife, odd and even, excess and defect, or what? Indeed, this question seems to arise with all the more force in view of the fact that Aristotle apparently claims that only one pair of opposites will be required.

At the beginning of chapter 6 (189a11–20) he praises Empedocles for having achieved with a limited number what Anaxagoras could do only by using infinitely many opposites, and he goes on to remark that sweet and bitter, white and black, are derivative opposites, which reminds us of the atomistic reduction of these opposites given by Democritus and Plato's *Timaeus*. In the same passage he mentions an argument, which is given more fully at the end of the chapter (189a13–14, 189b22–7), and which allegedly establishes that only one pair of opposites will be needed. I will comment on the argument later (p. 194), but clearly the run of the discussion very strongly suggests that Aristotle is wishing to say that in physical enquiry we need take only one opposition as fundamental. This claim is the more surprising when we recall that in his own explanation of the physical world Aristotle employs *two* pairs of opposites to characterise the sublunary elements, viz. hot and cold, wet and dry,[2] and uses a different (triple) opposition when he comes to consider the heavens, viz. motion towards the centre, away from the centre, and round the centre.[3] Even if we suppose (as is perfectly possible[4]) that Aristotle had not yet formulated these theories when he wrote *Physics* I, still it seems outrageous for him to claim, in advance of any empirical enquiry, that only one pair of opposites will be needed. Naturally we shall ask *which* pair of opposites Aristotle here recommends, and it must seem very strange that on the face of it he shows no interest in answering that question.

But this must be to misconstrue his intention. He cannot have meant to put forward the strong claim that only one pair of opposites will be required and then said nothing at all about which they are. So I think we must understand that the particular pair of opposites he has in mind is the pair that emerges as a result of his discussion in chapter 7, namely the pair 'form and privation' (*eidos kai sterēsis*).[5] But *this* alleged pair of opposites is not in any sense a rival to the various pairs employed by the older physicists, and it is quite incongruous to suggest that this is *the* opposition which should be taken as fundamental in physical enquiry. It is as if one were to say that the fundamental opposition in physical enquiry is that between 'a thing and its opposite', for there is no more content to the pair 'form and privation' than this – and in fact there is less, as I shall show later (p. 189–90). So Aristotle is not after all engaging in physical enquiry himself, as it had seemed from the beginning of the book that he was going to, but rather trying to lay down in advance the general form which any physical enquiry must have. Despite appearances he is not – or should not be – engaging in a dispute with the older physicists as to how many oppositions need to be taken as fundamental in physics, but is rather saying that however many principles the physicist needs to invoke some of them must be classifiable as 'forms' and others as the corresponding 'privations' (and still others as 'underlying things'). Roughly, what is introduced as if it were a continuation of the physicists' investigation of nature has instead become a

---

2 See *de Generatione et Corruptione* II 1–5. The two pairs are explicitly stated to be irreducible at .330a25–29.
3 See *de Caelo* passim, but especially 268b12–27.
4 For the early date of *Physics* I see Ross's commentary, p. 7.
5 Note that *Metaphysics* x 4 is as a whole an argument designed to show that all opposites reduce to ἕξις (or ἕξις τοῦ εἴδους) καὶ στέρησις. See especially 1055a33 ff.

meta-investigation of the general form which any account of change must take, whether it is an account of *natural* change or not. Commentators have remarked on this change of topic,[6] but I think they have not always noticed that it has some unfortunate consequences for the discussion in chapters 5 and 6. But before I come to this it will be convenient to say something of Aristotle's final doctrine in chapter 7.

As we have just seen, the doctrine is that in any change there will be three 'principles' involved, namely a form, a privation, and an underlying thing (*eidos, sterēsis, hupokeimenon*). This doctrine, properly understood, has the sort of generality which one might expect to result from a purely conceptual investigation, and there is no denying that most of the discussion in chapter 7 seems to be conducted on a conceptual level, indeed one that pays much attention to the niceties of linguistic usage. Thus we begin (189b32–190a31) with a detailed account of the kind of change which occurs when a man becomes musical, which is quite unconcerned to discuss the mechanisms and learning processes involved, but wholly devoted to the language we use to describe the change as a whole. Thus we speak of a man becoming musical, of an unmusical thing becoming musical, of an unmusical man becoming a musical man, and so on. Again we speak of a man becoming musical *from* being unmusical, but not *from* being a man. On the other hand we do speak of a statue coming to be *from* bronze, despite the fact that in this case the bronze remains throughout the change, as the man does. Whereas we do not (says Aristotle[7]) speak of the bronze becoming a statue. It is pefectly clear throughout these paragraphs that Aristotle is concerned to comment simply on the way we speak, and to show that it conforms to this general scheme:

6 E.g. W. Wieland, 'Aristotle's Physics & the Problem of Inquiry into Principles', translated in *Articles on Aristotle*, vol. I (London 1975), eds. Barnes, Schofield, and Sorabji.

7 190a25–6. This is a surprising statement, and I suspect a slip on Aristotle's part. Context demands that we take the Greek 'ὁ χαλκὸς ἀνδριὰς ἐγένετο' in the sense 'the bronze became a statue', but I suspect that Aristotle has been distracted by its other reading 'the bronze statue came to be', and is objecting to this on the ground that the noun-form 'bronze' is inappropriate for use as an adjective, and should be changed to 'bronzen'. (Cf. e.g. *Phys.* 245b9–246a4; *Metaph.* 1033a5–23; *Metaph.* 1049a18–b3.) There is a long and I think over-ingenious discussion of this sentence in B. Jones, 'Aristotle's Introduction of Matter', *Philosophical Review*, 83 (1974), 474–500. See also the reply by A. Code in *Philosophical Studies*, 30 (1976), 357–67.

When these distinctions are made one can gather from all cases of becoming this point, if one considers them in the way I suggest: namely that there must always be something which underlies and is what becomes, and this thing though numerically one is not the same in form. (I mean 'in form' in the sense of 'in definition': to be a man is not the same as to be unmusical.) The one remains and the other does not; that which is not an opposite remains, for the man remains, but what is not musical (or unmusical) does not remain (190a13–21).

The terminology is admittedly curious, but the main point seems to be quite clear. Before the change we have an object which can be described as a man (as an underlying thing) or as a thing that is not musical (as having a privation); it is the same thing that is described in these two ways. *Qua* underlying thing it persists throughout the change, in the sense that we have the same man at the end as we had at the beginning, but it can now be described rather as a musical thing (i.e. as having a certain form).

The discussion so far, then, is of a conceptual or linguistic nature, and aims to point out that we use three kinds of concepts – form, privation, and underlying thing – in describing this kind of change. But at the same time we should notice that in the passage just quoted Aristotle claims that the same trio of concepts will apply in *all* cases, and this is a claim which cannot be maintained on the basis of a purely conceptual analysis, as we may see by considering generations *ex nihilo*. The most general form of change, one might say, is simply this: 'At one time it was not the case that *p* and at a later time it was the case that *p*' (and to obtain the form of generation, in our sense of the word, one takes '*p*' as an existential proposition). Now if this is what change is, there is nothing in the concept to rule out generation *ex nihilo*, but it is clear that Aristotle does rule it out. Why? He may of course be influenced by the fact that no physicist had ever seriously embraced this possibility, and since Parmenides all had explicitly denied it (e.g. 187a26–31, 191b13–14), but I do not think he wishes to rest his case on this appeal to authority. Rather, he gives his own argument on the point, and this argument seems to me to rest squarely on empirical investigation.

The crucial passage is 190a31–b10, particularly b1–10, and runs as follows.

190a31    Now coming to be is predicated in many ways. Some things cannot be said to come to be – rather, something is said to come to be *them*[8] – but of substances and of them alone it may be said that they come to be without qualification.

a33     And in other cases it is clear that there must be some underlying thing which is what comes to be. Indeed it is possible to come to be somehow qualified, quantified, related, dated [?], or placed only if something underlies; for only substance is predicated of nothing further, and everything else is predicated of substance.

b1     But if one were to investigate it would become clear that substances too, and all other[9] things which are without qualification, come to be from some underlying thing. There is always something which underlies and from which there comes what comes to be, as for instance plants and animals come from seed.

b5     Things that come to be without qualification come to be either by change of shape, as a statue; or by addition, as those which grow; or by subtraction, as the Hermes from the block of stone; or by composition, as a house; or by alteration, as things which change in matter. But it is evident that whatever comes to be in one of these ways comes to be from some underlying thing.

In this passage Aristotle is arguing that any case of coming to be is a case of coming to be *from* something, so that there is always something that forms the starting point of the change. And the argument which is conducted in the third and fourth paragraphs quoted certainly appears to be an empirical one. This point is perhaps suggested by the opening clause 'if one were to investigate', but it is more strongly indicated by the enumeration in the last paragraph, which is surely not the *a priori* division of a concept but an empirical collection of cases. The argument hangs, of course, upon the contention that this collection of cases is exhaustive, and it is very difficult to see what *a priori* grounds one could bring in support of this.

The best way to take this passage, then, would seem to be as an empirical claim that all changes or generations that actually occur are of a certain sort: they are, as we may say, *becomings,* and becoming is distinguished from change in general in that a becoming requires both something which becomes and something which it becomes. Becoming thus includes turning into,

8  'καὶ τῶν μὲν οὐ γίγνεσθαι ἀλλὰ τόδε τι γίγνεσθαι'. To obtain my translation I take 'τι' as subject to 'γίγνεσθαι' and 'τόδε' as complement. ('τόδε' stands in for, e.g., 'white'). This sense seems demanded by the next two sentences, though it is not perhaps the most natural way of construing the Greek.
9  In view of the first sentence quoted ('and of them alone') commentators generally excise the word 'other', so that the preceding 'and' can be read as 'i.e.'

growing into, being made into, and so on, but it does not include generation *ex nihilo*, because if that were to occur there would be no underlying thing to function as the starting point of the change. But though it is an empirical claim that all actual changes are becomings, what follows this is I think best viewed as a piece of conceptual analysis. For considering now the mere concept of becoming we may argue that if one thing is properly said to become another then obviously there must be something which does not persist throughout the change, for otherwise there would be no change; but equally there must be something which does persist throughout the change, for otherwise the change would merely consist in one thing coming to be where another had ceased to be, and there would be no reason to say that the one *became* the other. This argument appears to have an *a priori* certainty, so in *all* cases of becoming we *must* be able to specify something that does persist as well as something that does not.

I suppose I should admit that this account of two different stages of argument in chapter 7 – one empirical and one conceptual – is rather idealised. For one thing, Aristotle very often seems to take no account of the distinction between an empirical and a conceptual enquiry,[10] and certainly he makes no attempt in this passage to draw the distinction as I suggest. For another, he never in fact states the *a priori* argument I have just supplied him with. But I think it is helpful to recognise that this argument is at work in his mind, for only so can we explain why he is so confident of his conclusion that in any case of becoming there will be something that persists and some form that it acquires or loses. For it is certainly *not* that he has shown us how this doctrine applies in particular cases, nor that its application is entirely straightforward. On the contrary he has discussed only one type of becoming in any detail, namely that typified by a man becoming musical, though he is perfectly well aware that there is another important type of case, namely when a substance comes into being, as when something becomes a tree, or a statue, or vinegar. And where substances are generated it is not always easy to see what it is that remains the same throughout the change. But at this point I should perhaps pause to defend my interpretation of the text, for

---

10 This emerges in many ways. For one aspect, see Owen's article on his use of the phrase 'τιθέναι τὰ φαινόμενα' in *Aristotle*, ed. Moravcsik (Garden City 1967).

Charlton[11] has claimed that it is *not* Aristotle's view that when a substance is generated there is always something that persists throughout the becoming.

I must begin by admitting that in my view of chapter 7 there is a serious ambiguity in the phrase 'what underlies' (*to hupokeimenon*), and Charlton's interpretation would avoid this ambiguity. For not until the last chapter of the book – which one may well suspect, for this reason, to be a later addition – do we find Aristotle using his technical term 'matter' (*hulē*) precisely as a technical term for whatever it is that persists, and until then the word seems to bear its ordinary sense of *stuff* or *material*.[12] In my view the expression which Aristotle does here use for what persists is 'what underlies'. But of course that expression is *also* his standard expression for a subject of predication, and Charlton's proposal is to take the expression consistently in the latter sense throughout. In that case what underlies is simply the subject said to become so-and-so, and though this subject may often persist throughout the change (as when a man is said to become musical) there is no reason to suppose that it always does. Perhaps, then, Aristotle is *only* intending to argue that every change has an underlying thing in the sense of a subject which becomes so-and-so, and is not *also* intending to claim that there is something which persists throughout the change.

One can certainly sympathise with the view that Aristotle's own arguments do not justify a conclusion any stronger than this. one might also sympathise with Charlton's claim (pp. 133–5) that there are several passages elsewhere, especially in the first book of the *De Generatione et Corruptione*, which are (as he puts it) 'not

---

11 W. Charlton, translation and commentary on *Physics* I–II, in the Clarendon Aristotle series, p. 77. Charlton's thesis is disputed by H. M. Robinson, 'Prime Matter in Aristotle', *Phronesis*, 19 (1974), 168–88.

12 Occurrences are at 187a18–19, 190b9, 190b25, and (according to all MSS) 191a10. The first is in a parenthesis (καθόλου, a16 – εἴδη, a20) which breaks the line of thought, and it is *possible* that 'ὕλη' is there intended technically, but I see no *need* to take it in that way. At 190b9 'ὕλη' *cannot* be taken as what persists, for τὰ τρεπόμενα κατὰ τὴν ὕλην are obviously things that change in the stuff they are made of, and not – whatever this would mean – things that change 'in respect of what persists'. The point is that their ὕλη, i.e. stuff, does *not* persist. At 190b25 the phrase 'ὁ χρυσὸς καὶ ὅλως ἡ ὕλη' is most naturally taken as a way of saying 'gold and any other such stuff', and the same interpretation fits 191a10. The reason why commentators excise the word in the latter passage is that they think the analogy is designed to explain how the word 'ὕλη' is to be understood in its technical sense (for in that case it would be unfortunate to use that same word untechnically in the explanans). But what Aristotle is trying to explain is the phrase 'ἡ ὑποκειμένη φύσις' (i.e. τὸ ὑποκείμενον), and he has not yet started to use 'ὕλη' as a synonym for this.

propitious' for interpreting Aristotle as claiming there that there is
something which persists when (say) air changes into water or
water into earth. But the question at issue is whether Aristotle
does, in *Physics* I,[13] claim that there is always something that
persists through any change, and it seems to me that the text is
quite unambiguous on this point. I have already quoted 190a13–21
(above, p. 184) which says quite unambiguously that in *all* cases of
becoming the thing that is not an opposite (e.g. the man) remains.
It may perhaps be suggested that Aristotle is writing loosely here;
perhaps he means to generalise from the example of the musical
man only to other cases in which what is acquired or lost is a
quality, quantity, relation, etc., and is still reserving for later
treatment the case where a new substance comes into being. After
all he has not yet mentioned the generation of substances. But
even this defence fails in view of the later passage, 190b9–14. This
passage comes immediately after Aristotle has been explicitly
discussing the generations of substances, and listing the various
ways in which they occur (quote above, p. 185). He reaches his
result – 'it is evident that what comes to be in one of these ways
comes to be from an underlying thing' – and then at once
continues:

So it is clear from what we have just said that *everything* that comes into
being is *always* composite. There is one thing that comes into being,
another that comes to be it, and the latter in two ways – either as what
underlies or as what is opposite. By the opposite I mean the unmusical
thing, and by what underlies I mean the man. And generally the
shapelessness, formlessness, and disorder are opposite; the bronze, the
stone, and the gold underlie (190b10–14).

The only ground Aristotle could have for saying that whatever
comes into being is composite (*sunthetos*) is that we can distinguish
in it two 'elements', one the persisting element (what underlies)
and the other the acquired element (the form). If the element said
to underlie did not persist in the end product there would be no
ground whatever for saying that the end product was composite,
and Aristotle explicitly claims that *all* products of becoming are
composite. He here makes this claim *immediately after* a passage
enumerating the different ways in which substances come into

---

13  For the reason mentioned earlier (text to note 12) I shall waive the evidence of *Physics* I 9
    (192a28–34). But clearly in that passage ὕλη is analytically what persists through
    change.

being, and *immediately before* an explanation of how the claim applies to substances (i.e. what underlies, and persists in, the statue is its bronze). So he must hold, contrary to Charlton's view, that any substance which comes into being contains both a persisting element and a form. And therefore, as I say, the expression 'what underlies' is being made to do double duty, both for the starting point of the change (i.e. the subject said to become so-and-so) and for what persists throughout the change.

So much, then, in defence of my reading of the doctrine of chapter 7. This doctrine raises a number of important questions, of which the most important seems to be this: is the *a priori* argument on becoming, which I supplied to support the Aristotelian doctrine, correct? Is it in fact true that in any case of becoming there must be something that persists as well as something that does not? Another question one might well wish to raise, now as a matter of Aristotelian exegesis, is the question whether Aristotle himself consistently espouses this principle, or whether he dropped it as a result of the difficulties that arise in trying to apply it to the case where what comes into being is a substance. But I do not intend to pursue either of these questions here. Rather, I shall return to the point that Aristotle fails to dissociate his own enquiry from that of the earlier physicists, for this creates some difficulties in chapters 5 and 6.

Aristotle's conclusion is that any becoming can be viewed as a case of one and the same thing persisting all through, but acquiring or losing a certain 'form' (*eidos*); a change is always from form to privation or vice versa. This is *not* to say that all change is, in the traditional sense, between opposites. Equally, the older physicists need not be saddled with the view that *all* change is between opposites, for their practice would rather support the generalisation that we shall always have to invoke opposites *when describing the fundamental processes of nature*. Of course, opposites may be fundamental *in physical science* without it following that they are needed to characterise non-natural changes, such as the generation of a house or a statue. What is characteristic of a genuine pair of traditional opposites is that they are opposite ends of a spectrum, an ordering, a scale – e.g. in respect of temperature, density, and so on – and neither is merely the negation of the other. (So you could perhaps represent the traditional view, a bit anachronistically, as the view that in basic physics *quantitative* concepts will be fundamental.) However, form and privation are practically the negations of one another, for anything which is of the right sort to have a certain form but does not have it will be said to have the corresponding privation, and vice versa. Thus form and privation are much more *general* concepts than that of an opposite, but Aristotle seems not to have noticed this point. I say this because in chapter 5 he offers himself to argue *for* the thesis that change is always between opposites (188a31 ff.), though this is not the doctrine of chapter 7. And the argument of chapter 5 is of course mistaken.

Aristotle begins with the unexceptionable remark that if something becomes white it comes to be white from being *not* white (188a37), but then he goes on to add: 'not every case of not white is appropriate here but only cases of black or an intermediate'. One must allow that the Greeks did commonly regard all colours as mixtures of white and black (or better, of pale and dark), but it is obvious that a thing can also come to be white from being colourless, and that is neither opposite to white nor intermediate between white and its opposite. Again if a man ceases to be 'musical' because, for example, he has suffered extensive brain-damage and permanently lost all power of thought, would it be right to say either that he has become 'unmusical' or that he has come to some state intermediate between the two? But the error is clearer still a few lines later, when Aristotle considers the generation of a house or a statue. For with these examples in mind he says (188b12–15) that everything that is organised (*hērmosmenon*) must be destroyed by degenerating into disorganisation (*eis anarmostian*), and indeed into the *opposite* disorganisation. But there is no organisation of bricks which is *opposite* to their being organised into a house, and no shape of bronze which is *opposite* to the shape of a statue, because there is no linear ordering of organisations and shapes with that of a house or statue at one end and all others appropriately placed as nearer or further removed from it. Indeed if Aristotle had been thinking clearly he must have seen that this doctrine about opposites is in error, for it is actually incompatible with his own account in chapter 7.

In chapter 7 the concept of form must clearly be taken to cover *any* property which a thing may acquire or lose, with the sole proviso that this acquisition or loss is one that counts as a case of the thing becoming something. It may be suggested that this proviso rules out properties in the category of time, for if something occurs at a certain date, or throughout a certain period, we can hardly represent that as a change in the thing or use the notion of becoming to describe it.[14] But all sorts of other properties will count as forms, and in particular properties *in the category of substance* will count as forms wherever it is possible for them to be acquired or lost (as e.g. when there comes to be a tree, or a house, or a statue, or vinegar). All of these must be counted as forms (or privations), and it is of course standard Aristotelian doctrine that substances *have no opposites* (e.g. *Cat.* 3b24–32).

The same confusion, between form and privation on the one hand and the traditional pairs of opposites on the other, infects the arguments of chapter 6. In this chapter Aristotle begins to argue that we must recognise a 'third principle' in addition to our opposites, and he is still writing with traditional pairs of opposites in mind. So his first argument is that an opposite (such as density) cannot act on, or make things out of, its opposite (rarity), but must rather act on and make things out of something else which is characterised by that opposite (189a22–6). The point is here presented in language that is only appropriate to the traditional conception of opposites, for it is surely difficult to conceive of a merely negative privation *acting* on anything, and it seems to be this line of thought which is later illustrated from the thinking of the Milesians and their followers (189b2–8). Nevertheless in this case it would seem reasonable to say that the argument survives the change to the more general concepts of form and privation, for just as Aristotle (wrongly?) thinks of the traditional opposites as predicates, so form and privation too are predicates, and therefore apt to characterise other (underlying) things, and not one another. In fact, by the argument of *Categories* 2a34–b6 every predicate must in the end be predicated of a primary substance, so no inventory of the world's ingredients could be complete if it only mentioned properties. Now it does not automatically follow from this that the subject of our predicates would have to rank as one of the 'principles' we are seeking for, but this is the point which the next argument seems designed to establish.

14 For this reason the commentators often excise 'or dated' at 190a35 (quoted above, p. 185). But the slip is quite likely to be Aristotle's.

The main thrust of this next argument (189a27–32) is just the claim that a subject of predication is always prior to its predicates, from which we are invited to infer that it must count as a principle. One thing that is surprising about this argument is that, as Aristotle presents it, it claims that *nothing* that is predicated of a subject can be a principle at all, for the subject would be *the principle of* its predicate, and there cannot be a principle of a principle. If we were right in saying just now that Aristotle's form and privation are both predicative in character, it therefore follows from this argument that they are not principles after all. It seems better, then, not to press the argument to this disagreeably strong conclusion, but to rest content with the claim that a subject of predication must be a principle if its predicate is. (There is, however, no very strong reason to agree with this claim.) A second surprising feature of this argument is that it is introduced by the remark that the opposites are not *the substance of* any existing thing, which presumably must be taken to mean that they are not the substance of anything that Aristotle classes as *a substance*, i.e. that no opposite gives the essential nature (*ti estin*) of any substance. No doubt this may be accepted so far as the traditional opposites are concerned, but we have seen that it does not hold of form and privation, for 'form' must here be taken to include the essential nature (*ti estin*) of any generable substance. As a matter of fact, the point appears to be quite irrelevant to the second argument as stated, but it is crucial to the third.

The third argument (189a32–4) begins by recalling that no substance is opposite to any other substance and then continues 'How then can substance be composed of what is not substance, and how can what is not substance be prior to substance?' The reasoning is somewhat elliptical, but I take it that the first point is that, since no substance is an opposite, if we only admit opposites as principles we shall not have any substance as principle. If so, then the best we could do to explain (the generation of?) substances would be to say that they are somehow made up of opposites that are not substances. But then Aristotle adds that this would be impossible, for what substances are made from would have to be 'prior' to the substances they compose, but nothing else could be 'prior' to substance. Again this argument makes use of the notion of priority in a way that would be hard to justify, but it is clear that the only conclusion to be drawn from it is that our principles must somehow include (a) substance, which they would not do if they consisted just of opposites: the required 'third principle' *must* apparently be (a) substance. But it is not very clear what happens to this argument when we generalise the notion of a pair of opposites to that of a form and its privation. Perhaps if forms may themselves include (secondary) substances, that would satisfy the requirement that the principles must include at least one substance?

The question that thus arises is: does Aristotle in the end wish to endorse the argument of chapter 6 that the missing 'third principle' is *substance?* At first sight it is not clear how much weight we can place on the present paragraph. On the one hand Aristotle does not here commit himself to the cogency of these arguments. He says that they 'provide some support' for the conclusion that there is a third thing (*echein tina logon*, 189a21–2, b17–18) but adds that the question is still full of difficulty (*aporian echei pollēn*, b28–9). On the other hand at the end of chapter 7 where he is summing up he refers back to these arguments in a way which apparently commits him to accepting them:

First we said [sc. in chapter 5] that only the opposites were principles, but then [sc. in chapter 6] that there must also be something else which underlies, and that the principles were therefore three. From what we have said now [sc. in chapter 7] it is clear what sort of opposites they are,[15] how the principles are related to one another, and what the underlying thing is (191a15–19).

The natural implication of this passage would be that just as chapter 5 established that the principles would at least include opposites, but did not tell us which, so equally chapter 6 established that they would include a third underlying thing, but did not tell us what it was. The difficulty with this line of interpretation, of course, is that the whole drift of the arguments in chapter 6 seems to be that something important has so far been left out, *namely substance.*

Another relevant consideration is that chapter 6 closes with two arguments designed to show that only one pair of opposites will

---

15 τίς ἡ διαφορὰ τῶν ἐναντίων. I take this to mean: what is the differentia distinguishing our opposites from others (so also Charlton, op. cit., p. 47). The reference is to the fact that Aristotle's alleged pair of opposites is the (fraudulent) pair 'form and privation', and not, e.g., 'hot and cold'.

be needed, and Aristotle evidently endorses this conclusion. So
you would certainly expect him to endorse the arguments he
gives for it, and these arguments both presuppose that there is
indeed a 'third principle' while the second of them presupposes
further that the 'third principle' is substance. The first of these
arguments (189b18–22) is obscure to me, so I here pass over it,
but the second (189b22–7) seems tolerably clear. It is claimed
that substance is itself a genus, and that there is only one
primary opposition within each genus. Clearly this point
would be irrelevant unless it was being assumed that the 'third
thing', which our opposites are to characterise, is substance.[16]
When we add this point to the previous ones, Aristotle's
profession to regard the arguments of 189a20–b2 as tentative
does not seem very convincing.

We can develop this line of argument more strongly. It is
clear that in chapters 5 and 6 Aristotle represents himself as
developing the thought of his predecessors, and in chapter 7 as
making a new start and giving us his own views. This would
leave it open to us to suggest that in chapters 5 and 6 he is
giving us something like a preliminary development of problems (aporiai), presenting merely plausible arguments which he
does not himself subscribe to. But I think the suggestion is
really not very convincing. There can be little doubt that in
chapter 5 he is sincerely arguing in his own person for the
(mistaken) view that all change is between opposites or an
intermediate. So he takes chapter 5 to have established that the
principles we are concerned with must include at least one
pair of opposites, and the remaining questions are then: how
many pairs, and which are they? The answer that he wishes to
give to these questions is that the principles include only one
pair of opposites – namely the (fraudulent) pair 'form and
privation' – and it seems clear that by the end of chapter 6 he
takes himself as having established that only one pair of
opposites is required. So chapter 5 is not wholly aporematic,
and nor is chapter 6, for each concludes with a statement that
something has now been established – viz. that the principles

16 The 'argument' is surely very shaky. In several other places Aristotle states that all
oppositions somehow reduce to one fundamental opposition (e.g. Metaph. 1004a1–2;
Metaph. 1055a33 ff.), but the point is not a very plausible one. The thesis that substance
is a genus is denied in Metaph. 1053b21–24, perhaps as a consequence of the many facets
of substance revealed in Metaph. VII–VIII.

must include opposites, and that they include only one pair of opposites – and Aristotle has no wish to go back on these statements.

The arguments concerning the 'third principle' in chapter 6 might be viewed as aporematic on the ground that Aristotle presents them tentatively and ends the chapter by saying that the question is still full of difficulty. But the difficulty is presumably that resolved in chapter 7, 190b23–191a5 – a passage which surely does not reveal any weakness in the arguments of chapter 6. Besides, the arguments that he goes on to give in that chapter for his *other* conclusion, that only one pair of opposites is required, seem to presuppose the correctness of the earlier 'tentative' arguments for the view that there is a third principle, namely substance. One could also note that this conclusion is entirely in harmony with the discussion of chapter 7, where the third principle appears now as *what persists* through change, and all the examples we are offered are substances. At this point the reader may well recall the doctrine of the *Categories* (4a10–21) that it is peculiar to substances that they and only they are capable of persisting through change, and he will surely be feeling confident that in Aristotle's own view the relevant trio is '*substance*, form, and privation'. I have developed the case for this interpretation at some length because of course our text in fact denies it. Right at the end of chapter 7 we read, to our surprise, 'it is *not* yet clear whether the form or the underlying thing is substance' (191a19–20). But surely it is perfectly clear. How could Aristotle in fact avoid the conclusion which he here explicitly disavows?

In fact I see two possible ways of avoiding it while still preserving Aristotle's main doctrine of becoming. One possibility would be to abandon the doctrine of the *Categories* on predication, and to say that there are subjects of (accidental) predication which are not substances; in particular, a form may be predicated of *matter*, and matter is not substance. Evidently *Metaphysics* VII 3 could be adduced in support of this view. But a more appealing possibility would be to retain the view that forms are always predicated of substances but to deny that that makes substance into the third principle. For according to the most plausible version of the doctrine of chapter 7 the third principle is not what underlies in the sense of what is a subject of predicates (i.e. the thing said to become so-and-so), but rather what underlies in the sense of what persists through change. And this need *not* be a substance (but might, for example, be spatio-temporal continuity, or mass). So here we deliberately split the two senses of 'what underlies', and we abandon a different doctrine of the *Categories*, that only substances persist through change. And we might perhaps cull some support for an Aristotelian version of this alternative by drawing on Aristotle's rather disputed views on 'prime matter'. In fact it is probably fair to say that Aristotle at least toyed with both these lines of thought at one time or another. Of course he also toyed with the thought that chapter 6 was right after all.[17]

17 I am glad to acknowledge my debt to Gwil Owen, whose teaching first led me to an enthusiasm for Greek philosophy and who has encouraged my thoughts on the subject in many ways since then.

# 10  Aristotle on natural teleology

JOHN M. COOPER

Aristotle believed that many (not, of course, all) natural events and facts need to be explained by reference to natural goals. He understands by a goal (*hou heneka*) whether natural or not, something good (from some point of view) that something else causes or makes possible, where this other thing exists or happens (at least in part) because of that good.[1] So in holding that some natural events and facts have to be explained by reference to natural goals, he is holding that some things exist or happen in the course of nature because of some good that they do or make possible. Thus he holds that living things have many of the organic and other parts that they have because of the good it does them, so that these parts exist, and are formed, for the sake of the animal or plant itself whose good they subserve. To explain why they have them, and why as they are being formed they come to have them, one must refer to the whole animal or plant who needs them as the goal for which they exist. Aristotle gives or suggests, at one place or another, several arguments in favour of this thesis. Some of these press the analogy between artistic activity, which is admittedly goal-directed, and natural processes, thus extending

---

1 See *Ph.* II 2, 194a32–3, II 3, 195a23–5, *Pol.* I 2, 1252b34–5, *EE* I 8, 1218b9–11, and the many passages where Aristotle routinely explicates 'that for the sake of which' by linking it with the good, the fine, the better, etc. (e.g. *Metaph.* I 3, 983a31–2, *PA* I 1, 639b19–20). That the concept of a goal is the concept of something good is a view Aristotle inherited from Plato's *Phaedo* (cf. e.g. 97C6–D3, E1–4, 98A6–B3, 99A7–C7); unless one bears the connection between goal and good clearly in mind one will fail to understand much that Aristotle says about natural teleology, and many applications he makes of it (see further n. 11 below). Andrew Woodfield (*Teleology* (Cambridge 1976), 205–6), correctly notes that according to Aristotle all teleological explanations are claims that something happened *because it is good*, and makes this theme central to his own unifying account of teleological description.

explanation by appeal to goals from human action to non-human, even non-animal nature. But these are not very good arguments and there are reasons for thinking that Aristotle did not think his view rested primarily on them.[2] So I will leave these arguments aside and concentrate on two lines of thought that argue directly from considerations of physical theory to the conclusion that there are goals in nature. I first sketch Aristotle's theory that living things have two natures, a material and a formal nature, and explain how his belief in the goal-directedness of nature derives from this theory. Then I turn to consider his reasons for the doctrine that living things do have these two different natures, with its teleological implications.

## I

Natural substances – and, in particular, living things – have, according to Aristotle, two natures, a formal nature and a material nature (*Physics* II 1, 193a28–31). A thing's nature is declared to be whatever, internal to it, is the source of (a) the changes it undergoes, under various circumstances, and (b) the ways it remains the same despite changing conditions (*Ph.* 192b13–14, 20–3). So according to Aristotle living things have within them two different such sources of change and/or continuity. Some of a living thing's behaviour is due to the *matter* it is made of, but some is not due to that at all, but to its being the actual thing it is – a human being, or an elm tree, or whatever – that is, to its form. Thus that a certain thing has and maintains a certain size, shape, texture, etc., and grows and drops leaves of a certain character at certain times of the year, etc. – all this is due to its being, say, an apple tree. On the other hand, that any part of it yields to an axe or a saw and divides, ignites at a certain temperature and produces ashes of a certain kind and consistency, that it falls down under certain conditions, etc. – all this is due to its being made of wood

2 In *Ph.* II 8 the argument for natural teleology that Aristotle places first makes no appeal to the analogy between art and nature (198b32–199a8; see below, pp. 207 ff.). Only then does he add, for good measure, the three arguments (199a8–15, 15–20, 20–30) which do develop this analogy. As early as Philoponus one can find cogent objections to Aristotle's use of the analogy in at least the first two of these arguments (*CIAG* XVI, 309.9–310.15 and 310.23–9). And since the first and most extensive argument Aristotle gives in this chapter is entirely independent of the art–nature analogy, one must reject the suggestion that is sometimes made that this analogy is central and fundamental to Aristotelian natural teleology.

of a certain kind and consistency. Of course, it does not do or undergo any of these things entirely of its own accord; if there is no water and no sunlight it will not grow or maintain itself, if no fire is applied to it it will not turn to ashes. To account for its behaviour one has to refer to things outside it as well, and Aristotle is not denying this; but what it does when these outside things act upon it is determined also by what *it* is, and Aristotle holds that the contribution that the thing itself makes is to be traced not to one but to two sources, its matter (the particular wood it is made of) and its form (the particular kind of tree it is). It is the nature of that kind of wood to be hard but not too hard to cut with an axe, to burn in that kind of way, in the conditions specified, with just those results, and so on; and it is the nature of that kind of tree to have and maintain a certain size and shape, and grow leaves and fruit of just that kind, under normal favourable conditions.

Since, then, there actually exist in the world these two distinct kinds of natures, two kinds of source in natural things of their behaviours, explanation in the study of nature, if it is to be true to the facts, must correspondingly take place at two levels: the level of matter and its properties, and the level of form, that is, the level of the natural kinds and their properties. It is a fundamental principle of Aristotle's theory of nature that explanations of these two sorts are both of them basic to the understanding of natural phenomena generally, and equally so – they cannot be dispensed with in favour of anything more basic than they, nor can either be discarded in favour of the other. In particular, explanation by reference to form is not in the final analysis eliminable in favour of explanation by reference merely to matter. I will return to this point in the next section, once I have brought into my account the other two Aristotelian 'causes' or bases for explaining things – the final cause (or end or goal) of something and the moving cause (or thing that set in motion the events leading up to it).[3] How does

3 I use the term 'cause' here and in what immediately follows simply as conventional translation for Aristotle's αἰτία. I do not mean to prejudge thereby the question whether the explanations provided by reference to such 'causes' are to be interpreted as causal explanations, rather than explanations of some other sort. In particular, in speaking of the irreducibility of formal and final 'causes' to material and moving 'causes' I want to leave open the question whether Aristotle means to be saying (a) that causal explanations (explanations by appeal to matter and motion) are not enough, and another sort of explanation is required as well (explanation by appeal to forms and natural outcomes), or (b) that in giving causal explanations of what happens in nature explanations by appeal to matter and motion do not suffice, and explanation by appeal to forms and outcomes is sometimes necessary as well. I return to this issue below, pp. 214–16.

Aristotle connect these further two types of explanation with the two so far considered?

Let us begin with the 'final' cause. Aristotle regularly identifies formal and final causes where natural substances are concerned (e.g. *Ph.* II 7, 198a25–6; *de An.* II 4, 415b10–12; *GA* I 1, 715a4–6, 8–9). In doing so, he has, I think, two points in mind. Consider first the process of formation by which a seed is developed into a mature living thing. If one inquires why at a certain stage in its growth the trunk divides in a certain way, the answer may be that what we have to deal with is an apple tree – if it had been a different sort of tree this division would not have taken place. This division occurs then because mature apple trees have a certain structure and shape, and this growing thing, being an apple tree, is taking on that shape and structure. And since each thing's nature, its mature natural condition, is a good for it, reference to the form here is reference also to the goal of the process of growth by relation to which, therefore, it is to be understood. Because the formal nature which the shoot has (that of an apple tree) is something it does not yet have fully, explaining what happens at such a stage by saying that it is an *apple* tree is at the same time to invoke a goal – the form of a natural kind is always defined by reference to the mature member of the species, and here that form is responsible for what happens only insofar as it is in prospect. Thus explanation by a thing's form is also explanation by its goal wherever one is attempting to account for some fact about the process whereby an immature or embryonic thing belonging to a certain species turns into a mature member of the kind. But formal explanation is also explanation by a goal even in the case where what one is explaining is the characteristic behaviour of a mature specimen. The form of any natural living kind consists of an interlocking and mutually supportive set of capacities, so that to explain the exercise of any one of these capacities by reference to the form is to link it to the further exercise of some other capacity for which it provides a supporting condition. Thus when Aristotle says a tree puts out leaves of a certain sort because it is an apple tree this explanation will be expressed more fully by saying it does this in order to protect the fruit which, because it is an apple tree, will grow beneath the leaves. The reference to the tree's nature thus refers implicitly to a whole connected pattern of behaviours on its part, each one of which occurs in order to make possible later ones. Explanation by the formal cause thus involves explanation by final cause both in the formation and in the behaviour of mature plant and animal specimens. The form that is appealed to in such explanations always functions partly as goal.

Final and formal explanation are, then, for Aristotle very closely linked, and jointly contrasted with explanation by the properties of matter. Where does the remaining kind of cause, the moving cause, stand in this contrast? Sometimes Aristotle connects the moving cause with the formal and final causes, but sometimes (particularly in the biological works) he associates it rather with the material. When he says at *Physics* II 7, 198a24–5, for example, that the formal, final and moving causes often coincide he means that the immediate source of the motions that lead eventually to the existence of a living thing of a certain kind is always another living thing of precisely the same kind; and, furthermore, it is *qua* being a thing of that kind that the parent is the source of these particular motions. 'A human being generates a human being', for example (*Ph.* 198a26–7). Thus where what you are explaining is the generation of a whole, fully-formed living creature, the source of the motions must be a living creature of the same kind. But (and this is the level at which in the biological works he mostly invokes the moving cause) when one is explaining something that happens in the course of the formation of such a creature, then the moving cause will often be assigned not on the side of form and goal but on that of matter. Thus in a well-known passage of the *Generation of Animals* Aristotle says that 'An eye is for some end, but a blue one is not . . . we must take it that these things [viz. eye colour and other such features that serve no end] come about of necessity, and refer to the matter and the source of the movement as their causes' (v 1, 778a32–b1; cf. also 731b21–2, 789b7–8). That is, one can explain why an eye is blue on the basis of the characteristics of the particular matter from which it was made, together with the motions present in the matter as the process of formation took place. If, then, one thinks of moving causes not at the level of the end-products of these processes but at that of the stage-by-stage development, there will often be two contrasting sets of explanatory factors. On the one side we have matter and moving cause (the nature of the materials together with the motions that arise in and around it); these are responsible for what happens, wherever and to whatever extent they are responsible at all, by being antecedent conditions from which what happens follows on what we may provisionally think of as mechanical principles. But on the other side we have form and goal, which are responsible not by being antecedent conditions but by being the end in view by which the earlier developments are, somehow or other, regulated.

## II

There are then two distinct and independent levels of facts and correspondingly two levels of principles that Aristotle holds are responsible for what happens in the course of nature. There are facts about the various kinds of matter there are, and principles of a mechanical sort governing their behaviour in given conditions. And there are facts about the natural kinds of living thing and principles of a teleological sort governing their development and behaviour. Aristotle's predecessors and contemporaries were all agreed, as we would also agree, that there are facts and principles of the first sort. This can be accepted as non-controversial. But what ground does Aristotle have for thinking there is, in addition to and independent of these, a second level of facts and principles such as he postulates?

In answering this question one must begin by taking note of certain assumptions Aristotle makes about the character of physical reality. The most important of these is his belief that the world – the whole ordered arrangement of things, from outer heavens right down to the earth and its animal and plant life – is eternal. That the heavens are eternal and move at a fixed rate in daily rotation by strict necessity is, of course, not a mere assumption of Aristotle's, it is in fact the conclusion of certain *a priori* arguments in *Physics* VIII. This does not, however, immediately imply that the sublunary world has forever been arranged as it now is. That there has always been and always will be an annual cycle of warm and cold periods, as the sun moves round the ecliptic, is perhaps arguable on this basis. But that the distribution of land and water and air, and the kinds of plant and animal life that now exist, should be permanent parts of the world order seems clearly to need further argument; these features are certainly not determined merely by the constancy of the movements of the heavenly bodies. Nonetheless, Aristotle did believe that the world's climate and the existence of the animal and plant life that depends on it were further permanent structural facts – as it were, part of the given framework of the world, over and above that provided by the celestial movements.[4] Partly, no doubt, he thought that even fairly cursory acquaintance with the basic facts about animal and plant life should convince anyone that our world is a self-maintaining system, with a built-in tendency to preserve fundamentally the same distribution of air, land and water and the same balance of animal and plant populations as it had in his own time. The seasonal variation of hot and cold, wet and dry periods seems to have the effect that no permanent dislocation in the ecology takes place. Furthermore, every plant and animal species reproduces itself (or, in the case of spontaneously generated things, the conditions in which they are produced are regularly

4 In GA II 1, 731b24–732a3 (cf. also *de An.* II 4, 415a25–b7) Aristotle appeals to the permanence of animal and plant life to explain why there is sexual differentiation and animal reproduction in general. Living things are better than non-living and existence than non-existence, so the continuous existence of living things is an important good; but since individual animals and plants are all perishable it is only by constant replenishment that this good can be achieved. Since there cannot be eternal individuals, there is instead 'always a *genos* of human beings, of animals and of plants' (b35 f.), and it is in order to sustain these genera in existence that reproduction through sexual differentiation takes place. It is true that in this argument Aristotle explicitly presupposes only that there are always plants and animals, not (except for human beings!) that there are always the *same* kinds. But the context shows that he is making this stronger assumption; for he goes on to speak of the arrangements which make possible the constant generation of the *existing* species. The stronger thesis is also found at GA II 6, 742b17–743a1, where Aristotle takes Democritus to task for saying that if something is always (ἀεί) so then that is sufficient explanation for it: what is *always* is infinite (τὸ δ' ἀεὶ ἄπειρον), i.e. lasts through infinite time, and there is no origin (ἀρχή) of the infinite, but to give an explanation of something is precisely to cite an origin (ἀρχή – but in another sense!) for it. If this were right, Aristotle says, we would be barred from seeking an explanation for why in animal generation we find just the organs and other parts we do find being formed in just the order in which they are actually formed. For the Democritean argument to be the threat he takes it to be Aristotle must be holding that the existing species of animals, whose structure and generation he is investigating, are existent through infinite time. The strict interpretation required for 'always' in this passage should put us on notice that when Aristotle speaks elsewhere of some arrangement as being so 'always or for the most part' (ἀεὶ ἢ ὡς ἐπὶ τὸ πολύ) he means to say that that arrangement is found existing eternally or recurring regularly throughout all time, with only the occasional exceptions implied in the 'for the most part' rider. Thus if he says that in some particular animal certain organic parts are formed always or for the most part in a certain way or order he does *not* just intend the hypothetical, '*if* or *when* these animals are formed, this is the way it always happens'; he means to assert the categorical conjunction, 'these animals regularly are generated through all time, and this is the way it always happens'. Some rare, fortuitous event that nonetheless happened in the same way every time would not be counted by Aristotle as something that happens 'always or mostly' in a certain way; nor would he count animal generation as happening 'always or mostly' in some particular way if animals were found in the universe only in a certain finite period of its existence, even though *when* they exist they are always or mostly generated in that way.

recurring); moreover, there appears to be an effective balance of nature, whereby no plant or animal is so constituted by its nature as to be permanently destructive of any other. Everything seems to fit together – the environment is permanently such as is needed to support the kinds of plants and animals there actually are, and the natural processes of generation and growth seem to maintain permanently a fairly fixed population of those same plants and animals. One observes in the world itself, then, no internal disharmony or imbalance that could lead to its eventual destruction; and since there is nothing outside it that could attack it and cause its disintegration, it seems only reasonable to believe that in these respects no change is to be anticipated. And if none is to be anticipated in the future, there is *pari passu* no reason to believe that things were ever any different in the past.

Now for Aristotle the fact, as he thought it, that the species of living things are permanent features of the natural world has a very special significance. It is not simply as if nature, by some mechanism or other, managed to keep in existence a stock of arbitrarily shaped and structured, but complex, objects (specially shaped and coloured stones, for example). For each plant and animal is structured in such a way that its parts *work together* to make possible the specific form of life characteristic of its species, and (in almost all cases) so that they make possible the continuation of the species by enabling some appropriate kind of reproduction. It is important to realise that things might not have been this way. The organs and other internal parts of animals and plants might not have been as highly adapted to one another as in fact they are. Empedocles hypothesised that during one stage of the world's history all manner of animals were constantly being formed by chance collocations of varied animal parts more or less like those of animals known to us; some of these individual animals, having the parts necessary to make a go of it, survived to old age, others only for a short time if at all. While this situation continued all kinds of odd creatures were constantly being produced which clung to life with difficulty or not at all, and the adaptedness for life of the animals and plants known to us would be distinctly the exception, by no means the rule. If the world were permanently that way, one could perhaps speak of the permanence of all those weird kinds of 'animals', produced as they would continue to be by chance collocations of limbs springing up from the earth equally by chance, but in such a world the permanence of animal kinds would mean something very different from what it meant for Aristotle. For him, it meant the permanence of a set of well-adapted, well-functioning life forms. The preservation of the species of living things is therefore, as Aristotle understands it, the preservation of a fixed set of good things, things economically and efficiently organised so that they function in their environment for their own good.

The view that the world, together with its animal and plant life, is eternal was obviously quite a reasonable view in fourth-century Greece. But if it is *permanently* true that there *are* these given kinds of good, well-adapted plants and animals, and that the seasons follow upon each other in this given way, with those good effects, it becomes at once a condition of adequacy on any physical theory that it should be able to accommodate these facts. There are several possibilities. One might attempt to explain them by arguing, so to speak, from below: the materials of the world being what they are, and having the natures they do, the world naturally tends, by the operation of nothing but material principles, to produce and maintain just those kinds of living things that are actually observed. Or, one might attempt to explain them by arguing from above: for example, by claiming that it is a fundamental fact about nature, not to be further explained, that it tends toward maximal richness and variety, and then arguing that precisely the natural kinds that are actually observed, taken together with the environing inorganic stuffs, constitute the maximally rich and varied world. Thirdly, one might simply accept as a fundamental postulate of physical theory that the world *permanently has* whatever species it contains; that is, one might hold that it is an irreducible fact about the natural world, not further to be explained, that it so governs itself as to preserve in existence the species of well-adapted living thing that it actually contains. Of these alternatives Aristotle chose, and evidently thought one could not reasonably avoid, the last. He does not ever explicitly consider, so far as I can tell, a theory of the second sort. Perhaps he thought any such theory conflicts with well-established metaphysical principles, so that he could safely dismiss this alternative without discussion. For any such theory is committed to the idea that standards of goodness – in particular, of richness and variety – can be clearly conceived and specified in purely intellectual terms, in advance of study of the actual world, and that these standards can then be thought of as imposed on the world, as principles it must conform to, whether by its own inherent nature or by external compulsion. And Aristotle's metaphysics of the good rules out any such abstractly conceived standards. All our ideas about goodness, he thinks, are derived from familiarity with the actual world, and though we can extend these to conceive of possible arrangements that, if taken in isolation, might be better than actual ones, there is no Idea of the Good to provide us with absolute standards worked out by the pure intellect on its own, by which one might securely judge that the actual world either is or is not the best possible. In fact the world may *be* maximally rich and varied, but we cannot argue that it is by appeal to self-justifying standards independent of and prior to the good things we find in the world as it is actually constituted. Our best *idea* of richness and variety is, as a matter of fact, probably given by the actual world: in any event, we have no independent idea of these things by which to judge the world, so there cannot be any such principle of physics as this second sort of theory demands.[5]

Whether for this reason or another, Aristotle does not consider the possibility of deriving the permanence of the species in this Platonic sort of way, from above. He does, however, argue against the first sort of theory. He represents his materialist predecessors as having favoured this sort of view: they supposed one could explain why there are the species there are, why they are preserved, and why the seasons follow one another as they do, in terms of nothing but the natures of the various materials the world contains and the ways in which, given their distribution at any given time, they interact with one another. In other words, they thought that ultimately only the first of Aristotle's two levels of facts and principles ever needs to be appealed to in explaining anything. His second level they proposed to account for entirely in terms of material causes and moving causes involving nothing but the motions that arise in matter, given its nature, under given conditions.

---

5 This line of thought explains why Aristotle's teleology does not extend to arguing that the good of the world as a whole requires any particular species or any particular interlocking arrangements among whatever species are to exist. He consistently takes the existing species as given; *they* are the good things by reference to which to explain those features of reality that he thinks need to be explained teleologically. (The class of exceptions to this rule noted below, pp. 220-1, do not damage this point.)

One can distinguish two lines of argument in Aristotle against any such supposition. One of these, which I shall explore at some length below, consists in an outright denial of the materialists' claim that their principles enable them to explain the occurrence of living things with the organic parts we actually observe them to have. But first I want to discuss more briefly a weaker line of argument, weaker in the sense that in it Aristotle grants, for the sake of argument, this major claim of his materialist opponents: even granted this outrageous claim, Aristotle argues, the materialists cannot explain *everything* that the fact of the permanence of the species involves.

This argument is found at *Physics* II 8, 198b32–199a8 (and see *Metaph.* I 3, 984b8–15). Interpreters have found this a difficult passage, but I believe the argument itself is rather straightforward. Without attempting a full-scale defence of my interpretation I shall simply state what I take the argument to be.

As I noted above, the animal and plant species we observe in nature are well-adapted. Their organs and other parts work together to promote their existence and functioning in their actual environments – a plant or animal's organs are, and do, *good* for it. Is there an explanation for this? The materialists argue that the various parts that are produced in the course of a creature's formation are produced by nothing but material necessity: the natures of the materials are such that *this* kind of tooth (a sharp one) necessarily comes up in the front of the mouth, and other material necessities result in *that* kind (a flat one) coming up in the back. But what explains the *fit* between these dental arrangements and the creature's need for food? The front ones, for example, are not just sharp, but useful for tearing food off, which is something the creature needs to do to survive and flourish. What account of *this* fact can the materialists give? Aristotle argues that the materialists' answer to this question is insupportable. (1) Where some thing occurs that in fact works to the advantage of someone or some thing, there are only two choices: either it is advantageous by coincidence or it happens for that reason, i.e. *because* of the good it does. If one admits that something is good, as the natural arrangements here in question indubitably are, one must either hold that this was a lucky coincidence, or grant that it happened that way (perhaps as a result of some agent's design, perhaps not) *for* the good of the person or thing in question. (2) Our materialists deny that in nature anything happens *for the sake of* any good that results, so they are forced to say, as Aristotle represents them as saying (198b16–32), that these good results are only coincidences: the teeth come up sharp in front by material necessity, but only *happen* to serve the creature's interests by doing so.[6] But, he argues, (3) a coincidence is necessarily an exceptional occurrence, and (4) animals' organs are *always* (with only occasional failures) formed in such a way as to serve the creature's needs. Hence it cannot be a coincidence, as the materialists say it is, that they do serve those needs. And if it is no coincidence, it must have the other explanation allowed: it happens that way *in order to* promote the creature's welfare.

Aristotle's conclusion here does, clearly enough, follow from the premises he provides. Whether the opponents would have to grant all the premises is less clear. The premises about coincidences, (1) and (3), perhaps most often strike interpreters as questionable, though actually I believe each of them can be fairly vigorously defended.[7] What is quite certain, however, is that

---

6 See 198b24–7; the sense of the ἐπεί-clause in b27 is given by this expansion: ἐπεὶ οὐχ ἕνεκα τοῦ ἐπιτηδείους εἶναι, γενέσθαι τοὺς ὀδόντας ὀξεῖς, ἀλλὰ συμπεσεῖν τοῦτο ἐκείνῳ. It is essential for assessing this argument to notice that the opponents are represented as saying that the organs are *formed* as they are by necessity, but are *good* by coincidence. They do not claim they are *good* by necessity (whatever that would mean).

7 It might be objected, against (1), that while one may grant that any good outcome is either a coincidence or has *some* special explanation, this explanation *need* not be the teleological one asserted in (1). For if one has a run of heads in flipping a coin, and this is not a coincidence, it only follows that it has *some* cause (perhaps simply that the coin is untrue), not that it must have been produced for some purpose. But this reply overlooks that what premise (1) claims is not that *every* apparent coincidence that turns out not to be one must be explained teleologically, but only that when something *good* happens its being good must, if it is not a coincidence, have a teleological explanation. Thus the alleged counterexample must be expanded to make the run of heads a good thing for some reason (for example, because it means money for some particular person); but now we no longer have a counterexample, since this good that was done will remain a coincidence after the run of heads has itself been explained as due to the coin's weighting. Thus Aristotle's claim that if something good has an explanation and is no coincidence, the explanation must be teleological, is actually quite plausible. And even if it is not finally true, this will not give comfort to Aristotle's opponents. For certainly if some conjunction of phenomena is not a coincidence, it must at least have an explanation that connects the conjoined phenomena in a single, joint explanation (on this see Richard Sorabji, *Necessity, Cause and Blame* (London 1980), 10–11); and materialists driven to deny that the good done by the organs' arrangement is surely cannot replace their separate explanations of how *each* organ is produced with a unified one claiming that the natures of the various materials in the world are in themselves such that this conjunction necessarily results every time.

The other premise, premise (3), can be seen to be perfectly unobjectionable if it is borne in mind that the criterion of the exceptional is defined against what happens throughout all time. For of course there is no assurance that any finite run of similar outcomes is not nonetheless a coincidence; but an *infinite* run with a preponderance of similar outcomes surely cannot be a coincidence but must have some special explanation. Strictly, perhaps, coincidences don't have to be exceptional, when taken in an infinite run, but they must not count for more than 50% of the cases, and that is good enough for the purposes of Aristotle's argument.

materialists like Democritus and Empedocles do not accept premise (4) in the sense in which Aristotle intends it (and the sense in which it must be taken to make the argument valid). It must be remembered (see n. 4 above) that when Aristotle says that the parts of animals and plants are *always* formed serviceably for the creature's needs he means that this has been going on *throughout all time*. And unless that is how (4) is taken the conclusion will not follow. If, for example, as Democritus is reported to have held, there have been infinitely many worlds (*kosmoi*), some of them larger than others, some with no sun or moon, some without plants and animals or even water (Hippol. *Haer.* 1 13 = DK 68A40), there have *not* always existed serviceably structured living things, reproducing themselves in the ways that now appear to be regular. And, as we have seen, according to Empedocles there are periods in the world's history during which all kinds of *unserviceable* combinations are produced (Simp. *in Ph.* 371.33–372. 9 = DK 31B61). On either of these views one could only hold the orderly and good arrangements presently prevailing to be an extended run of luck; viewed *sub specie aeternitatis* the good outcomes with which our experience makes us familiar are distinctly the exception, not the rule, and therefore the materialists' classification of them as coincidences would after all satisfy the requirements imposed by premises (1) and (3). Of course, Aristotle would insist that Democritus' theory of infinitely many world-orders and Empedocles' story about the alternating epochs of control by Love and by Strife are nothing but unsupported fancies, and that his own theory of the eternity of the actual world is more reasonable. One can well sympathise with this contention, and it is worth emphasising that if one does accept Aristotle's theory, and I am right that premises (1) and (3) are defensible, then this argument provides quite a good defence of Aristotle's teleological hypothesis. It must at least be granted that Aristotle was on stronger ground than his actual materialist opponents, even if we would ourselves, for different reasons from theirs, side rather with them in rejecting Aristotle's thesis of the eternity of the actual kinds of living things.

Aristotle's more thorough-going confrontation with the materialists is found in the following chapter of *Physics* II, chapter 9, where he explains and defends his claim that in the structure and formation of plants and animals and their functional parts the materials are not a necessitating factor in the way the materialists claim, but are only 'hypothetically' necessary – necessary *if* the end-result of a fully-formed creature of the kind in question in any given case is to be attained.[8] The materialists, as we have seen, claim that the given natures of the materials making up the world are such that under the conditions prevailing in animal generation they necessarily interact in such a way as to produce the organs we actually observe the living things to have, and in that arrangement

---

8 Aristotle's doctrine of hypothetical necessity (*Ph.* II 9, *PA* I I, 639b21–640a10, 642a1–13, *GC* II 11, 337b14–33) is nowadays usually interpreted as maintaining the very implausible view that in natural processes *nothing* is necessitated except hypothetically: that, as Sorabji puts it (op. cit., 148), 'in natural events' (not counting the motion of the stars and other such everlasting processes) there is no necessity other than 'the merely hypothetical necessity of certain prerequisites, if a certain goal is to be achieved'. (See also Ross, *Aristotle's Physics* (Oxford 1936), 43, and Balme, *Aristotle's De Partibus* . . ., 76–7.) On this view, Aristotle is committed to denying all material necessities of a Democritean sort, things that happen because the materials present simply interact by their natures to cause them. One then faces the formidable task of understanding how if this is his theoretical position he nonetheless constantly invokes in his actual biological explanations material necessities that he sometimes explicitly *contrasts* with hypothetical ones; he does this even in *PA* I I less than twenty lines after the second of the two passages on hypothetical necessity cited above (642a31–b4, cf. esp. a32–5; for other similar passages see Balme, op. cit., 76–84). I believe Balme's attempt to accommodate these invocations of necessity to the prevailing interpretation of Aristotle's official position is quite unsatisfactory (Sorabji, op. cit., 149–50, 152–4, 162–3, gives a partial rebuttal of Balme's argument). But, more importantly, it is unnecessary; Aristotle's official position does not in fact deny *all* material necessity of an unhypothetical kind, and easily accommodates all the passages in the biological works where non-hypothetical necessities are invoked (if one discounts the occasional overgenerous concession to his materialist opponents, e.g. *GA* v 8, 789b2–5). What he denies is only that a natural *goal* (the whole living thing, with its fully formed organs) is ever produced by material necessity of a Democritean kind: that is, you cannot argue simply from the natures and powers of the materials present at the beginning of the process to their transformation into the fully-formed living thing that eventually results. This is implied already by the way in expounding his view he makes comparisons to artifacts, e.g. walls and whole houses: the claim (see *PA* 639b27–30, *Ph.* 200a1–8, b1–4) is just that neither the whole artifact nor the whole animal is brought into being by material necessities. *Mete.* IV 12, 390b12–14 makes the point very clearly: 'though cold and heat and their motion cause bronze or silver to come to be they do not cause a saw or a cup or a box to come to be; here craftsmanship is the cause, and in the other cases [the cases of natural generation] nature'. If the passages about hypothetical necessity are read carefully and their contexts are borne in mind, I think the intended limitations emerge quite clearly enough: *some* things that happen in the course of formation of a living thing *do* happen by material necessity (e.g., *GA* II 4, 739b26–30, a membrane takes shape round the newly forming animal fetation by this kind of necessity – from one point of view, it's like any other thickish fluid, milk for example, acted on by heat), but, Aristotle insists, the *whole sequence* of events leading up to the fully-formed creature does not. (Of course any talk in Aristotle of the necessity of events in the sublunary world must be understood not to apply strictly, since according to him such events only happen for the most part in any given way and never absolutely always so; strictly therefore Aristotle's material necessities do not conform to the Democritean idea of *absolute* necessity. But this difference must not be allowed to distract attention from the fact that Aristotle does allow significant scope to material necessity of essentially the type for which Democritus argued.)

which constitutes the normal, fully-formed specimen of the species in question. But Aristotle argues that as a matter of fact it is not possible to complete the project of derivation thus envisaged. Acquaintance with the various kinds of matter there are and the ways in which by their natures they behave under various conditions does not permit one to think that there *are* any true principles at this level sufficiently strong and comprehensive to make any such derivation possible. The Democritean hypothesis that there is a set of fixed, true principles specifying how material particles of different sizes and shapes behave under various conditions, and that everything that happens happens as a result of these principles ('by brute necessity') is mere fantasy. *Some* things do happen by this kind of necessity; but not very much does, and it is certainly not possible to start merely from a description in materialist terms of, say, a sperm and some female matter, together with a similar description of the environing conditions, and build up, step-by-step, with appeal only to material necessity, the complex and highly organised newborn animal that *always*, unless something specifiable goes wrong, results. If one actually studies how matter, as such, behaves, instead of inventing theories about such things, Aristotle thought, one will see at once that this is so.

It is easy for us, with the hindsight made possible by post-Renaissance experimental physics and chemistry to suppose that Aristotle's atomist opponents had the better of this dispute. But such an attitude is quite unhistorical. The ancient atomists had no *empirical* reason to think that the powers attributable to matter of different kinds were sufficient to determine any of the actually observed outcomes. No Greek theorist had any conception of what controlled experiment might show about the powers of matter; insofar as empirical evidence bearing on this question was available either to Aristotle or to his opponents it amounted to no more than what ordinary observation could yield. And there is no doubt that ordinary observation, so far from suggesting any universal necessitation of such outcomes by the inherent properties of matter, leads to Aristotle's more modest estimate of what can be explained by reference to the material and moving causes. Who, having observed what happens when fire is applied to a stick of wood, would suppose that the material characteristics of that stick and that fire, together with the prevailing conditions of air-flow, and so on, dictate that just *so* much ash will result, and in just *that* arrangement? That the stick will be consumed, that it will be turned to ashes – that is clear; but ordinary observation does not license the belief that the outcome is in further particulars determined one way or the other. Similarly, when wet warm stuff, such as fourth-century scientists thought gave rise to an animal fetus, was affected by the watery, mobile stuff of the male semen, there might be grounds, taking into account only what follows from their constitution as stuffs of a certain consistency, etc., for thinking that some congealing and setting effect will result. But that the congealing and setting should be precisely that which constitutes an animal fetus? There was no reason at all to believe that *this* was determined on *that* sort of ground. So insofar as either Aristotle or the atomists had an empirical basis for their views about the powers of matter, Aristotle's position was far stronger. I do not mean to deny, of course, the inherent theoretical strengths of the atomists' 'programme'; but insofar as the dispute between them and Aristotle turned on actual evidence, Aristotle clearly had the better of this argument.

What then does account for the production of an animal fetus under the conditions in which we know such a fetus is produced? In his account in *Metaphysics* 1 of his predecessors' views on explanation, Aristotle remarks that some earlier philosophers (e.g. Anaxagoras) recognised that material necessity did not suffice, and also saw that one could not well say that there is no general explanation at all, that this outcome was due simply to chance – holding that *some* particular arrangement or other of the materials as they are congealed and set has to result, and that it just happens each time that what results is a properly constructed fetus of the appropriate kind (984b11–15). One might, I suppose, say that it is only a long run of luck that, so far as we know, has produced this regular-seeming result up to now, and that things may soon start turning out differently. But, as we have seen, Aristotle plausibly argued there was reason to believe that this is how things *always* have been and *always* will be. And if it *always* happens like this, throughout all time, some further explanation is required; it cannot be a matter of luck. So if this fact cannot be explained by deriving it from more basic natural facts about the material constitution of the world, then one must either invoke supernatu-

ral powers as responsible for it, or else posit as a second level of
basic natural fact that the world permanently contains plants and
animals (in addition to matter of various kinds), and indeed
precisely the *same* plants and animals at all times. In other words: *if*
one is determined to treat these regularities as a fact of nature, and
they cannot be derived from other natural principles, one must
take them as expressing a natural principle all on their own. Thus
Aristotle's response, that it is an inherent, non-derivative fact
about the natural world that it consists in part of the natural kinds
and works to maintain them permanently in existence, is an
eminently reasonable, even scientific, one.

But now – and this is the crucial point for our present discussion
– by adopting the view that plants and animals are a basic, and not
a derived, constituent of physical reality, one provides the theoretical background necessary to justify the appeal to goals in
explaining the recurrent processes of animal and plant generation
that we have been discussing. For, on this view, there is inherent
in the world a fundamental tendency to preserve permanently the
species of living things it contains. But the living things in
question are so structured that each one's organs and other parts
work together to make it possible for it to achieve to a rather high
degree its own specific good, the full and active life characteristic
of its kind, including the leaving of offspring behind; the actual
plant and animal life that is preserved is all of it *good*. One can
therefore claim to discover in any given process of animal
generation one of those processes in which the tendency to
preserve the species of living things is concretely realised. And because the regular outcome of each such process is something good,
one is also entitled to interpret the process itself as directed at that
outcome as its goal. For if it is a fundamental fact about the world,
not derivable from other natural principles, that it maintains
forever these good life-forms, then the processes by which it does
so, being processes by which something good is achieved, are for
the sake of the outcomes. Thus, for example, fetal materials
coming from a female dog and acted upon by a male dog's sperm
are transformed by certain definite stages into a puppy. This
transformation cannot be explained by reference to the material
constitution of these antecedent stuffs; left to themselves these
materials would not, or would not certainly, have produced just
those formations in which the features and organs that characterise

a dog are developed. What happens in this case needs to be explained by referring to the fundamental tendency of the natural kinds of living things to be preserved in existence, and recognising that this process is one of those by which a species, the dog, preserves itself by reproduction. This tendency, which is not ultimately reducible to the powers and properties of matter-kinds, is irreducibly teleological; it is the tendency of certain materials to interact, be formed and transformed in certain ways, *so as* to produce a well-formed, well-adapted, viable new specimen of the same species as the animals from which they came. So, given his view that living things are basic to the permanent structure of the world, Aristotle can argue that those stages in the formation of a fetus in which one can discern the development of the features and organs of the mature animal being produced are *for the sake of* that animal nature which is the final outcome of the process.

It is, then, by two related arguments professing to address observed natural facts and the need to explain them that Aristotle offers his best and most interesting reasons for accepting teleological explanations in the study of nature. In each of these the permanence of the natural kinds of living things figures prominently. In the first it is the fact that the permanent natural kinds are all of them well-adapted – that living things' organic and other parts serve their needs by enabling them to survive and flourish in their natural environments – that is said to demand teleological explanation, even if mechanical principles sufficed to explain everything else about them. In the argument just examined the focus is on the more elementary (alleged) fact that plants and animals are very complex objects whose regular and permanent production the natural powers of the matter-kinds are not sufficient to explain; that this nonetheless happens is only explicable, according to Aristotle, if we suppose the regular production of these objects is a fundamental goal (or rather, set of goals) in nature, so that the presence in nature of these goals is what makes the processes of animal and plant generation come about always in the way that they do.

It is worth emphasising that, as I have just implied, the teleological explanations that these arguments of Aristotle's are meant to endorse are best construed as causal explanations of a certain kind, whatever one may think of them so construed. On

Aristotle's view, certain goals *actually exist* in *rerum natura*; there *are* in reality those plants and animal forms that he argues are natural goals. Their existence there is what controls and directs those aspects of the processes of generation that need to be explained by reference to them, and that, indeed, is why they need to be so explained. Thus one could put Aristotle's view by saying that *one* kind of causal explanation refers to antecedent material conditions and powers: what *makes* wood burn when fire is applied to it is that fire is hot and so has the power to act in this way on wood. The given material natures of fire and wood are simply such that this happens. But similarly what *makes* a particular series of transformations take place in the generation of a dog is that it is a fundamental fact about nature that each kind of living thing reproduces so as to preserve itself. That series is made to happen *because* what is being formed is a dog, and it is a dog's nature to have certain particular organs and other features. Here what Aristotle thinks of as the cause of what happens is located not in the material nature of anything but in a certain formal nature, that of the dog. The recent tendency to explicate and defend Aristotelian teleology exclusively by appeal to essentially epistemological considerations leaves out of account this crucial fact about Aristotle's theory, that he grounds his teleological explanations thus in the very nature of things. It is quite true, and important, as for example Richard Sorabji says, that we will certainly always need teleological explanations, no matter how much we learn about causal mechanisms, because, among other reasons, our interests in asking 'Why?' sometimes cannot be satisfied otherwise than by noticing some good that the thing inquired into does.[9] But it would be misleading to put such considerations forward as providing insight into Aristotle's theory or his reasons for holding it. For they leave out of account the fact that for Aristotle such explanations only *truly* explain where, and because, reality is *actually governed* in the ways the explanations claim; what our interests demand is only of significance where they may be satisfied by pointing to something about the actual workings of things. Here as elsewhere for Aristotle ontology takes precedence over epistemology. His

9 Sorabji, op. cit., 165–6. See the similar remarks of Martha Nussbaum, *Aristotle's De Motu Animalium* (Princeton 1978), 69–70, 78–80. Both authors record their indebtedness here to Charles Taylor's work on teleological explanation.

commitment to teleological explanation is fundamentally misunderstood where this fact is not borne clearly in mind.[10]

## III

We have now, I believe, uncovered the key to the interpretation of Aristotelian natural teleology: it is the alleged *fact* of the permanence of the species of livings things, not explicable, as Aristotle plausibly thinks, on other natural principles, that constitutes the foundation and justification for all the types of teleological arguments he ever accepts in the natural sciences, with only one small class of exceptions. In my discussion so far I have emphasised the teleological explanation of processes of animal and plant generation. But it is easy to see that this same principle of the preservation of the species licenses other sorts of teleological explanation as well. Three of these are worth mentioning here because they are sorts of teleological explanation that Aristotle himself does, at one place or another and with apparent conviction, actually offer in his scientific writings. And since these three, together with the explanation of the processes of generation of living things, constitute all the principal kinds of teleological explanation to be found in Aristotle, one is entitled to conclude that it is on the principle of the permanence of the species that Aristotle ultimately rests his belief in the goal-directedness of nature in general.

To begin with, then, this principle allows full scope for functional analyses of living things, and for teleological arguments based upon them. Given Aristotle's assumption that natural kinds are preserved, the normal member of each kind must be viable in its natural habitat; it must grow to adulthood, preserve itself for some normal period and arrange for the continuance of the species through successful reproductive activities. On this basis one can appeal, as Aristotle attempts to do *in extenso* in the *De Partibus*, to the contribution to a creature's life made by a given organ or other part as

10 This difference between Aristotle and contemporary defenders of teleological (or, as people now for no very good reason say, teleonomic) argument in biology is well brought out by a comment of David Hull. Focusing on the issue of reductionism Hull points out that the dispute nowadays is over 'methodological reduction' and 'theory reduction', not 'ontological reduction'. 'Nowadays both scientists and philosophers take ontological reduction for granted. . . . Organisms are "nothing but" atoms, and that is that' (Hull, 'Philosophy and Biology', forthcoming in G. Fløistad, ed., *Contemporary Philosophy: A Survey*, vol. II (The Hague 1981), typescript, p. 3). When Aristotle opposes the reduction of teleological explanation to mechanical-efficient causation he is opposing ontological reduction just as much as methodological (and theory) reduction.

the explanation for its having that organ or part. Because every animal and plant must have a structure and organisation that makes it a viable form of life, one is entitled to examine each species to see what in *its* organisation contributes to viability; in discovering what each single organ or part does to this end (given what the others do), one discovers what makes the animal have that part.[11]

Secondly, Aristotle's assumption of the preservation of the species also licenses a wide variety of teleological explanations of facts about the physical environment. For if the species are to be preserved, the environment must both support the continued existence of the mature members of the species, and provide the conditions under which new generations are produced and brought to maturity. So one is entitled, on Aristotle's assumption, to study the physical environment with a view to discovering the features of it that support the life-cycles of the natural kinds the world contains. In discovering, for example, that heavy rain in winter and spring and warmth in summer and fall are necessary first to bring to life and then to promote the maturation of the world's plant-life, one discovers why there is rain in winter and heat in summer.[12] So far as I am aware the frequency of rain in

11 In this summary I do not distinguish the several different ways in which Aristotle argues that an animal has an organ because it needs it. He says (e.g. at *PA* 11, 640a33–b1, *GA* 14, 717a15–16) that some organs are necessary for an animal (or a given animal) to have (all animals must have sense-organs, blooded ones a heart, those that eat certain kinds of food multiple stomachs), while others that are not strictly necessary (the creature could survive without them) nonetheless do the animal good (flexible bone joints allow ease of movement, the kidney enables the bladder to do its job better, external testes free the animal from the need for urgent and violent sexual activity). It should be observed that despite these differences the patterns of argument here are basically the same: in both types of case an animal is argued to have an organ because it is *good* for it to have it. In one case, having it is good because otherwise it would not exist or survive at all; in the other, having it is good because otherwise its existence would be encumbered in some respect. The difference is thus just that between two aspects of the single natural goal associated with each species; if nature makes animals viable because that is for their good, it is only to be expected that it advances their good in further ways, too. Sorabji in an interesting account of Aristotle's teleological analyses of animal organs (op. cit., ch. 10, esp. 155–60) neglects this common connection to the animal's good and as a result overemphasises the differences between these two patterns of argument.

12 See *Ph.* 198b36–a5. It is sometimes overlooked that here, in preparing his defence against the anti-teleological argument stated just previously, Aristotle unequivocally endorses the teleological explanation of these meteorological regularities: these things, he says, do not happen by coincidence (ἀπὸ συμπτώματος), but must happen either in that way or for the sake of an end (ἕνεκά του), so that (199a5) they must be for the sake of an end (ἕνεκά του ἂν εἴη). The fact that he endorses the non-teleological view of these phenomena in giving his opponents' argument just before (198b18–23) is perfectly natural, since he is there speaking for them and not for himself. What his response shows is that he rejects both their premises and their conclusion. Nussbaum (op. cit., 94) is therefore wrong to cite 198b18–21 as evidence that Aristotle rejected such arguments as illegitimate.

winter and heat in summer are the only features of the physical environment that Aristotle ever explicitly offers to explain teleologically: in the *Meteorologica* and other places where he discusses such matters he seems to concentrate on material and moving causes in explaining the phenomena. Perhaps he thought these processes were too remote for us to gain knowledge about how they operate sufficient to say what they were for; possibly with greater knowledge he would have begun to find a more extensive set of patterns of a teleological kind. In any event, it is clear both that his fundamental assumption about the preservation of the species makes teleological explanations possible here, and that he himself, in the case of winter rain and summer heat, actually gives some.

Lastly, the account I have just given of the basis on which Aristotle explains the cycle of the seasons suggests the possibility of similar explanations of certain interactions among species. After all, an important part of the environmental needs of any species is the need for food of an appropriate sort, and this means that one should be in a position to say of some given plant and animal species, which serve as food for given other species, that the former exist *in part* for the sake of the latter. And there are other ways in which the species serve one another, e.g. the complementarity of plants and animals vis-à-vis carbon dioxide and oxygen. Where such adaptation exists Aristotle's principle of the preservation of the species will support the claim that the species which contributes to the continuance of another exists in part for the sake of the latter. And in a well-known passage of the *Politics* (1 8, 1256b15–22), Aristotle argues in precisely this way, though in considering primarily the relation of plants and animals to human needs he fails to represent accurately the full state of affairs.

We must suppose that plants are for the sake of the animals and that the other animals are for the sake of human beings – the domesticated ones both for their usefulness and for food, the wild ones (most of them, at any rate, if not all) for the sake of food and for support in other ways, to provide clothing and other instruments. If then nature makes nothing incomplete or without a point it is necessary that nature has made them all [i.e. I take it, all the other *animals*] for the sake of human beings.

Given the assumption of the permanence of the natural kinds what Aristotle says here seems perfectly justified (provided that one takes seriously his disclaimer that perhaps not *all* animals can be seen as supporting human life). Of course, he omits to mention either the ways in which animals serve plants, which support the reverse judgement that animals are for the sake of plants (think of bees), or the ways in which human beings serve the animals that they make use of and eat. (Presumably many domesticated species would long ago have passed out of existence if human beings had not protected them.) But though Aristotle's account is objectionably one-sided, the basic idea that plant and animal species exist for one another's sake is sound, if his general principle of the preservation of the kinds is true. It is worth noting that it also follows from this principle that any species that makes use of another for its own survival must not so reduce it that it fails to continue in existence. And that fact might be made the basis for a further application of teleology. In one passage (but, it seems, only one) Aristotle does argue in such a way. He mentions that some fish (dolphins, he wrongly says, and sharks) have their mouths underneath and therefore turn on their backs to get their food, and explains this as follows:

It looks as if nature does this not only for the sake of preserving other animals (for while they take time to turn on their backs the other animals save themselves – all the species in question feed on animals), but also to prevent them from indulging their insatiable appetite for food. For if they got food more easily they would quickly destroy themselves through overeating (*PA* IV 13, 696b25–32).

Thus as a fourth class of teleological explanations, though it is one he almost entirely neglects in his biological writings, we can add explanations drawn from the adaptedness of plant and animal species to one another.[13]

13 There is no need to apologise as Nussbaum seeks to do (op. cit., 95–8) for Aristotle's occasional indulgence in this fourth kind of argument. The principles which support the other sorts of teleological argument, even those (the first two) which Nussbaum approves, equally support arguments of this fourth kind. She does not explain very clearly why she deprecates them, but I suspect that a certain looseness in her use of the expression 'universal teleology of nature' leads her astray. Aristotle does indeed deny, what Plato is at least verbally committed to, that 'the universe as a whole is an organism with its own *logos* and its own good' (p. 97), but that is perfectly compatible with holding that one species subserves the needs of another and exists partly for that reason. For here the good appealed to is not the proprietary good of the universe as a whole, but only that of that other species. I do not see why this should be described, as Nussbaum describes it, as a 'universal teleology of nature': but if it *is* so described the expression is plainly being used in a sense different from that Platonic sense to which Nussbaum rightly objects on Aristotle's behalf. It is true that the good appealed to in this fourth class of explanations is not the good of the species whose characteristics are being

In four contexts in nature, then, where Aristotle actually offers teleological explanations, such explanations are clearly authorised by the principle of the permanence of the species. There remains one class of cases that cannot be made to fit my account, because they appeal to a good that does not reduce to what some living thing needs to survive and flourish in its environment. In a number of places Aristotle appeals to a notion of fittingness derived from some conception of what is inherently well-ordered.[14] Thus he explains (*PA* II 14, 658a18–24) that in general body-hair exists for the sake of protection, which is why quadrupeds have more hair on their backs than their undersides; but because human beings stand upright (so that they are equally exposed front and back) if this need alone were operative human beings would be equally hairy in back and front. Yet in fact men have more hair on their chests. Aristotle's explanation is that the front is nobler than the back – in this case, as always, nature uses the given conditions to make *what is better*, and it is better to devote scarce resources to protect the nobler parts. In several similar cases (*PA* 665a18–26, b18–21, 667b32–5, 672b19–24, *IA* 5, 705b3–16) Aristotle explains the location of an animal organ or other part by appeal to a general principle of 'nobility' to the effect that front is better than back, above than below and right than left (stated at *PA* 665a22–6, *IA* 706b10–16); and in attributing to nature the tendency to favour the front, top and right parts *where there is no reason not to*, he attributes to it goals that are quite independent of anything required by the preservation of the species. The good aimed at here is not any living thing's good, in the sense of its survival or well-functioning. In these passages

explained, but I know of no passage in Aristotle which says or implies that teleological explanation in nature must appeal only to that kind of good. Certainly *Ph.* II 7, 198b7–8, to which Nussbaum refers, does not do so; it offers as an example the most common situation, where an organ or other part exists for the good of the creature itself which has it, but rules out only the Platonic kind of universal teleology. Our fourth kind of explanation introduces no new *goals* at all; only the good of living things is appealed to. It is just that there, as in the third kind of case, what contributes to the good of an animal kind is something that lies outside it.

14 Aristotle's argument in these cases is that the arrangements in question are 'for the better' (as he says explicitly at 658a24) but it is important not to confuse these cases with those cited above (n. 11) where e.g. an animal is said to have a kidney because it is 'for the better', i.e., better for *it*. The cases here in question are quite different, because the good in prospect is *not* the good of the species whose features are being explained. In fact, unlike all the teleological arguments so far considered, the good achieved in these cases is not the good of *any* animal or plant species at all.

Aristotle adopts a further fundamental principle about nature, that it tends to organise itself, subject to the prior satisfaction of the principle of the preservation of the species, so as to favour the front, top and right parts over the rear, bottom, and left of anything. His motivation for accepting this principle certainly has the appearance of being somewhat pre-scientific, so there is on any interpretation no alternative but to treat it and the explanations it yields as separate from the explanations we have been concentrating on. The failure of my account to rank these further cases alongside the others and range them all under a single basic principle is no ground for objecting to the account I have given of the other cases; we have to do here with two separate aspects of Aristotle's philosophy of nature, and no unified account of them is presumably to be looked for.

## IV

An attractive consequence of the account of Aristotle's commitment to natural teleology that I have given is that it explains one distinctive fact about his version of the teleological hypothesis. This is that Aristotle, unlike other teleologists of nature (Plato, the medievals, Leibniz), finds goal-directedness in natural processes without feeling any need at all to find intentions (whether God's or, somehow or other, nature itself's) lying behind and explaining it. In both the arguments we have examined in section II the central claim on which Aristotle rests his case, the principle of the permanence of the species, is offered as a *fact* about the natural world, his acceptance of which is based on ordinary observation and reasonable inference from it. And if that fact requires to be understood as the result of a tendency in nature *to* preserve these species, the goals thus postulated stand on their own without any need for support by thought processes whether in or antecedent to the arrangements of nature itself. In this crucial respect there is no difference for Aristotle between the existence of the goals of nature and the natural powers of the various kinds of matter one finds in the world. The teleological explanations based on the principle of the preservation of the species are no more mysteriously anthropomorphic and no more problematic than the mechanical explanations by reference to material and moving causes which invoke the natural powers of the various kinds of matter. Aristotle's theory that goals are at work in nature though without the support of thought-processes of any kind turns out to be both coherent and philosophically well-motivated.[15]

15 An early version of this paper was read to audiences at the Catholic University of America, Yale University and Rice University, and I profited greatly from the discussion on those occasions. In preparing the final version I benefited from comments by Jonathan Lear, James Lennox, Alexander Nehamas and Malcolm Schofield on earlier efforts. My oldest debt goes much further back, however: to 1963, when in the course of his marvellous graduate class on Aristotle, in which over a two-year period Oxford students would read and discuss Aristotle's major philosophical works, G. E. L. Owen devoted several sessions to *Physics* II. Those discussions brought out how questionable Aristotle's arguments for teleology in nature are, but also made it clear that behind them lay something quite profound, if only one could put one's finger on it. Later, in the spring of 1971, in meetings of the monthly Ancient Philosophy Colloquium that Owen presided over in New York during his Harvard years, I enjoyed further stimulating discussion of these topics. Since Owen's enormous contributions to ancient philosophy through such discussions may tend to go unrecorded, I am specially pleased to be able to offer in his honour a paper whose seed was planted and nourished in that soil.

# 11 Accidental unities

## GARETH B. MATTHEWS

> For if not the philosopher, who will it be who investigates whether Socrates and Socrates seated are the same? (*Metaph.* IV 2, 1004b1–3)

## I

In chapter 11 of his *de Interpretatione* Aristotle tries to explain why certain features of a thing go together to make up a unity, whereas others do not. 'For example,' he says, 'a man is perhaps an animal and two-footed and tame, and from these there does come to be some one thing' (20b16–8). But 'from white and man and walking,' he adds, 'there is not one thing' (20b18–19).

The reasoning in this chapter is intricate; but without tracing out the intricacies we can perhaps say that the unity Aristotle is seeking here is the oneness of an individual substance. In this passage he is unwilling to count as a unity the parasitic oneness that is enjoyed by features only accidentally compresent in a single substance. Though it may be true to say, he remarks later on in the chapter, 'The white is musical' (that is, presumably, 'The white *person* is musical'), still, he warns, *musical white* and *white musical* (contrast: *two-footed animal*) are not one thing (21a7–14).

Aristotle later softens his position. He allows, in *Metaphysics* V 6, for example, that there is such a thing as an accidental unity (*hen kata sumbebēkos*).[1] *The musical* and *the just*, he says, make up an accidental unity because musicality and justice are accidents of one substance (1015b21–2). Other examples of accidental unities that Aristotle mentions in this chapter are

Coriscus and the musical,
musical Coriscus, and
musical Coriscus and just Coriscus.

---

1 Better: unity in the accidental sense of 'unity'.

It is hard for modern readers to take Aristotle's accidental unities seriously. Yet anyone who would take Aristotle seriously must make the effort.

To be sure, Aristotle himself often ridicules those who concern themselves with such entities.[2] Thus at *Metaphysics* VI 2 he remarks, derisively, that 'the arguments of the sophists deal . . . above all with the accidental, e.g., with the question whether the musical [*mousikon*] and the literate [*grammatikon*] are different or the same and whether musical Coriscus and Coriscus are the same' (1026b15–18). Yet it isn't only the arguments of the sophists that deal with the accidental; so do the arguments of Aristotle.

Aristotle's picture of an accidental unity is that of an ephemeral object – an object whose very existence rests on the accidental presence, or compresence, of some feature, or features, in a substance. Accidental unities exist, he supposes, but not in their own right; indeed it is, Aristotle says, only in an accidental sense of the verb 'to be' that they can be said to be (*Metaph.* VI 2).

So far it may seem that accidental unities are only the harmless inventions of an idle metaphysics. But the commitment to accidental unities becomes a serious affair when Aristotle appeals to these very objects – 'kooky objects', I shall call them – to give a semantics for ordinary language.

Perhaps it isn't so alarming when Aristotle supposes that expressions like 'musical Coriscus' and 'Socrates seated' pick out kooky objects. Those expressions are odd anyway. Apart from Homeric epithets, one associates phrases of their syntactic ilk with breezy journalism ('Hollow-cheeked Jimmy Carter flashed a forced smile') and cheap novels. It is when Aristotle suggests that standard definite descriptions like 'the musical man' and 'the man in the corner' pick out kooky objects that we have trouble taking him with appropriate seriousness. For ourselves, we suppose that, in a suitable context, the expression 'the musical man' might simply pick out Coriscus, and that the expression 'the man in the corner' might simply pick out Socrates. Aristotle doesn't.

That Aristotle sees things quite differently from us comes out very clearly in, for example, *Physics* I 7. He is there considering the change that takes place when a man becomes musical; he says:

This survives but that doesn't . . . the man survives . . . but the

---

2 Or better: with entities in such a sense of 'entity'.

not-musical, or unmusical, doesn't survive, nor does the compound of the two, viz., the unmusical man (190a17–21).

In this context 'the not-musical' is the not-musical *person* (rather than nonmusicality) and 'the unmusical' is the unmusical person. What Aristotle is telling us is that, when the man becomes musical, the man survives but each of these kooky objects perishes:

the not-musical (one)
the unmusical (one)
the unmusical man.

The implications of this doctrine are staggering. When the man rises, the seated man ceases to be; when the woman awakens, the sleeping woman passes away; when the baby cries, the silent baby perishes.

Before we go any further I should admit that there is one passage in which Aristotle does seem to suggest that an accidental description might simply pick out a 'straight', rather than a kooky, object. In the first book of the *Topics* he says this:

That what I have just said is true may be best seen where one form of appellation is substituted for another. For often when we give the order to call one of the people who are sitting down, indicating him by name, we change our description, whenever the person to whom we give the order happens not to understand us; he will, we think, understand better from some accidental feature; so we bid him call to us 'the man who is sitting' or 'who is conversing over there' – clearly supposing ourselves to be indicating the same object by its name and by its accident (*Top.* I 7, 103a32–9).

At first glance it seems that Aristotle is here treating 'the man who is sitting' (*ton kathēmenon*) and 'the man who is talking over there' (*ton dialegomenon*) as alternative descriptions for, say, Coriscus. After all, Aristotle says we suppose 'ourselves to be indicating the same object (*hōs tauton . . . semainein*) by its name and by its accident'.

In fact a closer examination of this passage tells against the idea that, even here, Aristotle supposes 'the man who is sitting' or 'the musical man' might simply pick out Socrates. Aristotle has announced earlier in the chapter that he will canvass the ways in which 'same' is said or used. He has discussed 'same' meaning 'same in species' and 'same' meaning 'same in genus' and he has now come to 'same' meaning 'same in number'. Under this heading he makes three further distinctions, as follows:

It is generally supposed that the term 'the same' is most used in a sense agreed on by every one when applied to what is numerically one. But even so, it is apt to be rendered in more than one sense (*apodidosthai pleonachōs*); its most literal and primary use (*kuriōtata men kai prōtōs*) is found whenever the sameness is rendered in reference to an alternative name or definition, as when a cloak is said to be the same as a covering, or an animal that walks on two feet is said to be the same as a man: a second sense is when it is rendered in reference to a *proprium*, as when the one that can acquire knowledge is said to be the same as the man, and the thing that naturally travels upward is said to be the same as the fire: while a third use is found when it is rendered in reference to some term drawn from accident, as when the creature who is sitting, or who is musical, is called the same as Socrates (103a23–31).

Anyone who thinks that, according to Aristotle, 'the man who is sitting' and 'the musical one' simply pick out Socrates must explain why Aristotle distinguishes the sense of 'same' in which one says 'The man who is sitting and Socrates are the same' from the sense of 'same' (that of 'its most literal and primary use') in which one says, 'The man and the animal that walks on two feet are the same'. One who takes Aristotle to suppose here, as elsewhere, that accidental descriptions pick out kooky objects will have no difficulty understanding why Aristotle wants to distinguish as less favoured the sense of 'same' in which the man who is sitting may be said to be the same as Socrates. After all, the man who is sitting will perish when Socrates stands, even though Socrates will not. Although Socrates and the man who is sitting are the same (person or thing), even numerically the same (person or thing), it is only in an accidental sense that they can be said to be the same (person or thing).

So Socrates and Socrates seated (to pick up the epigram with which this paper begins) are only in a sense the same (people). Yet they are not two people, nor, indeed, two of anything else. There is not even, according to Aristotle, a univocal sense of the verb 'to be' in which they can both be said to be.

By now it may seem even more clear that talk of kooky objects is only a rather silly metaphysical parlour game. Is there any serious purpose behind such talk, anything more consequential than a simple-minded effort to find the referent of accidental descriptions like 'musical Coriscus' and 'the seated (one)'?

There is at least one use to which Aristotle puts the distinction between kooky objects and 'straight' ones (that is, substances) that will strike modern readers as certainly important. It is illustrated in Aristotle's treatment of the famous puzzle of the Masked Man (*SE* 179ab). Simplifying matters somewhat, we can perhaps say that Aristotle asks how it can be that this is true:

(1) Coriscus has the attribute of being known by Socrates to be Coriscus

and also this:

(2) Coriscus and the masked man are the same (man),

even though this is false:

(3) The masked man has the attribute of being known by Socrates to be Coriscus.

Readers of contemporary philosophy may be disconcerted by this way of stating the problem. They will be accustomed to distinguishing between (3) and

(4) Socrates knows that the masked man is Coriscus

in such a way that (3) can be true even though (4) is false. For they will be used to understanding (3) in such a way that it is hospitable to the commentary in this expanded version:

(3*) The masked man (who is, after all, Coriscus, even though Socrates doesn't realise this) has the attribute of being known by Socrates to be Coriscus.

It will be useful for my purposes, however, to understand (3) in such a way as to make the commentary in (3*) quite inappropriate; I shall take (3) as a rough equivalent of (4). Such a reading of (3), even if it does violence to a familiar philosophical convention, does none, I think, to ordinary, pedantic English.

Puzzles like the Masked Man are familiar to us today as problems about opaque contexts – contexts in which we are not guaranteed to be able to substitute co-referential expressions *salva veritate*. For Aristotle, of course, the point must be something rather different. For him, after all, 'Coriscus' and 'the masked man' are not really co-referential expressions at all. The one picks out a kooky object that perishes when Coriscus takes off his mask; the other doesn't. To be sure, the masked man is accidentally the same[3] as Coriscus. But accidental sameness is not identity and accidental sameness does not guarantee that every attribute of

---

3 For stylistic reasons I shall use 'accidentally the same' to mean 'the same in the accidental sense of "same"' and 'accidental sameness' to mean 'sameness in the accidental sense of "same"'. For warnings against such looseness, see my 'Senses and Kinds', *Journal of Philosophy*, 69 (1972), 149–57.

Coriscus is an attribute of the masked man. Only identity could give that guarantee. And so the inference from (1) and (2) to (3) fails.

I have mentioned the Masked-Man passage to illustrate the importance for Aristotle of the doctrine of kooky objects. That doctrine explains how it can be that, though Coriscus is the masked man, Coriscus and the masked man are not identical. But, of course, this will not be a point we can suppose Aristotle to be making unless we think he has, as I have already suggested that he does have, not only the concept of accidental sameness, but also the concept of identity. Recently doubt has been cast on the assumption that Aristotle has either of these concepts.


## II

One person who has cast doubt on the view that Aristotle has what I have identified as the concept of accidental sameness is Jonathan Barnes. In a review of Edwin Hartman's book, *Substance, Body and Soul*, Barnes writes as follows:

Hartman's gloss on accidental identity is puzzling. 'The man sitting over there is Socrates' expresses an accidental identity, according to Aristotle; for it is at best an accident – a contingent truth – that Socrates is sitting (cf. *Top.* 103a29ff.) But the relation in question is ordinary identity, not 'a weak sort of identity'; and it is said of Socrates and the seated man, not of *qua*-Socrates and some *qua*-man. I am not sure why Hartman ascribes a bizarre view to Aristotle; but the point is of little consequence: what matters is that the identities . . . are contingent, not necessary (*Philosophical Books*, 20 (1979), 59).

The interpretation of Aristotle that Barnes is criticising in this passage includes a doctrine considerably broader than what I call the 'doctrine of kooky objects'. I shall not discuss the broader doctrine here. But it is an implication of the broader doctrine that Socrates and the man sitting over there are not strictly identical. In this respect Hartman's interpretation agrees with the one I have been trying to set out here.

By contrast, Barnes's interpretation of Aristotle makes accidental sameness simply non-necessary identity. Thus, on his interpretation of Aristotle,

(5) Socrates is accidentally the same as musical Socrates amounts to this:

(6) (Socrates = musical Socrates) and ~ □ (Socrates = musical Socrates)

Barnes cites *Topics* I 7, 103a29ff. (which I have already discussed) to substantiate his interpretation. But neither that passage, nor any other passage I know of, glosses 'accidental sameness' as 'non-necessary identity.'

There is perhaps a further objection to Barnes's interpretation. The *Topics* passage by implication, and other passages by explicit assertion, tell us that if *A* is accidentally the same as *B*, then *A* and *B* are in a way (*pōs*), or in a sense, the same, and in a way, or in a sense, different – though not absolutely (*haplōs*) different. This is the implication of the *Topics* passage because, in it, the accidental sense of 'same' is distinguished from that most strict and primary sense of 'same' in which a cloak is said to be the same as a covering, or a man the same as a two-footed animal. (One takes Aristotle to be supposing here that 'two-footed animal' is at least a stand-in definition of 'man'.) It is quite explicit in other passages, for example in these:

A thing and the thing modified are in a way (*pōs*) the same, for example, Socrates and musical Socrates (*Metaph.* v 29, 1024b30–1).
. . . you should say that the subject of an accident is not absolutely (*haplōs*) different from the accident taken along with its subject [for example, the man and the white man] (*Top.* v 4, 133b31–6).

If Barnes were right in thinking that, for Aristotle, accidental sameness is merely contingent identity, then Aristotle would have no reason to say of things he tells us are accidentally the same that, while they are in a way, or in a sense, the same, they are in a way, or sense, different – though not absolutely different. Things that are contingently identical are not in a way the same and in a way different. Being identical they are absolutely the same, even if it is only a contingent fact that they are absolutely the same.

It is important to note that Aristotle's concept of accidental sameness has little to do with what has been discussed in the recent philosophical literature as 'relative identity'. The Doctrine of Relative Identity comes in at least two forms. In its weaker form, it is the claim that every assertion that something, *x*, is identical with something, *y*, must be understood as a claim that could be put in this form: *x* is the same *F* as *y*. For example, the claim that Dr Jekyll is identical with Mr Hyde might be understood as the claim that Dr Jekyll is the same *man*, or the same *person*, as Mr

Hyde. (This is what David Wiggins calls 'D' or 'Sortal Dependency' in his *Sameness and Substance* (Cambridge, Mass. 1980, 15ff.).)

In its strong form the Doctrine of Relative Identity adds to the above claim that a conjunction of this form might conceivably be true:

$x$ is the same $F$ as $y$;

$x$ is a $G$ and yet

$x$ is not the same $G$ as $y$.

(This is what Wiggins in *Sameness and Substance* calls 'R' or 'the Relativity of Identity'.)

Locke, for example, might be thought to hold views that commit him to supposing that, although Dr Jekyll is the same *man* as Mr Hyde and Dr Jekyll is a person, still Dr Jekyll is perhaps not the same *person* as Mr Hyde. The reason would presumably have to do with the fact that, whereas for Locke some sort of memory criterion is both necessary and sufficient for sameness of person, that criterion is neither necessary nor sufficient for sameness of man. (Cf. John Locke, *Essay Concerning Human Understanding* II 27, 'Of Ideas of Identity and Diversity'.)

I agree with Nicholas White when he says, in a seminal article on these issues, that, although Aristotle 'maintains that the word "same" carries many senses, he does not offer to resolve its ambiguity by coupling it with general terms'. ('Aristotle on Sameness and Oneness', *Philosophical Review*, 80(1971), 178). Even if one succeeded in extracting the weaker form of the Doctrine of Relative Identity from Aristotle's writings (perhaps by paying special attention to the opening chapters of *Metaphysics* x), that doctrine would have little direct bearing on the claim that it is only accidentally that Coriscus and the masked man are the same. One would simply have to add (what it is a good idea to add anyway, namely) that it is only accidentally that they are the same *man*.

## III

Let's suppose, then, that Aristotle really does have the concept of accidental sameness. Does he also have the concept of identity?

In 'Aristotle on Sameness and Oneness' Nicholas White claims that Aristotle begins, in the *Topics*, with a 'relatively firm grasp of something like the notion of identity', but that Aristotle's grasp soon slips – already, in fact, in his *Sophistical Refutations*. It is puzzling to think that someone might go, indeed go rather quickly, from having a relatively good grasp of something like the notion of identity to having a poor grasp of that notion. It is especially puzzling if that someone is Aristotle.

White has an explanation to offer. It has to do with (i) a connection between 'same' (*'tauton'*) and 'one' (*'hen'*), (ii) an apparent ambiguity in expressions of the form, '*x* and *y* are one', and (iii) a philosophical legacy that, White says, Aristotle takes from Plato. These three points are interesting and important in themselves and can be discussed on their own. I shall not discuss them here. (For a discussion of (i) and (ii) see Fred D. Miller, Jr, 'Did Aristotle Have the Concept of Identity?' *Philosophical Review*, 82 (1973), 483–90.)

Is there really anything to explain? What is the evidence that Aristotle loses his relatively firm grasp on something like the notion of identity? What is the evidence he ever had such a grasp?

First, let's consider the evidence White offers for saying that Aristotle has, in the *Topics* anyway, a 'relatively good grasp of something like the notion of identity'. The evidence seems to consist in the fact that Aristotle offers a statement that looks to us very much like the Principle of the Indiscernibility of Identicals. Following modern practice, White calls the principle 'Leibniz's Law' (or 'LL' for short) and formulates it this way:

(7) If *A* and *B* are identical, then whatever is true of the one is true of the other (178–9).

White tells us that Aristotle states (7) at *Topics* VII 1, 152b25–9, after first having produced these two restricted versions of it:

(8a) If *A* and *B* are the same, then any accident of *A* is an accident of *B* and vice versa (178).

(8b) If *A* and *B* are the same, then whatever is a 'property' (*proprium, idion*) of the one is a 'property of the other' (179).

White finds (8a) stated at 152a31–2 and (8b) stated already at *Topics* v 4, 133a32–4.

It is worth noting that (7) contains the word 'identical' whereas (8a) and (8b) use only the vaguer word 'same' to translate Aristotle's *'tauton'*. Since the point at issue is whether Aristotle gives evidence here of having the concept of identity, it would be well to have this formulation in play as well:

(7*) If *A* and *B* are the same, then whatever is true of the one is true of the other.

Now the question is whether Aristotle affirms (7) at 152b25–9, or only (7★) instead.

White is, of course, well aware that '*tauton*' is more elastic than 'identical'. He warns us in his very first sentence that '*tauton*' 'cannot by any means be uniformly translated by the word "identical"' (177). Why then should he, or we, suppose that it can and should be so translated in the relevant part of *Topics* VII 1?

I can think of only two reasons. The first is that the general form of what Aristotle says at 152b25–9 reminds us of LL. That, of course, is not a very good reason. The second is that, unless 'same' in (7★) is taken to mean 'identical', the statement will be open to countless counter-examples. For example, though this Barbie doll and that Barbie doll are the same – indeed, as the salesperson rightly assures me, they are *exactly* the same – it is true of one, but not of the other, that I am holding it in my right hand. Is this last reason a good reason to read (7★) at 152b25–9 as (7)? It is not, I think, a very good reason unless we can find Aristotle confidently turning aside what would be counter-examples to (7★) on its looser reading. If, instead, we find him amending (7★), or qualifying it, so as to be able to cope with counter-examples to it, we have, I think, reason for supposing that '*tauton*' in this passage means something looser than 'identical'.

In fact White cites two passages (*SE* 24, 179a, and *Ph.* III 3, 202b14–16) in which Aristotle tries to cope with apparent counter-examples to (7★) by producing a more restricted principle. The first is the Masked-Man passage, which we have already discussed. The second passage is one in which Aristotle points out that, though the road from Thebes to Athens and the road from Athens to Thebes are the same (road), it is true of one that it is uphill and the other that it is downhill. What Aristotle does in each of these cases is to produce a tighter and more restricted principle than (7★). At 179a37–9 he offers this:

(9) If *A* and *B* are without difference and one in being (*ousia*), then whatever belongs to one belongs to the other.

At 202b14–16 he offers this:

(10) If *A* and *B* are the same, not just in a way (*pōs*), but such that their being (*to einai*) is the same, then whatever belongs to one belongs to the other.

These two passages seem to show Aristotle coping with counter-examples to (7★) by amending and tightening up that principle.

Thus they count against our saying that what Aristotle means at 152b25–9 is already (7), and not just something as vague and loose as (7★).

On the other hand, these two passages seem to show that when Aristotle wrote them he was indeed working towards something like our notion of identity. Indeed the progression from (7★) to (9) and (10) seems to show a movement towards, rather than away from, the concept of identity. For ourselves, we might want to say that Coriscus is identical with the masked man, and that the road from Thebes to Athens is identical with the road from Athens to Thebes. But we would have to admit that if Coriscus has an attribute that the masked man lacks (such as the attribute of being known by Socrates to be Coriscus), he is not identical with the masked man. Similarly, if the road from Thebes to Athens has an attribute that the road from Athens to Thebes lacks (say, the attribute of being downhill), then the road from Thebes to Athens is not identical with the road from Athens to Thebes. It is very natural to understand Aristotle as getting at just this point with his clumsy expressions, 'without difference and one in being (*ousia*)' and 'not just the same in a way, but such that their being (*to einai*) is the same'.

Perversely, the very evidence I have offered for saying that Aristotle does not display a good grasp of the notion of identity at 152b25–9, but begins to do so at 179a37–9 and 202b14–16, is offered by White as evidence that Aristotle loses his grip on the notion of identity. How can this be?

The first thing to note is that White supposes the substitution of (9) for (7★) 'clearly retracts some of what has been said at 152b25–9'. What does it retract? White speaks of 'this new restriction' embodied in (9) in a way that suggests that, according to him, Aristotle means to be limiting the force or application of LL.

There are, I take it, two general ways in which one might try to limit the force or application of LL. One would be by limiting the range of identicals to which it applies; thus some identicals would be guaranteed to be indiscernible, others not. The other way to restrict LL would be to restrict the indiscernibility it guarantees; thus identicals would be guaranteed to be indiscernible with respect to attributes of one class, but not another.

Let's consider the second approach first. A natural suggestion for limiting the force of LL is this:

(7a) If *A and B* are identical, then whatever non-intentional attribute belongs to the one belongs to the other.

One could then allow that, although Coriscus and the masked man are identical, and though Coriscus has the attribute of being known by Socrates to be Coriscus, yet the masked man does not have that attribute. That situation would not flout (7a), since the attribute of being known by Socrates to be Coriscus is an intentional one.

Whatever Aristotle's 'restriction' is at 179a37–9, it is not this one. In fact it is not a restriction on kinds of indiscernibility at all. If anything, (9) offers a restriction on the identicals guaranteed to be indiscernible (the other possible approach mentioned above). Perhaps it amounts to this:

(9a) If *A* and *B* are identical and if they are also without difference and one in being, then whatever belongs to one belongs to the other.

But now how is 'identical' to be understood in (9a)? Either what it means guarantees indiscernibility or it doesn't. Suppose it does. Then it guarantees that *A* and *B* are without difference. It also guarantees that *A* and *B* are one in being. For surely *A* is one in being with *A* and *B* is one in being with *B*. If *A* is not one in being with *B*, or *B* one in being with *A*, then *A* has an attribute (being one in being with *A*) that *B* lacks and *B* has an attribute (being one in being with *B*) that *A* lacks and so *A* and *B* are not indiscernible. Thus if 'identical' in (9a) is understood in such a way that it guarantees indiscernibility, the rest of the antecedent is otiose and constitutes no restriction whatsoever.

Suppose, on the other hand, that 'identical' in (9a) is not understood in such a way that what it means guarantees indiscernibility. Then there is no reason to think that it is Leibniz's Law that is being restricted by the second clause of the antecedent. In fact, as I have already suggested, there is reason to think that (9), and hence (9a), are simply cumbersome ways of *stating* LL.

People sometimes say that the force or application of LL needs to be restricted when what they have in mind restricting is not (7) but rather a second-order analogue of LL, such as this:

(7b) If $\alpha$ and $\beta$ are co-referential singular terms, they may be substituted, one for the other, in all contexts, *salva veritate*.

Aristotle's Masked-Man example might be thought to show us that we don't want to allow the substitution of the expression 'the masked man' for, say, the first occurrence of 'Coriscus' in

Socrates knows that Coriscus is Coriscus

even if 'Coriscus' and 'the masked man' are co-referential singular terms. So we might try amending (7b) to this:

(7c) If $\alpha$ and $\beta$ are co-referential singular terms, they may be substituted, one for the other, in all purely extensional contexts, *salva veritate*.

But Aristotle doesn't move in that direction either. So far as I know, he never formulates anything like either (7b) or (7c).

So the situation is this. Aristotle seems to have come to suppose that something more than mere sameness is required to guarantee indiscernibility. Should we understand him as supposing that something more than *identity* is required? I think not, for two reasons. First, the main reason for thinking he demands something more than identity rests on reading 'same' in (7★) to mean 'identical' and we have seen that there is inadequate reason for doing that. Second, it is hard to see how anyone could suppose that identity plus some other condition would succeed in guaranteeing indiscernibility where 'mere' identity had failed; the thought seems incoherent.

I can think of only one other reason for taking 179a37–9 and 202b14–16 to constitute evidence that Aristotle was losing whatever grasp he might have had on something like the concept of identity. One might think it so obvious that Coriscus and the masked man are identical and also so obvious that the road from Thebes to Athens is identical with the road from Athens to Thebes that one would view any hesitation to agree with these judgements as evidence that the hesitator lacks a good grasp of the concept of identity.

We can't attribute this reasoning to White, however. It is a great merit of his discussion that he takes seriously Aristotle's doctrine of kooky objects. Unless White supposes that the notion of an accidental unity is incoherent, and he seems not to suppose that, then he would understand the view that Coriscus is not identical with the masked man, even if he doesn't agree with it.

## IV

What is one to make of the doctrine of kooky objects? perhaps the best way to conceive it is to think of it as a way of trying to understand how it is we are justified in rejecting certain unwarranted arguments.

To facilitate conceiving the doctrine in this way one could construct a formal, or linguistic, model of the doctrine of kooky objects. Premises to the effect that $x$ is the same person or thing as $y$ would be reconstrued as premises to the effect that $\alpha$ and $\beta$ are (as we, *but not Aristotle*, would want to say) co-referential. For example, 'Coriscus and the masked man are the same person' would go over into'"Coriscus" and "the masked man" are co-referential.' Then one could distinguish between 'hard' singular terms and 'soft' ones. The hard ones would be either proper names or expressions made up of a definite article or demonstrative plus the proper term for a real species or genus, or its logical equivalent (e.g., 'the man', 'this two-legged animal'). The substitution rule would limit guaranteed substitutivity, *salva veritate*, to co-referential singular terms that are both hard. The idea would be that all and only arguments that could be validated with such a restrictive substitution rule would have material analogues that the doctrine of kooky objects allows to be valid.

On this formal model the Masked-Man example might be reconstrued as the problem about how 'Socrates knows that Coriscus is Coriscus' can be true and 'Socrates knows that the masked man is Coriscus' false when 'Socrates' and 'the masked man' are co-referential singular terms. The solution would be that 'the masked man' is a soft singular term and thus fails to fall under the substitution rule.

Of course the Masked Man is not the only sort of argument Aristotle hopes to use the doctrine of kooky objects to extricate himself from; he has other epistemic and doxastic arguments in mind as well. Moreover, Aristotle is perhaps even more interested in arguments concerning time and change than in those that concern knowledge, belief and intention.

In a resourceful and thoughtful paper, 'Aristotle's Response to Quine's Objections to Modal Logic' (*Journal of Philosophical Logic,* 5 (1976), 159–86), Alan Code has called our attention to an argument that Aristotle mentions at *Metaphysics* VI 2, 1026b18–20. We can render the argument, somewhat loosely, this way:

*Argument A*

(11) The musical (one) has become the literate (one).

So: (12) The musical (one) and the literate (one) are the same (person).

So: (13) The literate (one) has become the musical (one).

Quite obviously (13) is an unwanted conclusion. Moreover, the same means we use to get (13) we can also use to get these further unwanted conclusions:

(14) The musical (one) has become the musical (one).

(15) The literate (one) has become the literate (one).

We aren't going to be very clear about metaphysical problems of change unless we known how to deal with such arguments as these. Aristotle's solvent is, again, the doctrine of kooky objects, according to which (12) should be read as a claim of merely accidental sameness. So understood, it fails to support (13), (14) or (15).

Incidentally, Code, like White before him, suggests that a kooky object might be thought of as a segment of a four-dimensional object (a 'space–time worm', as it is sometimes called); but this can't be right. White concedes that Aristotle 'does not . . . have the notion of four-dimensional spatiotemporal objects' (195). And Code supplies no evidence to show otherwise. Without the concept of a space–time worm Aristotle can hardly be thought to have the concept of a segment of a space–time worm.

Code is perhaps attracted to the space–time worm idea by concentrating on puzzles of time and change in Aristotle. When one notes, however, that the doctrine of kooky objects is meant to deal with epistemic puzzles as well as temporal ones, the attractiveness fades. After all, there is no reason why a kooky object could not have the same temporal boundaries as the substance it rides on. Thus suppose that Coriscus is, from birth, the favourite son of Electra. Then the favourite son of Electra could lack the attribute of being known by Socrates to be Coriscus even though Coriscus has it and is accidentally the same person as he.

I have already suggested that the impulse to fault the doctrine of kooky objects for ontological extravagance is not obviously justified. Aristotle's doctrine that 'to be' is said in many ways seems to save him from the charge that kooky objects bloat being (certainly they do not bloat being in the sense of 'being' in which substances may be said to be).

Perhaps the doctrine could be challenged on the ground that it flouts the ideal of simplicity in theory construction. Certainly it does have about it what is, to us, an unwelcome complexity. But I don't know how to make that charge stick.

More obviously to the point, one might ask what pernicious 'sameness' arguments the doctrine of kooky objects fails to save us from and what benign 'sameness' arguments it forces us to discard. One pernicious argument it fails to save us from is this one:

## Argument B

> (16) Cicero has the attribute of being known by $S$ to be Cicero.
> (17) Cicero and Tully are the same (person).

So: (18) Tully has the attribute of being known by $S$ to be Cicero. (17) cannot plausibly be treated as a statement of accidental sameness and yet, on one important reading of these statements,[4] (18) should not follow from (16) and (17).

Though Argument B is not dissolved by the doctrine of kooky objects, it would be unfair to make very much of this inadequacy. The reason it would be unfair is that, so far as I know, no very good way of handling this argument has ever been proposed.[5]

On the other side, one might say that the doctrine of kooky objects is much too restrictive; it leads us to exclude as unsound many perfectly benign arguments, such as this one:

## Argument C

> (19) Walter Cronkite has the attribute of being a millionaire.
> (20) Walter Cronkite and America's favourite newscaster are the same person.

So: (21) America's favourite newscaster has the attribute of being a millionaire.

Aristotle might reply that eliminating this argument is no serious loss, since one can easily preserve what is worth preserving in it by recasting it this way:

## Argument C*

> (19) Walter Cronkite has the attribute of being a millionaire.

---

4 It is, of course, the reading that makes (18) roughly equivalent to '$S$ knows that Tully is Cicero.'

5 That is, so far as I know, no very good way of handling this argument has ever been proposed:
> (18*) $S$ knows that Cicero is Cicero.
> (19) Cicero and Tully are the same (person).
So:
> (20*) $S$ knows that Tully is Cicero.

(20★) Walter Cronkite has the attribute of being America's favourite newscaster.

So: (21★) There is someone who has both the attribute of being America's favourite newscaster and also the attribute of being a millionaire.

To show Argument $C^\star$ valid one would need only a principle of conjunction and a principle of existential generalisation.

Why, one might ask, won't a similar manoeuvre work for the paradox of the Masked Man? The similar manoeuvre would yield this:

*Argument D*

(22) Coriscus has the attribute of being known by Socrates to be Coriscus.

(23) Coriscus has the attribute of being the masked man.

So: (24) There is someone who has both the attribute of being known by Socrates to be Coriscus and also the attribute of being the masked man.

More simply, one might just conclude this:

(25) Coriscus has both the attribute of being known by Socrates to be Coriscus and also the attribute of being the masked man.

Both (24) and (25) are benign. Neither amounts to

(26) Socrates knows that Coriscus is the masked man.

Nor could one get (26) from (22) and (23) by other, legitimate, means. To see that (25) does not amount to (26) we need only note that (25) is compatible with this:

(27) Coriscus has both the attribute of being known by Socrates to be Coriscus and also, *unknown to Socrates*, the attribute of being the masked man.

To evaluate fully Aristotle's doctrine of kooky objects one would need to do much more than I have been able to do in this chapter. For one thing, one would need to assess Aristotle's claim that sameness in the accidental sense of 'same' is a variety of numerical sameness. To accomplish that task one would need to say a great deal about how we count persons and things – a daunting task.

Even if it should turn out, on fuller examination, that the doctrine of kooky objects is a defective or excessively costly or cumbersome way of weeding out pernicious 'sameness' arguments, still it stands as an ingenious way of trying to cope with philosophical perplexities that vex us yet. That, in itself, is a significant accomplishment.[6]

6 The long passages I quote from *Topics* 1 7 follow, quite faithfully, the Pickard–Cambridge translation; otherwise the translations I use are of rather mixed parentage.

I first began to worry about the matters discussed here when, some ten years ago, Anthony Willing began writing, under my direction, his PhD dissertation, *Aristotle on the Paradoxes of Accidence* (University of Massachusetts, 1974). I think my own conclusions are compatible with Willing's, but reading my paper is certainly no substitute for working through his careful study. Willing and I both profited enormously from reading, and trying to come to terms with, Nicholas White's 'Aristotle on Sameness and Oneness', and also his 'Origins of Aristotle's Essentialism' (*Review of Metaphysics*, 26(1972), 57–85).

Richard Bidgood made several suggestions for improving this chapter; I thank him.

My debt to Gwil Owen is fundamental. Without the stunning example of his teaching and scholarship, I should never have tried to read Aristotle freshly for myself.

# 12 Aristotle's concept of signification

T. H. IRWIN

## 1 Meaning and signification

Professor Owen has taught us to attend to Aristotle's, no less than to Plato's, views on the relation between language and reality. Some of his work is the distinguished result of his attention to these views. In 'Logic and Metaphysics' and 'Aristotle on the Snares of Ontology' he has argued that Aristotle's views on the proper way to inquire into Being are influenced by his views on the irreducibly different senses of 'being'. In *'Tithenai ta Phainomena'* he has shown how Aristotle's questions 'What is time?', 'What is place?', 'Does anyone ever act incontinently?' and so on are approached by methods and arguments different from those of empirical science: 'By such arguments the *Physics* ranks itself not with physics in our sense of the word, but with philosophy. Its data are for the most part the materials not of natural history but of dialectic, and its problems are accordingly not questions of empirical fact but conceptual puzzles.'[1]

This account of Aristotle's results reflects a clear and influential picture of his questions and his aims. Aristotle asks the Socratic 'What is it?' question to find out what a word means, to give an analysis of the concept associated with the word; he wants to set out the meaning that competent speakers implicitly grasp but cannot always state in clear, paradox-free terms. Sometimes he

1 *'Tithenai ta Phainomena'*, in *Aristote et les Problèmes de la Méthode*, ed. S. Mansion (Louvain 1961), 88; reprinted in *Aristotle*, ed. J. M. E. Moravcsik (New York 1968) and in *Articles on Aristotle* I, ed. J. Barnes, M. Schofield, R. Sorabji (London 1975). Other references to Owen's papers are to 'Logic and Metaphysics in some Earlier Works of Aristotle', in *Aristotle and Plato in the Mid-Fourth Century*, ed. I. Düring and G. E. L. Owen (Göteborg 1960), repr. in *Articles on Aristotle* III; 'Aristotle on the Snares of Ontology', in *New Essays on Plato and Aristotle*, ed. R. Bambrough (London 1965).

denies that there is just one answer to the Socratic question, because the word is homonymous; and then he means that it has more than one sense.

Are these Aristotle's questions and aims? Is he concerned with senses, meanings and concepts? We may try to answer this question in various ways. We may consider sample definitions to see if they display the meanings of words; we may consider homonymous words to see if different senses or meanings are distinguished. Here I want to raise a more general question: do Aristotle's works reflect a concern with meaning at all? Roughly speaking, the meaning of a word is what is entered in a dictionary; what the learner grasps implicitly when he learns a word; what a competent speaker and hearer grasp but a non-speaker does not grasp; what two synonymous words share; what a word shares with its translation in another language. To be concerned with these aspects of a word is to be concerned with its meaning and with the concept it expresses.

Someone could be concerned with meaning in these ways without having a word that means 'mean'. However, this does not seem to be a difficulty with Aristotle. If our previous account of his questions and aims is right, he is certainly concerned with meaning; and he seems to have the right word too. For his term *sēmainein*, 'signify', is the etymological origin of our word 'semantic'; surely it means 'mean'?[2]

To have a concept of meaning and to have a word meaning 'mean' is not yet to have a theory of meaning. To have a theory of

---

2 For examples of readers who understand signification as meaning see: W. and M. Kneale, *The Development of Logic* (Oxford 1962), 45; Owen, 'Snares', 73; J. Barnes, *Aristotle: Posterior Analytics* (Oxford 1975), 205. C. A. Kirwan, *Aristotle: Metaphysics IV, V, VI* (Oxford 1971), 94, suggests that in *Metaph.* IV 4 the significate is a sense or explication, while in *Int.* 18a25, 20a13, 16b24, *Poet.* 1456b38–1457a10 *sēmainein* means something more like 'denote'. The connexion with reference is exploited by D. W. Hamlyn, 'Focal Meaning', *Proceedings of the Aristotelian Society*, 78 (1977–8), 1–18, who ascribes to Aristotle 'a theory of meaning according to which meaning amounts to reference' (11); 'Aristotle's theory of meaning is . . . a realist one. He thinks, that is, of the meaning of a term as what is picked out by it, and he does not operate with anything approaching a distinction between sense and reference. Such a theory may not be explicitly stated, but it is implicit in much of what Aristotle says' (12). A thorough confusion is found by R. Haller, 'Untersuchungen zur Bedeutungsproblem in der antiken und mittelalterlichen Philosophie', *Archiv für Begriffsgeschichte*, 7 (1962), 57–119, at 65–75. He thinks Aristotle has a concept of meaning (Bedeutung), but fails to distinguish meaning from signification (Bezeichnung). To show that in speaking of *sēmainein* Aristotle is sometimes speaking of meaning, Haller claims that sameness of *sēmainein* is sometimes established by sameness of concept (Begriff) (70, citing *Metaph.* 1006b25 f.), while sameness of signification is just sameness of reference (Denotierung). If we offer only these two options to Aristotle, it is easy to conclude that he hopelessly confuses them.

meaning is to have a general account of sentences of the form '*F* means *G*' – what the terms of the relation are, and when the sentences are true; this account will in turn describe a speaker's and hearer's competence, conditions of synonymy and correct translation. Now Aristotle makes some general comments about signification; do these comments express a schematic theory of meaning?[3]

I want to ask whether Aristotle's concept of signification is really a concept of meaning, and whether his remarks about signification are about meaning or about something else. I will begin with his practice, by considering some of his examples of signification, and only later turn to his apparently theoretical comments. A way to test our account is to see how it works in arguments that crucially appeal to signification. I will briefly consider two of these arguments, in *Posterior Analytics* II and in *Metaphysics* IV. I hope to show that Aristotle's concept of signification does not primarily reflect an interest in meanings and concepts, though it does express interests that fit naturally into some of Aristotle's other philosophical concerns.

## 2   Conditions of signification

When Aristotle describes signifiers and their significates, does he describe words and their meanings? We might well suppose so. For he thinks names, verbs, phrases and sentences signify, while parts of names and parts of verbs – e.g. the 'ig' in 'pig' and the 'rat' in 'rattle' – do not (*Int.* 16b28–33); nor do particles signify (*Poet.* 1456b38–1457a6). Surely Aristotle intends to distinguish sounds with independent meaning from sounds without it?[4]

Similarly, words that signify the same, for instance 'cloak' and

3 The theory of meaning is a flourishing industry in contemporary philosophy; perhaps it is really several flourishing industries with different theories addressed to different questions. For some views of the problems that a theory should answer see M. Dummett, 'What is a Theory of Meaning?', in *Mind and Language*, ed. S. D. Guttenplan (Oxford 1975), ch. 6; P. F. Strawson, 'Meaning and Truth', in *Logico-Linguistic Papers* (London 1971), ch. 9; H. Putnam, 'The Meaning of "Meaning"', in *Philosophical Papers* II (Cambridge 1975), ch. 12. It would be rash to claim that Aristotle's claims about signification do not overlap with the claims of any theory of meaning. But I have tried to describe meaning fairly non-committally, to show what he does not have a theory of. Putnam claims 'the traditional problem of meaning splits into two problems. The first problem is to account for the determination of extension. . . The other problem is to describe individual competence' (246). I do not think Aristotle has a theory of meaning that tries to perform either of these tasks.
4 I have discussed *sēmainein* as the most plausible candidate for being Aristotle's word for 'mean'. On *boulesthai* see n. 11. The other relevant term is *dēloun*, 'reveal'. I see no clear or consistent difference of use or truth-conditions between it and *sēmainein* in the relevant contexts. They seem to be interchangeable in, e.g., *Top.* 102a18 with 101a38, 120b26–8, *Cat.* 3b10–21, *Int.* 16a19, 28, *APo.* 85b19–20. R. Bolton, 'Essentialism and Semantic

'coat' (see *Top.* 103a9–10, 168a28–33, *Ph.* 185b7–9, 19–21, *Metaph.* 1006b25–7), seem to mean the same. When Aristotle says that these words are 'synonymous' (*Top.* 167a24) because they have the same definition, he seems to use 'synonymous' as we do. Conversely, 'one' and 'being' belong to everything (cf. *Top.* 121b7–8) and so 'follow each other' (*Metaph.* 1003b22–5), but signify the same only 'in a way' (*Metaph.* 1054a13–19) because they have different definitions. We might suppose that for Aristotle they are co-referential terms with different senses. So far the remarks about signification seem to be sensible remarks about meaning.

However, other remarks are very odd if they are remarks about meaning. Aristotle thinks that negative names such as 'not-man' and negative verbs such as 'not walking' are not really names or verbs at all, but just 'indefinite' names and verbs (*Int.* 16a29–31, b11–15). An indefinite term does not signify one thing; 'it signifies something in a way one and indefinite' (19b9). Why should a negative term mean something indefinite? The meaning of 'not-man' seems no less definite than the meaning of 'man'.

Aristotle requires a genuinely single assertion to say and signify one thing about one thing (17a15–17, 18a12–13), as 'Man is white' does. But an assertion containing a single univocal word as its grammatical subject and another as its predicate does not necessarily signify one thing about one thing. If we coin a term 'whitewalker' (meaning 'white walking man'), it will not signify one thing, nor will an assertion with it as subject or predicate signify one thing about one thing (20b15–19). Aristotle's demands are more easily understood from his comments on two other invented terms, 'manorhorse' (whatever is a man or a horse is a manorhorse) and 'manandhorse' (whatever is both a man and a horse is a manandhorse). Aristotle believes that the assertion 'Manorhorse is white' signifies two things and is really two assertions ('Man is white' and

---

Theory in Aristotle', *Philosophical Review*, 85 (1976), 514–44, at 527 f., assumes a sharp distinction between *sēmainein* and *dēloun*; to *sēmainein* something is just to fix on it, while to *dēloun* is to display it explicitly. He cites *APo.* 93b29–94a2, at b29 f. and b39 f., 'where *dēloun* (treated as a synonym of *deiknunai*) is contrasted with *sēmainein*' (528 n. 27). But *dēloun* is not clearly treated as a synonym of *deiknunai*; 94a1–2 suggests that signifying is contrasted with demonstrating, and *dēloun* need not be demonstrating. Aristotle does not even say that the nominal definition signifies the very thing that the real definition *deiknusi*. Nor does he imply that the nominal definition signifies without revealing; at 92b27–8 *logos onomati to auto sēmainōn* must indicate the same fact as *tounoma touti dēloi* in 92b33. Bolton remarks that Plato regularly uses 'reveal' and 'signify' interchangeably, and contrasts his practice with Aristotle's. I do not think there is any contrast.

'Horse is white'), while 'Manandhorse is white' signifies nothing since no man is also a horse (18a19–26).[5]

Now if 'signify' means 'mean' here, Aristotle's claims are evidently false. Both 'manorhorse' and 'manandhorse' have clear, definite single meanings, no less than 'man' and 'horse' have. 'Manorhorse is white' does not signify two things because it has two meanings – since it has only one meaning; and 'Manandhorse is white' does not signify nothing because it is meaningless – since it evidently has a meaning. Aristotle says that 'Manandhorse is white' signifies nothing because no man is also a horse; does he then assume that all non-referring terms are meaningless?[6]

If signifying one thing is not having one definite meaning, what is it? 'Not-man' signifies something indefinite because 'it belongs alike to anything that is and that is not' (16b15). Not-men include centaurs, fleas, numbers and mountains, an utterly heterogeneous class with no common features besides being not-men. 'Whitewalker', 'manorhorse' and 'manandhorse' all in their different ways fail to signify a single thing because they do not signify a genuine single subject. Ammonius comments correctly on 'not-man': 'he does not add the "in a way" superfluously, but to show that it does not signify one nature as a definite name does' (*in Int.* 156.21–3). If a word signifies one definite thing, what it signifies is a single nature, not a single meaning. Aristotle does not think a single nature corresponds to every term with a single meaning. Indeed, he criticises the Platonists because one of their arguments for Forms requires a Form for every predicate, including 'not-man'; this is an absurd result, in Aristotle's view, since 'not-man' corresponds to no genuine nature (Alexander, *in Metaph.* 80.15–81.7).[7]

## 3 Signification, definition and essence

So far we have found reasons to deny that what words signify is their meaning. We can confirm this view by examining the

5 Aristotle actually uses his favourite term *himation*, understood first as 'manorhorse', 18a21–5, then as 'manandhorse', a25–6 (with *ou gar* explaining *ē ouden* in a25).

6 J. L. Ackrill comments, in *Aristotle: Categories and De Int.* (Oxford 1963), ad loc.: 'It is of course very doubtful whether Aristotle is entitled to deny significance to "a cloak is white" . . The reason he gives – "because no man is a horse" – would seem to commit him to the over-strong thesis that no empty class can be significantly mentioned.' Ackrill seems to assume that signification is something like meaning.

7 In fact Aristotle's view here is not so simple. See G. Fine, 'The One over Many', *Philosophical Review*, 89 (1980), 197–240.

relations between words, definitions and signification. Aristotle thinks that a name can be replaced by a formula (*logos*) that preserves truth (e.g. *Top.* 106a1–4). The name is a sign (*sēmeion*) of the formula (*Metaph.* 1012a22–4, 1045a26); and the name and the formula signify the same (*Top.* 162b37–163a1; cf. 129b30–5). The relevant 'formula' here expresses the definition (*horismos*) corresponding to the name (*Metaph.* 1012a22–4, *Top.* 106a1–4, 107a36–8).

It is safe to assume, then, that the name and the definition signify the same. This is what we might expect if signifying is meaning – the definition will replace the name with a formula that states its meaning; on this view the definition will signify the meaning of the term that it replaces. But what does Aristotle think the definition signifies?

He says that the definition of F signifies the essence of F (*Top.* 101b38). Now an essence is a universal, a definable property of things in the world; it is not the sense or meaning of a name or a linguistic expression. As we have seen, Aristotle does not think a universal corresponds to every name. The definition corresponding to 'F' signifies the same as 'F' not because it means the same, but because it is correlated with the same non-linguistic essence; both 'biped animal' and 'man' are correlated with the real essence of men. The relation of name to definition and significate does not after all show that signification is meaning. On the contrary, it shows why signification cannot be meaning. It cannot be meaning, because names signify essences and essences are not meanings, but belong to non-linguistic reality; Aristotle thinks they are real features of the world, though not separate from particulars (*APo.* 85b15–22).[8]

To say that signifying is signifying a real essence is not to say that signifying is referring, though it implies that non-referring terms cannot signify anything, since they cannot be replaced by a

8 Some identify universals and properties with meanings and intensions. See R. Carnap, *Meaning and Necessity* (2nd ed., Chicago 1956), 15, 22 (though he also claims, 20, that properties are what physicists investigate). This identification is rejected by D. M. Armstrong, *Universals and Scientific Realism* (Cambridge 1978), 1 5f, 64f, II 7–14, and by Putnam, 'On Properties', *Papers*, 1, ch. 19. For further discussion of Aristotelian essences see, e.g., R. R. K. Sorabji, *Necessity, Causes and Blame* (London and Ithaca 1980), ch. 12. With Sorabji, Bolton and others I am indebted to the views of Kripke, Putnam and other recent writers on natural kinds. I have not, however, compared them directly with Aristotle; this would require a lengthy account both of similarities and of some important differences.

definition true of any feature of reality. If signifying is signifying essences, it must have a non-extensional element that distinguishes it from reference. Two names may be co-referential, for instance 'man' and 'haircomber' if all and only men comb their hair, without signifying the same, since the essence of man is not the essence of haircomber. Though 'one' and 'being' are co-referential, they signify the same only 'in a way' because the essence of one and the essence of being are not the same (*Metaph.* 1054a13–19). Even though the form of a house is found only in the compound of form and matter, it may still be unclear whether the name signifies the compound or the form alone (1043a29–37). Two names signify the same only if the corresponding account is the same, as it is for 'cloak' and 'coat' (*Metaph.* 1006b25–7). The same account will be true of the same essence, since accounts are of essences; and so two co-referential, even necessarily co-referential, terms with two corresponding accounts will signify two essences, and will not signify the same. Definitions signify essences and properties, and so do names. But these non-extensional aspects of signification do not show that signification is meaning.

It will be easy to see that meaning is not signification if we see that meaning the same is neither necessary nor sufficient for signifying the same. It is hard to find examples in Aristotle of two words that evidently have two different meanings, but have the same signification. But perhaps he offers one. The constitutional authority (*politeuma*) and the constitution (*politeia*) of a state are the same (*Pol.* 1278b8–15), and the names of them signify the same. It does not follow that the two names mean the same: when we speak of the *politeuma* we speak of the supreme power, and when we speak of the *politeia* we speak of the relation of the supreme power to subordinate powers. 'The *politeuma* of Athens is a democracy' and 'The *politeia* of Athens is a democracy' describe the same facts about Athens and signify the same, but describe them from different points of view, and so do not mean the same.

It is easier to see that meaning one thing is not enough for signifying one thing. Aristotle allows a single formula to replace the word 'life', but still insists that 'life' signifies many different essences (*Top.* 148a26–31). When he claims that 'good' is homonymous and signifies many essences, he does not imply that it has many meanings. There is no reason why a homonymous word, signifying many essences, should not have a single meaning.[9]

For these reasons we should agree that what a word signifies is not what it means, but the nature, essence, property correlated with it. Aristotle's concept of signification cannot be a concept of meaning.

## 4    Words, beliefs, signification

How do words signify essences? Aristotle assumes that a word signifies an essence even if we do not know what the essence is; if we find out what the essence of sharks is we find out what 'shark' signifies and always has signified, and do not change its signification. Many competent speakers do not know what the essence of sharks, place, time, happiness or courage is, but they signify these essences by the use of the words none the less. We might expect from a competent speaker some implicit grasp of the meaning of his words; but it is unreasonable to expect knowledge of their signification, as Aristotle understands it. We might determine what a word means by what the user intends to communicate by it, or by its role in his conceptual scheme; but these approaches will be useless with signification. How then are words associated with the essences they signify?

When we use a name 'F' we apply it to certain objects, and we count these objects as Fs because we think they satisfy our beliefs about Fs. To find out what 'F' signifies we might attend either to the objects or to the beliefs. If we attend to the objects, our inquiry will be retrospective; for we will want to know what objects the name was originally applied to. If 'Lycurgus' was originally the name of a statue of Zeus at Sparta, but the Spartans came to believe that someone called Lycurgus had been their lawgiver, when in fact their actual lawgiver was called Morus, the name 'Lycurgus' is still the name of the statue of Zeus, even though the Spartans' beliefs associated with the name are true of Morus. Similarly, if the word 'gold' was originally applied to samples of iron pyrites, but speakers came to associate the name with beliefs that are false of iron pyrites, none the less 'gold' would have to be

---

9 Here I am not distinguishing homonymy and multivocity. For further discussion see 'Homonymy in Aristotle', *Review of Metaphysics*, 34 (1981) 523–44.

a name of iron pyrites. If the word 'happiness' was originally applied to the lives of Archelaus and Sardanapallus, but speakers associate it with beliefs that are false of these lives, it must still name a property of these lives. If Aristotle conceives signification this way, he will have to say that a word signifies the essence of the actual things it was originally applied to; it will signify the essence in something like the way an effect signifies, is a sign of, its cause.

This retrospective view of signification does not seem to be Aristotle's. He concentrates instead on the beliefs associated with the name, and seeks to determine its significance prospectively. Users of a name have some beliefs about the sort of thing that it names; as Aristotle remarks, everyone who uses 'happiness' agrees that it is the name of the final good, and that happiness is the same as living well and faring well (*EN* 1095a18–20); those who speak of time agree that it includes the past which is over and the future which is not yet (*Ph.* 217b34). Aristotle characteristically begins with these sorts of common beliefs associated with a name, and then tries to say, by using the methods appropriate to the question, which beliefs are true and which false of some real essence. His treatment of the common beliefs has been analysed in Owen's fundamental study, *'Tithenai'*. As Owen shows, it is unlikely, on Aristotle's view, that all the common beliefs will turn out to be true of one real essence; before they can be accepted they must be revised and reconstructed. Knowledge of the appropriate real essences will show us what the name really signifies. On this view the name signifies the real essence which the reconstructed beliefs associated with the name are true of.

Aristotle does not definitely reject the retrospective view of signification. If the right assumptions are made about the original use of the name and the original associated beliefs, the retrospective and the prospective accounts may even produce the same results. In the *Cratylus* Plato makes the right assumptions, and combines the two accounts; the correct name was first given by a lawgiver with a true view of reality, but our present names only preserve the outline of the truth, which must be revealed by further rational reconstruction. Plato rejects a historical inquiry as a way of finding out the true significate of a name, and relies on the prospective method (cf. *Cra.* 432E).[10] Aristotle's position is

10 On the *Cratylus* see further G. Fine, 'Plato on Naming', *Philosophical Quarterly*, 27 (1977), 289–301.

less clear; he has nothing to correspond to Plato's well-informed lawgiver. But while the retrospective view is hard to connect with his other philosophical views, the prospective view fits them well. Both empirical inquiry – into the structure of animals, say – and dialectical inquiry of the sort found in the *Physics* and *Ethics* begin with our initial beliefs and seek a rational reconstruction and revision of them. Though Aristotle does not say so, he is committed to the view that this inquiry discovers what our names signify, since names signify essences and essences are discovered by inquiry.

It is reasonable to attribute this account of the relation between a name and its significate to Aristotle, even though he does not present it himself as a view about signification. We have simply combined three things: (1) his claim that names signify essences; (2) his project of reconstructing common beliefs so that they are true of real essences; (3) the obvious fact that these common beliefs are associated with names. Aristotle can readily explain how names signify essences even if their users have false beliefs about the essences that they signify. His reconstructive approach to common beliefs is a familiar part of his inquiry into real essences, since he wants to show that common beliefs should be reconstructed and not rejected; for the same reasons and by the same methods he wants to show that ordinary names signify real essences. He rejects any attempt to argue that because common names are associated with some false beliefs they should be rejected and replaced (*Top.* 148b16–22; cf. 110a14–22, 140a3–5).

If this is a reasonable conception of signification for Aristotle to hold, it can reasonably be extended by appeal to other doctrines of his. Aristotle often distinguishes different stages of inquiry by contrasting what is 'known to us' (*gnōrima hēmin*) with what is 'known by nature' (*gnōrima phusei*) (*APo.* 71b23–72a5). What is known to us is the starting-point for inquiry, our common beliefs; what is known by nature is the true theory resulting from inquiry. This contrast affects Aristotle's conception of an adequate definition. The only correct definition corresponding to '*F*' is the one that says what *F* really is, revealing the real essence, what is known by nature. But sometimes, in some arguments, before the inquiry is completed, we may need a definition that says what is known to us, expressing the common beliefs (*Top.* 141b14–19). Now since Aristotle sometimes says that the name is a sign of the definition (*Metaph.* 1012a22–4, 1045a26), we might expect the two sorts of definition to reflect different aspects of signification. One sort of definition, mentioning what is known to us, will tell us what the name signifies to us; the other sort of definition will tell us what the name signifies by nature because it will mention the real essence that is known by nature.

This distinction between signification to us and by nature is not mentioned by Aristotle. But it is a fair inference from his linking of names, signification and definition, and it fits easily into his normal inquiries. He can readily say that 'incontinence' signifies to us a condition in which someone knows quite clearly that he is doing the worse thing when he does it; for that is a common belief about incontinence. It does not signify this by nature; for, Aristotle believes, there is no such condition, and this common belief must be modified before it is true of a real condition; 'incontinence' signifies by nature the condition that Aristotle describes. Aristotle could easily allow himself this contrast between aspects of signification; and he may accept it implicitly if not explicitly. We will find it useful to consider this possibility to explain some remarks about signification that would otherwise be inconsistent.

## 5   Types of signifiers

So far we have considered how words signify. But these are not the only signifiers that Aristotle recognises; for he also allows assertions, speakers and things to signify. Our account should explain how all these appear to be legitimate signifiers. If we can show this, we can extend the comparison and contrast between signification and meaning. Two of Aristotle's three candidates are no surprise if we think of meaning; for sentences and speakers mean. But the third signifier is a surprise; if Aristotle suggests that man as well as 'man' signifies rational animal, is he simply confusing use and mention? Or is his claim more plausible if signification is not meaning?

We saw that a single assertion is held to signify one thing of one thing, as in 'Man is white' (*Int.* 18a13–14); we see what an assertion signifies by seeing what genuine things its subject-term and predicate-term signify, and by seeing how how the sentence relates them (e.g. it says that white belongs to Socrates, not the other way round). Apparently an assertion cannot signify one thing unless it signifies about one thing. For 'Manorhorse is white' signifies two things, while 'Manandhorse is white' signifies nothing (cf. 18a24–6). The trouble with these sentences is that their subject-terms signify two natures or no nature. The same sorts of reasons should require Aristotle to say that 'Not-man is white' only signifies something indefinite, since it signifies about an indefinite subject. Why should these sentences not signify one thing, however, when 'white' signifies a single property? Aristotle might argue that the assertion with 'white' as the predicate-term signifies the belonging of the predicate to the subject, and that the belonging will be one state of affairs only if it is true of one subject. While the predicate-term may signify only one property (so that it is not homonymous), the assertion including that predicate-term does not merely signify one property, but the state of affairs that is the belonging of that property to a subject, and different states of affairs correspond to different subjects.

It is harder to see how Aristotle will explain the signification of an assertion such as '(A) tailor is white.' It does not signify about one thing, since 'tailor', unlike 'man', does not signify a single subject; it signifies a compound subject, a man with the accident of having clothes-making skill. But it does not signify two things in the way that 'Manorhorse is white' did, since we cannot analyse 'Tailor is white' into two assertions. It seems to say one thing, though not about one thing; and so it seems to be a single assertion. Aristotle clearly rejects this conclusion; he insists that if we say one thing not of one thing, we have not made one assertion (*Int.* 20b12–22). We must suppose that we make the two assertions: 'Tailoring skill belongs to some men; these are white'; or perhaps: 'These have bodies and their bodies are white.' The analysis explains the relation between the real subject and the subject-term of the sentence, showing that 'tailor' signifies a man with an accident; and it explains the relation between the real subject and the property signified by the predicate-term. Sometimes the paraphrase (e.g. for 'Some sunburnt tailors are ugly cobblers') will be quite complicated, but Aristotle insists on it to reveal the real relations between things and properties (cf. *Metaph.* 1015b16–34, 1017a17–22).

These paraphrases may seem awkward to us. Perhaps that is because a single assertion, as Aristotle conceives it, is not the same as a single sentence. He multiplies assertions to make clear the relations of the subject and the properties talked about. His ontology determines his account of the structure and nature of assertions. This does not mean he has a strange view of the structure and meaning of sentences. His criteria for counting assertions are guided by the real natures that are signified.

Aristotle thinks a speaker or thinker signifies something. We might think he is saying what we say when we say that someone can mean something by a word or sentence. What I mean is determined by what I intend. If Warden Spooner in his sermon said 'Aristotle was a great theologian', his words clearly meant that the Stagirite was a great theologian. But when he explained 'When I said "Aristotle" I meant St Paul', he showed that what he meant was 'St Paul was a great theologian', and that he was actually speaking about St Paul. Aristotle considers someone who wants (*bouletai*) to say what belongs to man by nature and who says 'Being a biped is a *proprium* of man.'[11] In fact a *proprium* belongs always (not just by nature) to its subject. Here we might say that the speaker meant that being a biped belongs by nature to man, or that by '*proprium*' he meant 'natural property'. Aristotle, however, does not use 'signify' as we might use 'mean'. He does not think that what someone signifies is what he means; the speaker signifies what the word he uses signifies. Since '*proprium*' signifies what belongs always to a subject, that is also what the speaker 'signifies by his speech' (*Top.* 134a9) in using '*proprium*' (134a5–17).

Aristotle's reasons for treating signification as he does may be clearer if we compare signification not with meaning, but with signalling, as the etymology of '*sēmainein*' suggests. If I use the wrong flags to signal, I may mean 'Full ahead', but signal 'Abandon ship'. Similarly Aristotle thinks that what I signify is determined by the character of the word and its signification; I signify the nature that is signified by the word. These differences between 'I signify' and 'I mean' do not by themselves show that signification is not meaning; for we might say that I signify what my words mean or what I actually say, rather than what I mean. But if we have considered the other reasons for denying that

---

11 For *boulesthai* cf. *Cat.* 9a4, *EN* 1126b21, 1129a7; *boulesthai sēmainein*, *Top.* 103a31, 142b27–8; *boulesthai legesthai*, *EN* 1110b30–1. Sometimes *boulesthai legein* suggests 'wants (tries) to say without fully succeeding'; *Int.* 16a25 (Bonitz, *Index* 140b58), *Metaph.* 989b19–21, 1002b27–8, *GA* 769a36–b4, *Top.* 134a9.

signification is meaning, we will not be surprised by this one; Aristotle's treatment of 'I signify' fits his general views on signification quite well.

Readers are usually surprised to find Aristotle saying not only that 'man' signifies rational animal, but also that man signifies rational animal (e.g. *Cat.* 3b10–23, *Top.* 122b16–17, 139a21–31, 142b27–9, 146a17, *APo.* 85b18–21, *Metaph.* 1017a22–7, 1028a10–16, 1042b27, 1043a21, *Pol.* 1279a25–6). Indeed some readers have inferred that he just confuses the use and the mention of a word.[12] This is a natural reaction if we think signification is meaning. But if Aristotle thinks significates are real properties, it may be easier to see how non-linguistic items can be correlated with real properties too.

Non-linguistic items that signify are natural signs; clouds are signs of rain, smoke of fire, and so on (*APr.* 70a10–38). These are natural signs because they are correlated with their significates apart from any human convention.[13] Clouds signify rain by nature, while 'rain' signifies rain only because it is a word in a particular language. For 'man' to signify rational animal it must be associated with the right beliefs, the ones true of rational animal; but man is correlated with rational animal whatever anyone believes or decides. Man indicates, and is correlated with, the essence rational animal because that is what man really is. The correlation between man and rational animal is much closer than between smoke and fire, since men are essentially rational animals; but that is no objection to our taking man to signify rational animal.

From this point of view the relation between signifiers and significates is different for natural and conventional signs; natural signs signify apart from anyone's beliefs while conventional signs

12 See, e. g., Ackrill, 88; 'It is careless of him to speak as if it were substances (and not names of substances) that signify.' Unfortunately Aristotle has no unambiguous device for quotation. The neuter article *to* plus nominative often indicates quotation (e.g. *Int.* 16a14), but the nominative is not always retained (e.g. 16b30–1); and the *to* does not always indicate quotation (e.g. *Metaph.* 1030a1). Sometimes an ungrammatical nominative without *to* indicates quotation (e.g. *APo.* 92a7). These conventions often result in ambiguity (e.g. with a neuter nominative singular). Sometimes Aristotle uses no quoting convention when he clearly means to quote a word; see *Int.* 16a16, *ho tragelaphos*, with 16a14, *to anthrōpos*; *Metaph.* 1043a29, *Top.* 174a8 (a striking example). Often it is hard to tell (e.g. at *Metaph.* 1006a32, 104b25–9) whether quotation is intended or not.

13 On natural and conventional signs see N. Kretzmann, 'Aristotle on Spoken Sound Significant by Convention', in *Ancient Logic and its Modern Interpretations*, ed. J. Corcoran (Dordrecht 1974), 7 f.; H. P. Grice, 'Meaning', *Philosophical Review*, 66 (1957), 377–88.

signify only because of beliefs. But natural signs signify 'to us', and not merely 'by nature', only in so far as we have the right beliefs about them; for we will not know that man signifies rational animal unless we know what man essentially is. With natural and conventional signs alike our only access to the significate is through our beliefs.

Aristotle need not be foolish or confused, then, when he implies that both 'man' and man signify rational animal. His claim would be puzzling if we supposed that words signify their meanings; for then it would be hard to see how man could signify a meaning. If words signify meanings, then either Aristotle is confused or he must agree that words and things signify different sorts of significates, and then his easy move from words signifying to things signifying would be unjustified. But if words and things signify the same non-linguistic items, real properties, Aristotle's practice is intelligible. He is not necessarily misled or confused; and he makes no illegitimate assumptions when he speaks inter-changeably of words signifying and things signifying. As before, the range of signifiers recognised by Aristotle is easier to under-stand once his view of the significate is understood.

## 6   Types of significates

So far we have assumed that the significate of a word is the real property that the reconstructed beliefs are true of; this account can be modified to deal with words that signify more than one property (e.g. 'manorhorse') or signify something indefinite (e.g. 'not-man'). However, Aristotle recognises two other sorts of significates that raise difficulties for this account. First, he takes words to signify thoughts. Second, he sometimes assumes that non-referring terms, with associated beliefs true of no real prop-erties, nonetheless signify something. How are these claims to be understood?

Aristotle claims that spoken sounds are symbols and signs of conditions of soul, and that conditions of soul are likenesses of things (*Int.* 16a3–8). He argues that verbs by themselves signify something – 'for the speaker stops his thought and the hearer pauses' (16b20–1); the verb apparently signifies some thought of the speaker's and brings the hearer's thought to a pause by signifying something to him. This does not prevent Aristotle from saying that words are symbols of things (*Top.* 165a7–8) and that words and thoughts signify things (*Metaph.* 1006a18–24, b8–11).[14] What is the relation between words, thoughts and things?[15]

Ammonius suggests 'Aristotle teaches through these things what are the things primarily and immediately signified by sounds, and that they are thoughts, and that things are signified through thoughts as intermediaries' (*in Int.* 17.24–6). Aristotle does not clearly endorse this two-stage theory of signification. But he might find it attractive. Words signify real properties through our beliefs about them; and what they signify to us is determined by our beliefs. Since beliefs determine the signification of a word, it is not suprising if Aristotle also says that the word signifies the thoughts and beliefs through which it signifies the thing that the beliefs are true of. A word need not really signify the thing that we think it signifies, what it signifies to us, since some of our beliefs about the significate may be false; our actual beliefs determine what a word signifies to us, but only our reconstructed true beliefs determine what it really signifies. When beliefs and thoughts are so important in relating words to their significates, it is natural for Aristotle to say that thoughts are themselves primary significates, since we must pass through them to find the extra-mental significates. The treatment of thoughts as significates requires no radical or disastrous change in the general view that words signify things.[16]

Non-existent significates raise harder problems; for here the word signifies no genuine property. Aristotle, however, thinks that 'goatstag' signifies something (*Int.* 16a16–17); and he thinks we

14  In 1006a22–4 Aristotle insists that signifying something is necessary for someone to have any *logos* with himself or with another; 1006b8–11 implies that if names do not signify, a man cannot have discourse with himself either; for thought requires us to think of one thing and a name can be applied to that one thing. If we combine this with the previous passage, Aristotle implies that the name 'F' and the thought of F both signify F.

15  This passage is clearly and helpfully discussed by Kretzmann, 'Spoken Sound', though I doubt two of his claims; (1) *sēmeia*, 16a5, are intended to be natural signs, and *sumbola*, 16a4, conventional signs; (2) the claim in 16a7 that conditions of soul are likenesses of things is not meant to apply to *noēmata*, 16a10. Against (1) see 16a17, b10, 20 for *sēmainein* and *sēmeion* applied to conventional signs (Kretzmann cites the last two passages himself). Against (2) *de An.* 429a15–18 suggests that the claim about likeness should apply to thoughts.

Kretzmann rightly insists that Aristotle does not explicitly accept the traditional theory of mediate and immediate signification.

16  Aristotle might sometimes be taken to suggest that universals are only contents of thoughts, with no independent existence; see *de An.* 417b22–4, 426a6–26, 429a13–18, 429b10–430a5. Normally this is not his view of universals and signification.

can say what 'goatstag' signifies even though we cannot say what goatstags are, since non-existents have no essence (*APo.* 92b4–8). Essences are the properties explaining the other properties of the subject; we discover them by revising our initial beliefs after inquiry. There is nothing to explain and nothing to discover about non-existent subjects, and so they have no essence. Aristotle's claim that 'goatstag' signifies something without signifying a real essence seems to conflict with his implied view that 'manand-horse' signifies nothing, because it signifies no genuine essence, because there are no manandhorses (*Int.* 18a25). This is only his implied view – he says only that 'Manandhorse is white' signifies nothing – but the implication is clear, and the conflict with his claim about goatstags is hard to avoid. This particular conflict indicates the larger anomaly created by the goatstag. For he normally thinks that the name signifies the real property that the associated beliefs are true of; and he cannot say this if he allows 'goatstag' to signify something.

Perhaps, however, the anomaly is removed if we remember that names signify through associated beliefs, and that they can signify something to us as well as something in nature. 'Goatstag' is associated with beliefs that purport to describe a goatstag; and the animal they purport to describe is what 'goatstag' signifies to us, what it appears to us to signify. We can still say what the word signifies to us even if we know quite well that there are no goatstags, and that therefore the word signifies nothing by nature. 'To us' need not mean 'as we believe', implying that we believe there are goatstags; with 'goatstag' it will mean 'as we imagine it'.

Non-referring terms differ from referring terms because they correspond to no real properties. They do not even signify an indefinite thing as 'not-man' does. They signify the thoughts and beliefs associated with them; as the *de Interpretatione* might suggest, they have a primary significate. They signify something to us. But they signify nothing further by nature. Normally we cannot determine what a word signifies simply by examining the associated beliefs; for they may not be completely right, and may need reconstruction in the light of further knowledge about the world. But with non-referring terms examination of the world shows us that they refer to nothing; there is nothing we can examine to find out more about their significates; and therefore the associated beliefs tell us all that there is to be told about the significates. Further study of the features of dolphins might cause us to change our minds about the essence of dolphins, and hence about the signification of 'dolphin'; but no further study of goatstags will change our mind about the signification of 'goatstag'.

Aristotle need not, then, be contradicting himself when he both implies that non-referring terms signify nothing, and elsewhere says that they signify something. His remarks are consistent if he means that 'goatstag' signifies thoughts, but no reality, and that it signifies something to us but nothing by nature. He does not explicitly draw the distinctions we must draw to show how his account is consistent. But the distinctions are easily derived from the other things he says; and they show how his views on signification might be presented coherently, with the resources available to him.

### 7    Signification and essence in the Analytics

Now that we have examined some of Aristotle's views about signification and its varieties we may consider some arguments in which the appeal to signification is important. Aristotle's remarks here do not always fit smoothly into the views we have described so far; we must see if some revision of our account is needed.

*Posterior Analytics* II raises questions for us because it separates definitions that say what a name signifies from those that describe the essence of something. To begin with, Aristotle wonders whether a definition can just say what a name signifies; if it just said that, we would be allowing definitions of non-essences and of things that are not, since it is possible to signify things that are not (92b26–30).[17] Here Aristotle plainly must assume that definitions are of essences, but non-essences as well as essences may be signified. He answers these difficulties by allowing several sorts of definitions; one of them is an account of what a name signifies, while the others say what something is, and so reveal the essence (93b29–30).[18] The suggestion of this passage, that the significate

17 Following W. D. Ross, *Analytics* (Oxford 1949) ad loc. and Bolton, 'Essentialism', 527 n. 1, I take *mē ousiōn* in 92b29 to be 'non-essences' (e.g. not-man, manorhorse), rather than 'non-existents', preferred by Barnes, *Analytics*.

18 Bolton, 'Essentialism', 523 f., argues that since (a) Aristotle insists that a definition is always of what something is, 90b3–4, 30–1, 93b29, and (b) there is no account of what non-existent things are, therefore (c) nominal definitions, 93b30, are of existents only, and hence (d) there is no nominal definition of goatstags. But 92b26–30 with 93b29–32

of '*F*' and the essence of *F* are not the same, is accepted elsewhere in the *Posterior Analytics*. Learning must begin with some grasp of what triangle, say, signifies (71a14–15, 76a32, b7, 15); this is the initial 'understanding' (*sunienai*, 71a13, b32, 76b37) that precedes the full knowledge of something's essence.

The difficulty in these remarks is plain. While we found previously that Aristotle thinks names signify real essences, he seems to deny it in the *Posterior Analytics*. He seems to think at least that essences are not the only things that can be signified, and sometimes even seems to suggest that they are never signified – that the essence is always different from the significate. Must we then revise our earlier account of signification?

We should notice that the *Analytics* also seems to conflict with Aristotle's general views on definition. A correct definition signifies the same as the name it replaces, and it signifies the essence (*Top.* 101b38–102a2).[19] On this view the *Analytics*' 'nominal definitions', those which say what the name signifies, but do not reveal the essence, cannot be definitions at all. Aristotle's different claims can be reconciled, however, if we notice the distinction between definitions that mention what is known to us and those that mention what is really known. A definition through what is known to us cannot define the essence, unless we are lucky enough to have hit on the right natural kinds already (*Top.* 141b22–8); nor can it be the really correct definition; for there is only one really correct definition, but there may be several definitions 'to us', reflecting different people's knowledge at different times (141b34–142a9). None the less, Aristotle thinks that definitions 'to us' are quite suitable at the beginning of inquiry or instruction; and this is the stage he considers when he speaks in the *Analytics* about signification.[20]

make it doubtful that (d) is Aristotle's view. Probably he rejects both (d) and (a) (90b3–4, 93b29 do not clearly endorse (a), while 90b3–4, 30–1 are in the aporetic discussion). 93a17–29 suggests that a grasp of the 'that it is' precedes a grasp of 'what it is', and 93b32–5 suggests that a grasp of 'that it is' follows a grasp of nominal definition. I therefore doubt Bolton's further claim that the nominal definition is always the definition that is the conclusion of the demonstration (94a7–9; this suggests a grasp of the 'thing itself' (cf. 93a22–3) which 93b32–5 may contrast with a nominal definition). These passages are lucidly discussed by Ackrill, 'Aristotle's Theory of Definition: Some Questions on *Posterior Analytics* II 8–10', in *Aristotle on Science: "The Posterior Analytics"*, ed. E. Berti (Padua 1981). Bolton's views are discussed by Sorabji, *Necessity*, 195–8.

19 102a1–2 says 'for it is possible to define also some of those things signified by a *logos*' (sc. a phrase). 'Also' implies that we define the things signified by a name.

20 *Topics* VI 4 does not suggest that real definitions fail to say what the name signifies; contrast Bolton, 533 n.

If a similar distinction can be drawn with signification, Aristotle's remarks will be consistent. We begin with a definition 'to us', mentioning what is known to us, and saying what the word signifies to us, through our initial beliefs. We try to find the one correct definition 'by nature', saying what is known by nature, and what the word signifies by nature. Here as before the distinction between signifying to us and signifying by nature is useful; it allows us to see how Aristotle's remarks are not necessarily inconsistent, and how they may be parts of one intelligible theory.

The remarks in the *Analytics* should not, then, encourage any over-hasty generalisations about signification. Understood one way, they conflict with the view that a name signifies a real essence. But they need not be understood that way. They are easily reconciled with Aristotle's other remarks if he means that what a name signifies to us at the start of an inquiry is not the same as what it signifies by nature.

If Aristotle meant that what a name signifies is what it signifies to us at the start of our inquiry, we might expect him to say in other works that he begins with what the name 'F' signifies and inquires into what F is. Normally he does not say this. His dialectical inquiries often begin with some account of the common beliefs; these tell us what 'F' signifies to us, but Aristotle does not say that they tell us what 'F' signifies.[21]

There is one exception to this rule. Aristotle implies that the common beliefs about void tell us what the word 'void' signifies (*Ph.* 213b30–1), though they do not tell us what void really is, since there is no such thing. However, we cannot infer from this remark about 'void' that the common beliefs always say what the name signifies. For 'void', like 'goatstag', applies to no real essence; we cannot find out what it signifies by nature, and the only signification it has is its signification to us. It is not surprising if Aristotle thinks we can say what 'void' signifies just by inspection of the common beliefs, when we know there is no void, but cannot say what 'time' or 'incontinence' signifies before we have reconstructed the associated beliefs. At the beginning all we can say about 'incontinence' is what it signifies to us; but further inquiry will show what it signifies by nature.

---

21 For claims that other works show a passage from what the name signifies to a real definition see H. H. Joachim, *Aristotle on Coming-to-be and Passing-away* (Oxford 1922), 123, 127; Bolton, 'Aristotle's Definitions of the Soul', *Phronesis*, 23 (1978), 248–78.

Aristotle's remarks are consistent if he is allowed the distinction between signifying to us and by nature. Some names signify nothing more than what they signify to us; some do signify more. Aristotle is justified in not usually saying that the common beliefs tell us what a name signifies; for when the common beliefs can be reconstructed so that they are true of some real essence, only the reconstruction tells us what the name really signifies.[22]

## 8  Signification and essence in Metaphysics IV

Aristotle's argument in *Metaphysics* IV 4 for the Principle of Non-Contradiction (PNC) relies on an appeal to signification. One premise of the argument assumes that the opponent who challenges PNC signifies something 'to himself and to another' (1006a21–2). Aristotle argues that if the opponent signifies something by the name 'man', he cannot maintain that it is possible that man has both all his properties and their contradictories; in particular he cannot maintain that man is both a biped animal and not a biped animal; and so he cannot reject PNC. What conception of signification does Aristotle appeal to here, and is it the conception we have found elsewhere?

Two of Aristotle's claims seem to suggest two different conceptions of signification:

1.  Signifying something is necessary for speaking and thinking of something (1006a21–2, b10–11).[23] Speaking and thinking of something is necessary, in turn, for having any discourse with oneself or with another (1006a22–4, b8–11). It follows that signifying something is taken to be necessary for all thought and discourse.

2.  Signifying something requires the existence of essences. For signifying something by '*F*' is signifying some one thing (1006b7); signifying something by 'man' is signifying what it is to be man (1006a31–4); what it is to be man is the essence of man

---

22  Bolton, 'Essentialism', 529 ff., argues that nominal definitions give the meaning of a word, as Putnam understands it (see n. 3 above). The evidence (e.g. the claim that *tis*, 93a22–3, indicates an essentially demonstrative element) seems slim to me.

23  In 1006a21–2, b10–11 *legein ti* and *noein ti* might mean 'saying (thinking) that *p*' or 'speaking (thinking) of *x*'. Since *legein ti* is taken to imply *sēmainein ti*, and what is signified is a thing, *zōion dipoun*, rather than a proposition, 'speak of' is probably the right rendering of *legein ti* here. This is uncertain, however, when *to zōion dipoun* is unclear – the *to* might or might not indicate quotation (see n.12); and *logos*, 1006b3, might also be linguistic or non-linguistic.

(1007a25–7); therefore signifying requires the signifying of essences.[24]

These two claims reflect two aspects of signification that we have found elsewhere. The first claim seems to require signifying to us; if the opponent has any definite thought or discourse, he must have some conception of what he is talking about; if he uses the word 'man' he must have beliefs associated with it, to say what the name signifies to him. Aristotle will then argue that if he contradicts every one of these associated beliefs, he will have no definite thought when he utters the name and will not be saying anything.

This would be an intelligible defence of PNC. But Aristotle's later remarks suggest that it is not quite what he intends. For the later remarks assume that the name 'F' and the definition of F signify the same thing, the essence of F. Here signification points us to how things are, not simply to the speaker's beliefs. Aristotle implies here that the opponent of PNC must be taken to signify some essence, and that a subject cannot have both its essential property and the contradictory property. Here Aristotle argues that thought and speech require not only associated beliefs, but also signification of essences. The names must signify something, not only to us but also by nature. While some of Aristotle's arguments suggest that 'goatstag' would do as well as 'man' in the examples, the claims about essence should apply only to 'man', since 'goatstag' does not signify an essence.

What could justify Aristotle's second claim about signification in this argument? Why must the opponent of PNC, and any speaker and thinker, signify an essence? We might decide that Aristotle is simply confused. Perhaps he begins with a name signifying something to us, assumes that it must also signify something by nature, and that its significate must be an essence, and mistakenly infers that signifying an essence is necessary for thought and speech; but the demand that the name should signify something by nature is much less immediately plausible.[25] Has

---

24  1006a33 mentions *to anthrōpō(i) einai*; 1007a20 mentions *ousia* and *to ti ēn einai*. But no new account of signification is introduced. Aristotle simply assumes that if we agree that 'man' signifies being a man we are thereby agreeing that it signifies the essence and substance of man; 'for to signify substance is to signify that it [sc. man] is nothing else', 1007a26–7. Most probably Aristotle thinks the commitment to essence has been implied from the start.

25  For different views of signification here see G. E. M. Anscombe, *Three Philosophers* (Oxford 1961), 39; Kirwan, 95 f; R. M. Dancy, *Sense and Contradiction* (Dordrecht 1975), 107–14, 131–9; H. W. Noonan, 'An Argument of Aristotle on Non-

Aristotle some better argument to show that he is not confusing signification to us with signification by nature? Can he defend his second claim about signification?

It is easiest to see the possible defence by considering the opponent's claim. The opponent of PNC wants to say that for any property of a subject, it is possible for the subject to have the contradictory property as well; and so in the example discussed he is committed to the possibility of 'Man is a biped animal and not a biped animal.'[26] Now Aristotle insists that if we are to assess the opponent's claim we must know what subject he is speaking of; for he must be speaking of one and the same subject and ascribing contradictory properties to it in the same respect – otherwise he does not really deny PNC (1005b20–2; cf. *Top.* 180a26–31, 167a10–14, *Int.* 17a34–7). If he does not signify one essence with a name, his alleged contradictions may be spurious. 'Not-man' does not signify one essence, and 'Not-man is a horse and not-horse' is no genuine contradiction, since horses and non-horses are obviously included in non-men. 'Horse' does not signify one essence either, since equine animals and vaulting-horses may be called horses; and so 'Horse is animal and not-animal' is no genuine contradiction.[27] The opponent must be speaking of one and the same subject. But one and the same subject must have one and the same essence. 'Man is white' and 'Man is biped' signify one and the same subject because 'man' signifies a single essence whose

Contradiction', *Analysis*, 37 (1976–7), 163–9. On Anscombe's view (41) a single signification is a single sort of reference; since 'being large' can signify something (e.g. a two foot length) that 'not being large' can also signify, 'being large' does not signify one thing, and only names of substances signify one thing. However, Aristotle never endorses any such view either in *Metaph.* IV 4, or even in VII 4. Dancy sees the connexion between signification and essence; he is surprised by Aristotle's failure to mention the sort of nominal definition described in the *Analytics*. Noonan suggests that the signification of the predicate '*F*' is designated by 'to be (an) *F*', and that '*to be (an) F* will be *to be (a) G* just in case it is necessarily true that (*x*) (F*x* iff G*x*)'. These identity-conditions for significates are not Aristotle's, because of 1003b22 taken with 1054a13; see section 3 above.

26 Is the subject meant to be a particular man or the species man? Aristotle may intend the argument to apply to both; but he seems to have primarily species and other universals in mind.

27 A word can signify many things either (a) because, like 'manorhorse', it signifies a plurality of essences, *Int.* 18a23–6, or (b) because, like 'good', it is multivocal, *Top.* 129b30–130a5. For (a) but not (b) the same definition applies to all uses of the name; for (b) but not (a) each definition may signify just one essence. In *Metaph.* IV 4 Aristotle probably intends to rule out both ways of signifying many things. See further Ackrill, *Categories*, 131. The differences between (a) and (b) could be made clearer if Aristotle more clearly distinguished word-tokens and word-types.

definition can be truly substituted for both these occurrences of the name.

If the opponent must signify a single subject with a single essence, he must signify a subject that is the same subject only as long as it has the property that constitutes its essence. And so if he both affirms and denies that property of the subject, he both affirms and denies that he is speaking of a single subject; and so he must both affirm and deny that he ascribes contradictory properties to a single subject.

Is this the argument that Aristotle intends to present? That is hard to say without a full analysis of a complex and sometimes obscure series of moves. But if this argument is ascribed to him, his procedure is fairly clear and coherent in outline. If we suppose that phrases such as 'being a man' and 'biped animal' first indicate the meaning attached to 'man', and then indicate Aristotelian essences, Aristotle makes an abrupt and unjustified transition. If we assume that he is arguing about essences all along, he makes no unjustified transition in mid-argument, and his strategy is fairly clear.

This argument is different from an argument from a single meaning of 'man', because it assumes something different about the opponent. If Aristotle wants to insist that 'man' has a single meaning, he will suggest what the speaker must have in mind and what he must communicate to a hearer; 'biped animal' will indicate what one must mean and the other must grasp. But an argument about essences does not assume this about the mental states of the speaker and the hearer. If biped animal is the essence of man, neither speaker nor hearer need believe this; they need have no views about what the essence of man is. Aristotle's point is not about what must be true of their beliefs, but about what must be true of a subject that they speak of; if it is a single subject it must have an essence. Aristotle does not present his argument as though he is concerned with the beliefs of speakers and hearers or with the meanings to be attached to their words; he seems to be concerned with the properties that must be ascribed to the non-linguistic subject that is spoken of. If we have understood the argument correctly, he presents it accurately.

We are justified, then, in taking the argument to be about signification, understood the same way throughout. Aristotle need not be taken to use 'signify' as he uses it in the *Analytics*, meaning 'signify to us'. He uses it in the way we have noticed elsewhere, for what names signify by nature; and here as usual they signify essences. In *Metaphysics* IV he argues that we must speak and think about definite subjects, and that these definite subjects must have essences.

## 9  Conclusion

It is hard to discuss Aristotle's views on signification without overinterpreting them. For he offers no full general account of signification to explain what he says about it. When we try to construct some general account from what he says, it is not surprising that a tidy result is hard to find. However, an attempt at a general account is fruitful if it exposes some difficulties in Aristotle's claims, and even more fruitful if it suggests solutions to the difficulties – even if Aristotle himself does not explicitly notice the difficulties or the solutions.

We can say enough with reasonable confidence about signification in Aristotle to conclude that he is not talking primarily about meaning; he is not sketching, well or badly, a theory of meaning, or even asking the sorts of questions that it would answer. An inquiry into the signification of words is not concerned with sense, communication, translation or linguistic competence, but with the discovery of the real properties there are and their relation to words.

However, signification by nature must be distinguished from signification to us; and is signification to us not meaning? It looks rather like it, since signification to us is discovered by examination of our beliefs; and certainly knowledge of our beliefs about F will help us in finding out the meaning of 'F'. Still, it is not mere pedantry to distinguish Aristotle's interest in signification to us from an interest in meaning. He is not interested in what 'incontinence' signifies to us because he is interested in communication or translation, but because what 'incontinence' signifies to us is what we believe about incontinence; and these common beliefs are the starting-point of inquiry into what incontinence really is, what 'incontinence' signifies by nature. We will hardly suppose that all our beliefs about incontinence determine the meaning of 'incontinence'; some will be more and less central than others. Aristotle will also discriminate among the common beliefs; but he will not look for those that tell us the meaning of the word; he will look for those that are true of incontinence as it really is. The meaning of 'incontinence' may be determined by a verbal formula 'choosing what you know to be worse', or by agreement on some range of paradigm cases. Aristotle's inquiries may not discover the meaning of the word; for he may reject the generally-accepted formula as false of incontinence, or decide that the paradigm cases are not genuine cases at all. The ordinary beliefs must be reconstructed to find their significate.

If this is true, it does not follow that we cannot speak of meaning or concepts in talking about Aristotle. We are free to say that he has an implicit grasp of the meanings of terms, and that his remarks show what meaning he attributes to them. We are free to say that sometimes he in fact supplies an analysis of a concept. The notions of meaning and conceptual truth are rich in philosophical difficulties; but they may still accurately reflect Aristotle's practice. I have argued that his concern with signification does not primarily reflect a concern with these notions; we should not suppose that he aims at explaining meanings or analysing concepts. At the same time we should be cautious about supposing that he is implicitly talking about meaning, when other accounts of his practice are at least as plausible. If I am right about signification, he is often interested in something that may look like meaning, but really is not.

Our account of Aristotle's views of signification has relied heavily on appeals to 'essences', 'real properties', 'reconstructed beliefs'. What he is looking for, and whether there is anything there to be found, will not be clear until we have a clearer grasp of these difficult notions and Aristotle's use of them. But we know that Aristotle faces these questions anyhow; his views on signification raise familiar difficulties. One benefit of our account is that it shows the connexion between Aristotle's views on signification and his other philosophical interests. Inquiry into words and their signification is part of inquiry into the world and the real essences in it.[28]

28 I am grateful to Julia Annas, Gail Fine, Malcolm Schofield and especially Norman Kretzmann, for helpful comments on an earlier version of this paper.

# 13   Saving Aristotle's appearances

## MARTHA CRAVEN NUSSBAUM

We shall not cease from exploration
And the end of all our exploring
Will be to arrive where we started
And know the place for the first time.

T. S. Eliot, 'Little Gidding'

That with which people most continuously associate – the discourse that orders
their whole lives – with this they are at variance; and what they encounter every
day seems strange to them.

Heraclitus, Fragment B72

At the beginning of Book VII of the *Nicomachean Ethics*, just before
his discussion of *akrasia*, Aristotle pauses to make some observations about his philosophical method:

Here, as in all other cases, we must set down the appearances (*phainomena*) and, first working through the puzzles (*diaporēsantes*), in this way go
on to show, if possible, the truth of all the beliefs we hold (*ta endoxa*)
about these experiences; and, if this is not possible, the truth of the
greatest number and the most authoritative. For if the difficulties are
resolved and the beliefs (*endoxa*) are left in place, we will have done
enough showing (1145b1 ff.).

Aristotle tells us that his method, 'here as in all other cases',[1] is to
set down what he calls *phainomena*, and what we shall translate as
'the appearances'. Proper philosophical method is committed to
and limited by these. If we work through the difficulties with
which the *phainomena* confront us and leave the greatest number

---

1  I follow Ross's rendering of *epi tois allois*. Although the word 'all' is not explicitly
present, I agree with Ross that this is the force of the unqualified *tois allois*; it certainly
cannot mean 'in some other cases'. *APr.* 46a17–22 makes explicit the crucial role of the
*phainomena* (there interchangeable with *empeiria*, 'experience') in providing the starting
point for 'any art (*technē*) and understanding (*epistēmē*) whatever'. On *endoxa*, cf. *Top.*
100b21.

and the most basic intact, we will have gone as far as philosophy can, or should, go.

This theoretical remark is closely followed by an application of the method. Aristotle first reports some of our most common beliefs and sayings about *akrasia*, concluding his summary with the words, 'These, then, are the things we say (*ta legomena*)' (1145b20). Next he presents the Socratic view that nobody does wrong willingly: we choose the lesser good only as a result of ignorance. Of this theory he says brusquely, 'This story (*logos*) is obviously at variance with the *phainomena*.' He then sets himself to finding an account of akratic behaviour that will remain faithful to the 'appearances' in a way that the rejected Socratic account does not.

Here, then, is an ambitious and exciting philosophical view, one that asks us to revise much of what we ordinarily think and say about weakness. What kind of reply has Aristotle made to this view when he dismisses it because it is at variance with the *phainomena* – by which, from the context, he seems to mean our beliefs and sayings? What sort of philosophical method is this that so thoroughly commits itself to and circumscribes itself by the ordinary?

I have indicated by my title that I believe that Aristotle's *phainomena* need saving. This implies that they are in trouble, or under attack. This I believe to be true, on two quite different levels. First, on the level of the text itself, the *phainomena* are in danger of vanishing altogether. Aristotle's word '*phainomena*' receives so many different translations that a reader of the standard English of the passages that I shall discuss would have no clue that they had anything in common. Ross, in the passage from *EN* VII, uses 'observed facts'.[2] Elsewhere we find 'data of perception', 'admitted facts', 'facts', 'observations' – almost everything *but* the literal 'appearances', or the frequently interchangeable 'what we believe', or 'what we say'. Even G. E. L. Owen, who did so much to salvage the close connection of the *phainomena* with language and ordinary belief, did so, as we shall see, only by charging Aristotle with serious ambiguity of usage.[3] To understand Aristotle's method we must, then, salvage and be more precise about

2 W. D. Ross, trans. *Ethica Nicomachea, The Works of Aristotle* (Oxford 1915), vol. IX.
3 G. E. L. Owen, '*Tithenai ta phainomena*', in *Aristote et les problèmes de méthode* (Louvain 1961), 83–103.

these *phainomena*, which are, as Aristotle tells us in the *Eudemian Ethics*, both the 'witnesses' and the 'paradigms' that we are to use in philosophical inquiry (1216b26).[4]

Second, as a philosophical method, the method that announces appearance-saving as its goal was when it was introduced, and still is now, in danger of abrupt philosophical dismissal. It can strike us as hopelessly flat, tedious, underambitious. All philosophy does, apparently, is to leave things where they are; when it has done that it has, Aristotle tells us, done 'enough showing'. Enough, we might ask, for what? For whom?

Aristotle was, as we shall see, well aware of such questions. In fact, he seems to have chosen the term 'appearances' deliberately, so as to confront them. By using this term for his philosophical 'paradigms', he announces that he is taking a position about philosophical method and philosophical limits that is very unusual in his tradition. 'Appearances' standardly occurs, in pre-Aristotelian Greek epistemology, as one arm of a polarity, on the other side of which is 'the real' or 'the true'. The appearances – by which Plato and his predecessors usually mean the world as perceived, demarcated, interpreted by human beings and their beliefs – are taken to be insufficient 'witnesses' of truth. Philosophy begins when we acknowledge the possibility that the way we pre-philosophically see the world might be radically in error. There is a true nature out there that 'loves to hide itself' (Heraclitus, B123) beneath our human ways of speaking and believing. Revealing, uncovering, getting behind, getting beyond – these are early Greek philosophy's guiding images for the philosophical endeavour. The Greek word for truth itself means, etymologically, 'what is revealed', 'what is brought out from concealment'.[5] Parmenides, the boldest of the philosophers whom Aristotle will be charging with violation of basic appearances, tells us unequivocally that truth is to be found only in a place 'far from the beaten path of human beings', after you depart from 'all the cities'.[6] He puts the contrast between the true and appearances this way:

---

4 *EE* 1216a26–32.
5 See H. Boeder, 'Der frühgriechische Wortgebrauch von *Logos* und *Alētheia*', *Archiv für Begriffsgeschichte*, 4 (1959), 82–112; T. Krischer, '*Etymos* und *alēthēs*', *Philologus*, 109 (1965), 161–74.
6 On Parmenides' attack on 'convention' and one early answer, see my 'Eleatic Conventionalism and Philolaus on the Conditions of Thought', *Harvard Studies in Classical Philosophy*, 83 (1979), 63–108.

You will learn the unshakeable heart of well-rounded Truth. You will, on the other hand, also learn the opinions of mortals, in which there is no true confidence.

The opinions of finite and limited beings provide no good evidence at all for the truth; far less do they provide truth with its 'witnesses' and 'paradigms'.

Plato inherited and developed this tradition; and it is clearly against Plato's metaphilosophical strictures that Aristotle is most deeply rebelling when he tells us that the *phainomena* are our best and only *paradeigmata*. Throughout the middle dialogues Plato repeatedly argues against the philosophical adequacy of any method that consists in setting down and adjusting our opinions and sayings. It is Plato who most explicitly opposes *phainomena*, and the cognitive states concerned with them, to truth and genuine understanding.[7] It is also Plato who argues that the *paradeigmata* that we require for understanding of the most important philosophical and scientific subjects are not to be found in the world of human belief and perception at all. In Book VI of the *Republic*, we see a proto-Aristotelian endeavour scathingly criticised. The interlocutors look back at the procedures they had used in Book IV in talking about desire and the elements of the person. Their method there had been to set down various common beliefs about psychological conflict and to work through puzzles in order to arrive at a harmonious adjustment of their pre-theoretical beliefs. Glaucon still seems content with this; but Socrates chides him for his complacency:

Any measure, my friend, which in these matters falls short of the real [or: the true] to any degree is not good measure. Nothing imperfect is a measure of anything, though sometimes people think that it is enough and that there is no need to search further. – They do this [says Glaukon] out of laziness. – Laziness, however, [Socrates replies] is a quality that the guardian of a city and of laws can do without.

Plato here flatly rejects the famous dictum of Protagoras, 'The human being is the measure of all things.' Nothing imperfect, that is, no limited being, *a fortiori* no human being or human agreement, is ever 'good measure' of anything. It is philosophical 'laziness' to stop with our beliefs and sayings. A willingness to go outside shared human conceptions and beliefs is here, as in

---

7 For only a few representative passages, see *Rep.* 476A, 598B, 602D; '*phainomena*' is significantly replaced by '*nomima*', 'conventional beliefs', at *Rep.* 479D.

Parmenides' poem, made a necessary condition of being a philosopher; and extra-human philosophy is a necessary prop for human discourse and human society. The city was said earlier to exist because 'each of us is not self-sufficient, but needs many things' (*Rep.* 369B). It now emerges that we are not sufficient, even in community, to satisfy our needs; we require paradigms that are more stable, clearer, purer than we are. Philosophy's purpose is to supply us with that exemplary purity. For the response of the interlocutors is to go on to search for a 'longer route' to truth: a route that searches for unmixed, unconditioned paradigms that are what they are no matter what we say or think.

Nor is this a claim concerned with the ethical alone; for an adjacent passage criticises mathematicians on the grounds that they practise their science starting from hypotheses – from something 'laid down' by human beings.[8] They never attain to a pure and unhypothetical point, not relative in any way to the conditions and contexts of human life and language. Such starting points are alleged to be the only adequate basis for any science.

When Aristotle declares that his aim, in science and metaphysics as well as in ethics, is to save the appearances and their truth, he is not, then, saying something cosy and acceptable. Viewed against the background of Eleatic and Platonic philosophising, these remarks have, instead, a defiant look. Aristotle is promising to do his philosophical work in a place from which Plato and Parmenides had spent their careers contriving an exit. He insists that he will find his truth *inside* what we say, see, and believe, rather than 'far from the beaten path of human beings' or (in Plato's words) 'out there'. When he writes that the person who orders these appearances and shows their truth has done 'enough showing', he is replying to the view expressed in *Republic* VI by insisting that it is not laziness, but good philosophy, that makes one operate within these limits. I want to arrive at a deeper and more precise account of Aristotle's method and of his reply to these opponents of anthropocentricity. Three questions (or groups of questions) will be important:

(1) What are Aristotle's *phainomena*? How is the term '*phainom-*

---

8 For Aristotle's own use of the notion of the 'unhypothetical', cf. *infra*, p. 288. Aristotle tends, in a similar way, to reserve the word 'conventional' for the arbitrary and replaceable (cf. *EN* 1134b19–30); the deeper human principles and practices are called 'natural' by contrast.

*ena'* best translated? How are *phainomena* related to observation? to language?

(2) What, more exactly, is the philosophical method described? How does the philosopher gather and set down the appearances, and what does he do with them then? For what reasons might he throw out some of them, and what has been accomplished when he has done that?

(3) Why should we, or our philosophers, be committed to appearances? Where do they get their claim to truth? What can Aristotle say to an opponent who claims that some of our deepest and most widely shared beliefs are wrong?

## The phainomena

'*Phainomena*' is the neuter plural of the present participle of '*phainesthai*', 'appear'. The (*prima facie* unlikely) translation of '*phainomena*' as 'observed facts' comes out of a long tradition in the interpretation of Aristotelian science. The tradition ascribes to Aristotle a Baconian picture of scientific/philosophical method that it also believes to be the most acceptable characterisation of the scientist's procedure. The scientist or philosopher, in each area, begins by gathering data through precise empirical observation, scrupulously avoiding any kind of interpreting or theorising; he or she then searches for a theory that explains the data. Aristotle's *phainomena* are his Baconian observation-data; the attempt to 'save' them is the attempt to find a comprehensive theory.

It is readily evident that in many contexts this cannot be the meaning of '*phainomena*'. In our *Ethics* passage, for example, Ross's translation plainly does not fit. The passage goes directly on to substitute for the word '*phainomena*' the word '*endoxa*'; *endoxa* are the common conceptions or beliefs on the subject. What Aristotle actually goes on to collect and set down are, in fact, our common beliefs about *akrasia*, usually as revealed in things we say. There is no attempt to describe the incontinent agent's behaviour in language free of interpretation; instead Aristotle looks at the ways we standardly do interpret such behaviour. And the summary of *phainomena* concludes, as we noticed, with the words, 'These, then, are the things we say (*ta legomena*)' (1145b8–20). Again, Socrates' theory clashes not with some hard

Baconian facts or some theory-neutral description – how could it? – but with what we commonly say, our shared interpretations.

In his justly famous article, G. E. L. Owen convincingly established that not only in the ethical works, but also in *Physics, de Caelo*, and other scientific works, Aristotle's *phainomena* must be understood to be our beliefs and interpretations, often as revealed in linguistic usage. To set down the *phainomena* is not to look for belief-free fact, but to record our usage and the structure of thought and belief which usage displays. For example, the *Physics* accounts of place and time begin not with an attempt to gather 'hard' data, but with observations about what we say on this subject, designed to give us a perspicuous view of our current conceptions. By showing us the prevalence of conceptual and linguistic considerations in the scientific works, Owen went a long way towards correcting a previously prevalent view, according to which Aristotle makes a sharp distinction between 'science' and 'metaphysics' or *Weltanschauung* – a view in which the *Physics* had always figured as a problematic, or even a confused work.

But Owen did not, I think, go far enough in his criticism of the Baconian picture. He still held on to the view that in certain scientific contexts the Baconian translations are appropriate, and that Aristotle's defence of a method concerned with *phainomena* is, in these cases, a defence of what Owen explicitly calls a 'Baconian picture'. His criticism of the traditional view limits itself to pointing out that it does not fit *all* the evidence; in particular, that it does not even fit all the evidence of all the scientific works. But Owen is then forced to conclude that Aristotle uses the term '*phainomena*' ambiguously. There are two distinct senses – and, we must add, therefore two distinct methods. In one sense, '*phainomena*' means 'observed data' and is associated with a Baconian picture of natural science. In the other, it means 'what we say' or 'our common beliefs', and is associated with a method that aims at sorting out and arranging our descriptions and interpretations of the world.[9]

Owen's article is a major contribution to the study of Aristotle. But its uncharacteristically conservative stopping place does Aristotle an injustice. First, Owen forces us to charge Aristotle with

9 Owen, '*Tithenai*'; Owen considers and rejects, on the basis of the evidence, the suggestion that we should distinguish senses of '*phainomena*' in a way that corresponds to the distinction between '*phainesthai*' with the infinitive and with the participle (n. 4).

equivocation concerning his method and several of its central terms.[10] This would be a serious lapse, without any cautionary note, in just the area where Aristotle's precision and attentiveness are usually most striking. Fortunately, however, we do not need to charge him with this. For the entire problem arises only because of a second difficulty in Owen's account, one whose removal will remove this one with it. There is, in fact, no case for crediting Aristotle with anything like the Baconian picture of science based on theory-neutral observation. He was not concerned, in his talk of experience or how the world 'appears', to separate off one privileged group of observations and to call them the 'uninterpreted' or 'hard' data. Such a bounding-off of a part of the data of experience as 'hard' or 'theory-free' was, in fact, unknown to any early Greek scientist. Instead of the sharp Baconian distinction between perception-data and communal belief, we find in Aristotle, as in his predecessors, a loose and inclusive notion of 'experience', or the way(s) a human observer sees or 'takes' the world, using his cognitive faculties (all of which Aristotle calls *'kritika'*, 'concerned with making distinctions'[11]).

This, I suggest, is the meaning of Aristotle's talk of *phainomena*. It is a loose notion, one that invites (and receives) further subdivisions; but it is neither ambiguous nor vacuous. If we do not insist on introducing an anachronistic scientific conception, the alleged two senses and two methods can be one. When Aristotle sits on the shore of Lesbos taking notes on shellfish, he will be doing something that is not, if we look at it from his point of view, so far removed from his activity when he records what we say about *akrasia*. He will be describing the world *as it appears to*, as it is experienced by, observers who are members of our kind.[12] Certainly there are important differences between these

10  Owen even claims (86–7) that 'this ambiguity in *phainomena* . . . carries with it a corresponding distinction in the use of various connected expressions'. These turn out to include *'aporiai'* ('puzzles') and *'epagōgē'* (usually rendered 'induction'), two central terms in Aristotle's epistemology whose ambiguity, on this story, also remains concealed or unnoticed by him. This makes the cost of this interpretation even clearer.

11  For further discussion of the active and selective character of Aristotelian perception, see my 'The Role of *phantasia* in Aristotle's Explanation of Action', Essay 5 in *Aristotle's De Motu Animalium* (Princeton 1978), 221–69.

12  It has often been noted with alarm that the *HA*, Aristotle's data-book, mentions beliefs and stories side by side with the records of field-work. Properly understood, this should not alarm us. Cf. also *Cael.* 303a22–3, where Aristotle criticises a vew on the grounds that it 'does away with many common beliefs (*endoxa*) and many perceptual appearances (*phainomena kata tēn aisthēsin*)': apparently two subdivisions of the *phainomena*, broadly construed.

two activities; but there is also an important link, and it is legitimate for him to stress it. We distinguish sharply between 'science' and 'the humanities'. Aristotle would be reminding us of the humanness of good science. Owen correctly emphasises that Aristotle is composing these methodological remarks in the shadow of Parmenides, who repudiated together, without distinction, both the evidence of sense-perception and the data of shared language and belief; all this he derides as mere 'convention' or 'habit'. Aristotle, answering him, promises to work within and to defend a method that is thoroughly committed to the data of human experience and accepts these as its limits.

## How the method works

If Aristotle simply spoke in vague terms of preserving perceptions and beliefs, his method would be no substantial contribution. But we can elicit from his theoretical remarks and from his practice a rich account of philosophical procedure and philosophical limits.

First the philosopher must 'set down' the relevant appearances. These will be different (and differently gathered) in each area. But in all areas we are to include both a study of ordinary beliefs and sayings and a review of previous scientific or philosophical treatments of the problem, the views of 'the many and the wise'.[13] To judge from what Aristotle sees fit to set down, the 'we' that bounds the class of relevant appearances is a group whose members share with each other not only species membership, but also some general features of a way of life. The scientific community around Aristotle was fascinated by ethnography and by parallels between animal and human customs. It is not simply cultural chauvinism that leads Aristotle to omit their more remote material. In *Politics* I, he tells us that the ethical concepts with which his study deals grow out of, and get their sense only in connection with, ways of life that 'bestial beings' and beings without any needs do not share. It seems to follow, if we generalise this principle, that data for an inquiry into our conception of $F$ can come only from peoples whose ways of life are similar to ours with respect to those conditions that gave rise to

13 Cf. *Top.* 100b21, 104a8–12.

our use of the term 'F'. Other groups and species not so related
to us could not have 'F' (or a term closely enough related to our
'F') in their language, and we do not, therefore, need to ask them
what they think about it. (We shall see later that these observations derive support from Aristotle's general remarks about
discourse.)

The philosopher has now gathered together all the relevant
*phainomena*. His next job, Aristotle argues, is to set out the
puzzles or dilemmas with which they confront us. The *phainomena* present us with a confused array, often with direct contradiction. They reflect our disagreements and ambivalences. The first
step must, therefore, be to bring conflicting opinions to the
surface and set them out clearly, marshalling the considerations
for and against each side, showing clearly how the adoption of a
certain position on one issue would affect our positions on
others. Without this serious attempt to describe the puzzles, the
philosopher is likely to accept too quickly a solution that dis-
guises or merely avoids the problem. 'It is not possible to resolve
anything if you do not see how you are bound; but the puzzles of
the intellect show you this about the issue. For insofar as the
intellect is puzzled, thus far its experience is similar to that of
someone in bonds: it cannot go forward in either direction'
(*Metaph.* 995a29–33).

If philosophy simply preserved the *status quo*, it would stop
here. Some people think this, but some think this. There are
these good reasons for *p*, these other good reasons for not-*p*. The
Greek sceptic did stop at this point. The conflict of opinion, and
the apparently equal weight of opposing beliefs displayed in the
puzzles, left him poised in the middle, released from all intellectual commitment.[14] And he found this experience of dissociation
from belief so delightfully pleasant that he sought it out as the
human good, designing his arguments, from now on, so as to
*produce* this 'equal weight'. Aristotle does not stop here. His
imagery of bondage and freedom indicates that *he* found the
experience of dilemma anything but delightful. (Here we begin
to notice some of the deep human differences that can separate
one metaphilosophical position from another.) Our deepest in-

---

14  There is a valuable discussion of this and other points concerning the relationship of
   Aristotle to Hellenistic scepticism in A. A. Long, 'Aristotle and the History of Greek
   Skepticism', forthcoming.

tellectual commitment (as we shall see) is to the Principle of Non-Contradiction, the most basic of all our shared beliefs. The method of appearance-saving therefore demands that we press for consistency.

But in resolving our difficulties we are not, Aristotle insists, free to follow a logical argument anywhere it leads. We must, at the end of our work on the puzzles, bring our account back to the *phainomena* and show that our account does, in fact, preserve them as true – or, at any rate, the greatest number and the most basic. Aristotle repeatedly criticises philosophers and scientists who attend to internal clarity and consistency, ignoring this return. For example, in *de Caelo* III, he criticises the Platonist theory that physical bodies are generated from triangular surfaces: 'What happens to these people is that in a discussion about the *phainomena* they say what is not in confirmity with the *phainomena*. The reason for this is that they have the wrong notion of first principles and want to bring everything into line with some hard-and-fast theories' (*Cael.* 306a5 ff.; cf. 293a27).[15] Similarly, in *On Generation and Corruption* (325a13 ff.), he criticises the Eleatics for being 'led to overstep' experience by their view that 'one ought to follow the argument' (325a13). What all these thinkers did, evidently, was to begin in the right way, with the *phainomena*; but then they got fascinated with the internal progress of their argument and trusted the argument, even though it ended in a place incredibly remote from, and at odds with, human beliefs. (Of the Eleatic conclusion, the denial that plurality is a genuine feature of the world, Aristotle goes on to say: 'Although these opinions appear to follow if one looks at the arguments, still to believe them seems next door to lunacy when one considers practice. For in fact no lunatic seems to stand so far outside as to suppose that fire and ice are one' [*GC* 325a18–22].) Instead, in such cases, they should have regarded the inhuman strangeness of the conclusion as a sign that something was wrong with the argument.

But what principles and procedures can we, then, use in deciding what appearances to keep and what to throw out, as we press for consistency? Here Aristotle's procedures vary, as we might expect,

15 Contrast *Cael.* 270b5, where arguments and *phainomena* are seen to support one another. *Top.* 104a8 ff. insists that the views of 'the wise' will be entertained only so long as they do not contradict 'the opinions of most people'. Presumably this would not prevent the scientist from attempting to show that an apparently appearance-violating theory really did 'save' basic appearances better than any other (cf. *infra*).

with the subject matter and the problem, and it is difficult to say anything illuminating at this level of generality. But we can make a few remarks. First, nothing universally believed is entirely discarded. 'For that which seems so to everyone, this we say is' (*EN* 1172a36). Earlier in the *Ethics*, Aristotle quotes with approval the poetic lines: 'No report is altogether wiped out, which many peoples . . .' (*EN* 1155b27–8).[16] (Here the context [concerning pleasure] shows that this does not prevent us from qualifying the belief in the light of other beliefs.) Second, nothing that we have to be using in order to argue or inquire can get thrown out. We shall look at that point in the following section.

Beyond this, we must, Aristotle believes, ask ourselves whether, in the inquiry at hand, we share some conception of the good judge, of the person or persons whom we will trust to arbitrate our disputes. Very rarely is truth a matter of majority vote. Often our idea of the competent judge is more broadly shared among us, and less subject to disagreement, than is our view of the subject-matter concerning which this judge is to render a verdict. In ethics, for example, we agree more readily about the characteristics of intellect, temper, imagination, and experience that a competent judge must have than we do about the particular practical judgements that we expect him to make. The same is true in other areas as well. In *Metaphysics* IV, Aristotle answers thinkers who create puzzles about perception by pointing out that our practices reveal a set of standards for arbitrating disagreements:

It is worthy of amazement if they create a puzzle about whether magnitudes are of such a size, and colors of such a quality, as they appear (*phainetai*) to those at a distance or to those who are near, and whether they are such as they appear to the healthy or to the sick; and whether those things are quite heavy which appear so to the weak or to the strong; and whether those things are true which appear so to the sleeping or to the waking. It is obvious that they do not really think that these are matters for doubt. At any rate nobody, if, while he is in Libya, he has imagined one night that he is in Athens, [wakes up and] heads for the Odeion.[17] Again, as for the future, as even Plato says, the opinions of the

16  The fact that both of these passages occur in ethical contexts may be significant. In science we are more likely to be forced to revise radically some pre-theoretical beliefs; and yet even here Aristotle would insist that the theory must return to and account for our original experience.

17  The whole context indicates that the issue here is probably not the Cartesian question of distinguishing dream-states from real, but rather the question whether a waking person regards his (previous) dream experience as having equal weight with his waking experience.

doctor and the ignorant man are not equally authoritative as to whether someone is or is not going to be healthy (1010b3–14).

Aristotle asks us to look at our practices, seeing, in the different areas, what sorts of judges we do, in fact, trust. The judgement about whom to trust and when seems to come, like the appearances, from us. We turn to doctors because we do, in fact, rely on doctors. This reliance, Aristotle insists, does not need to be justified by producing a further judge to certify the judge (1011a3 ff.); it is sufficiently 'justified' by the facts of what we do. The expert, and our reasons for choosing him, are not behind our practices; they are inside them. And yet such experts do, in fact, help us to unravel puzzles.

The importance of the expert emerges clearly if we consider Aristotle's account of our basic linguistic practices of introducing into discourse and defining. In *Posterior Analytics* II 8, Aristotle develops an account of the transition from our initial use of a natural kind term to its scientific definition.[18] The kind term enters our use on the basis of some communal experience or experiences (the pronoun 'we' is used throughout). For example, 'We are aware of thunder as a noise in the clouds, of eclipse as a privation of light, or of the human being as a certain species of animal' (93a22–24). At this point we are able to 'indicate' (*sēmainein*) human beings or eclipses, to introduce them into discourse or refer to them; but we do not yet have the scientific definition that states the nature of things of this kind. We may have sorted our experience and assigned our kind terms very roughly – 'sometimes incidentally, sometimes by grasping something of the item in question' (93a21–2). We move from this rough grouping and this thin account to the full definition only when we have some account or theory that states the 'nature' of the phenomenon: in the case of thunder, he tells us, when we have a theory that tells us that it is the quenching of fire in the clouds, and how this produces the sound we hear. The expert, not the layman, uncovers this theory. In the case of most species of animals, we do not yet, Aristotle believes, have a theory that

18  Some related points receive an interesting discussion in R. Bolton, 'Essentialism and Semantic Theory in Aristotle', *Philosophical Review*, 85 (1976), 514–55; Bolton's account of this passage is convincingly criticised by T. Irwin in chapter 12, above. The passage is discussed in connection with the Putnam/Kripke account of the meaning of natural-kind terms by David Wiggins, *Sameness and Substance* (Oxford and Cambridge, Mass. 1980), ch. 3.

satisfies our demands. But our broadly shared belief that natural beings are 'things that have within themselves a principle of change' (*Ph.* II 1) implies a commitment to abide by the results of scientific investigation into these inner structures.[19] When the scientist comes up with a theory that offers a satisfactory account of the growth and movement of some type of natural being, we are committed to regarding this theory as defining and bounding (at least *pro tempore*) the nature of this being – even if some individuals whom we have previously tended to include in the extension of the term will have to be excluded. Our agreement in a commitment to scientific exploration proves more basic than our *prima facie* disagreement with the biologist over the extension of the term.

We can use Aristotle's account of defining to make progress on two of our previous problems. First, we can now see more clearly why Aristotle gathers his *phainomena* only from communities relevantly like ours. The suggestion of the *Politics* passage is confirmed by his general account of discourse. We take our evidence about *F*s only from communities where the relevant conditions of experience are similar to those that obtain in our own community, because our ability to introduce *F*s into discourse arises from actual experience, and the nature of *F*s is given by a scientific account arrived at by research in and into the world of our experience.

We can now also begin to give Aristotle an answer to the charge that his method shuns the hard work involved in making real philosophical or scientific progress. Aristotle can insist that there is no tension – or at least no *simple* tension – between the appearances-method and the scientist's aims. This is so because our practices and our language embody a reliance on such experts, frequently making their judgements constitutive of truth. This method is attempting at once to be seriously respectful of human language and ordinary ways of believing and to do justice to the fact that these very practices reveal a demand for scientific understanding. The method should not be taken to prevent us from doing what we in fact do. It is, however, also crucial to see that the expert plays here no deeper role than the role that he in fact plays. He is normative for our use only to the extent that we

19 On this point, see Wiggins, op. cit., ch. 3.

in fact agree in accepting his authority. Aristotle shows no tendency to convert these descriptive remarks about discourse into a thick theory of discourse; we, in reading him, should not build in more structure than is present in the text, whose main aim is to argue against those who create specious puzzles by denying an actual feature of our practice.

I have so far said little about how this account of Aristotle's philosophical/scientific method, constructed largely from the *Metaphysics* and the specific scientific treatises, is to be put together with the account of scientific understanding developed in the *Posterior Analytics*. Two pressing questions might be raised at this point. The first concerns the *Analytics'* ideal of a finished science as a hierarchical deductive system: how does this norm cohere with Aristotle's aims and procedures in the appearance-saving passages on which I have drawn? This is clearly a huge question, which can barely be broached here. But we can provisionally say that the appearance-saving method could be fully compatible with the *Analytics'* demand that, in the natural sciences (as opposed to ethics), the expert should in the end be able to validate his claim to understanding by giving systematic demonstrations of the type described. The two aims would be compatible if the deductive ideal were seen as something that arises, itself, from the appearances, a commitment which we believe ourselves to undertake when we do science. And this, in fact, is how Aristotle presents his account of *epistēmē* there: as an articulation of what 'we' believe scientific understanding should be and do. He begins from an account of the conditions under which 'we' 'think we understand' something (*APo.* 71b9), and goes on to show what this shared conception requires of the scientist. Similarly, the *Physics* discussion of explanation begins from the ways in which 'we' ask and answer 'Why?' questions, and criticises earlier scientists for insufficient attention to the variety of our usage. At every step Aristotle is concerned to show how his norm arises out of the appearances and embodies their requirements.[20] In ethics, on the other hand, he takes pains to argue that our beliefs about practice do *not* yield

20 It is yet another problem, of course, to relate this norm to the practice of Aristotle's scientific treatises, where deductions of this sort are very rarely present. This discrepancy may indicate only that Aristotle does not believe he is ready to claim full *epistēmē*; on the other hand, it is plausible, as I argue in *Aristotle's De Motu*, Essay 2, that the evidence uncovered in actual scientific work led Aristotle to make some revisions in his methodological norms, especially with regard to the autonomy of the sciences.

the demand for a deductive system.[21] He is evidently not interested in assimilating the appearances to a theoretical ideal where the appearances themselves do not reveal a commitment to such an ideal.

But a more troublesome question arises when we consider that the first principles of science in the *Analytics* have been thought by centuries of commentators, *via* the medieval tradition, to be *a priori* truths grasped by special acts of intellectual intuition, apart from all experience. Surely, we might object, the finished structure of an Aristotelian science rests on these, and not, ultimately, on the appearances. Or, if the scientific works do rest on appearances, they depart, in so placing themselves, from the ideal set forth in the *Analytics*.

The objector and I can agree on a number of points about the principles mentioned in the *Analytics*: that they are to be true, indemonstrable, necessary, primary, both prior to and more knowable than the conclusion; that they transmit their truth to the conclusion; even (as it will turn out) that they are *a priori* according to *some* understanding of the *a priori*. But this leaves, it is plain, much scope for disagreement: for a deep and basic human appearance can be all of those things, as I shall show; and to say this about a principle commits us neither to special acts of rational intuition, nor to the notion that the principles are true outside of all conceptual schemes, all language. The objector, it emerges, derives these extra elements of this famous interpretation from an exiguous amount of evidence, especially from some alleged evidence in *Posterior Analytics* II 19. Fortunately (since I have no space here to argue the case in detail) recent work on *nous* (intellect) and *epistēmē* (understanding) in the *Analytics* has convincingly shown that the objector's picture is a misreading of the text. Work by A. Kosman, J. Lesher, and, most recently, an excellent article by Myles Burnyeat, have established that the model of understanding that emerges from this and connected texts does not introduce either intuition or extra-experiential truth.[22] To have *nous*, or insight, concerning first principles is to

---

21  There will be some significant differences between the sciences and ethics (of which there is, in Aristotle's view, no *epistēmē*), in two areas above all: (1) the degree to which *consistency* is a requirement, and the nature of the consistency sought; (2) the amount of vagueness or indeterminacy in the subject-matter, which will have implications for the usefulness and feasibility of general accounts. These issues are discussed in essay 4 of my *Aristotle's De Motu*.

22  A. Kosman, 'Explanation and Understanding in Aristotle's *Posterior Analytics*', in *Exegesis and Argument: Studies . . . presented to Gregory Vlastos*, ed. E. N. Lee, et al. (Assen 1973: *Phronesis*, suppl. vol. I), 374–92; J. Lesher, 'The Role of *Nous* in Aristotle's *Posterior Analytics*', *Phronesis*, 18 (1973), 44–68; M. F. Burnyeat, 'Aristotle on Under-

come to see the fundamental role that principles we have been using all along play in the structure of a science. What is needed is not to grasp the first principles – we grasp them and use them already, inside our experience, as the text of II 19 asserts. As Burnyeat puts it: 'What [the student's belief] is not yet is understanding and the kind of [grasp] that goes with understanding. To acquire this at the level of first principles what we need is greater familiarity, perhaps some more dialectical practice; in short, intellectual habituation.'[23] We move from the confused mass of the appearances to a perspicuous ordering, from the grasp that goes with use to the ability to give accounts. There is no reason to posit two philosophical methods here, one dealing with appearances, one resting on the *a priori*; dialectic and first philosophy have, as Aristotle insists in *Metaphysics* IV 2 (cf. *infra*) exactly the same subject matter. The appearances, then, can go all the way down.

## Saving the most authoritative

But if the *Analytics* does not help the objector, neither does it really answer our remaining questions about the status of Aristotelian first principles. What *is*, then, meant by the claim that they must be both 'true' and 'undemonstrated', and where do we get our conviction of their truth, if undemonstrated is what they are? If they are found in and through experience, it then becomes all the more pressing to inquire how they get their claim to truth and to priority. The *Analytics* tells us some of the characteristics of first principles; it also tells us how, through experience, we can acquire insight into their fundamental status. It does not yet answer our question concerning that status, since it does not encounter any sort of sceptical challenge.[24] Now we must turn, therefore, to *Metaphysics* IV, where we shall see how Aristotle defends their claim against the sceptic's attack.

standing Knowledge', in *Aristotle on Science: "The Posterior Analytics"*, ed. E. Berti (Padua 1981). The standard interpretation is defended by T. H. Irwin; 'Aristotle's Discovery of Metaphysics', *Rev. Metaph.*, 31 (1977), 210–29. Cf. also the helpful related account of Aristotelian *epagōgē* in T. Engberg-Pedersen, 'More on Aristotelian Epagoge', *Phronesis*, 24 (1979), 301–19.

23 Burnyeat, op. cit.
24 Burnyeat, op. cit., argues this convincingly; this forms part of his case that *epistēmē* is understanding, rather than knowledge.

In *Metaphysics* IV 4, Aristotle considers how we should deal with an opponent who challenges the Principle of Non-Contradiction (contradictory predicates cannot belong to the same subject at the same time). He calls this principle 'the most secure starting-point (*archē*) of all'. It looks like something that underlies and is used in every inquiry. How then, are we to deal with the opponent who challenges us to justify our inquiry by demonstrating its truth? Aristotle's answer is revealing. 'They demand a demonstration,' he says, 'out of *apaideusia*. For it is *apaideusia* not to recognise of what things you should look for a demonstration, and of what you should not.' Now *apaideusia* is not stupidity, absurdity, logical error, even wrong-headedness. It is lack of *paideia*, the education by practice and precept that initiates a young Greek into the ways of his or her community; the word is usually translated 'acculturation' or 'moral education'. *Apaideusia* is, for example, the condition of the Cyclopes (Euripides, *Cycl.* 493), humanoid creatures who live in isolation from human community. 'They have no assemblies that make decisions, nor do they have binding conventions, but they inhabit the summits of lofty mountains . . . and they have no concern for one another' (Hom. *Od.* 9.112–115).[25] It looks significant that the opponent is charged with this defect, rather than with ignorance or dumbness. It is not so much that he is stupid; he just does not know how to do things (or he refuses to do things) the way we do them. He lacks what Burnyeat has called 'intellectual habituation' – the sensitive awareness, produced by education and experience, of the fundamental role this principle plays in all our practices, all our discourse. (Cf. *GC* 316a5: 'The reason for their deficient ability to survey what we all agree on is their inexperience [*apeiria*].') And, for some reason, he has decided to dissociate himself even from the incomplete *paideia* that characterises the person in the street; for he is assailing a principle that that person *uses* as fundamental, whether he is aware of this or not.

Aristotle now goes on to propose a way of dealing with this objector. First, he says, you must find out whether this person will say anything to you or not. If he will not say anything, then you can stop worrying about him. 'It is comical to look for

25 An examination of the uses of '*apaideusia*' both before and in Aristotle supports the interpretation given here. Though the results of this inquiry cannot be detailed here, important passages are: Democritus B212; Thuc. 3.42; Plato, *Gorg.* 523E, *Alc.* 1 123D7, *Phd.* 90E–91A, esp. *Tht.* 175A–176A; Aristotle *Rhet.* 1391a17, 1395a6, 1356a29, *EN* 1128a20 ff., *EE* 1217a8, *PA* 639a1 ff.

something to say to someone who won't say anything. A person like that, insofar as he is like that, is pretty well like a vegetable' (1006a13–15). But if he *does* say something, something definite, then you can go on to show him that in so doing he is in fact believing and making use of the very principle he attacks. For in order to be saying something definite he has to be ruling out something else as incompatible: at the very least, the contradictory of what he has asserted.[26]

So if the person does not speak, he ceases to be one of us, and we are not required to take account of him. If he does speak, we can urge him to take a close look at his linguistic practices and what they rest on. In doing this we are giving him the *paideia* he lacks, a kind of initiation into the way we do things. Sometimes the opponent will not listen. 'Some need persuasion, others need violence', Aristotle remarks somewhat grimly in the next chapter (1009a17–18). Philosophy, at the level of basic principles, seems to be a matter of bringing the isolated person into line, of dispelling illusions that cause the breakdown of communication. Sometimes this can be done gently, sometimes only with violence; and sometimes not at all.

Several things strike us in this reply to the sceptical challenger. First, it is not the sort of reply he demands. In the century after Aristotle, Stoic philosophers answered sceptical attacks against basic beliefs by arguing that these beliefs rest on a perceptual foundation that is absolutely indubitable. The 'cataleptic impression' was a perception that certified its own accuracy; this foundation was, they felt, secure against the sceptic.[27] But Aristotle does not point to this sort of foundation for our knowledge of the world. He says that the Principle is true and primary; that we are entitled to assert it; that, in fact, we cannot be wrong about it; that it is what any thinking person must believe. He does not

---

26 In fact, Aristotle claims that he can handle the opponent even if he says just a single word, so long as he gives it some definite sense; the argument is complex, and it would take a detailed analysis to show whether he succeeds in this enterprise. I therefore confine myself to a more cautious statement of what is to be shown.

27 Long (op. cit.) assimilates Aristotle's reply to that of the Stoics claiming (wrongly, in my view) that he means to provide the demanded certainty by developing a foundationalist theory of knowledge based on perception. (Long has told me in correspondence that he no longer holds this.) Irwin ('Aristotle's Discovery') advances very briefly an account of elenctic demonstration that seems to be somewhat closer to the one being developed here, although there would, I believe, be important differences; and Irwin links it in quite a different way with other features of Aristotle's scientific method.

say that this basic principle is true apart from the 'appearances' and from human conceptual schemes, true of the way the world is *behind* or *beyond* the categories of our thought and discourse. In fact, in the next chapter he even refuses to take up the popular contemporary question, which animate species is the standard of truth? All he says is that *we* cannot assail the principle; but neither, he insists, can we demonstrate it in the demanded way. It is, for us, the starting-point of all discourse, and to get outside it would be to cease to think and to speak. So in a very important way Aristotle does *not* answer the opponent's challenge. He does not offer him the exterior, Platonic certainty he wants. And if the opponent does choose to isolate himself from discourse, even the limited 'elenctic demonstration' will not succeed. In a penetrating account of this passage, the third-century A.D. Greek commentator Alexander of Aphrodisias writes that to attempt to converse with such a silent opponent is 'to try to communicate something through discourse to someone who has no discourse, and through discourse to try to establish fellowship with someone who is bereft of fellowship' (272,36–273,1). We cannot satisfy the sceptic's demand for external purity; we can ask him to accept our fellowship. But perhaps, if he is a sceptic bent on securing his equanimity against the risks attendant on community and human involvement, he will welcome that. We cannot, in any harder sense, show him that he is *wrong*. (This is why Aristotle's crucial next step, in chapter 5, is to search for a diagnosis of the opponent's motivations, asking what beliefs and aims might lead an intelligent person to take up this position, and how we might cure the motivating error in each case.)

A similar position is implied in the passage we examined earlier, where Aristotle rejected the Eleatic One on the grounds that not even a lunatic believes in it, if we judge from his actions. Here, too, Aristotle stops short of calling Parmenides' conclusion wrong of the world as it is apart from all conceptualisation. All he says is that no human being who undertakes to act in the human world – no human being who does not 'stand so far outside' as not to be acting *among* us at all – can be seriously holding the view. Action, even bizarre and abnormal action, commits itself to the existence of movement and plurality. Aristotle makes this same point later in *Metaphysics* IV 4, extending his discourse argument for the Principle of Non-Contradiction to cover cases in which the opponent, though possibly silent with respect to the argument's verbal demands, reveals his commitment to the principle through his practices:

It is most obvious that nobody really is in this condition [sc. of believing the denial of the Principle of Non-Contradiction], neither those who make the argument, nor anybody else. For why does he go to Megara and not stay put, when he thinks he should go? Why doesn't he go straight out early in the morning and throw himself into a well or off a precipice, if there chance to be one, but instead obviously avoids this, as though he does not actually hold that it is not good and good to fall in? It's clear, then, that he believes one thing better and the other thing not better (1008b14–19).

The opponent can defeat us, then, only by ceasing to act humanly in our world, as well as by ceasing to speak. As soon as he acts in some definite fashion, he is being responsive to definite features of the world as it strikes a human being, namely himself. He is accepting certain appearances, both perceptions and common human beliefs – e.g. beliefs about the badness of early death, about the danger of being killed if one walks off a precipice, about the fact that he is a mortal, bodily creature with bones that can be broken and blood that can be spilled – as having a bearing on his life and actions. He is not accepting their contradictories as having equal force. He is allowing the humanity that he shares with us to govern his choice.[28] But this Aristotelian reply, once again, comes from within human practices. It makes clear the cost of refusing the principle: immobility as well as silence, the utter loss of community. It does not seek to ground the principle in anything firmer than this. But this is firm enough; this is true, necessary, as firm as anything could be.

Aristotle does not, however, assert that there is *nothing more* to non-contradiction than *paideia* or our practices. He would say, I think, that we are not in a position to judge this; that this claim, like the sceptic's denial of the principle, asks us to stand outside language and life, and is therefore doomed to incoherence.

Is the principle then for Aristotle an *a priori* principle?[29] This question is frequently raised, but often without sufficient care to define the type of *a priority* involved. It is certainly *a priori* if an *a priori* principle is one that is basic or unrevisable, relative to a certain body

---

28 Cf. M. Burnyeat, 'Can the Sceptic Live his Scepticism?', in *Doubt and Dogmatism*, ed. M. Schofield, et al. (Oxford 1980), 20–53.

29 A valuable discussion of the different varieties of the *a priori*, and a defence of a position closely related to Aristotle's, is in Hilary Putnam, 'There Is At Least One A Priori Truth', *Erkenntnis*, 13 (1978), 153–70.

of knowledge (what has sometimes been called contextual *a priority*). It is even *a priori* in a somewhat stronger sense: it is so basic that it cannot significantly be defended, explained, or questioned at all from within the appearances, that is to say the lives and practices of human beings, as long as human beings are anything like us. But it is not an *a priori* principle if that is a principle that can be known to hold independently of all experience and all ways of life, all conceptual schemes. This is the question that we are in no position either to ask or to answer. This is what the sceptic wanted to be shown, and this we do not offer him.

We cannot illustrate this point more clearly than by contrasting the Aristotelian and the Platonic notions of the 'unhypothetical' foundations of a science. For Plato, as we said, each science must start from a principle or principles that are 'unhypothetical' in the sense that they are known to hold 'themselves by themselves', entirely independently of all conceptualisation and thought. Aristotle also calls his 'most secure principle' an 'unhypothetical' principle. But his account makes clear the difference of his position: 'For that which it is necessary for anyone who understands anything at all to have, this is not a hypothesis' (1005b15–16). A hypothesis is, in his view, quite literally something 'set down beneath' something else. Anything that we must use in order to think at all obviously cannot be posited or 'set down' at will; therefore, we are justified in calling such a principle 'unhypothetical'. But this Kantian kind of non-hypothetical status is all that Aristotle ever endeavours to claim for it. To try to say 'more' would be, in his view, to say less, or perhaps nothing at all. Scientific truths are certainly true *of* or *about* the world of nature; they are not (any more than they were for Kant) all *about* human beings or their mental states. But the status of the basic truths on which science is based is a status of necessity *for* discourse and thought. It is this necessity, and only this, that they can transmit to their dependants.

One further example will show us a connection between Aristotle's replies to sceptical opponents and his views about language. In *Physics* II, Aristotle considers Parmenides' claim that change and motion are merely conventional. As in the *Metaphysics*, he rejects the Eleatic demand that he demonstrate this basic appearance:

To try to show that nature exists is comical; for it is obvious that there are many such [i.e. changing] things. And to show the obvious through the obscure is what someone does who is unable to distinguish what is self-evident from what is not. It's possible to be in that state: a man blind from birth might try to give a proof from premises concerning colours. But it is necessary that the talk of such people will be mere words, and that they will have no *nous* about anything (193a1 ff.).

Once again, we notice that there is a sense in which the challenger goes unanswered. Aristotle says not that the opponent is *wrong* about the way things really are apart from the categories of thought, not that he says that can be decisively falsified by appeal to some foundational evidence, but that what he says is comical. He is trying to say what *he*, at any rate, is in no position to say. Just as a person blind from birth is in no position to use in an argument premises about colours, since he can have had no experience of colour, so the Eleatic is in no position to use premises having to do with the unitary, unchanging Being of the universe. Change and plurality are in everything we experience; even Parmenides grants this. How then, Aristotle asks, can he make his argument?

These remarks can be better understood if we recall Aristotle's views about linguistic indicating. The Eleatic is 'comical' because he does not succeed in singling out or indicating the unchanging, undivided One. This unity is, by the Eleatic's own story, 'far from the beaten path of human beings'. Neither he nor anyone else in his community can have had experience of it.[30] Therefore, Aristotle would say, he cannot introduce it into discourse; discourse, even when vague and imprecise, is bounded by the experience of the group. Therefore, although the Eleatic believes that he is saying something bold and strange, he is really saying nothing at all. This is why we can say that his talk is 'mere words' without understanding.

And as for the Platonist, who charges with 'laziness' any philosopher who refuses to take the 'longer route' that moves away from appearances to grasp the form of the Good, Aristotle says, elsewhere, that this opponent, too, fails to 'indicate' or refer to his cherished entities. In a remarkable passage in the *Posterior Analytics*, he remarks how queer it is that the Platonist introduces

---

30 Aristotle's actual example is not entirely appropriate, since the blind man would, presumably, be able to refer to colours because colour-words are parts of his language, even if they enter the language on the basis of others' experience, and not his own.

monadic, self-subsistent forms of properties which, like colours, always occur in our experience as the properties of some substance or other. Then, with a burst of exuberant malice that shows us aspects of Aristotle's temperament usually masked by a measured sobriety, he exclaims: 'So goodbye to the Platonic forms. They are *teretismata*, and have nothing to do with our speech' (*APo.* 83a32–4). *Teretismata* are meaningless sounds you make when you are singing to yourself; we might render them as 'dum-de-dum-dums'. Jonathan Barnes's new translation calls them 'noninoes'. But, besides the fact that this suggestion of highbrow musical taste makes the criticism too polite, we also miss the emphasis on solitude and isolation conveyed by the Greek. We are supposed to think not of a madrigal society, but of a completely self-absorbed individual saying to himself what neither anyone else, nor, ultimately, he, can understand. When the Platonist speaks of The Good or The White, he is not referring to anything, much less communicating anything to us. He is just crooning away in a corner. For forms are self-subsistent, monadic, where our experience makes properties dependent on substance; forms are non-relational, even where the property (e.g. equality, doubleness) always turns up, in our experience, in a relational context. (In *Metaphysics* I, Aristotle says that Plato's arguments tried to create a non-relative class of relative terms, 'of which *we say* there is no all-by-themselves class' [990b16–17].)

But to say 'goodbye' to the forms is not to assert that they do not exist entirely outside of the world of our experience and thought. That we could not say either. Even the contrast between the world as it is for us and the world as it is behind or apart from our thought may not be a contrast that the defender of a human internal realism should allow himself to make using human language. Here we might say that Aristotle usually maintains his internality more consistently than Kant, refusing, most of the time, even to try to articulate what it is that we cannot say. Aristotelian reason is not so much in bonds, cut off *from* something that we can, nonetheless, describe or point to, as it is committed *to* something, to language and thought, and the limits of these. Appearances and truth are not opposed, as Plato believed they were. We can have truth only *inside* the circle of the appearances, because only there can we communicate, even refer, at all.

This is, then, a kind of realism, neither idealism of any sort nor scepticism. It has no tendency to confine us to internal representations, nor to ask us to suspend or qualify our deeply grounded judgements. It is fully hospitable to truth, to necessity (properly understood), and to a full-blooded notion of objectivity. It is not relativism, since it insists that truth is one for all thinking, speaking beings. It is a realism, however, that articulates very carefully the limits within which any realism must live. Talk of the eternal or the immortal has its place in such a realism – but, as Aristotle makes clear, only because such talk is an important part of our world. 'It is well to join in by persuading oneself that the ancient beliefs deeply belonging to our native tradition are true, according to which there is something deathless and divine' (*Cael.* 285a1–4; and cf. the preservation of the theistic 'appearances' of 'all human beings' at *Cael.* 270b5 ff.). The belief in the divinity and eternity of the heavenly bodies has weight in philosophy because of its depth for us, because it has survived so many changes of social and political belief of a more superficial nature (*Metaph.* 1074a39 ff.). But, by the same token, an 'internal' truth is all we are entitled to claim for such beliefs.[31] Even the existence of an unmoved mover is established as one of the conclusions of a physical science, none of whose principles has a deeper status than the Principle of Non-Contradiction, and many of which are obviously less firmly grounded.

To opt out of a basic 'appearance' will not always entail silence or inaction. Appearances come at different levels of depth: by which we mean that the cost of doing without one will vary with the case, and must be individually scrutinised. To deny the prevalent belief in gods will lead to a certain loss of community: there will be a very real sense in which theist and atheist do not inhabit the same world or look at the same stars. But the gulf will not be totally unbridgeable. Similarly, to opt out of very basic communal ethical judgements will lead to a way of life that more normal humans may judge bestial or inhuman. A life of extreme intemperance does bring a communication problem with it, for 'the person who lives according to his impulses will not listen to an argument that dissuades him' (*EN* 1179b26–7); and, at the other end of the spectrum, the extreme ascetic also ceases to be

31 On some of these points, see my *Aristotle's De Motu*, Essay 2, esp. 133–8.

one of us, 'for insensibility of this sort is not human . . . and if there should be someone to whom nothing is pleasant, he would be far from being a human being' (*EN* 1119a6–10). But the cost of asceticism is not the same as the cost of denying the Principle of Non-Contradiction; presumably this is a life that could be lived among us, though the liver would in significant ways fail to be one of us.

Furthermore, whereas the opponent of the Principle of Non-Contradiction could not find a place from which to argue with us, the opponent of a prevalent but less basic appearance can always try to show us (relying on the Principle) that some other, more basic appearances conflict with this one and ought to lead us to abandon it. For example, a feminist opponent of Aristotle's conservative view about the social role of women could try to show Aristotle that a progressive position actually preserves certain deep human beliefs about the equal humanity of other human beings better than his own political theory does. If Aristotle agreed about the conflict, and agreed that these other beliefs were deeper (i.e. that the cost of giving them up would be greater, or one we are less inclined to pay), then we would expect him to change his view. The method does not make new discoveries, radical departures, or sharp changes of position impossible, either in science or in ethics.[32] What it does do is to explain to us how any radical or new view must commend itself to our attention: by giving evidence of its superior ability to integrate and organise features of our lived experience of the world. Sometimes it may remain unclear over a long period of time whether a bold hypothesis (including some of Aristotle's own) has or has not successfully made this return – whether it is the truth, or just empty words.

There is much more to be said about this Aristotelian conception of philosophising, and especially about the relationship, in it, between the negative goal of deflating inappropriate metaphysical pictures and the positive aim of satisfying what Aristotle takes to be a natural human demand for understanding (*Metaph.* 980a1).[33]

32 We should remember that Aristotle's final answer to the problem of *akrasia* is not simply a list of popular truisms, but a complex and controversial account which is *argued* to be the best way of preserving the most important appearances on the subject.
33 I have written more about these issues in a longer version of this paper, which will appear as a section of a longer forthcoming manuscript on contingency and practical reason in Greek ethics. Some pertinent material is also included in my 'Aristotle', in *Ancient Writers*, ed. T. J. Luce (New York: Charles Scribner's Sons, forthcoming 1982).

We philosophise, Aristotle tells us, because we do not like to be at a loss in the world: wonder and bewilderment lead us to undertake studies that promise an orderly grasp (982b12–19). Given this motivation, we suspect that oversimplification and reduction will remain deep and ever-present human dangers. (The views that Aristotle attacks for violation of appearances are not all the theories of professional specialists; many exercise a great hold over the imaginations of ordinary people, people who at the same time, in their daily life and speech, reveal their commitment to a more complicated world.) The perspicuous mapping of serious researchers should, ideally, enable us to satisfy our demand for comprehension without making us strangers to the world of our language and our practices. But this is a delicate undertaking, requiring keen perception of the mean between too much order and disorder, excessive and deficient simplicity. Aristotle summarised the problem neatly in his lost work *On the Good,* where he is said to have written: 'You ought to remember that you are a human being – not only in living well, but also in doing philosophy.'[34] Concerning which the ancient biographer who reports the sentence observes: 'Aristotle must have been a very balanced character.'[35]

34 *On the Good*, fr. 1 Ross, from *Vita Marciana*, p. 433, 10–15 (Rose).
35 I would like to thank audiences at Stanford University and at the University of Massachusetts at Amherst for discussion that contributed to the revisions of this chapter. I am also grateful to the many people who have generously helped me with comments on earlier versions: especially Julia Annas, Myles Burnyeat, John Carriero, Randall Havas, Geoffrey Lloyd, Julius Moravcsik, Edward Minar, Hilary Putnam, Malcolm Schofield, Gregory Vlastos, and David Wiggins. My gratitude to Gwil Owen is fundamental. Concerning the delicate and difficult philosophical enterprise I have described here, Aristotle once remarked, 'To do it well is something rare and praised and noble'. We see this in Gwil Owen's work. It gives me great pleasure to dedicate this chapter to him.

# 14 Myths about non-propositional thought

RICHARD SORABJI

G. E. L. Owen's papers tend not only to transform their professed subject matter, but also to spread illumination into quite distant regions. The present distant region is no exception, as the footnotes will reveal.

Plotinus distinguished at least two kinds of thinking. There is *dianoia*, which is often called discursive thinking, and which is the activity of the soul (*psuchē*). And then there is the different activity of the intellect (*nous*), which is often called non-discursive thinking. It is commonly held that non-discursive thinking does not involve entertaining propositions. That is, it does not involve thinking *that* something is the case. Instead, one contemplates concepts in isolation from each other, and does not string them together in the way they are strung together in 'that'-clauses. It is further supposed that Plato and Aristotle anticipated Plotinus in postulating this non-propositional thinking.

I have three aims in this chapter, The main one is to deny that non-propositional thinking is to be found in any of these three thinkers at the points where it has most commonly been detected. In order to show this for the case of Plotinus, I shall have to explain some of Aristotle's ideas about thinking and how Plotinus transformed them. He certainly did believe that there is a mystical state in which we have contact with something much simpler than any proposition. But I shall maintain that he regards this mystical experience as *above* the level of thinking, while thinking in its highest form he treats as propositional.

Among the many Aristotelian ideas about thinking which influence Plotinus, one is especially interesting. It is that non-discursive thought does not involve seeking, and that in general contemplating the truth is more rewarding than seeking it. This was certainly a majority view in Greek Philosophy. But I shall want, as one subsidiary aim, to trace and to endorse the minority view which takes 'perpetual progress' as an ideal, as opposed to static contemplation.

I shall start with Aristotle's account of thinking, which has proved very difficult to understand. I do not believe that he is at his strongest on this subject. But I think that it can be seen why he says what he says. So a further subsidiary aim will be to explain, if not to justify, his position.

## Aristotle: non-discursive thought is propositional

Let us consider Aristotle's account of non-discursive thinking, which comes in two related chapters.[1] The usual interpretation is most clearly articulated in an important article by A. C. Lloyd, although he is more concerned with Plotinus than with Aristotle. It is that non-discursive thought involves contemplating things in isolation without thinking anything *about* them.[2] In thinking that beauty is truth, my mind passes from beauty to truth. That is offered as an example of ordinary discursive thinking. But the suggestion is that this passage from concept to concept already implies the possibility of contemplating something in isolation. For will there not be a stage at which my mind is contemplating beauty without yet having passed to truth? Admittedly, I do not allow the concept of beauty to remain in isolation, for I promptly link it up with the concept of truth. But (it is suggested) if I were knocked down by a number 68 bus before I had done so, I should then have thought of beauty in isolation. One objection to this suggestion is that I could hardly be said to have thought of beauty,

---

1 *Metaph.* IX 10, 1051b27–1052a4 and *de An.* III 6, 430b26–31.
2 A. C. Lloyd, 'Non-discursive thought – an enigma of Greek philosophy', *Proceedings of the Aristotelian Society*, 70 (1969–70), 261–74. Lloyd criticises the idea of non-discursive thought, so understood, as incoherent. For a valuable survey of interpretations of Aristotle, see E. Berti, 'The intellection of indivisibles according to Aristotle *De Anima* III 6,' in *Aristotle on Mind and the Senses:* Proceedings of the Seventh Symposium Aristotelicum, ed. G. E. L. Owen and G. E. R. Lloyd (Cambridge 1978). Berti expresses agreement with the kind of interpretation which I offered in discussion on that occasion, and which I later put into print in *Necessity, Cause and Blame* (London 1980), 217–18, and in *Aristotle on Science: "The Posterior Analytics"*, ed. E. Berti (Padua 1981).

if I did not go on to think something about it, even if only that I wanted to know what its attributes were.

It must also be doubtful that Aristotle can be considering the kind of interrupted thinking just described. For one thing, he seems to regard the kind of thinking in question as the loftiest achievement of man in his happiest moments and the permanent activity of God.[3] That is suggested, at any rate, by the fact that these kinds of thinking are all compared with touching.[4] It is hard to see what is so lofty about interrupted thinking. It is also hard to see how contemplating something in isolation, without thinking anything about it, could lead to *truth*, as Aristotle says that non-discursive thinking does.[5] For we should expect there to be neither truth nor falsehood, unless we are in some sense *combining* concepts, and indeed Aristotle himself sometimes expresses this view.[6]

Why should it be supposed that Aristotle has in mind the contemplation of isolated concepts? The most important reason is his saying that in this kind of thinking we do not predicate anything of anything (*ti kata tinos, de An.* III 6, 430b28), nor is there any assertion (*kataphasis, Metaph.* IX 10, 1051b24). But I think there is a better interpretation available.

One of the loftiest achievements for a human being, according to Aristotle, is to engage in theoretical science, and this involves knowing the essences, that is, roughly speaking, the defining characteristics,[7] of the various subject matters. For Aristotle's account of a science is that one knows the definitions of the basic entities in that science, and by reference to these definitions can explain the further characteristics of all the entities concerned. In our two chapters, Aristotle is talking about subjects which are incomposite (*asuntheta* 1051b17; *adiaireta* 430a26), in the sense, I believe, that they do not involve matter as well as form. He is

---

3 *Metaph.* XII 7, 1072b14–26; *EN* X 8.    4 *Metaph.* IX 10, 1051b24–5; XII 7, 1072b21.
5 *de An.* III 6, 430b28; *Metaph.* IX 10, 1051b24.
6 *de An.* III 6, 430a27–b6; *Cat.* 4, 2a7–10; *Int.* 1, 16a9–18.
7 It is a slight oversimplification to identify form or essence with defining characteristics. That is the picture given by early works such as *Posterior Analytics*: form or essence consists of genus and differentia, and the form or essence of lunar eclipse (to take one example) would be the moon's loss of light due to screening by the earth. In later works, however, the form is restricted to something less than the full defining characteristics, for certain material characteristics are excluded. Thus (*de An.* I 1, 403a25–b9) the form of a house is a shelter protecting from wind, rain and heat, whereas the full defining characteristics would include being made of stones, bricks and timbers.

further discussing, I believe, *definitions* of these incomposite subjects, which state what their essences are. Hence the reference to 'what it is' (*ti esti* 1051b26; b32), and to 'what it is in respect of essence' (*ti esti kata to ti ēn einai*, 430b28). Aristotle's non-discursive thinking will then involve contemplating the definitions of incomposite subjects. But in that case, the thinking must be *propositional*; for it will involve thinking *that* such-and-such an essence belongs to such-and-such a subject. How can this be squared with the claim that there is no asserting, nor predicating something of something?

I think the answer is that Aristotle often views definitions as being statements of *identity*. They do not therefore require us to predicate one thing of another, but involve simply referring to the same thing twice. This is not assertion or predication as Aristotle usually understands it. That Aristotle sometimes thinks of statements which give the essence of something, or part of its essence, as *identity* statements has been argued by G. E. L. Owen.[8] The evidence is that he says that it is by being something *other* than a pale thing (viz. a man) that a man is pale, but it is not by being something *other* than an animal that he is an animal.[9] Again, pale is predicated of an individual man as one thing of *another*, whereas man is not predicated of him as one thing of *another*.[10] There is a further statement even closer to our interests. For, in *Metaph.* VII 11, 1037a33–b7, Aristotle is talking of a subject which is not a composite involving matter as well as form (*suneilēmmenon tēi hulēi*). Here at least, he says, the subject is *identical* with its essence.

We are now in a position to understand what is perhaps the most surprising statement of all. Aristotle says that in this kind of thinking you cannot be mistaken, but can only touch or not touch (*thigein, thinganein*, 1051b24–33). The idea is, perhaps, that, if you try to state the essence of an incomposite subject and fail, you are not in error, because you have not succeeded in talking about the subject at all. You have not made contact with it. The contact metaphor is more useful than the seeing metaphor here, because there are degrees of clarity in seeing, but contact is an all-or-nothing affair. Plato had also maintained that one could not be

---

8 G. E. L. Owen 'The Platonism of Aristotle', *Proc. Brit. Acad.*, 50(1965), 125–50, esp. 136–9 (repr. in *Articles on Aristotle* I); so also Christopher Kirwan, *Aristotle's Metaphysics Books Γ, Δ and E*, Clarendon Aristotle Series (Oxford 1971), 100.

9 *APo.* I 4, 73b5–10; I 22, 83a 32; *Ph.* I 4, 188a8; *Metaph.* XIV 1, 1087a35; 1088a28.

10 *Metaph.* VII 4, 1031a2–6; 10–14.

mistaken about certain identity statements. No-one, mad or sane, has ever said to himself that a horse was an ox.[11] And Plato like Aristotle uses a tactual metaphor, namely, that of grasping (*ephaptesthai, Tht.* 190C6).

## Plato's *Republic*: knowledge of the Forms is propositional

There is another kind of thinking which I believe to be propositional. In Plato's *Republic* 509D–541B, there is a discussion, which strongly influenced Plotinus, of how philosophers can ascend through dialectical training to knowledge of the ideal Forms. It is very commonly taken that the knowledge they acquire is some kind of 'knowledge by acquaintance'.[12] By that is meant a knowledge like that involved in knowing a person, and it is usually supposed to be non-propositional. As to whether Plato later renounced this conception of knowledge in the *Theaetetus* there is controversy.[13] But on the *Republic*, there is fairly widespread agreement. I do not think, however, that the common interpretation is right.

Progress towards knowledge of the Forms is said in this passage of the *Republic* to start from questions like 'what is largeness?'; 'what is smallness?'.[14] For many years, there will be an intensive course in dialectical argument, which involves[15] question and answer. The questions are designed to trap the answerer into a

11 Plato *Theaetetus* 190B–C; cf. 188B and *Phaedo* 74C1–2. For Plato's contact simile a little earlier at 189A3–10, see G. E. L. Owen, 'Plato on Not-Being', in *Plato*, 1, ed. G. Vlastos (New York 1971), 245; 262–5.

12 I think I can fairly ascribe this view to Gilbert Ryle, commenting on *Tht.* 184B–186E, in 'Plato's Parmenides', *Mind*, 48(1939), 129–51 and 302–25 (repr. in *Studies in Plato's Metaphysics*, ed. R. E. Allen, London and New York 1965, see pp. 136–41); D. W. Hamlyn, 'The communion of forms and the development of Plato's logic', *Philosophical Quarterly*, 5(1955), 289–302; R. S. Bluck, 'Logos and forms in Plato: a reply to Professor Cross', *Mind*, 65(1956), 522–9; and '"Knowledge by acquaintance" in Plato's *Theaetetus*', *Mind*, 72 (1963), 259–63; W. G. Runciman, *Plato's Later Epistemology* (Cambridge 1962), 40–5; J. H. Lesher, Γνῶσις and Ἐπιστήμη in Socrates' dream in the *Theaetetus*', *Journal of Hellenic Studies*, 89 (1969), 72–8; John McDowell, *Plato, Theaetetus*, Clarendon Plato Series (Oxford 1973) 115–16. For Owen's rather different contribution to this subject, see his 'Plato on Not-Being', loc. cit. In disagreeing with the common interpretation, I have been anticipated by Myles Burnyeat in an unpublished paper delivered at Princeton in 1970, 'The simple and the complex in the *Theaetetus*'. Burnyeat also draws attention to the wording in *R.* 534B–C. Another dissenter is Gail Fine, 'Knowledge and logos in the *Theaetetus*', *Philosophical Review*, 88 (1979), 366–97; and 'False belief in the *Theaetetus*', *Phronesis*, 24 (1979), 70–80.

13 Ryle postulated a renunciation, and was followed by Hamlyn, but Bluck (1963) and McDowell (p. 193) disagree.

14 Plato *R.* 524C11.    15 Plato *R.* 534D9.

contradiction and so to refute him (*elenchein*).[16] The method is meant to enable one to grasp what (or that which?) each thing is (*ho estin hekaston*),[17] and eventually what (or that which?) goodness itself is (*auto ho estin agathon*).[18] In 534B3–534C5, Plato concludes:

> Do you not call a man a dialectician, if he gets an account (*logos*) of the being (*ousia*) of each thing? And will you not deny that a man understands something, if he does not have such an account, and insofar as he cannot give an account of the thing to himself or others? . . . And is it not, then, similar with goodness? If someone cannot define (*dihorisasthai*) the Form of the Good with an account, separating it from all other things; if he cannot come through all refutations (*elenchoi*) as if in battle; if he does not desire to produce real refutations rather than merely seeming ones; if he does not in all these things journey through with an unfaltering account; will you not deny that such a man knows goodness itself, or anything else that is good?

The thinking described here seems to me to be propositional. For the questions, answers and refutations all bear on propositions, and what is being sought is definitions.

It may be protested that apprehending the Form of the Good is described as if it were a kind of vision, and is compared with coming to see the sun. Such experiences are certainly non-propositional. Moreover, Plato is insistent that this kind of knowledge cannot be conveyed in writing.[19] Why not, if it is propositional? I would answer that these comments of Plato's are entirely appropriate to definitional knowledge in philosophy, and do not at all imply a non-propositional knowledge. Definitional knowledge cannot be conveyed in writing, because one cannot be said really to know that goodness is so-and-so, until one has gone through the dialectical process. One must try one definition after another, seeing how the others fail, and how the successful one exactly surmounts all previous difficulties, and achieves all that the others could not. As for the comparison with a vision, that is a very good account of what it is like to realise that the new formula does at last achieve all that the others could not. The Form of the Good, or goodness, is not itself a proposition, but to know it is to know the proposition that goodness is so-and-so.

This propositional interpretation is quite compatible with Plato's giving to apprehension of the Forms an almost religious significance, and with his expecting it to have practical conse-

16 Plato *R.* 534C1; C3.   17 Plato *R.* 532A7; 533B2.   18 Plato *R.* 532B1.
19 Plato *Prt.* 329A; 347E; *Phdr.* 274B–277A; and (if genuine) *7th Letter* 341C–344D.

quences in the understanding of mundane questions of justice and injustice in the state. The religious significance is not out of place, when so much importance has been attached to the ascent, and when so much of life had been devoted to it. The dialectical training is not completed until the age of thirty-five, and it is not expected that the supreme Form will be understood until a further fifteen years of practical experience has been gained in public service (535A–541B). The requirement of public service makes it all the more plausible that the understanding gained will be of a kind to have appropriate practical consequences.

If Plato compares apprehension of the Forms to seeing the sun, or to other kinds of awareness which could be classed as *acquaintance*, this is perfectly legitimate, so long as the respect of comparison is a just one. It would take more than this to show that Plato intends the knowledge in question to be non-propositional. Some commentators have argued for a *different* thesis, namely, that when Plato later goes on to *analyse* what knowledge is, he is *confused* between propositions and more ordinary objects of acquaintance. On this larger and more complex issue I shall not comment. The evidence on it is drawn from a *later* work, the *Theaetetus*.[20]

I must now return to Aristotle, because, in order to understand Plotinus, it will first be necessary to understand some of the ideas which Aristotle bequeathed him.

## Aristotle: thinking and its object

One difficult saying of Aristotle is that the act of thinking is identical with the object of thought. The basis of this idea can safely be traced (although this is not always recognised) to a discussion in *Ph.* III 3. When an agent acts on a patient, the activity of the agent is in a certain sense identical with the activity of the patient, and both are located in the patient. For example, the activity of some teacher and the activity of his pupil can be called a single activity, and can be located in the pupil. Aristotle wants this result, because at the end of the *Physics* he will make his God an unmoved mover, and he wants no activity of causing motion to

20 Runciman op. cit. p. 45; McDowell op. cit. pp. 115–16 and see index under '*connaître* and *savoir*'.

go on within the deity. But he spells out very carefully what kind of identity is to be found here. It is not, he says five times, an identity of essence,[21] for the essence of teaching and the essence of learning are quite different things. He might have put his point by saying that it is a merely numerical identity: if you are counting activities on a particular occasion, there are not two different activities to be counted. In fact, he tries out various other formulations. Properly speaking (*kuriōs*), teaching is not the same as learning; it is rather that teaching and learning are predicated of a single process.[22] It is not like the identity of cloak and mantle, but more like that of the road from Thebes to Athens and the road from Athens to Thebes. Nor should you expect, since the identity is not one of essence, that the activities we are identifying will have all their predicates in common.[23]

This idea is re-applied in the *De Anima*. The activity of the man who hears and the activity of a resounding object in arousing his hearing can be viewed as a single activity.[24] Again, and by analogy, the activity of thinking is identical with the actively working object of thought; not, admittedly, with a stone, if you are thinking of a stone (for there is no stone in the soul), but with the intelligible *form* of the stone,[25] that is, roughly speaking, with its defining characteristics.[26]

What does this idea mean, when it is applied to the case of thinking? Aristotle maintains that, when we think of something, its intelligible form is in the soul,[27] and that the thinking part of the soul must *receive* the form,[28] and is the *place* of forms.[29] We might initially understand this by saying that the defining characteristics of the thing will be in one's mind. Aristotle's idea will then be that, if we are counting, we should not count the act of thinking and the defining characteristics at work in our minds as if they were two distinct things.

G. E. M. Anscombe has defended the idea that we should not speak of two distinct things here.[30] If we want to know whether a person understands a theorem, it is the theorem which we ask him

---

21 *Ph.* III 3, 202a20; b9; b12; b16; b22.    22 *Ph.* III 3, 202b19–21.
23 *Ph.* III 3, 202b14–16.    24 *de An.* III 2, 425b26–426a26.
25 Esp. *de An.* III 8, 431b20–432a1; also III 4, 429b6; b30–1; 430a3–7; III 5, 430a14–15; a19–20; III 7, 431a1–2; *Metaph.* XII 7, 1072b21; XII 9, 1074b38–1075a5.
26 See above on the identification of intelligible form with defining characteristics.
27 *de An.* III 8, 431b28–432a1.    28 *de An.* III 4, 429a15.    29 *de An.* III 4, 429a27–8.
30 G. E. M. Anscombe, in G. E. M. Anscombe and P. T. Geach, *Three Philosophers* (Oxford 1961), 60.

to expound. There is not a second thing, the understanding of the theorem, which we must ask him to expound as well.

The idea that the defining characteristics of a thing are in the soul can be given a more concrete sense, if we consider some further remarks of Aristotle's. One way for them to be in the soul would be for them to be embodied in a mental image. And Aristotle does say that the object of thought, or intelligible form, is in, or is thought within, an image.[31] As to how it can be within an image, there is a revealing passage in the *De Memoria*.[32] If you want to think of a triangle you will place before your mind's eye a triangular image, but will attend to its features selectively, ignoring the irrelevant ones. You will ignore its exact size, for example, since this is irrelevant to its triangularity. Aristotle points out that the same treatment is given to physically drawn diagrams in geometry. In the example which he chooses, that of a triangle, it is easy to understand the idea that the defining characteristics are in the image. For the image can simply be a plane figure with three straight sides.

Aristotle further distinguishes between the intelligible form in its potential state and in its actual state.[33] We can perhaps speculate that the defining characteristics of the triangle are considered to be present only potentially, until they are separated out from other characteristics by the act of attending to which he refers. Be that as it may, it is the *actualised* form which Aristotle declares identical with the act of thinking.

The idea that the defining characteristics are within the image will be harder to understand for some examples. When I think of man, the form of man (rationality) can hardly be embodied in an image in the same way as the form of triangle. Nonetheless, Aristotle clearly thinks that his account will apply to all cases. You may, he says, want to think of something altogether sizeless. In that case, you will still put before your mental gaze an image which has a size, but you will ignore the fact that it has a size.

Since the act of thinking is numerically identical with the object of thought, Aristotle is equally willing to say, in some of the passages

31 *de An.* III 7, 431b2; cf. 432a4–5.
32 *Mem.* 449b30–450a7. See Sorabji, *Aristotle on Memory* (London 1972), 6–8: the *de Memoria* is an important, though under-used, source for Aristotle's theory of thinking.
33 *de An.* III 8, 431b24.

cited above, that the *intellect* is identical with that object. This would not mean, in normal cases, that the *thinker* was identical with it. For a human thinker is more than an intellect. But God constitutes a special case, because Aristotle conceives his God as being *nothing but* an intellect. Accordingly, God is identical with the object of his thought.

On one persuasive interpretation, which is followed among others by Plotinus, this last point explains Aristotle's further claim that intellects, including God, think of themselves:[34] naturally so, if they are identical with the objects of their thought. Self-thinking is guaranteed, for in thinking of the objects, they will be thinking of themselves. There need be nothing narcissistic in the claim that God thinks of himself, or regressive in the claim that he thinks of his own thinking.

Aristotle believes that all human thinking requires images.[35] He is indeed committed to believing this, if the thought process is one of attending to the right features, in the way described above. But he also has a more metaphysical reason for thinking images required.[36] Thus he accepts Plato's view that forms are objects of thought, but rejects his view that intelligible forms can exist separately from the sensible world. Rather, they need a sensible vehicle, and a convenient vehicle for *intelligible* forms is provided by the so-called *sensible* forms. An example of a sensible form would be the colours of external objects, which during perception are taken on by one's eye-jelly.[37] Subsequently, these colours in the eye-jelly can leave behind an imprint in the central sense organ, which in turn gives rise to images. First, the colours in the eye-jelly, and subsequently the images, can provide a vehicle for the intelligible forms. There is a further disagreement here with

---

34 This interpretation is most fully defended by Richard Norman, 'Aristotle's Philosopher–God', *Phronesis*, 14 (1969), 63–74 (repr. in *Articles on Aristotle* IV). The connexion of thought is also made by Plotinus, *Enneads* v.3.5. (21–48), and perhaps by pseudo-Alexander, *in Metaph.* 671, 8–18. Among modern commentators, G. E. M. Anscombe has a related interpretation in *Three Philosophers*, 60. For Aristotle's claim that intellects think of themselves, see *de An.* III 4, 429b9; *Metaph.* XII 7, 1072b19–21; XII 9, 1074b33–5; 1074b38–1075a5.

35 *Mem.* 449b31; *de An.* III 7, 431a16; b2; III 8, 432a8; a13.

36 *de An.* III 8, 432a3–9. I have discussed these points in *Aristotle on Memory*, 6–8.

37 That Aristotle thinks our eye-jelly takes on colour patches when we see I have argued in more than one place, most fully in the revised version of 'Body and soul in Aristotle' in *Articles on Aristotle*, IV, 49–53, with notes 22 and 28, which expands the earlier version in *Philosophy*, 49 (1974), 72–6, with notes 30 and 35.

Plato, who explicitly maintained that dialectical thought rises above the need for images.[38] We shall see that Plotinus makes a parallel claim.

God's thought, in Aristotle's view, is evidently different. For images depend on physiological organs, whereas God is immaterial, so that his thinking must be imageless. Aristotle never explains, however, how God escapes the need for images, or how the disagreement with Plato can be maintained, once imageless thought has been allowed.

In *DA* III 5, Aristotle briefly introduces the agent intellect. His account of the intellect so far has made it seem analogous to a material cause, because it passively receives forms. But it depends for being activated on there also being an active efficient cause to bring it from potentiality to actuality. To serve this purpose, Aristotle postulates that there is a second intellect which thinks incessantly and for ever. It can reside both in us and separately from us, and it involves no memory. He makes little more of this 'agent' intellect, but the commentators made a great deal of it. The Aristotelian Alexander of Aphrodisias maintained that it was God,[39] and also that what he called our 'material' intellect could somehow *become* this 'agent' intellect, since when it thinks of the agent intellect it becomes the object of its thought.[40]

There are two last points to be made about Aristotle's theory of thinking. He classes thinking as an *energeia* (activity) rather than a *kinēsis* (process).[41] The English renderings do not properly bring out the distinction. Aristotle's idea is that as soon as you can use the present tense 'is thinking', you can use the perfect 'has thought'. For thinking is not, like building a temple, a process which has to *wait* before it is complete.[42] It might be protested that this ought to be said only of certain kinds of thinking. Proving a theorem surely does remain incomplete until the end, even if contemplating a premise does not.

It may be a connected fact that Aristotle describes the happiest and most pleasant possible life as one of *contemplating* philosophical truths rather than *seeking* them (*zētein*).[43] For seeking is defined by reference to the goal of finding, and is in a certain sense

38 Plato *R.* 510B; 511C; 532A.    39 Alexander, *de An.* 80,16–92,11.
40 Alexander, *de An.* 89,21–2.    41 *Metaph.* IX 6, 1048b24; b34; IX 8, 1050a36.
42 *Metaph.* IX 6, 1048b18–35; *Sens.* 6, 446b2–3; *EN* X 4, 1174a14–29.
43 *EN* X 7, 1177a25–7.

(admittedly, a different sense) incomplete until it gets there. Moreover, it was a view which appealed at least to some members of Plato's Academy that the goal must always be better than the process of reaching it.[44] Even if this view is not plausible, when taken so generally, it is at least fairly natural to suppose that the whole point of seeking is to possess the object sought.

Personally, I think this natural supposition overlooks the fact that part of the pleasure of philosophical activity is emerging from the state of perplexity which Aristotle describes in *Metaph.* 1 2 (982b11–983a21). Aristotle's God, who has always known and contemplated the truth, has missed this peculiar philosophical excitement. If we too had been so born, or so educated, that we never got into a state of perplexity, we should, I think, have missed something of value. Perhaps the point would be clearer, if we distinguished three states rather than two: seeking the truth, winning it and contemplating it. Philosophers differ on whether they enjoy the search: some find it exciting, others agonising. But, for many of them, winning the truth, if they reach that stage, provides the greatest pleasure of all. After that they typically want not to stay contemplating it, but to tackle a new perplexity. To remain in contemplation, so far from being the most rewarding activity, would soon become tedious.

## Two rival traditions

There are still disputes, however, about the value of philosophical perplexity. Wittgenstein compared the person caught in philosophical perplexity with a fly trapped in a fly bottle, or with a man scratching an itch. And after him, John Wisdom compared philosophical perplexity with mental illness which calls for therapy. These similes would suggest that emerging from perplexity is a relief rather than an exhilaration. Indeed, they invite the question whether it would not have been better to avoid entering the fly bottle in the first place. Wittgenstein may have been ambivalent on this question; but Peter Winch has shown me a passage which he has translated for publication, in which Wittgenstein says:[45] 'I am by no means sure that I should prefer a

---

44 *EN* vii 12, 1153a8–9, with reference to Speusippus.
45 Wittgenstein, *Vermischte Bermerkungen*, translated by Peter Winch as *Culture and Value* (Oxford 1980). The passage cited was written in 1947.

continuation of my work by others to a change in the way people live which would make all these questions superfluous. (For this reason I could never found a school.)' Wittgenstein speaks here as if it would have been better, like Aristotle's God, never to have suffered perplexity at all.

In antiquity, Plato was on the same side as Aristotle. He did not, like Wittgenstein, speak of search as disagreeable, but he did speak of contemplation as the superior state. Thus he records with approval the claim that the gods are not eager for wisdom as philosophers are, because they already have it,[46] and that philosophers after death may hope to be rewarded with full knowledge.[47]

Another view, closer to Wittgenstein's in its dislike of perplexity, was that of the ancient Pyrrhonian sceptics, represented by Sextus Empiricus.[48] They found philosophical perplexity profoundly disturbing, but expected to attain equanimity by suspending judgement on every issue. Their method for achieving this was to convince themselves that the philosophical arguments were equally strong on either side of every case, so that no conclusions could be drawn.

There was, however, a minority tradition. Augustine records one version of it,[49] putting it into the mouth of Licentius, who represents the sceptics of Plato's Academy, and ascribing it to Cicero. It was presumably expounded in Cicero's lost work, *Hortensius*. The view is that for man, as opposed to God, happiness consists in *seeking* the truth. Some sceptics must have felt forced to say this, when they reflected that their scepticism denied to man all hope of knowing the truth. Augustine's own preferred answer, however, is that the truth has been revealed to us in Scripture.

At a more trivial level Plutarch, who is also in the Platonist tradition, records two relevant anecdotes. One concerns a man who did not want his uncertainty resolved, because he wanted the pleasure of seeking. Another concerns Democritus, who was annoyed at being told a simple explanation of why his cucumber tasted of honey – it had been stored in a jar used for honey – and

---

46 Plato *Smp.* 204A; cf. *Phdr.* 278D.     47 Plato *Phd.* 64A–69E.     48 E.g. *PH* I 1–30.
49 Augustine *Against the Academics* I § 7 (=Cicero, *Hortensius* frag. 101, Müller); 9; 23; III 1.
   I am indebted for this reference and the next to Myles Burnyeat.

insisted that he would continue to seek an explanation, as if the phenomenon were a natural one.[50]

But the most influential expression of the minority tradition is found in the Christian philosopher Gregory of Nyssa (c. A.D. 331–396), who wrote after Plotinus but before Augustine. He differed from both of them in viewing the supreme mystical experience of God not as a static experience, but as a perpetual discovery. Since the distance between the soul and God is infinite, there will always be more to understand. Thus he describes the soul as: 'conforming itself to that which is always being apprehended and discovered'.[51] Again, he describes the beatific vision as follows:

Then, when the soul has partaken of as many beautiful things as it has room for, the Word draws it again afresh, as if it had not yet partaken in beautiful things, drawing it to share in the supreme beauty. Thus its desire is increased in proportion as it progresses towards that which is always shining forth, and because of the excess of good things which are all the time being discovered in that which is supreme, the soul seems to be touching the ascent for the first time. For this reason the Word says again to the awakened soul 'arise', and to the soul which has come 'come'. For to him who really arises there will be no end of always arising. And for him who runs towards the Lord, the space for this divine race will never be used up. For we must always be aroused, and never cease from coming closer by running.[52]

Gregory's brother, Basil of Caesarea, had expressed a somewhat similar view. We shall not be able to understand God even in eternity, or He would be finite. We shall only know Him more perfectly.[53] To some extent, Gregory's conception is also prepared for by an earlier theologian, Origen (c. A.D. 185–253). For Origen thinks that we should try ever to *increase* our apprehension of the blessed life, and our longing for it, and our acceptance of God. But he also recognises that we are subject to the risk of *satiety*, even when we stand on the highest rung.[54] Still earlier, Irenaeus had said, at the end of the second century, that even in the

---

50  Plutarch *ap*. Montaigne, *Apologie de Raimond Sebond* (=*Essays* II 12), somewhat less than half way through. The Democritus story comes from Plutarch *Quaestiones Conviales* I 10 (*Moralia* 628B–D), but I have not been able to track down the other.

51  *On the Soul and Resurrection (De Anima et Resurrectione)* PG vol. 46, col. 93C.

52  Gregory of Nyssa, *On the Song of Songs (In Canticum Canticorum)* v, PG vol. 44, col. 876B–C.

53  Basil of Caesarea, *Letters* 233–5; *Against Eunomius* 1.5.11.

54  Origen, *On Principles* 1.3.8.

world to come there are things which God must teach and we must learn, although his motive was only to dissuade us from expecting the answers now.[55]

A. H. Armstrong has argued that, surprisingly enough, even in Plotinus there are hints of the idea of mystical experience as involving a constant succession of experience. Of course, Plotinus' official position is that the intellect is timelessly eternal, and he repeatedly asks us to discount passages which may suggest the contrary. But Armstrong thinks it hard to discount some of Plotinus' phrases, without evacuating the passages of content. Plotinus may, therefore, have been inconsistent, and in any case the passages in question may have helped to inspire Gregory.[56]

Arthur Lovejoy has described how the idea of a perpetual progress after death suddenly became popular in the eighteenth century and recurred in thinker after thinker.[57] It was embraced even by thinkers whose systems made it difficult to accommodate. Leibniz, for example, held ours to be the best of all possible worlds. But the best possible world turns out to be one in which there is room for everyone getting better. More surprisingly, Lovejoy maintains, each individual is defined by its position on the great scale of being, and every rung on the ladder is filled, but filled by only one specimen. If this is really Leibniz's view, it is hard to see how it leaves room for the progress of individuals up the ladder.

## Plotinus: three levels of experience

I come now to Plotinus' three levels of experience. His descriptions are likely to seem obscure and off-putting at first sight. But I do not think that we should be deterred. I shall return to this question at the end. Plotinus thinks that with suitable discipline we can progress from one kind of experience to another. At the bottom comes discursive thinking which he calls *dianoia*. Above that is the non-discursive thinking of the intellect. He believes that

---

55 Irenaeus, *Adversus Haereses* II. 28.3.
56 *The Cambridge History of Later Greek and Early Mediaeval Philosophy*, ed. A. H. Armstrong (Cambridge 1967), 246–7 and 455; see also Armstrong's article 'Eternity, life and movement in Plotinus' account of νοῦς', in *Le Néoplatonisme*: Report of the International Conference on Neoplatonism held at Royaumont 9–13 June 1969 (Paris 1971), 67–74. The references are to Plotinus v.8.4; VI.2.8 (26–41); VI.7.13.
57 Arthur Lovejoy, *The Great Chain of Being* (Cambridge Mass. 1936), ch. 9.

we can 'become' this intellect and engage in the same kind of thinking. Finally, there is union with the One, a union which is above thinking altogether. I shall argue that Plotinus transforms Aristotle's conception of non-discursive thinking by treating quite differently the idea of contact with the incomposite. On the other hand, he is like Aristotle in making non-discursive thought propositional. To establish this last point, I shall have to combat a rival interpretation of A. C. Lloyd's, although I cannot regard this as an easy task, when I have learnt so much about the Neoplatonists from him.

Lloyd ascribes to non-discursive thought four attributes which I think belong only to the higher level of union with the One.[58] He mentions that non-discursive thought involves no complexity, and hence (secondly) is not directed to propositions, since these are complex. He believes, thirdly, that it involves no self-consciousness, and fourthly that it is typically described in terms of contact. To make up our minds what Plotinus' view is, let us consider his three levels of experience in turn.

An important mark of discursive thought for Plotinus is that it takes one thing after another progressively, and is consequently spread out in time.[59] Indeed, the discursive thought in which the soul engages actually constitutes time.[60] It also depends, unlike non-discursive thought, on contemplating imprinted images.[61]

In contrast, non-discursive thought, in which the intellect engages, is not spread out, but timeless.[62] Indeed, this kind of thinking constitutes the timeless eternity which Plotinus describes as neither extended nor progressing.[63] He further declares that it does not involve seeking (zētein), but possessing knowledge.[64] He maintains that the intellect in action is identical with its objects.[65] And from this several consequences flow. Firstly, the intellect does not depend on mere images of its objects, since it can actually be identical with them.[66] Secondly, Plotinus is able to represent his theory as more akin to Plato's than it would otherwise have been. For it is no longer so big a divergence that the eternal realm

58 A. C. Lloyd, op. cit., 263; 266; 268.
59 E.g. Plotinus III.7.11 (36–40); V.3.17 (23–5); VI 9.5 (7–12).    60 III.7.11.
61 V.3.2; V.3.5 (23–5).    62 IV.4.1.
63 III.7.3. I shall argue elsewhere for the interpretation of eternity as timelessness.
64 V.1.4 (16).
65 I.8.2(16); V.1.4 (21); V.3.5 (21–48); V.9.5 (7–48); V.9.8 (3–4); VI.9.5 (14–15).
66 III.9.1 (8–9); V.3.5 (21–5).

for Plato is the realm of Forms, while for Plotinus it is the intellect, once it can be maintained that the intellect is *identical* with the forms which are its objects.[67] Thirdly, Plotinus maintains that the intellect thinks of itself.[68] And he supports this idea in just the way I took it to be supported in Aristotle. For if the intellect is identical with its object, then, in thinking of its object, it will be thinking of itself.[69]

Now why should it be supposed that Plotinus makes non-discursive thought non-propositional? Lloyd gives as one reason that this kind of thinking involves no transition from concept to concept. This is true, if by transition is meant a chronological passage which occupies time. But if there is no chronological transition, it does not follow that there is no complexity in the thought. Indeed, Plotinus repeatedly maintains that the intellect and its thinking are complex,[70] and that the object of thought is complex.[71] This seems to exclude the idea that non-discursive thought is directed to concepts taken in isolation.

I see no barrier, then, to supposing that non-discursive thought is directed to propositions. And there is actually evidence in favour of this. For, as we shall see, the route by which we attain to non-discursive thought is through discovering the definitions of things, in terms of genus and differentia.[72] The stage of non-discursive thought seems to involve contemplating these definitions arranged into a unified network.[73] And definitions are propositional in form, since they tell us *that* so-and-so is so-and-so.

A further issue on which I interpret Plotinus differently from Lloyd concerns self-thought. Lloyd takes it that, since the intellect is identical with its object, it cannot think of itself, at least not in the primary sense.[74] But, so far as I can see, Plotinus' view is the opposite. For he argues that the identity of intellect and object actually *guarantees* self-thought.[75] Moreover, he adds that this is self-thinking in the proper sense, whereas discursive thought involves self-thinking only in a secondary sense.[76]

From this I conclude that the four descriptions considered by Lloyd (non-complex, non-propositional, not self-directed, tactual) do not belong primarily to non-discursive thought. They belong rather to the higher level of union with the One, although I would

67 III.9.1 (1–20).    68 II.9.1 (33); V.3.2–6.    69 V.3.5 (21–48).
70 E.g. V.3.10–13; VI.4.4 (23–6); VI.7.39 (10–19); VI.9.4 (3–6); VI.9.5 (14–16).
71 E.g. IV.4.1 (16–38); V.3.10; V.3.13; VI.4.4 (23–6); VI.9.5 (14–16).    72 I.3. 1–4.
73 IV.4.1 (16–38).    74 A. C. Lloyd, op. cit., 266.    75 V.3.5 (21–48).
76 V.3.6 (1–5).

not deny that occasionally[77] the metaphor of touch is applied to the lower level as well. Let us now consider the higher level.

At this stage, I believe, we find a significant departure from Aristotle. The object of thought is always complex for Plotinus as we have seen. Plotinus diverges from Aristotle in thinking that this is so, even in the case of an identity-statement, like 'I am this.' Even here, it will emerge in a passage to be quoted shortly, the I and the this would be two things. To avoid this duality, one would have (absurdly) to say 'am am', or 'I I'.[78] On the other hand, Plotinus would, for his own reasons, agree with Aristotle that we do have dealings with what is non-complex. For Plotinus' One lacks complexity altogether. Moreover, he would agree again that *contact* is an appropriate metaphor for these dealings. He uses the same words for touching as Plato and Aristotle had used, or cognate ones, namely, *thixis, thigein, thinganein, haphē, ephapsasthai, epaphē, sunaphē, sunaptein, prosaptesthai.*[79] But just because this touching is not directed towards a complex object, Plotinus would depart from Aristotle, by denying that the touching should be classed as thinking. He repeatedly says that, because the One is simple, it does not think,[80] and when we achieve contact or union with it, we are not thinking of it.[81] Our contact is rather a pre-thinking (*pronoousa,* v.3.10(43)). And the One engages not in thinking, but in a super-thinking (*hupernoēsis,* VI. 8.16(33)). It exists before thought (*pro tou noēsai; pro noēseōs,* v. 3.10 (48); VI. 9.6 (43)). I believe it is no accident that Plotinus refuses to describe experience of the supreme being in intellectual terms as a kind of thinking. For other mystics through the ages have insisted that their experience is unlike rational thought.

The nearest Plotinus comes to deviating from this view is in v. 4.2 (18), where he says that the One engages in a downright thinking (*katanoēsis*), and in a thinking different from the thinking of the intellect. But even this qualified ascription of thinking cannot be taken too seriously. For one thing, the treatise is an

---

77 E.g. I.1.9 (12).    78 V.3.10 (34–7).

79 V.3.10 (41–4); V.3.17 (25–34); VI. 7.36 (4); VI.7.39 (15–19); VI.7.40 (2); VI.9.4 (27); VI.9.7 (4); VI.9.8 (19–29); VI.9. 9 (19); VI.9.10 (27); VI.9.11 (24).

80 E.g. III 9.9 (1); V.3.13 (10); V.4.2 (18); V.6.4–5; VI.7.35 and 37–42; VI.8.16 (31–6); VI.9.6 (42–5).

81 E.g. V.3.10 (41–4); V.3.13 (37); V.3.14(3); VI.7.35 (30 and 44–5); VI.7.39 (18–19); VI.7.40 (1); VI.9.4 (1–6); VI.9.10 (7–21); VI.9.11 (11).

early one, and, for another, a contemporary Work, III.9.9 (22), denies *katanoein* to the One after all. When Plotinus wants to ascribe to us any apprehension of the One (III.8.9 (20); VI.8.11 (23)), or to ascribe to the One itself any apprehension (VI.7.38 (26); VI.7.39 (2)), he uses instead the Epicurean term *epibolē*, *epiballein*, which is meant to convey something different from any kind of thinking.

A passage which incorporates some of the most important ideas is V.3.10 (28–52).

What can you think of which does not contain diversity (*allo kai allo*)? For if every object of thought is a verbal formula (*logos*), it will be multiple (*polla*). A thing is conscious of itself by being a diversified (*poikilon*) eye, or an eye of diverse colours. For if it encountered an object that was one and indivisible, it would be rendered speechless (*alogeisthai*). For what would it have to say or know about itself? For if a wholly indivisible thing had to describe itself it would have first to say what is was not; so that in this way too it would be multiple (*polla*) in order to be one. Then when it says 'I am this', it will speak falsely if the this of which it speaks is other than itself; while if this is an accident of itself, it will be describing a multiplicity (*polla*). Otherwise it will simply say 'am am' or 'I I'. But what if it were only two things and were to say 'I and this'? Must it not rather be many things (*polla*)? For it is diverse (*hetera*) in kind and manner, and is a plurality (*arithmos*) and many other things. Hence a thinking thing must take a diversity of objects (*heteron kai heteron*), and what is being thought while it is being thought, must be diverse (*poikilon*). Without this [diversity], there will be no thinking (*noēsis*) of it, but only a contact (*thixis*) and, as it were, a grasping (*epaphē*), which is unsayable and unthinkable, but which pre-thinks (*pronoousa*). The intellect (*nous*) will not yet have come into existence, and that which is touching (*thinganon*) will not be thinking (*nooun*). In contrast, what is thinking must not remain simple especially if it is thinking of itself, for it will divide itself in two, even if it does not speak its thoughts.

Thus [the absolutely indivisible] will not need to make a fuss about itself. For what would it discover, if it thought? Its essence belongs to it before all thinking (*pro tou noēsai*). For consciousness (*gnōsis*) is a sort of desire and a sort of discovery after search (*zētein*). Hence that which contains absolutely no differences remains by itself and searches for nothing about itself; whereas a thing that unrolled itself would have to be multiple (*polla*).

I believe this tells us that thinking requires a complex object, and that the contact which one might make with a non-complex object is not a kind of thinking at all. If so, this contact will not be non-discursive thinking, as it is in Aristotle, and as Lloyd takes it to be in Plotinus. Aristotle, I have suggested, is prepared to assimilate non-discursive thought to contact, only because he has a way of representing the proposition thought as non-complex, provided it is an identity-proposition. But this possibility is rejected by Plotinus, and so for him thinking and contact with the simple are two separate things.

It might be objected that Plotinus is confining his remarks to *discursive* thought, when he says that thinking is directed to a complex object. Admittedly, the notion of *unrolling itself* in line 52 and of *search* in lines 50–1 are elsewhere declared inapplicable to the non-discursive thinking of the intellect.[82] But everything else suggests that it is discursive and non-discursive thinking alike for which Plotinus demands a complex object.

In 1.3.1–4, Plotinus describes the method of ascent from discursive to non-discursive thinking and finally to union with the One. A crucial part of the ascent to non-discursive thought involves dialectic. The account of dialectic in 1.3.4 is derived from Plato's *Republic*, *Phaedrus* and *Sophist*. It involves finding the definitions of all intelligible things, by using the method of division, which divides genera by their differentiae into species. It also involves seeing the interconnexions between all things, until the whole intelligible realm has been analysed. Finally, the dialectician rests from labour and quietly contemplates. The intellectual process here should not be viewed as something bizarre or unfamiliar. Even today, most philosophers concern themselves with definitions, even if they do not define by genus and differentia.

Less familiar, perhaps, to contemporary Anglo-Saxon philosophers is the description of the final stage of union with the One. But Plotinus' account greatly influenced Augustine, pseudo-Dionysius and the Christian tradition of mysticism. And in this tradition, Plotinus' account rings echo after echo. In some quarters, indeed, there is a danger of people *too readily* finding Plotinus' kind of description familiar. Thus takers of drugs such as the 'beatniks' (seekers of the beatific vision, on one derivation) have claimed to have a short cut to mystical experience, although their pretensions have been wittily exposed by R. C. Zaehner.[83]

---

82 III.7.6 (16); V.I.4 (16).
83 R. C. Zaehner, *Mysticism Sacred and Profane* (Oxford 1957).

# 15  Gods and heaps

M. F. BURNYEAT

*I*

The ancients were already well aware that the sorites is not just
about heaps. It brings into question the very existence of the gods,
or at least the rationality of religious belief. If modern philosophers of language (who in recent years have been much preoccu-
pied with the sorites paradox) seldom know this, a magisterial
paper by Jonathan Barnes has now made clear the range and
richness of the ancient material on the subject.[1] Some of this
material looks strange by modern lights. All the more reason,
therefore, why enthusiasts for the sorites should take an interest in
its history.

The history begins, as everybody knows, with a memorable
example fashioned by the past master of paradox, Eubulides of
Miletus (4th cent. B.C.), known also for his purveying of the Liar,
the Bald Man, the Nobody, and other logical delights (D.L. II
108).[2]

I say: tell me, do you think that a single grain of wheat is a heap?
Thereupon you say: No. Then I say: What do you say about 2 grains?
For it is my purpose to ask you questions in succession, and if you do not
admit that 2 grains are a heap then I shall ask you about 3 grains. Then I
shall proceed to interrogate you further with respect to 4 grains, then 5

---

1 'Medicine, Experience and Logic', in *Science and Speculation*, ed. J. Barnes, J. Brun-
schwig, M. Burnyeat and M. Schofield (Cambridge, forthcoming). The magnitude of
my debts, both scholarly and philosophical, to this article will be apparent to anyone
who comes to it after trying to make headway with the ancient sorites on their own.
ἀγαπητὸν γὰρ εἴ τις τὰ μὲν κάλλιον λέγει, τὰ δὲ μὴ χεῖρον.

2 For data on Eubulides, such as his not belonging to the Megarian school, see David
Sedley, 'Diodorus Cronus and Hellenistic Philosophy', *Proc. Camb. Philol. Soc.*, 203
(N.S. 23) (1977), 74–120.

and 6 and 7 and 8, and you will assuredly say that none of these makes a heap. (Galen, *On Medical Experience* XVII 1, p. 115 Walzer).

The Greek for 'heap' is *sōros*, and that, we are told (Galen, *Med. Exp.* XVI 2, p. 115 W, Cic. *Acad.* II 92), is where it all began. 'Sorites' means an accumulator or one who heaps things up.[3]

Eubulides himself can hardly have foreseen that his modest heap of grain would grow to menace Olympus and undermine the foundations of logic. But he may nonetheless have intended that the Heap, along with the logically analogous argument of the Bald Man, should serve as a memorable paradigm on which the dialectician could model any number of arguments of the same general pattern. If there are two arguments of the pattern, surely there are three . . . But even if he had no such general aspiration, and was content to propound an elegant paradox, a pleasing conundrum of logical interest in its own right,[4] the word 'sorites' itself quite soon ceased to be the proper name of Eubulides' example and became a general (descriptive) term designating a pattern of argument capable of many instantiations.[5] And it is from this that I propose to start.

My question is the following: With what degree of abstraction did the ancients grasp the pattern of argument they called sorites? Did they have a general conception of the conditions, formal or material, which an argument must satisfy to count as a sorites? An answer to this question would be useful for two reasons. It would help us to understand any general reflections we may find on the wider philosophical significance of the sorites. And it would help us to understand why certain arguments get called sorites which we might not expect to find so called. Conversely, the historian may, with all due caution, use both the general reflections and the terminological practice as evidence to help in reconstructing the ancients' conception of the sorites. In that case he will be inferring that a certain conception of the sorites provides the best explanation of the wider philosophical moral someone wishes to draw or of a surprising application of the sorites terminology.

---

3  -ιτης is an agentive suffix: Barnes (n. 18). I shall, however, continue to distinguish Eubulides' example from other sorites arguments by calling it the Heap, because it is too late now to undo established custom.

4  So Barnes, who convincingly rebuts *inter alia* the suggestion of J. Moline, 'Aristotle, Eubulides, and the Sorites', *Mind*, 78 (1969), 393–407, that the sorites was aimed from the start at an Aristotelian target.

5  Thus already Chrysippus' title περὶ τῶν πρὸς τὰς φωνὰς σωρίτῶν λόγων, 'On sorites arguments against words' (D.L. VII 192), which happens also to be the earliest extant occurrence of σωρίτης.

But first the dedication. No excuse is needed, I trust, for offering the pages which follow to such a connoisseur of Greek paradox as Gwil Owen. From the Eleatics to the second part of Plato's *Parmenides,* his genius at teasing out the subtleties of the challenge and at displaying the profundity of the Platonic or Aristotelian solution has been a model and an inspiration for those who believe that the history of philosophy is about the truth as well as the past. The question I have posed is a strictly historical one. But the investigation will not be worthy of the occasion unless it contributes something to the philosophical understanding of one of the deepest and most challenging paradoxes that antiquity devised.

## II

Let us then return to the excerpt just quoted from Galen's *On Medical Experience.* Galen is writing his own version of the Heap, not reporting Eubulides, but for that very reason he shows us how the example has crystallised in the tradition. Notice first – the narrative style makes it the more conspicuous – that Galen still thinks of the Heap as set in the context of a two-person dialectical debate. The paradox is propounded by the familiar Greek method of question and answer, not as an argument composed of premises and conclusion, and this despite the fact that (as will be seen) by Galen's time such formulations had long been available and the subject of intense discussion. The dialectical context will prove critical later, but already it gives point to a second, negative observation.

Galen shows no sign of thinking that the name 'sorites' had originally a double meaning and referred not only to a man heaping up grains but also to the dialectical procedure of heaping up questions (or premises) to set the puzzle. His etymological derivation of 'sorites' mentions only the content of the example.[6] If Galen is not aware of a procedural allusion, this may either be because it was never there or because by his time the sense of it had been lost.[7] In either case we lose one natural way of explaining

6  n. 8 below. Similarly Cicero, *Acad.* II 49 and 92.
7  The hypothesis that argument titles often have a double meaning was put forward by Sedley, (n. 132), citing Eubulides' ἐγκεκαλυμμένος as being a veiled argument about a veiled man and his κερατίνης as a horned argument, i.e. dilemma, about a man losing his horns; Barnes n. 18 extends the suggestion to 'sorites', as above. It is an attractive idea: even if grammar does not require it (cf. ὁ Ἀχιλλεὺς λόγος, D.L. IX 23), and ὁ φαλακρὸς λόγος is a recalcitrant exception, Cic. *Fat.* 29 plays on a double meaning in the 'Lazy argument'. But so far as 'sorites' is concerned, it seems that the secondary meaning, if any, got lost or was not thought relevant when the term was generalised to other examples.

the extension of the word 'sorites' beyond the original Heap: it becomes improbable that the word was simply transferred to other arguments which derive their conclusion from a pile of premises. Galen in fact cites another, different name as alluding to the method of the sorites: 'the argument of little by little' (*ho para mikron logos*).[8] This nomenclature, which occurs already in Chrysippus (D.L. VII 197, *SVF* II p. 106, 9–10), is more likely to contain the clue we are seeking.[9]

'The argument of little by little' is a descriptive phrase with a plain meaning: argument which proceeds by small transitions. The only uncertainty is, What counts as so proceeding? Galen promulgates a strictly quantitative view, and thereby gives us one ancient answer to the question set for inquiry.

According to what is demanded by the argument, there must not be such a thing in the world as a heap of grain, a mass or satiety, neither a mountain, nor strong love, nor a row, nor strong wind, nor city, nor anything else which is *known from its name and idea to have a measure of extent or multitude*, such as the wave, the open sea, a flock of sheep and herd of cattle, the nation and the crowd. And the doubt and confusion introduced by the logos leads to contradiction of fact in the transition of man from one stage of his life to another, and in the changes of time, and the changes of seasons. For in the case of the boy one is uncertain and doubtful as to when the actual moment arrives for his transition from boyhood to adolescence . . . [etc., etc.] . . . By the same reasoning, doubt and confusion enter into many other things which relate to the doings of men in spite of the fact that knowledge of these things is obvious and plain (*Med. Exp.* XVI 1, pp. 114–15 W).

The answer is that a sorites argument can be mounted, and will lead to contradiction of plain fact, with any term the meaning of which involves a measure of extent or multitude. Any term which

---

8 *Med. Exp.* XVI 2, p. 115 W: 'There are some Dogmatists and logicians who call the argument expressing this doubt "sorites" after the matter which first gave rise to this question, I mean the heap. Other people call it the argument of little by little. They have only named it thus in accordance with its method which leads to doubt and confusion'. Cf. also *Loc. Aff.* VIII 25 Kühn.

9 ἡ παρὰ μικρὸν ἐρώτησις, 'questioning little by little' (cf. S.E. *M* 1 68), is used in a definition of 'sorites' given at Simplicius, *in Ar. Phys.* 1177, 2–4 Diels: 'The sorites is a sophistical argument which from questioning little by little as our impressions get fainter draws a conclusion which is non-evident or manifestly false' (ὁ . . . σωρίτης σοφιστικός ἐστι λόγος ἐκ τῆς παρὰ μικρὸν . . . ἐρωτήσεως ἀπάγων κατὰ τὴν ἔκλυσιν τῶν φαντασιῶν ἐπ' ἄδηλον ἢ ψεῦδος). See further Barnes ns. 16–17. This idea of little by little is crucially omitted in the debased 'modern' logic book use of 'sorites' for an abbreviated chain of categorical syllogisms of the form 'All *A* is *B*, All *B* is *C*, . . . Therefore, All *A* is *Z*.' The *fortuna* of 'sorites' in late antiquity and beyond would repay study.

is implicitly quantitative[10] gives rise to a sorites paradox and does so because it is quantitative. The thesis is both general and diagnostic. Should there be any doubt about this, the context will confirm it.

Galen is recording a debate between two schools of medicine about the concept of experience, where by 'an experience' is meant a piece of general knowledge based on repeated observations. The question at issue is, How many observations make an experience, i.e. enable one to know or to be justified in believing that, e.g., vinegar aids digestion (XIII 2, p. 108 W)? A serious matter: your life may depend on which doctor you go to, and patients were expected to decide on the basis of the sort of debate that Galen records.[11] Well then, one observation is not enough, nor two, and if two is not enough it is no good adding just one more . . . and so on. The sorites argument is the Logical doctor's challenge to the claim that very many observations make an experience. To which the Empirical doctor replies, in the passage quoted, that if the argument proves the non-existence of experience, it proves the non-existence of a whole lot of other things as well, 'in spite of the fact that knowledge of these things is obvious and plain'. The paradox hits everyone. We all sink, or swim on regardless, together (cf. XX 6, p. 126 W). Whatever the merits of this reply,[12] it plainly rests on the contention that it is the notion of a measure of extent or multitude which makes a term vulnerable to the sorites.

I suppose that a modern philosopher who has concerned himself with the sorites will think this characterisation insufficiently general. It fits many of the examples that crop up in the modern literature, but not all. Think of the sorites paradox which Crispin Wright constructs with colour predicates.[13] It is possible to arrange a series of colour patches such that the first is undeniably red and such that it is equally undeniable that the second is red if the first is red, that the third is red if the second is, and so on, until we find ourselves concluding that something is red which plainly

10 Not, of course, explicitly quantitative terms such as '3 cubits long'. The contrast between explicitly and implicitly quantitative terms is the prosaic truth behind Hegel's claim that the sorites and the Bald Man dramatise the dialectic of quantity and quality passing into one another: *Lectures on the History of Philosophy*, tr. E. S. Haldane and F. H. Simson (London 1892), I 462–4.

11 See G. E. R. Lloyd, *Magic, Reason and Experience* (Cambridge 1979), 89 ff.

12 See Barnes for an exposition which leaves the Empirical doctor with an unexpectedly impressive case.

13 'Language-Mastery and the Sorites Paradox', in *Truth and Meaning: Essays in Semantics*, ed. Gareth Evans and John McDowell (Oxford 1976), 223–47. Also Michael Dummett, 'Wang's Paradox', in his *Truth and other Enigmas* (London 1978), 248–68.

is not red. The argument proceeds by small transitions but they are transitions of similarity, qualitative not quantitative. For 'red' does not involve a measure of extent or multitude. It has indeed been claimed that all empirical concepts lead to paradox if the sorites reasoning is allowed.[14] Others say that the predicates at issue suffer from vagueness, or from semantic tolerance, where hopefully this is a characteristic that can be elucidated independently of the claim that it makes a predicate liable to the sorites paradox. That a predicate involves a measure of extent or multitude is certainly something which can be elucidated independently of, and so could explain, liability to the sorites paradox. It is just not general enough to capture what is going on in all the sorites arguments that we, or the ancients, would want to have explained. If Galen's Empirical doctor does not look beyond the quantitative basis of the terms he considers, his diagnosis of our affliction is bound to be superficial.

## III

If this conclusion seems disappointing, it may nonetheless serve as a background against which to view the one surviving ancient presentation of the sorites that shows signs of an attempt to be abstract and formal. Here it is, a fragment of a handbook of Stoic logic:

It is not the case that two are few and three are not also; it is not the case that these are and four are not also (and so on up to ten thousand). But two are few: therefore ten thousand are also (D.L. VII 82).[15]

The dialectical context is suppressed and the argument regimented into premises (9,998 of them) and conclusion. But it is still only a specimen example of the sorites, not a general account of sorites arguments. If there was a general account to go with it, it has unfortunately dropped out of the text through damage or corruption.[16] Nevertheless, the example is designed to *display* certain

14  Max Black, 'Reasoning with Loose Concepts', *Dialogue* 2 (1963), 1–12.
15  Text and translation as in Barnes, who reads μυρίων and μύρια for δέκα and δέκα (cf. S. E. *M* VII 416–21), following U. Egli, *Zur stoischen Dialektik* (Basel 1967), 8 and 55.
16  When the writer goes on to the Nobody argument, he gives first a general specification, then an example, thus encouraging the thought that he might have done the same for the sorites. There would be room enough for a general specification in the lacuna which all editors mark before the sorites example. But if the lacuna comes after, not before, οἷον ὁ τοιοῦτος, it looks as though in dealing with the Veiled Man the writer led straight into the example. Moreover, the Nobody lends itself to abstract specification in a way that the Veiled Man does not. So our estimate of the size and content of the lacuna must wait upon the question whether ancient resources extend to a reasonably abstract specification of the sorites – the very question we are pursuing.

features which have become apparent to someone who tried to think about the sorites in a general way.

I say this because the intermediate premises of the argument – those that come between 'Two are few' and 'Ten thousand are few' – are exhibited not as a series of conditionals ('If two grains are too few to make a heap, so are three', 'If Zeus is a god, so is Poseidon'), which is the usual ancient practice, but as a series of negated conjuctions of the form 'not both $p$ and not $q$'. This makes no difference to the validity of the argument, nor would any Stoic logician (as opposed to a modern intuitionist) think it did. For it merely recasts an argument which can be analysed by repeated application of the first Stoic indemonstrable (*modus ponens*) into an argument which can be analysed by repeated application of the third indemonstrable plus double negation.[17] So the writer is not rejecting the more normal conditional form from considerations bearing on the validity of the argument. Nor, in fact, is he rejecting, or denying the appropriateness of, the conditional form at all. Rather, he is urging for present purposes Philo's interpretation of the conditional, whereby 'If $p$ then $q$' is true if and only if it is not the case that '$p$' is true and '$q$' false; in our terms, he is telling us to take the premises as material implications. For we know that there were occasions when Chrysippus would rewrite conditionals as negated conjunctions for this very reason, in order to insist that they be understood as material implications with the Philonian truth conditions, and, more specifically, in order to exclude the so called *sunartēsis* ('connection' or 'cohesion') reading of the conditional, whereby 'If $p$ then $q$' is true if and only if '$p$' and 'not $q$' are incompatible.[18] If, then, our writer is following Chrysippean precedent, he is telling us that the conditionals in a sorites argument are not to be understood as claiming a necessary connection between antecedent and consequent. He is going out

17 The third indemonstrable is: Not both the first and the second; but the first; therefore not the second. On double negation in Stoic logic, see Benson Mates, *Stoic Logic* (Berkeley and Los Angeles 1961), 31 n. 29; Michael Frede, *Die stoische Logik* (Göttingen 1974), 71–2.

18 The main evidence is Cic. *Fat.* 1 1–16. For other references and discussion of complications, see Frede, op. cit., 80–93; Richard Sorabji, *Necessity, Cause and Blame: Perspectives on Aristotle's Theory* (London 1980), 74–8; David Sedley, 'On Signs', in *Science and Speculation*, op. cit. In applying the point to D.L. VII 82 I am following Barnes, but I believe, with Sedley, that rather more is at stake than getting the argument into its strongest form by taking the weakest reading of the premises.

of his way to indicate that the truth or falsity of the conditionals in a sorites argument is not to be decided on logical or conceptual grounds.

But why not? Is it not our semantic intuitions which persuade us that if two grains are too few to make a heap, so are three?[19] This is the point at which to notice that in the example from the Stoic handbook the premises, as translated above, are nonsense. It is nonsense to say 'Two are few.' Two grains of wheat are few, if you like, or too few to make a heap, but two itself, the number two, is neither few nor many. Now if we are impressed by the evidence just adduced that our author (i.e. his source – with luck, Chrysippus) has tried to think about the sorites in a general way, we may be tempted to see in this apparent nonsense evidence that he has also thought about the content of the sorites premises. He means 'Two are few' to stand for 'Two so-and-so's are few.'[20] He wants to abstract from heaps and cities and the observations which ground a doctor's experience, so as to display a common form they all share. The idea behind his use of numbers is to mark out in an abstract way an ordered sequence of subjects – as we might write it, $<a_1, a_2, \ldots, a_n>$ – such that we are inclined to say, first, that $a_1$ is few, in a sense appropriate to the given context; second, that each $a_i$ is few if $a_{i-1}$ is few; but third, that $a_n$ is not few. And if we are persuaded that the writer's thought is moving at this level of abstractness, we may further suppose that the predicate 'few' is itself intended only as a specimen or representative example of a class of predicates, any one of which would give rise to the sorites paradox in connection with an appropriate sequence of subjects $<a_1, a_2, \ldots, a_n>$. So, finally, and assuming we are not being overoptimistic, we may credit Stoic logic with a quite abstract grasp of the idea that a sorites argument has a structure which, if we put all our results together and use modern symbolism, can be written as follows:[21]

19 Cf. Wright's account of 'semantic tolerance'.
20 Alternatively, as Charles Young suggested to me, the number words in the Greek may themselves mean two, three . . . *of* something.
21 Gratefully lifted from Barnes. At one stage I was worried that τὰ μὲν δύο ὀλίγα ἐστιν might mean simply 'Two is small' (sc. a small number), which is not nonsense and so would suggest that the example is merely that, not an attempt to be abstractly schematic. For the lexicon tells us that ὀλίγος means 'small' (e.g. of an ox, a space, a period of time) as well as 'few'. But Steve Strange pointed out to me that the question *tria pauca sint anne multa* at Cic. *Acad.* II 93 must reproduce a contrast between ὀλίγα and πολλά in the Greek source.

$$Fa_1$$
$$Fa_1 \supset Fa_2$$
$$Fa_2 \supset Fa_3$$
.
.
.
$$Fa_{n-1} \supset Fa_n$$

---

$$Fa_n$$

But this schema is misleading if it suggests that all specific semantic content has been abstracted away. In the original the word 'few' remains. So when we ask how the Stoic logician would fix the class of predicates whose substitution for '*F*' creates a sorites, we have no right to suppose that he has got further than the Empirical doctor. 'Two are few' represents 'Two so-and-so's are few for a such-and-such', where 'few' occurs essentially because the such-and-such is an implicitly quantitative notion like heap or city.[22] The difference between the Stoic and the Empiric is that the former denies, what the latter allows, that the quantitative analysis of these notions supplies a conceptual backing for the sorites premises. That is the claim implied by rejecting the *sunartēsis* conditional in favour of the Philonian. Or to put it another way, the Stoic does not agree that three are few *because* two are few.[23]

Well may we be surprised. Not only does the Stoic logician apparently refuse to accept that there are conceptual or semantic pressures on us to accept the premises of a sorites. He refuses this

22 Here I depart from Barnes, who thinks that 'few' represents a much wider class, because – and on this, of course, I agree – there are arguments, classified by the ancients as sorites, which do not use and cannot readily be formulated in terms of 'few'. Instead of asking how the Stoic logician would fix the class, Barnes gives his own account: '*F*' is a soritical predicate if and only if (i) to all appearances, '*F*' is true of $a_1$, (ii) to all appearances, '*F*' is false of $a_n$, (iii) each pair of adjacent $a_i$s is, to all appearances, indistinguishable with respect to '*F*'. Certainly, any predicate which gives rise to a successful sorites paradox meets these conditions (trivially so). But our question was, which these predicates are and why? Nevertheless, the choice of 'few' confirms, what is abundantly clear elsewhere, that the sorites was standardly taken to be about adding rather than subtracting, i.e. the conclusion was that you cannot make a heap, not that you cannot undo one.

23 For this interpretation of *sunartēsis*, see Jonathan Barnes, 'Proof Destroyed', in *Doubt and Dogmatism: Studies in Hellenistic Epistemology,* ed. M. Schofield, M. Burnyeat and J. Barnes (Oxford 1980), 161–81.

for the very cases where the idea is most compelling, because of the patently quantitative nature of the predicates involved. But there is evidence that we have not mistaken the Stoic stance.

One of two books that Chrysippus wrote on the sorites (D.L. VII 192, 197) was entitled 'On sorites arguments against words' (n. 5 above). At least some sorites arguments are viewed as attacking language: in modern terms, they purport to show that certain predicates are incoherent, in more ancient parlance (cf. S.E. M I 65–9) that, insofar as one is to judge by the definition of 'F', there can be no F. Consequently, to the extent that Chrysippus is a critic of the sorites (see below), to that extent he defends our language against Eubulides' invention.[24] If he succeeds, he can say, 'There's nothing wrong with the predicate "heap"; you are wrong to claim conceptual validity for the premises you propound.'

## IV

For the moment let us shelve the question what justification Chrysippus might have for his contention. Let us imagine ourselves schooled in Stoic logic to accept both that the sorites reasoning is formally valid and that it is no use blaming the predicate for the puzzle which results. Our only remaning option, it seems, is to claim that at least one of the premises is, as a matter of plain fact, false.[25] The Stoic insistence on reading the sorites premises as material conditionals records a decision to fight the battle on the field of epistemology rather than as an issue of logic and the philosophy of language. But the battle still has to be fought. Not everyone agrees that there is anything wrong with the sorites.

Cicero, speaking on behalf of the sceptical Academy against the pretensions of Stoic logic, declares that the fault lies not in the sorites argument but in ourselves; moreover, it is not an avoidable fault for which we can be blamed. For, he says:

24 Sedley, 'Diodorus Cronus and Hellenistic Philosophy', 91, suggest that sorites arguments against words (φωναί) would be Academic arguments against Stoic terminology. But φωναί is more likely to denote ordinary than technical language, and the title is listed among Chrysippus' works on language, not those on logic (the next entry is 'On solecisms'). So I agree with Barnes (n. 48) that we should expect a linguistic rather than a logical target; which is not of course to exclude philosophically important words of ordinary language.

25 If there is more than one false premise, the truth conditions for material implication ensure that no two of them are adjacent.

The nature of things has given us no knowledge of boundaries so that in any case we could determine how far to go; nor is this so only with that heap of wheat from which the name derives, but in no case at all if we are questioned little by little – Is he rich or poor? famous or obscure? Are they many or few? large or small? long or short? broad or narrow? – in no case can we say how much is to be added or subtracted for us to answer definitely (*Acad.* II 92).

The examples, and the latter part of the elucidation, still suggest a quantitative conception (How much money do you need to be rich?), but they sustain an epistemological moral which is stated quite generally: in no case at all do we know, nor can we know, where the boundary is.

Notice that Cicero does not say there are no boundaries (no heaps, no famous men), only that there is no knowing where they are. He takes a properly sceptical stance. He is properly sceptical also when it comes to the question what right he has to generalise about the significance of the sorites. All he says is: 'This kind of error spreads so widely that I do not see where it may not reach to' (II 93 *fin.*). A sceptic is not in the business of setting up a logical theory to explain the sorites. On the contrary, the sorites argument is a device he borrows from logic to make logic turn against itself, thereby revealing the incapacity of our reason to determine what is true and what is false (*Acad.* II 93 *init.*; cf. 95 *init.*). This is a strong claim,[26] but I think a fair one, not mere rhetoric, given that no justification has been offered for confining the sorites to quantitative notions. For how is the sceptic's opponent to show that the sorites does not spread further? Perhaps quantitative considerations can be brought to bear on virtually any predicate. Perhaps the fixing of boundaries is as problematic in non-quantitative cases as in the example cited. The alternative nomenclature 'the argument of little by little' is positive encouragement to think so – especially if it was the gloss via which 'sorites' was transformed (? by Chrysippus) into a general term (above, p. 318).[27] In the absence of a logical theory which sets limits on the scope of sorites reasoning by giving firmly characterised condi-

---

26 Cf. Black, op. cit., 12: 'To argue that the *sorites* shows that something is wrong with logic would be like maintaining that the coalescence of raindrops reveals an imperfection of simple arithmetic.'

27 Further evidence in support of this suggestion is that among the arguments called 'sorites' are some which proceed little by little through a series of closely similar predicates rather than applying a single predicate to a series of closely similar subjects (see Cic. *Acad.* II 49–50, *Fin.* IV 50, Sen. *Ben.* V xix 9 with Barnes n. 54).

tions for a predicate to be liable to the paradox, the sceptic is entitled to suggest that, for all we know, sorites paradoxes may crop up in any area. None is sacrosanct.

## V

Which brings me to the gods. In the second century B.C. the gods became the target of a celebrated series of arguments which the Academic Carneades propounded 'in sorites form' (*sōritikōs*); so Sextus Empiricus puts it (*M* IX 182; *sōritas* 190), and Sextus is drawing on Carneades' friend and eventual successor Clitomachus, who wrote up the arguments as being, in his view, most excellent and effective. I quote the first two arguments as Sextus records them:

If Zeus is a god, Poseidon also is a god:
  Brethren three were we, all children of Cronos and Rhea,
  Zeus and myself and Hades, the third, with the Shades for his kingdom.
All things were parted in three, and each hath his share of the glory.[28]
So that if Zeus is a god, Poseidon also, being his brother, will be a god. And if Poseidon is a god, Achelous, too, will be a god; and if Achelous, Neilos; and if Neilos, every river as well; and if every river, the streams also will be gods; and if the streams, the torrents; but the torrents[29] are not gods; neither, then, is Zeus a god. But if there had been gods, Zeus would have been a god. Therefore, there are no gods. – Further, if the sun is a god, day will also be a god; for day is nothing else than sun above the earth. And if day is god, the month too will be god; for it is a composite made up of days. And if the month is god, the year too will be god; for the year is a composite made up of months. But this is not <true>; neither then is the original supposition. And besides, they say, it is absurd to declare that the day is god, but not the dawn and midday and the evening (*M* IX 182–4, tr. Bury).

Some fifteen such arguments have come down to us, but there may well have been more (cf. *M* IX 190) – variations on a theme which was a regular topic of debate. (Remember that philosophical debate at this time was largely oral. We can picture Carneades, the unbeatable controversialist, varying the arguments to suit the occasion, while his faithful amanuensis Clitomachus sits by to take them down.) Sextus gives a relatively clear presentation of a

---

28 Homer, *Iliad* XV 187–9, Poseidon speaking.
29 Read αἱ χαράδραι for οἱ ῥύακες, with Sedley, op. cit., n. 89.

selection of the arguments (*M* IX 182–90), Cicero in his *De Natura Deorum* (III 43–52) a confused and garrulous presentation of rather more, together with some valuable information about the character and aims of Carneades' debating tactics on this subject.[30] That information will concern us in due course. Our first task is to take note of the classification of these arguments under the heading of 'sorites'.

It has indeed been denied by one modern scholar that they are properly so classified, on the grounds that all they have in common with the original Heap is the 'polysyllogistic structure'.[31] This claim presupposes that we have a clear conception of what the ancients standardly meant by calling an argument sorites and can see in the light of it that Carneades' arguments do not fit the bill.[32] Whereas the point I have been labouring is that the ancients' conception of the sorites is in important respects indeterminate. They can set out the 'polysyllogistic structure', as the Stoic handbook does, but so far as content is concerned no-one is in a position to say 'where this kind of error . . . may not reach to'.[33] Quantitative considerations are not prominent in Carneades' arguments, but it is not difficult to agree that they proceed by small transitions, 'little by little'. No doubt a Hellenistic audience will see differences as well as similarities between the theological sorites and the original Heap. But will they see the same differences as we do or assess their significance in quite the same terms?

When we compare the theological sorites with the original Heap, we are inclined to be struck by a procedural difference. The conditionals in Eubulides' argument accumulate automatically, one after another, in virtue of the general principle:

(*n*) if *n* grains are too few for a heap, *n* + 1 grains are too few.

Carneades seems to build his argument step by step. Cicero, who mixes conditionals with questions, probably gives a better impression of what an onslaught from Carneades actually sounded

---

30 The fundamental study is Pierre Couissin, 'Les Sorites de Carnéade contre le Polythéisme', *Revue des Études Grecques*, 54 (1941), 43–57.

31 Giovanna Sillitti, 'Alcune considerazioni sull' aporia del sorite', in *Scuole socratiche minori e filosofia ellenistica*, ed. Gabriele Giannantoni (Bologna 1977), 75–92.

32 Sillitti, to be fair, argues that every sorites properly so called proceeds both upwards and downwards to yield a contradiction such as 'Every number is both small and large.' The objection is that this specification rests on a misreading of Ar. *Top.* 179b34–7, which Barnes shows has nothing to do with the sorites.

33 Does Cicero hint here at a sorites of sorites arguments? *Manare* is used of the sorites process at *ND* III 49 *fin.* and *paucis additis* at *Acad.* II 92 attempts a related joke.

like, but Sextus shows us how it all adds up. The successive conditionals do not derive from a single general principle but from justificatory grounds which Carneades has to supply, and the justification stated or suggested varies within the argument. Why is Poseidon a god if Zeus is a god? Because we have it on the unimpeachable authority of Homer that they are brothers. Why is Achelous a god if Poseidon is? Because they are both masses of water (Poseidon the sea, Achelous a large river in Aetolia). Why is the Nile a god if Achelous is? Because they are both rivers, and so on. General principles are stated or implied: 'Every river is a god', 'All children of Cronos and Rhea are gods.' But no one principle will take us all the way through the argument. Or rather, we could try to formulate a principle that would do the trick. But it would not be the principle on which Carneades in fact relies.

To see more clearly what Carneades is missing, let us generalise the example so that monotheists find it easier to handle. In the ancient world the predicate 'is a god' designates a certain status, a status commanding for those (persons or things) fortunate enough to enjoy it specially privileged treatment (rooms in an architectural masterpiece, feasts, processions, and the like). Unlike the Fellows of a Cambridge college, however, the gods receive this treatment without having to qualify or be elected under man-made rules and conventions. It is simply what their pre-eminence deserves. So the analogue in our world would be such things as being an adult, where that is thought of as commanding certain kinds of treatment quite apart from any legal fixing of rights and responsibilities; being a person, where that is taken to be a moral concept; or being one of the needy poor, in the sense in which one might complain that there are more of them than are covered by existing social security provisions. The modern parallels to Carneades' theological sorites are those familiar slippery slope arguments by which conservatives on the abortion issue push the right to be considered a person little by little back towards the moment of conception, while liberals urge that current welfare provisions fail to recognise deserving cases of poverty or need. These analogies suggest that the following might be the principle we are looking for:

If $X$ deserves treatment $T$, and $Y$ does not differ significantly from $X$ in features relevant to deserving $T$, then $Y$ deserves $T$.

I do not think it is an objection to this formulation that there may be an overlapping series of features $F_1, F_2, \ldots F_n$ such that (i) if one is asked why $X$ deserves $T$ (why $X$ is a god, a person, needy), the first thing one would mention is $F_1$ ($X$ is a son of Cronos and Rhea, a safely delivered healthily functioning baby, without sufficient income to buy food); but (ii) what persuades one that $Y$ also deserves $T$ is a resemblance between $X$ and $Y$ in respect of $F_2$ (Poseidon and Achelous are both masses of water, the baby and the foetus both have the limbs, organs, etc. of humankind, Mrs Jones has a job but in circumstances detrimental to the children), and so on. In these matters second and third thoughts count as well as, and sometimes more than, first thoughts. It is an illusion to think one can say straight off exactly why $X$ deserves $T$, and it may be an illusion to think one can ever say it with finality. For it may be that what strikes one about $X$, and again about $Y$, as relevant to its deserving $T$ is itself something that gets modified when someone sets a new case beside the old.

By way of comparison, *Lyrical Ballads* is uncontroversially an example of the Romantic style. Why? Quite different answers may suggest themselves according as one takes it on its own or compares it with a novel by Scott on the one hand and with a painting by Caspar David Friedrich on the other. The admission or rejection of new candidates for the title 'Romantic' goes hand in hand with reassessment of the old, and the process can repeat itself once the new candidates have become part of the established canon. The semantics of these predicates is such as to allow not merely for variable realisation ($X$ deserves $T$ because $X$ has $F_1$, $Y$ deserves $T$ because $Y$ has $F_2$) but for what one might call elastic realisation ($X$ deserves $T$ because $X$ has $F_1$, $Y$ deserves $T$ because $X$ deserves $T$ and both $X$ and $Y$ have $F_2$, $Z$ deserves $T$ because $Y$ deserves $T$ and both $Y$ and $Z$ have $F_3$): the concept (some may prefer to say: our grasp of the concept) stretches from one example to another as social or historical circumstances make it possible or appropriate to perceive and respond to a significant resemblance with exemplary instances. And perhaps it belongs to the point of these predicates, to their role in our culture, that they should be in this way elastic, hence inherently contestable, hence properly and usefully subject to the Carneadean type of sorites reasoning. Such reasoning may be the result of insight and the instrument of progress.

I say 'perhaps' and 'maybe'. It would be interesting to develop these reflections further, but for our purposes the important thing is to notice how naturally they have led us into the philosophy of language. Take a class of predicates, look for the semantic characteristics which sorites reasoning exploits, and connect these characteristics with the role of the predicates in our language and thought. That is the modern style.[34] It is not Carneades' style. He offers a multiplicity of particular arguments, one after another, each of them built premise by premise on a multiplicity of different grounds. No general pattern emerges. We, with our craving for generality, may be disappointed. But after our examination of the Stoic handbook we should no longer be surprised. The general principle formulated above, if it is true, is presumably some sort of conceptual or analytic truth, deriving from the meaning of the verb 'deserve'. If this principle, or a less general principle of the same type, is what Carneades is missing, his practice is no other than the Stoic logic book prescribes.[35] When he advances his conditional premises, it is not with the thought that they can be supported on conceptual grounds. They are material conditionals which neither claim nor appeal to conceptual connections.[36]

We are lucky enough to know what consideration Carneades did mean to appeal to. Cicero states: 'These arguments were advanced by Carneades, not to refute the existence of the gods (for what could less befit a philosopher?),[37] but to show that the Stoics' account of the gods explains nothing' (ND III 44). Carneades' target is Stoic rational theology, the attempt to use reason to explain and justify religious belief. This attempt had two aspects. First, there was a good deal of argument to establish that the world itself, or its immanent governing principle, is god, because the whole world is a sentient rational living creature vastly superior to everything within it, endowed with every perfection and such that nothing more perfect can even be conceived (e.g. ND II 18 ff.).[38] Second, by reference to this philosophical monotheism the Stoics proposed to rationalise and thereby to vindicate the polytheism of popular belief (ND I 36 ff., II 63 ff., III 61 ff.).

34 Beautifully practised by Wright, op. cit.
35 The information that Carneades was taught logic by the Stoic Diogenes of Babylon is given by Cicero in a context (*Acad.* II 98) closely related to our main subject.
36 If it be objected that the second argument quoted rests on the definitions of day, month, etc., the reply is that the relevant definition for *sunartēsis* would be the definition of god.
37 One suspects that the aside is Cicero's own, to reassure his Roman audience. Elsewhere (*de Inv.* 46) he cites 'Philosophers are atheists' as a stock example of common belief.
38 For an illuminating recent discussion, see Malcolm Schofield, 'Preconception, Argument, and God', in *Doubt and Dogmatism*, op. cit., 283–308.

The plurality of popular gods is to be seen as a recognition by the tradition of aspects of the one cosmic deity. It is because Poseidon is the sea, for example, that we can continue to worship him under the name which custom has bestowed (*ND* II 71). People were shocked when Chrysippus interpreted a picture of Hera fellating Zeus in terms of the material element receiving the *spermatikoi logoi* (*SVF* II 1071–4). But it shows the lengths he was prepared to go in the project (not without its parallels in modern theology) of demonstrating that there can be a clean philosophical understanding even of the most primitive of the old ideas.

This is where Carneades comes in. The Stoic gives his own reasons, or finds some truth in the traditional reasons, for various applications of the predicate 'is a god'. Many of the steps in Carneades' sorites arguments can be supported by some precedent in popular religious belief. For example, Achelous was widely held to be a god, and in the *Iliad* (xx 7–8) all the rivers come to a gathering of the gods.[39] Other steps would have found some rationale in Stoic thought, for we hear that Zeno attributed divine power to the years, months and seasons (*ND* I 36). Probably, if we had more background information of this sort, we would feel the force of some of the steps which now look baffling or bizarre. In the context of this debate, given that $X$ is a god, it is fair evidence to show there is no relevant difference which justifies refusing the same status to $Y$, that in fact some popular thought or even Stoicism itself accepts $Y$ too as divine. It is fair evidence in the context of this debate because the Stoics are committed to the proposition that the predicate 'is a god' is applied on the basis of reasons; the ordinary worshipper has but a dim grasp of the reasons, but philosophy can provide a clear, clean understanding to vindicate the rationality of his beliefs and practices. The trouble is that this rationalisation programme faces a tradition which no more offers a single, determinate creed than our tradition has left us a single well-defined notion of personhood or need. The predicate 'is a god' is essentially elastic. As the sorites questioning proceeds, some groups of worshippers want to drop out earlier than others ('Yes, Achelous is a god, but not the Nile: leave that to the Egyptians'); and eventually we reach something like the torrents, or a puddle by the door, which nobody wants to

---

39 Cicero is so expansive on this side of the matter that sometimes he loses hold of the main thread of the argument: see Couissin, op. cit., for a rich collection of details.

worship. But, it has been argued, there is no good reason for this discrimination. The Stoic rationalisation programme aims to separate true religion from superstition (*ND* II 71–2), but can draw no justifiable dividing line between the two.

Thus the theological sorites arguments expose a deficiency in Stoic reason, not a deficiency or peculiarity in the predicate 'is a god'. Carneades does not expect his Stoic opponent to accept the ostensible conclusion of the argument 'Zeus is not a god', let alone the further conclusion 'There are no gods' added on the strength of a generalising premise which says, in effect, that if Zeus is not a god, nothing is.[40] On the contrary, the Stoic is expected to find these conclusions so unacceptable that he gives up, not the term 'god', but the idea that our use of it can be grounded in reason. 'These arguments were advanced by Carneades, not to refute the existence of the gods . . . but to show that the Stoics' account of the gods explains nothing.' Indeed, Gaius Cotta, to whom Cicero gives the role of delivering the Academic arguments in *de Natura Deorum*, is a priest and believer (*ND* I 61, III 5): his scepticism is about the reasoned defence of religious belief, which raises doubts where there were none before (*ND* I 62, III 5–10). According to Cotta, the only thing to say about the gods is, 'This is the tradition handed down from our forefathers' (*ND* III 9); as a modern philosopher might put it, 'This language game is played.' So conservative a moral would go down well with Cicero's Roman audience, and may indeed have been inserted by Cicero for that purpose.[41] For the arguments began life in the more demanding context of second century Athens, where Carneades' Stoic opponent is spokesman for the faculty of reason (above, p. 325). If his rationalisation programme fails, human reason itself is revealed to be deficient, because it is unable to decide the all-important question, what is a proper object of worship.[42] The

40 This step is what corresponds to the use of mathematical induction in modern versions of the sorites. Cf. Galen, *Med. Exp.* XVII 3, p. 116 W: 'You . . . will never admit at any time that the sum . . . is a heap, even if the number of grains of wheat reaches infinity by the constant and gradual addition of more. By reason of this denial the heap is proved to be non-existent.'

41 Couissin writes, 'Sans doute, a cet endroit, Cicéron ne suit-il pas encore de près son modèle grec; mais en mettant cette précaution oratoire dans la bouche de Cotta, il n'a pas cru trahir la pensée de la Nouvelle Académie' (op. cit., 56 n. 2). But cf. n. 37 above. Cicero is often quite nervous about making philosophy respectable at Rome.

42 Compare the way Carneades' discussion of the criterion of truth proceeds on the basis that the claim of sense-perception to provide a criterion stands or falls by the Stoic articulation of the claim: S.E. *M* VII 160 ff. and M. F. Burnyeat, 'Carneades was no probabilist', in D. Glidden ed., *Riverside Studies in Ancient Scepticism* (forthcoming).

fault does not lie in the predicate 'is a god' but in ourselves. The theological sorites teaches a lesson in epistemology, not in the philosophy of language.

Let us now return to earth and re-examine the original Heap in the light of these results. We inclined to say that the conditionals in Eubulides' argument accumulate automatically, in virtue of the general principle

(*n*) if *n* grains are too few for a heap, *n* + 1 grains are too few. Galen's Empirical doctor would agree. He says expressly that the addition of a single grain cannot make a heap out of what was not a heap before (*Med. Exp.* XVII 3–5, pp. 116–17 W), which is an equivalent formulation of the same principle. This goes with his readiness to see a characteristic of the predicate 'heap', namely its involving a measure of extent or multitude, as responsible for the paradox. The general principle and the conditional premises which instantiate it are true on conceptual grounds. So the doctor does regard the sorites as a problem for the logician and philosopher of language, for 'those whose business, aim, and intention it is to confute fallacious arguments and reject them' (XX 6, p. 126 W). And good luck to them. Sensible doctors have better things to do than worry about the fact that Eubulides invented a sound argument for a conclusion which is plainly and evidently false.

But when we look to what the logicians, i.e. Stoic logicians, have to say, we seem to find nothing but advice about how to cope when your opponent in a debate embarks on a sorites. One piece of advice that can be extracted from the texts (Cic. *Acad.* II 93–4, S.E. *PH* II 253, *M* VII 416–21) and ascribed to Chrysippus is this. Suppose you face a series of questions 'Are two few?' (e.g. too few for a heap), 'Are three few?', and so on. Answer 'Yes', to begin with, while the quantities determined by successive numbers are clearly and unmistakably few, until you see that the series of quantities which are clearly and unmistakably few will shortly terminate. Choose a number somewhere *before* that termination, i.e. a quantity which is still clearly and unmistakably few, and when your opponent asks whether that many are few, keep quiet and say nothing. Now, if this were all the advice Chrysippus had to offer, we should be at a loss to see the sense of it.[43] Why refuse

---

43 Barnes has a lengthy but aporeutic discussion, although it is his signal achievement to have brought Chrysippus' exact prescription to the light of day from the murky texts in which it had been hidden. With less patience J. S. Reid, *M. Tulli Ciceronis Academica* (London 1885), 288, characterises Chrysippus' contribution as 'feeble'.

to agree that the quantity is few when *ex hypothesi* you know for certain that it is few? What a target for Carneades' scorn:

So far as I am concerned, you may not only keep quiet but snore as well. What good will it do you? For here comes someone to rouse you from sleep and put questions in the same manner: 'If I add one to the number at which you fell silent, will that make many?' (Cic. *Acad.* II 93; cf. 94)

But I believe that this retort points the way to an answer. For it assumes that in the debating context which, like Galen (above, p. 317), both Chrysippus and Carneades have directly in mind, *the questioning will continue.*[44]

Imagine the Stoic in debate, silent at, say, 'Are ten few?' (*Acad.* II 94). Carneades asks whether adding one more will make many. Silence. 'Well then, are twelve few?' If Carneades goes on in the same manner ('for what does it matter to the adversary who wants to trap you whether you are silent or speaking when he catches you in his net?'), sooner or later he will enter the series of numbers representing quantities which are clearly and unmistakably not few. My hypothesis is that Chrysippus' further advice is precisely to wait until that has happened, then choose a quantity which is clearly and unmistakably not few, and when asked about it say, 'No, that is many, not few', in the confident tones of one who knows he is in the right.[45] A moment's reflection will show what this strategy achieves.

The Stoic can claim to know with complete certainty (1) that there is a quantity $n$ such that $n$ is few and every quantity given by a number prior to $n$ is few, (2) that there is a quantity $m > n$ such that $m$ is not few and every quantity given by a number posterior to $m$ is not few. (1) and (2) together entail that the principle

44 On the importance of the debating context for the understanding of Greek logical reflections, see my 'Protagoras and Self-Refutation in Later Greek Philosophy', *Phil. Rev.*, 85 (1976), 44–69, and 'The upside-down back-to-front sceptic of Lucretius IV 472', *Philologus*, 122 (1979), 197–206.

45 I reach this hypothesis by noticing (i) the questioner in Galen announces in advance, 'it is my purpose to ask you questions in succession' (quoted above, p. 315); (ii) at S.E. *PH* II 253 the Pyrrhonist who apes the Stoic procedure suspends judgement on each premise *until the completion of the whole argument*; (iii) at *M* VII 416–18 whether the Sage answers 'Yes' to 'Are fifty few?' or keeps quiet seems to depend on whether the next question is (going to be) 'Are ten thousand few?' (jumping to the conclusion of the argument) or 'Are fifty one few?'; (iv) the continuation of the questioning at *Acad.* II 93–4, as discussed above. One advantage of my interpretation (besides the result to which it will lead) is that it allows ἡσυχάζειν (*Acad.* II 93, *M* VII 416) to be a dialectical tactic and different from ἐπέχειν, the suspension of judgement appropriate to what is unclear, which the sceptic – and Barnes also – understandably but wrongly makes it out to be (Cic. *Acad.* II 94, *ad Att.* XIII 21, S.E. *PH* II 253).

(*n*) if *n* grains are too few for a heap, *n* + 1 grains are too few is false. There is a cross-over between few and not few and it occurs somewhere between *n* and *m*. That established, the Stoic is entitled to demand that the conditional premises of the sorites argument be taken as material conditionals. For if the above principle is false, they have no conceptual backing. The opponent can hope for no more than that each conditional premise will present itself independently as obvious to the mind. If one of the premises does not seem obviously true, too bad: he has no general principle to back it up.[46] Admittedly, he can press the Stoic to say where the cross-over between few and not few occurs, or where the numbers cease to give quantities that are clearly and unmistakably few; and he does (*Acad,* II 93–4). But it results from the way the strategy has been carried out that *this is a problem for epistemology*, not for logic and the philosophy of language.

It is Stoic doctrine that no two things are exactly alike (*Acad.* II 54–5): no hair or grain of sand (can the examples be accidental?) is in all respects the same as another hair or grain of sand (ibid. 85). But it may take a Wise Man to be able to tell them apart, and then only with practice and familiarity (ibid. 56–7). If Chrysippus cannot specify the last instance of 'few' or the first of 'many', the most this shows is that he is not a Wise Man, which he coolly admits in any case.[47] Carneades may fume and complain that this is no solution to the sorites (*Acad.* II 94). But it is. It is an indirect but not question-begging way to establish that the argument contains at least one false premise.

Moreover, someone who was willing to give up the principle of bivalence could adapt Chrysippus' strategy to establish that the argument contains at least one premise which is (not false but) not true or less than fully true. The Stoics defend bivalence with moralistic fervour. They insist on absolutely sharp cut-off points, with the result (to cite one notorious example) that anyone who is not perfectly wise and virtuous is according to them an idiot and a villain. But if they thought this was forced upon them by the

---

46 It will not help him to assert '(*n*) [*n* grains are too few for a heap] ⊃ [*n* + 1 grains are too few]'. By itself, if no stronger connection is assertible, that just says *that* each individual conditional premise is true.

47 This helps to explain why the advice at *Acad.* II 93–4 is to stop *before* the last quantity which is clearly few, while *M* VII 416 appears to say that the *Sage* will stop and keep quiet *at* the last quantity which is clearly few. Cicero speaks of what Chrysippus does, not the Sage, who alone can trust himself to tell when his impression is not kataleptic.

sorites,[48] technically they were wrong. To establish that there is a cross-over between few and many, saint and sinner, is not yet to prove that the cross-over is abrupt rather than gradual. Nowadays, a gradualist who follows Chrysippus' advice can opt for a fuzzy logic instead of rigid morals, and that is but one option among a number of sophisticated modern theories which have shown us how to reason without bivalence or without some other leading principle of classical logic.[49] But no ancient critic of bivalence knew how to reason without it. Classical logic was all they had.[50]

'But what motivates these modern constructions is that our semantic intuitions do pressure us to accept the individual conditionals of the sorites. Chrysippus has argued powerfully that there is a cross-over. He has not made the semantic grounds for believing that there cannot be a cross-over any less persuasive than they were. Unless he can do this, and do it independently of his critique of the sorites, the argument will continue to pull us, paradoxically, both ways.' There is nothing here with which a Stoic need disagree. Of course a paradoxical or puzzle argument (*aporos logos*) is one that pulls persuasively both ways (S.E. *M* VII 243), and the sorites is such an argument (D.L. VII 82). But persuasiveness is no more a criterion of truth in conceptual matters than elsewhere. Witness the textbook example illustrating the Stoic definition of the persuasive (*pithanon*):

$$(x)\ (y)\ \text{If } x \text{ gave birth to } y, x \text{ is } y\text{'s mother,}$$

a universally quantified conditional (can this be accidental?) which most people's semantic intuitions tell them to accept – until one reminds them that a bird is not the mother of its egg (D.L. VII 75).[51] And once Chrysippus has this general, but genuinely

---

48  As is plausibly suggested by Sedley, op. cit., 93–4.

49  The most illuminating discussion I know of the contemporary scene is J. A. W. Kamp, 'The Paradox of the Heap', in *Aspects of Philosophical Logic*, ed. U. Mönnich (forthcoming). For a truly stoical expression of willingness to accept the consequences of a decision to keep bivalence, see W. V. Quine, 'What Price Bivalence?', *J. Phil.*, 78 (1981), 90–5.

50  It is important here that the property of being clearly and unmistakably *F*, as spoken of above, is an epistemic property, connected with the Stoic theory of the kataleptic impression, and is not to be confused with the logical property of being determinately *F*; it contrasts not with borderline cases of *F* but with cases where we cannot be certain.

51  Anyone worried by the irrelevancy that Greek τίχτειν is more common for egg-production than English 'give birth to' may devise their own example. Mine would be this: 'A man is free to do something only if he is not compelled to do it.' Chrysippus wrote a 4-book work 'On persuasive conditionals' (D.L. VII 190; cf. 'Logical conditionals', D.L. VII 194).

independent ground for holding that our semantic intuitions are liable to mislead, he can take a G. E. Moore stand on (1) and (2): they are much *more* certain than any proposed semantic rule could possibly be.[52] Surprising it may seem, but what Eubulides invented was a perfect *reductio ad absurdum* of the principle

(*n*) If *n* grains are too few for a heap, $n + 1$ are too few.

One final hypothesis now lies close to hand: it was in part to circumvent this type of solution that in the theological sorites Carneades offered separate justification for each successive conditional instead of appealing to some more general conceptual principle. He submits to the Stoic insistence that the conditions stand as mutually independent material implications, and still wins through to his discomforting conclusion.[53]

So we reach what to all appearances is stalemate. On the one side, Carneades makes the dramatic charge that the sorites argument shows us reason bringing about its own downfall, with logic powerless to help. On the other side, Chrysippus yawns and says, 'Yes, it is sometimes hard to distinguish one thing from another.' The debate is endless because both sides agree (as against the Empirical doctor) that the predicate is not to blame, but some weakness in ourselves. The dispute is over where the weakness lies, in a precipitate, in principle avoidable assent to the persuasive or in a radical defect of our cognitive nature. And that dispute has to be fought out anew for each sorites argument that comes up. For Chrysippus' strategy does not require him to look for a general account of what constitutes a sorites or a general diagnosis of what makes a predicate liable to it. It requires him to be unshakably certain that the first premise is true and the conclusion false, and this is a certainty he can only achieve piecemeal, case by case. We really do know that ten thousand grains are enough to make a heap, so the argument *shows* the falsity of the conceptual principle on which its persuasiveness rests. But do we know that a puddle is not worthy of worship? The corollary of a piecemeal approach is that there is no saying ahead of time whether the next sorites may not teach us a surprising, non-

---

52 On G. E. Moore in the Stoa, see Schofield, op. cit.

53 It is not just a matter of making the premises as cogent as possible against the anticipated charge of falsity (Barnes' explanation) but of safeguarding them when all conceptual defences have been disallowed.

evident truth. Chrysippus himself used little by little arguments formulated with negated conjunctions to do just that (*SVF* II 665; cf. 1003, 1005, Cic. *ND* II 164–6). If it seems unlikely that he would call these 'sorites', that can only be because he restricts the term to cases – above all, the quantitative cases – where the conclusion of a little by little argument is manifestly false. Thus confined, 'sorites' is indeed the name of something unsound (*vitiosum interrogandi genus*, Cic. *Acad.* II 92; cf. 49). But it remains Chrysippus' position, commendably, that there is nothing wrong with slippery slope arguments as such. A good one may well show us that there are more needy persons than we had realised, or more persons; and in theology that if the world itself or any finite being is worthy of worship, so is the puddle by the door.[54]

54 This paper has benefited greatly from discussion of earlier drafts at Cornell and at a meeting of the American Philosophical Association in Portland, Oregon, where the commentators were Charlotte Stough and Charles M. Young. Other individuals whom I should like to thank for suggestions and discussion are Terence Irwin, Hans Kamp, Jonathan Lear, David Sedley, Steve Strange, David White and Richard Wollheim.

# Bibliography of the publications of G. E. L. Owen

## I. BOOKS EDITED

*Aristotle and Plato in the Mid-Fourth Century* (with I. Düring). Papers of the Symposium Aristotelicum held at Oxford in August, 1957. Studia Graeca et Latina Gothoburgensia XI (Göteborg: Elanders Boktryckeri Aktiebolag, 1960).

*Aristotle on Dialectic: the Topics.* Proceedings of the Third Symposium Aristotelicum (Oxford: Clarendon Press, 1968).

*Aristotle on Mind and the Senses* (with G. E. R. Lloyd). Proceedings of the Seventh Symposium Aristotelicum (Cambridge: Cambridge University Press, 1978).

## II. ARTICLES AND REVIEWS

Review of P. Kucharski, *Les Chemins du Savoir dans les Derniers Dialogues de Platon*, in *Mind*, 61 (1952), 289–90.

'The Place of the *Timaeus* in Plato's Dialogues', *Classical Quarterly*, NS 3 (1953), 79–95. Reprinted in *Studies in Plato's Metaphysics*, ed. R. E. Allen (London: Routledge and Kegan Paul, 1965), 313–38.

Review of J. B. Skemp, *Plato's Statesman*, in *Mind*, 62 (1953), 271–3.

Review of B. L. van der Waerden, *Science Awakening*, in *The Hibbert Journal*, 53 (1954–5), 419–21.

'A Proof in the *Peri Ideōn*', *Journal of Hellenic Studies*, 77 (1957), 103–11. Reprinted in *Studies in Plato's Metaphysics*, 293–312.

'Zeno and the Mathematicians', *Proceedings of the Aristotelian Society*, 58 (1957–8), 199–222. Reprinted in *Zeno's Paradoxes*, ed. Wesley C. Salmon (Indianapolis: Bobbs-Merrill, 1970), 139–63; and in *Studies in Presocratic Philosophy*, ed. D. J. Furley and R. E. Allen, vol. II (London: Routledge and Kegan Paul, 1975), 143–65.

'Eleatic Questions', *Classical Quarterly*, NS 10 (1960), 84–102. Reprinted in *Studies in Presocratic Philosophy*, vol. II, 48–81.

'Logic and Metaphysics in some Earlier Works of Aristotle', in *Aristotle and Plato in the Mid-Fourth Century*, ed. Düring and Owen, 163–90. Reprinted in German translation in *Metaphysik und Theologie des*

Aristoteles, ed. F.-P. Hager (Darmstadt: Wissenschaftliche Buch-gesellschaft, 1969), 399–435; and in *Articles on Aristotle*, ed. J. Barnes, M. Schofield, and R. Sorabji, vol. III (London: Duckworth, 1979), 13–32.

Review of J. H. Randall, *Aristotle*, in *Philosophical Books*, 2 (January 1961), 17–18.

Review of C. Kahn, *Anaximander and the Origins of Greek Cosmology*, in *Philosophical Books*, 2 (April 1961), 6–7.

'Tithenai ta phainomena', in *Aristote et les problèmes de méthode*, ed. S. Mansion (Louvain: Publications Universitaires de Louvain, 1961), 83–103. Reprinted in *Aristotle*, ed. J. M. E. Moravcsik (Garden City, N.Y.: Doubleday, 1957), 167–90; and in *Articles on Aristotle*, vol. I (1975), 113–26.

Commentary on papers by van der Waerden and Sambursky, in *Scientific Change*, ed. A. C. Crombie (London: Heinemann, 1963), 93–102.

'Aristotle on the Snares of Ontology', in *New Essays on Plato and Aristotle*, ed. R. Bambrough (London: Routledge and Kegan Paul, 1965), 69–95.

'Inherence', *Phronesis*, 10 (1965), 97–105. Reprinted in German translation in *Logik und Erkenntnislehre des Aristoteles*, ed. F.-P. Hager (Darmstadt: Wissenschaftliche Buchgesellschaft, 1972), 296–307.

'The Platonism of Aristotle', *Proceedings of the British Academy*, 51 (1965), 125–50. Reprinted in *Studies in the Philosophy of Thought and Action*, ed. P. F. Strawson (Oxford: Oxford University Press, 1968) 147–74; and in *Articles on Aristotle*, vol. I, 14–34.

'Plato and Parmenides on the Timeless Present', *The Monist*, 50 (1966), 317–40. Reprinted in *The Pre-Socratics*, ed. A. P. D. Mourelatos (Garden City, N.Y.: Doubleday, 1974), 271–92.

'Dialectic and Eristic in the Treatment of the Forms', in *Aristotle on Dialectic*, ed. Owen, 103–25.

'Aristotle: method, physics, and cosmology', in *Dictionary of Scientific Biography*, ed. C. C. Gillispie, vol. I (New York: 1970), 250–8.

'Notes on Ryle's Plato', in *Ryle*, ed. O. P. Wood and G. Pitcher (Garden City, N.Y.: Doubleday, 1970), 341–72.

'Plato on Not-Being', in *Plato I: Metaphysics and Epistemology*, ed. G. Vlastos (Garden City, N.Y.: Doubleday, 1970), 223–67.

'Aristotelian Pleasures', *Proceedings of the Aristotelian Society*, 72 (1971–2), 135–52. Reprinted in *Articles on Aristotle*, vol. II (1977), 92–103.

'Plato on the Undepictable', in *Exegesis and Argument*, ed. E. N. Lee, *et al., Phronesis*, Suppl Vol. I (Assen: Van Gorcum, 1973), 349–61.

'Aristotle on Time', in *Motion and Time, Space and Matter*, ed. P. Machamer and R. Turnbull (Columbus: Ohio State University Press, 1976), 3–27. Reprinted in *Articles on Aristotle*, vol. III (1979), 140–58.

'Gilbert Ryle', in *Proceedings of the Aristotelian Society*, 77 (1976–7), 265–70.

Review of Gregory Vlastos, *Plato's Universe*, in *The Times Literary Supplement*, 76 (1977), 646.

'Particular and General', *Proceedings of the Aristotelian Society,* 79 (1978–9), 1–21.

'Prolegomenon to Z7–9', in *Notes on Z,* recorded by M. Burnyeat and others (Sub-Faculty of Philosophy, Oxford, Study Aids Monograph No. 1: 1979), 43–53.

# Index Locorum*

*The editors wish to thank Dena Chasnoff for the many hours of dedicated work which she devoted to the preparation of these indices.

**Plutarch**

**Origen**

**Seneca**

**Sextus Empiricus**

**Simplicius**

**Sophocles**

**Thucydides**

**Xenophanes**

**Xenophon**

# Index of names